CONTEMPORARY ART
FROM CRESCENT MOON PUBLISHING

The Art of Andy Goldsworthy
by William Malpas

Andy Goldsworthy: Touching Nature
by William Malpas

Richard Long: The Art of Walking
by William Malpas

The Art of Richard Long
by William Malpas

Constantin Brancusi: Sculpting the Essence of Things
by James Pearson

Alison Wilding: The Embrace of Sculpture
by Susan Quinnell

Eric Gill: Nuptials of God
by Anthony Hoyland

The Erotic Object: Sexuality in Sculpture From Prehistory to the Present Day
by Susan Quinnell

Minimal Art and Artists in the 1960s and After
by Laura Garrard

Land Art, Earthworks, Installations, Environments, Sculpture
by William Malpas

*Land Art: A Complete Guide to Landscape, Environmental,
Earthworks, Nature, Sculpture and Installation Art*
by William Malpas

Andy Goldsworthy In Close-Up
by William Malpas

Land Art In Close-Up
by William Malpas

Installation Art In Close-Up
by William Malpas

*Colorfield Painting: Minimal, Cool, Hard Edge, Serial and
Post-Painterly Abstract Art From the Sixties to the Present*
by Stuart Morris

Mark Rothko: The Art of Transcendence
by Julia Davis

Jasper Johns: Painting By Numbers
by L.M. Poole

Brice Marden
by Laura Garrard

Frank Stella: American Abstract Artist
by James Pearson

Maurice Sendak and the Art of Children's Book Illustration
by L.M. Poole

The Erotic Object In Close-Up: Sexuality in Sculpture From Prehistory to the Present Day
By Susan Quinnell

Sacred Gardens: The Garden in Myth, Religion and Art
by Jeremy Robinson

Sex in Art: Pornography and Pleasure in Painting and Sculpture
by Cassidy Hughes

Postwar Art
by George Knighton

Minimal Art and Artists

In the 1960s and After

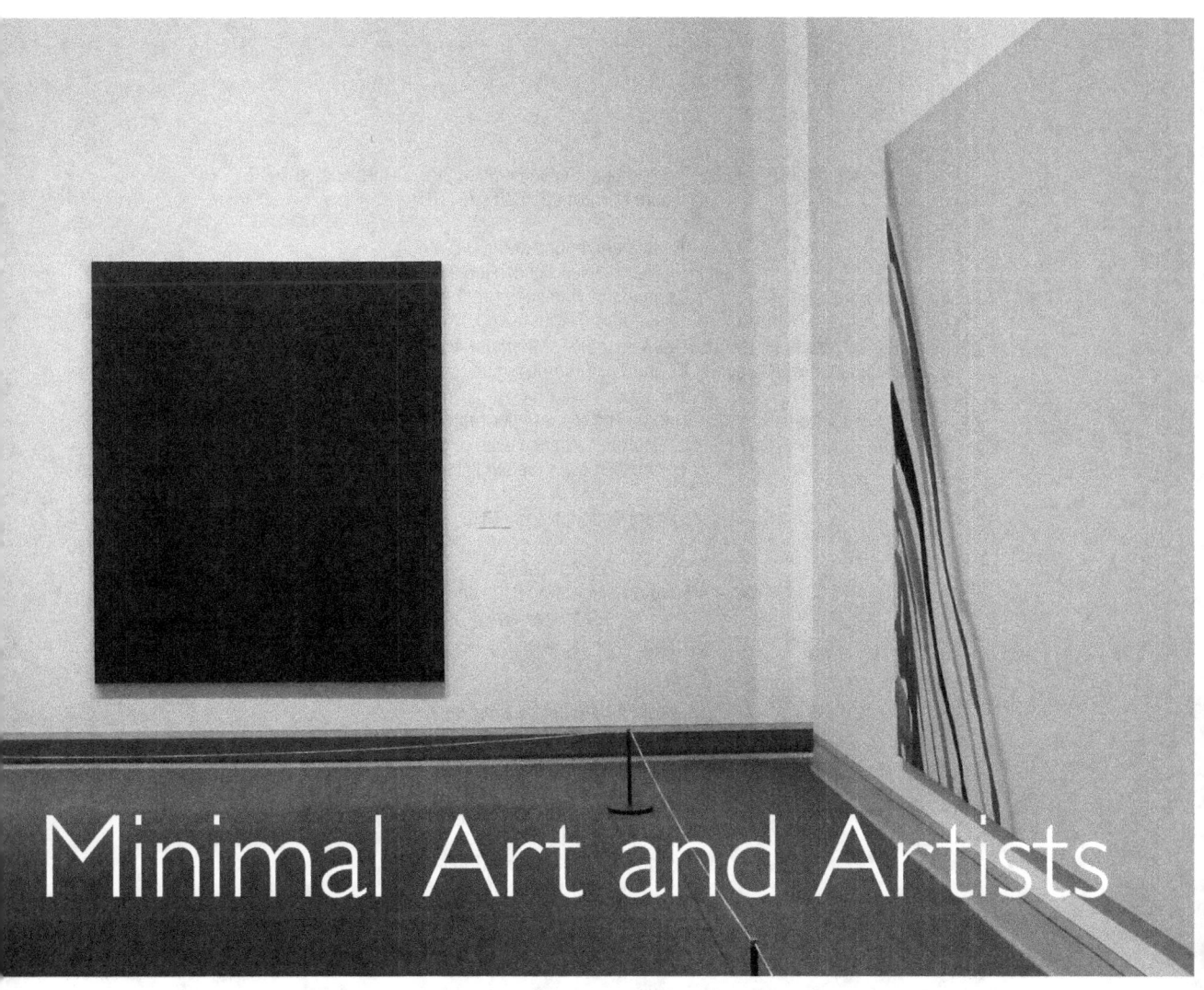

Minimal Art and Artists

In the 1960s and After

Laura Garrard

CRESCENT MOON

First published 2005. First edition. Second edition 2007. Third edition 2012.
© Laura Garrard 2005, 2007, 2012.

Printed and bound in the U.S.A.
Set in Helvetica Neue Condensed 9 on 12pt.
Designed by Radiance Graphics.

British Library Cataloguing in Publication data

Garrard, Laura
Minimal Art and Artists In the 1960s and After. 2nd ed.
1. Minimal Art
I. Title
709'.045

ISBN-13 9781861713926 (Pbk)
ISBN-13 9781861713742 (Hbk)

CRESCENT MOON PUBLISHING
P.O. Box 1312, Maidstone,
Kent, ME14 5XU, Great Britain
www.crmoon.com

CONTENTS

PART THREE:SCULPTURE

ACKNOWLEDGEMENTS

Thanks to the authors quoted and their publishers.

Illustrations © the artists and copyright holders.

Copyright holders:
Musée National d'Art Moderne, Paris. Philadelphia Museum of Art. National Gallery of Canada, Ontario. Lissom Gallery, London. Tate Modern, London. Kunstmuseum, Basel. Wallraf-Richartz Museum, Cologne. Pasadena Art Museum, California. Stedelijk Museum, Amsterdam. Saatchi Collection, London. National Gallery of Australia, Canberra. Rijksmuseum Kröller-Müller, Otterlo. Museum of Modern Art, New York. Whitney Museum of American Art, New York.

ABBREVIATIONS

B   Gregory Battock, ed. *Minimal Art: A Critical Anthology*
C   Frances Colpitt, *Minimal Art*
DJ   Donald Judd, *Complete Writings*
RS   Robert Smithson, *Selected Writings*
WS   Frank Stella, *Working Space*

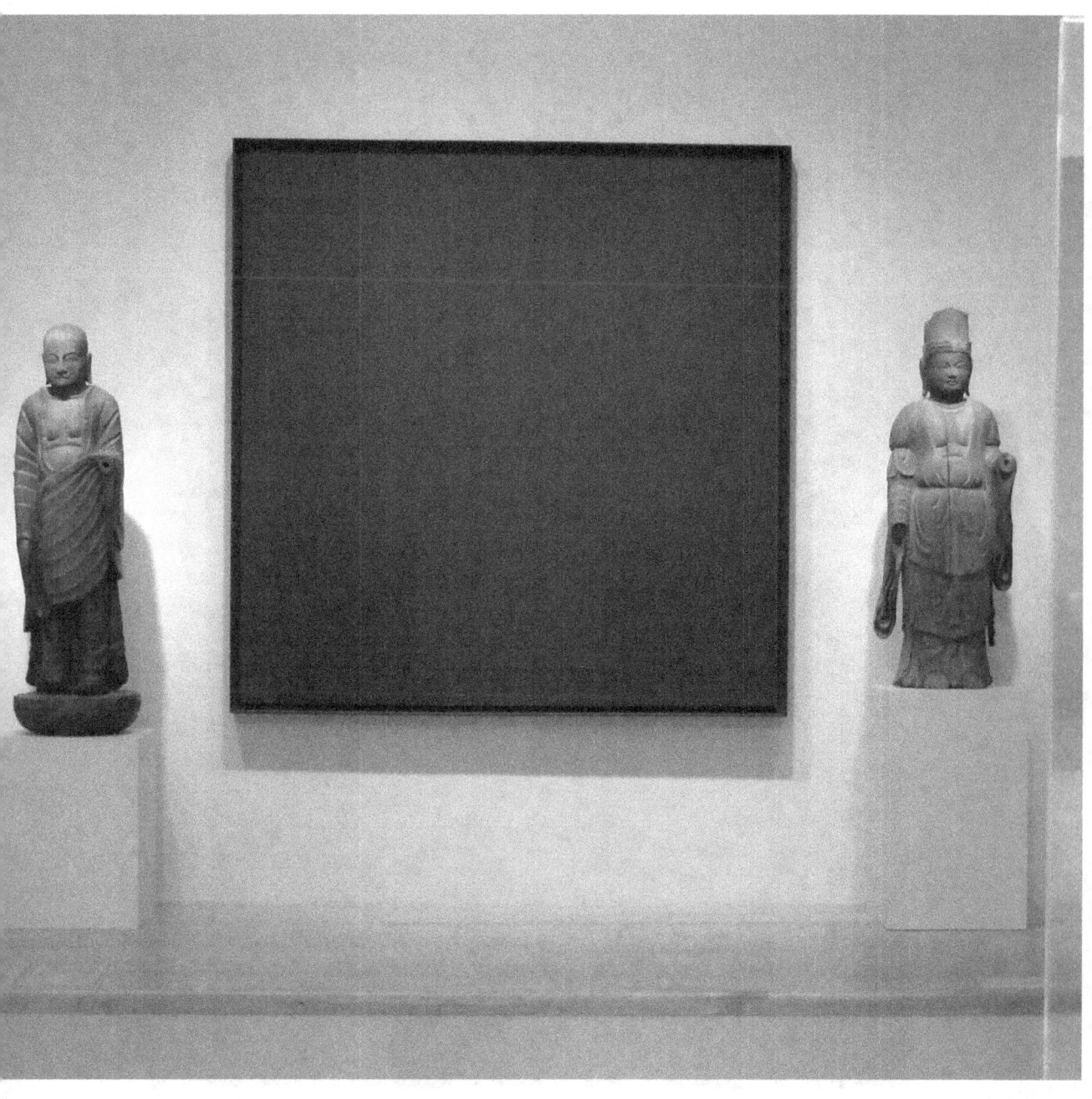

An inventive display of Ad Reinhardt's work in Princeton Art Museum, New Jersey, putting modern New York abstract art in amongst ancient Asian art

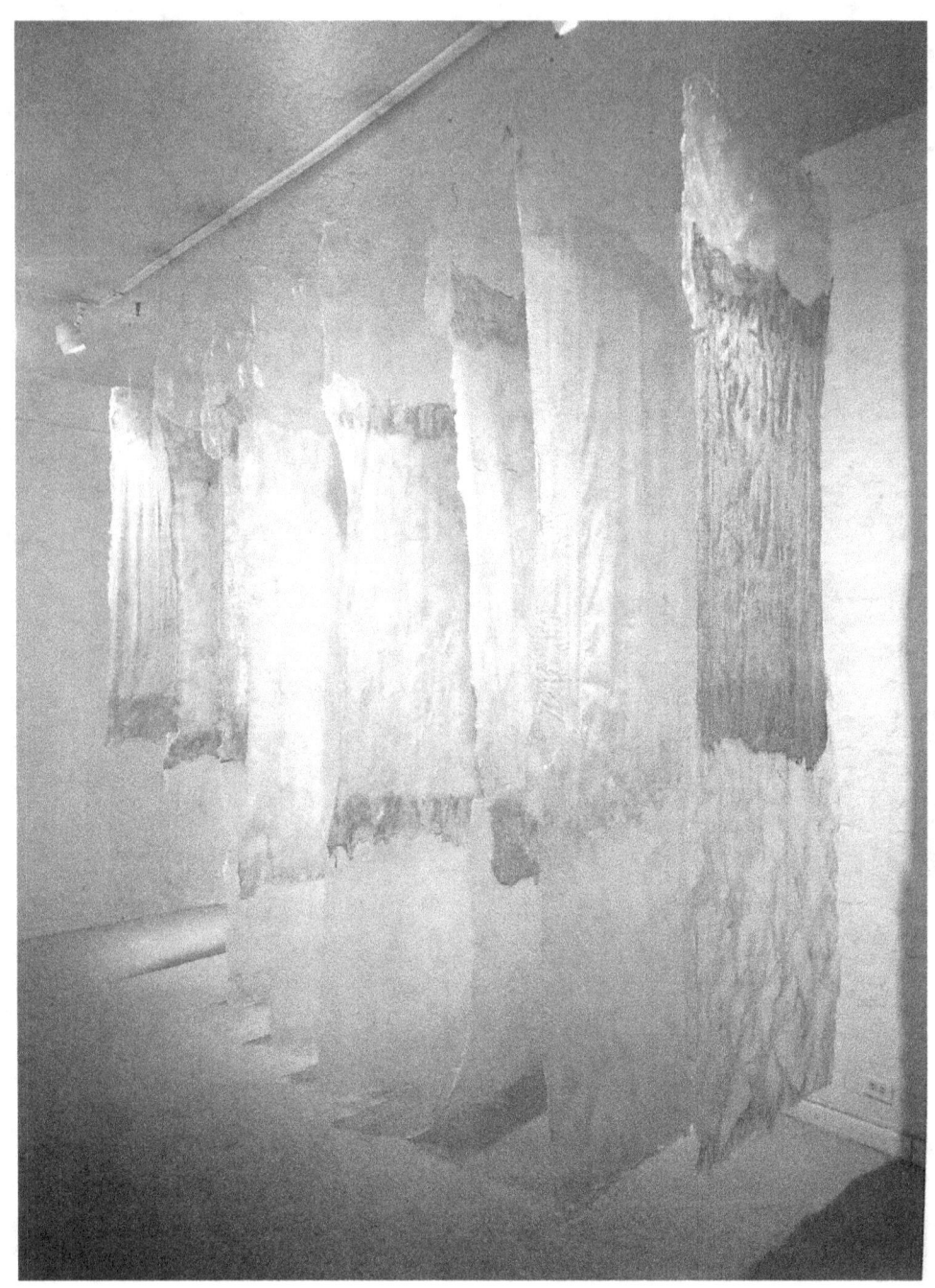

Eva Hesse, Contingent, 1969

PART ONE

THEORY

#1
MINIMAL ÆSTHETICS

MINIMAL ART AND ARTISTS

The key Minimal artists included Donald Judd, Carl Andre, Robert Morris, Sol LeWitt, Robert Smithson, Frank Stella, Brice Marden, Eva Hesse, Robert Ryman, Agnes Martin, Hans Haacke, Piero Manzoni, Yves Klein, Ad Reinhardt, Dan Flavin, and also Ellsworth Kelly, Richard Serra, Ronald Bladen, Robert Mangold and Tony Smith. Smithson, Stella, Judd, Reinhardt, Morris and Andre have been among the most lucid of theorists among artists. Probably the premier Minimal artist (and philosopher) is Donald Judd; Judd stands at the centre of Minimal art, and no account of Minimalism is complete without placing Judd in the foreground.

Some Minimalists have been taken up by feminists as icons (Eva Hesse). Some continued to work in mainly Minimal art throughout their careers (Ellsworth Kelly, Frank Stella, Brice Marden, Carl Andre), while others moved into Process art (Robert Morris), Conceptual art (Hans Haacke), performance art, body art, installation art, and feminist art (Judy Chicago). Some dipped in and out of Minimal art (Gerhard Richter). These artists, and the art they produced, form the main subject of this book.

There are many other Minimal artists (some are straightahead Minimalists, others were associated with Minimal art): Ursula Meyer, Brian O'Doherty, William Anastasi, Dean Fleming, Ludwig Sander, Milton Resnick, Dan Graham, David Budd, Paul Mogensen, Sigmar Polke, Lucio Fontana, On Kawara, Max Bill, Edward Avedisian, Jennifer Bartlett, Helen Frankenthaler, Imi Knoebel, Franz Erhard Walther, Mark Lammert, Ron Davis, John Hoyland, Beverly Pepper, Robert Irwin, Cy Twombly, Lucas Samaras, Scott Burton, Sean Scully, Larry Bell, Joel Shapiro, Daniel Buren, Phillip Taafe, David Hockney, Peter Halley, Blinky Palermo, Ross Bleckner, Claes Oldenburg, Alexander Liberman, Georges Sugarman, Charles Ross, Fred Sandback, Richard Artschwager, Jasper Johns, Kenneth Noland, Larry Zox, Michael Bolus, Sven Lukin, Joseph Beuys, John Baldessari, Antony Caro, James Rosenquist, Tony DeLap, Jim Dine, Andy Warhol, Bridget Riley, John Chamberlain, Robert Barry, Allan D'Arcangelo, Tony Doyle, Paul Frazier, Jannis Kounellis, Richard Long, Jan Dibbets, Mel Bochner, Michelangelo Pistelotto, Lawrence Weiner, Jules Olitski, Richard van Buren, Robert Duran, David Novros, Anne Truitt, James Turrell, Richard Tuttle, Richard Baringer, Donald Bernhouse, James Bishop, William Tucker, Phillip King, Bruce Nauman, Robert Murray, John Mc-Cracken, David Smith, Lee Valledor, Richard Deacon, Shirazeh Houshiary, Keith Sonnier, Charles Hinman, Paul Fraser, Jo Baer, Larry Poons, Walter de Maria, Mark di Suvero, Ralph Humphrey, Ronald Bladen, Lee Levine, Sherrie Levine, Richard Prince, Forrest Myers, Robert Neuwirth, Ed Kienholz, Judy Gerowitz, Graig Kauffman, Joseph Kosuth, David Lee, Al Held, Sam Francis, Jack Youngerman, Robert Grosvenor, David Lee, Doug Ohlson, Michael Steiner, Gianni Colombo, Stephen Antonakos, Bob Law, Peter Joseph, John Walker, Jeremy Moon, Patricia Johanson, Antoni Milkowski, Peter Tangen and Chris Wilmarth. There is not room to discuss them all here; some are explored in more depth than others.[1]

This book is concerned with Minimal art and artists, particularly painters, sculptors, 3-D, installation and land artists. But not Minimal art in architecture, graphic design, set design, dance, performance art, body art, advertizing, fashion, magazine publishing, book publishing, the internet, cinema or photography.

In the 1960s and 1970s, it seemed as if every artist went through a Minimal period at some time in their career, as well as a painting-as-sculpture period, and a brush with performance art (and perhaps body art). Both a Conceptual art phase and an on-going installation art preoccupation were mandatory for contemporary artists, it seems. All contemporary art can be viewed as basically Conceptual art, and a increasing proportion of it is installation art.

The influential critics on Minimal art in the

1960s included Clement Greenberg, Michael Fried, Lawrence Alloway, Bruce Glaser, Mel Bochner, David Bourdon, Barbara Rose, Lucy Lippard and Harold Rosenberg. Since the Sixties, important writings on Minimal art have appeared by Frances Colpitt, Gregory Battock, Rosalind Krauss, Robert Hobbs, Peter Schjeldahl, Kenneth Baker, Daniel Wheeler and Anna Chave.

If you're looking for a good place to start for a study of Minimal art, *Minimal Art: A Critical Anthology*, edited by Geoffrey Battock, is excellent. I would also recommend Frances Colpitt's book, Rosalind Krauss's book on sculpture, and anything by Lucy Lippard, Michael Fried or Barbara Rose. Daniel Wheeler's *Art Since Mid-Century* is still about the best single book on modern art: it covers everything, and in detail too, and has marvellous illustrations.

Important Minimal art shows included: *Sixteen Americans* (1959, MOMA, NY); *Towards a New Abstraction* (1963, Jewish Museum); *Black, White and Gray* (1964, Wadsworth Atheneum); *Eleven Artists* (1964, Kaymar Gallery); *Post Painterly Abstraction* (1964, Los Angeles County Museum of Art); *Shape and Structure* (1965, Tibor de Nagy Gallery), which included Andre, Morris, Judd, Murray, Hinman, Bell and Zox; *The Responsive Eye* (1965, MOMA); the Sao Paolo Biennial (1965); *Primary Structures* at the Jewish Museum (1966); *Systematic Painting* (1966, Guggenheim), featuring Novros, Ryman, Stella, Mangold, Baer and Noland; *Nine At Castelli* (1968), which included Nauman, Anselmo, Sonnier, Serra and Hesse; *Art In Process* (1966, Finch College); *Anti-Illusion* (1969), at the Whitney Museum of American Art, which featured Benglis, Hesse, Nauman, Ryman, Serra, Shapiro and Tuttle; *"10"* (1966, Dwan Gallery) included Smithson, Andre, Flavin, Judd, LeWitt, Baer, Martin, Reinhardt, Steiner and Morris; *American Sculpture of the Sixties* (curated by Maurice Tuchman in 1967, and probably the most expensive show, as well as the most famous show, of Minimalism in the 1960s); *A New Aesthetic* (1967, Washington, curated by Barbara Rose); *9 in a Warehouse*, which

featured Hesse, Nauman and Serra; *Scale As Content* (1967, Corcoran Gallery); *Art In Series* (1968, Finch College); *Art of the Real* (1968, MOMA); *Minimal Art* (1968, The Hague, curated by Enno Develing); *Live in Your Head* and *Square Pegs* (1969); *Information* (MOMA, 1970); and *Documenta 5* (which included Beuys, Buren, Christo, Gilbert & George, Hesse, Kounellis, LeWitt, Long, Nauman, Oppenheim, Ryman, Serra and Smithson). Galleries linked with Minimal art included Gotham's Tibor de Nagy, Leo Castelli, Dwan, Kaymar, Green, Pace, Guggenheim, the Jewish Museum, and MOMA.

To experience Minimal art firsthand, one would have to visit some of the main galleries of cities such as New York, Los Angeles, Tokyo, Berlin, London, and so on. Donald Judd's Marfa (Texas) is perhaps the premier Minimal art location in the world. Then there are land art sites, such as Michael Heizer's *Double Negative* in the Nevada desert, Walter de Maria's *Lightning Field* in Quemado, New Mexico, James Turrell's volcano transformation, *Roden Crater,* near Flagstaff, Arizona, Robert Smithson's *Spiral Jetty* in the Great Salt Lakes, his *Spiral Hill* and *Broken Circle* in Holland, and Nancy Holt's *Sun Tunnels* in Lucin, Utah.[2]

The Minimal artists did not consider themselves a group; they did not produce manifestos; they did not agree on æsthetics or working practices (though some were friends); they tended not to be directly involved in political art (Minimal art was more conservative than counter-culture); and they disliked the term 'minimalism'.

It tended to be the critics (as usual) who came up with the terms for the new art. Lucy Lippard used the term 'structurist', 'dematerialization' and 'eccentric abstraction'; Michael Fried had 'literalist' and 'objecthood'; Peter Hutchinson used 'Mannerist'; Barbara Rose coined 'ABC Art'; Lawrence Alloway had 'systematic painting'; Robert Morris took up 'unitary forms' and 'anti-form'; and Donald Judd employed 'specific objects'.

Terms for Minimalism like 'reductionist', 'Rejective Art', 'non-hierarchical', 'non-relational', 'non-anthropomorphic', 'Gestalt', 'environmental', 'Serial', 'Cool art', 'Know-Nothing Nihilism' and 'Idiot Art', were also employed. As Harold Rosenberg pointed out, few art movements had so many terms applied to it, and so many different definitions. For an art that was supposed to be about all things 'minimal', it attracted a lot of discussion. 'The rule applied is: The less there is to see, the more there is to say'.[3]

Many of the chief Minimal artists were not only artists, they also wrote plenty, publishing articles in the art magazines (*Artforum, Art In America, Arts Magazine, Avalanche* – all the 'A's – were among the chief art mags of the era). The Minimalists who theorized at length on art included Donald Judd, Robert Morris, Ad Reinhardt, Dan Flavin, Robert Smithson and Carl Andre; they were well-known for their written statements. Indeed, their essays and articles have become some of the key texts of the era (rather than the critics, or the patrons, or novelists, journalists and writers).

Friendships among the Minimal artists included Andre and Stella; Andre and Long; Long and Weiner; and Smithson, de Maria and Heizer. The co-operative of artists at the Park Place gallery included Novros, Grosvenor, Valledor, Fleming, di Suvero and Myers. A group of artists gathered around Smithson. Max's Kansas City was a favourite hang-out (and also for rock musicians and fans, fashion models, and Warhol's acolytes).[4] Bruce Kurtz wrote that:

> almost every night from 11 or 12 o'clock until closing... was Robert Smithson's territory. Carl Andre, Richard Serra, Mel Bochner, Don Judd, Larry Weiner, Joseph Kosuth, Ted Castle, Michael Heizer, Keith Sonnier, Dan Graham, and Dorothea Rockburne were often there, and occasionally Sol LeWitt.[5]

Minimal art, in its American manifestation (and American Minimal artists dominated Minimal art), tended to be based in New York City. Some Minimal artists later moved out of Gotham to more rural spots (such as Agnes Martin to New Mexico and

Donald Judd to Texas), but New York was always where many of the important shows were, where many artists worked, where the commercial galleries were based, where critics and art magazines were situated, and so on. Most of the Minimal artists, like most major artists since the 1950s, tended to be highly educated, often with degrees (and some took post-graduate courses too).

Minimal art has been criticized for being boring, cold, clinical, severe, fascistic, capitalist, and solemn. Minimal art does tend towards being a little po-faced, grave, and self-important. One might called it the ultimate neurotic art, or the ultimate art of repression. It deals with hi-falutin' ideas like scientific permutations of forms, or engages on radical reformulations of sculpture. Most Minimal art took itself very seriously, like its artists. The sedate art of Sol LeWitt, Donald Judd and Robert Ryman just seems a different fish from the ironic, throwaway camp Pop Art of Andy Warhol, Larry Rivers or Tom Wesselmann, or outsider art, or folk art. There is playfulness in Minimal art, but not nearly as much as in Pop Art or post-industrial art. It just doesn't possess much of a sense of humour: there aren't many laughs in Minimal art. Minimal art is not an art that tends to celebrate kitsch, or camp, irony. It's not an art, either, that is easily approachable and crowd-pleasing, like Claude Monet's *Waterlilies* or a nude statue by Auguste Rodin or Gianlorenzo Bernini. It's not an art that suits everybody's taste; it is, really, a highly cultured, highly educated and supremely refined art. It's modernism refined to the point of High Modernism in High Minimalism.

Postminimalism followed Minimalism, a term coined by critic Robert Pincus-Witten. Other names for Postminimal art of 1967-68 included Anti-Form and Process Art. Sixties painting, closely aligned with (Minimal) sculpture, was termed Colorfield, Hard Edge, Minimal and Post-Painterly Abstraction, and was linked with Pop Art, Op (optical) Art, chromatic and kinetic abstraction, wholistic art, pure-painting, geometric and organic abstraction, ABC Art, Cool Art, Systematic Painting, Non-Gestural Painting, Non-Relationalism, Abstract Mannerism and Abstract Sublime painting. Terms such as (Clement Greenberg's) Post-Painterly Abstraction seem unwieldy. New hyphenations and conjunctions had to be invented to describe the new painting. Ad Reinhardt, for example, might be described as a post-painterly, meta-structural, non-objective, post-religious, Minimal abstract-ionist. (Barbara Rose recalled that Reinhardt was also derided as 'the heretical black monk of Abstract Expressionism, or the legendary Mr. Pure' [B, 285-6]).

MINIMAL ART AND LITERATURE (AND SAMUEL BECKETT)

Also important in the world of the art of the 1960s and after was the literature of the time: Samuel Beckett's depressive reductionism ('I can't go on, I'll go on'), Alain Robbe-Grillet's self-conscious irony (with *Last Year At Marienbad* as a key film), Hermann Hesse's Existential explorations, Jorge Luis Borge's labyrinthine self-reflexivity, J.R.R. Tolkien's epic fantasy, and the Beat poets, of course (William Burroughs, Jack Kerouac, Allen Ginsberg and Lawrence Ferlingetti). And the 'sex mystics' (Henry Miller, D.H. Lawrence and Anaïs Nin), the European Existentialists (Albert Camus, Jean-Paul Sartre and Franz Kafka) and the visionary Romantics (Williams Blake and Wordsworth). And the great modernist novelists: Vladimir Nabokov, Norman Mailer and James Joyce. And science fiction (Frank Herbert, Arthur C. Clarke, Robert Heinlein and Isaac Asimov).

Sporting a beaten-up paperback seemed mandatory: *The Fall* and *The Stranger* (Albert Camus), *Nausea* (Jean-Paul Sartre), *On the Road* (Jack Kerouac), *Howl* (Allen Ginsberg), *Steppenwolf* and *The Glass Bead Game* (Hermann Hesse), *Dune* (Frank Herbert), *2001: A Space Odyssey* (Arthur C. Clarke), *Tropic of Cancer* or *Sexus* (Henry Miller), *The Trial* (Franz Kafka), *Lady Chatterley's Lover* (D.H. Lawrence), *Ulysses* (James Joyce), *The Lord of the Rings* (J.R.R. Tolkien) and the *Tao Te Ching* (Lao-tzu). And, for the more daring, or more intellectual: *A Season In Hell* (Arthur Rimbaud), *À Rebours* (J.-K. Huysmans), *The Magic Mountain* (Thomas Mann), *Lolita* (Vladimir Nabokov), *The Naked Lunch* (William Burroughs), *Last Exit To Brooklyn* (Hubert Selby), or *Journey To the End of Night* (Louis-Ferdinand Céline).

Contemporaneous with the development of High Minimalism in the 1960s was Samuel Beckett's exploration of self-referential fiction. Starting from the statement that there is 'nothing to express' and 'nothing with which to express', Beckett wrote short, condensed text pieces which he called 'fizzles', which have similarities with Minimalism's radical reductionism. Beckett, being a far better writer than any of the Minimal artists (or any of the critics of the period), was able to crystallize the prevailing philosophies of the time and put them into words. Indeed, if words themselves can be regarded as sculpture, as Lawrence Weiner asserted, then Samuel Beckett may be one of the great Minimal artists.

In his book of *Dialogues*, Samuel Beckett defined an extreme version of the position some of the Minimal artists took:

The expression that there is nothing to express, nothing with which to express, nothing from which to express, no power to express, no desire to express, together with the obligation to express.[1]

In conversation with Georges Dutuit, Beckett, speaking of the eternally paradoxical condition of the painter, put it another way:

B. – The situation is that of him who is helpless, cannot act, in the event cannot paint, since he is obliged to paint. The act is of him who, helpless, unable to act, acts, in the event paints, since he is obliged to paint.
D. – Why is he obliged to paint?
B. – I don't know.
D. – Why is he helpless to paint?
B. – Because there is nothing to paint and nothing to paint with. (ib., 142)

Samuel Beckett's poesie of absence, of 'lessness', of repetition, his spiritual negation, of having nothing to express but being 'obliged' to express, chimes with Minimal artists such as Donald Judd and Robert Ryman, and, most obviously, with Ad Reinhardt.

Samuel Beckett's short, later fictions – *Ping, Lessness, All Strange Away* and *Still* – with their mathematical descriptions of boxes, rotundas and cylinders, seem to be poetic equivalents of the smooth, rigid volumes of Minimal sculpture

(Donald Judd, Robert Morris, Carl Andre, Dan Flavin, etc). Indeed, Beckett's descriptions of square white rooms, which seemed so severe at the time, in the Sixties, now describe the contemporary art gallery. No one would've wanted to spend much time in the empty white rooms of Beckett's stories (too much like deprivation chambers), but now the typical art gallery is precisely that austere, rectilinear, 'minimal' space. The white box.

Samuel Beckett often employed the Minimalist's use of seriality, of doing one thing then another, in sequence. Plenty of Minimal artists based some of their artworks on series of numbers or patterns (J. Johns, 1993). Frank Stella and Richard Long referred to Samuel Beckett (though often the artists had the Beckettian affinities pointed out to them by others, rather than finding them for themselves).

I have read a few bits and pieces of Beckett's work [related Richard Long]… he does use things like country lanes and bicycles and stones and doing nothing… like an incredible minimal view of life, which is very attractive and powerful. So I think there are some similarities, in the same way there are similarities with Zen Buddhism. It is just sort of coincidental, human… we all live in the same world. It would be maybe very surprising if you could not find parallels with the work of other artists or other religions. (1985, 2, 7)

In *Working Space*, Frank Stella emphasized his roots in modernism, as well the Old Masters, and Samuel Beckett was one of the major modernists (like James Joyce, T.S. Eliot, Gertrude Stein, Marcel Proust and D.H. Lawrence). In the art of Beckett and Stella (and Minimalism), the actuality of the materials of their art is crucial. Stella's credo – what you see is what you get – is echoed by Beckett. Disliking discussing his art, Beckett insisted on the texts themselves, which needed no glosses to make them explicit. Likewise, Stella asserted the physicality of his painting, and there was no need for explanations. Of Beckett, Stella said:

The idea of repetition appealed to me, and there were certain literary things that were in the air that corresponded to it. At the time I was going to school, Samuel Beckett was very popular. Beckett is pretty lean, you might say, but he is also slightly repetitive to me in the sense that certain very simple situations in which not much happened are a lot like repetition. I don't know, it struck me that bands, repeated bands would be somewhat more like a Beckett-like situation than, say, a big, blank canvas... There was something Beckett did that seemed kind of insistent about what little was there. It also seemed to fit me. (E. de Antonio, 141)

In his late trilogy (*Company, Ill Seen Ill Said* and *Worstward Ho!*, 1980-83), Samuel Beckett composed highly economical, even poetically radical texts with the hard, crystalline surface of Minimal art. In *Company*, Beckett's narrator described an ecstatic memory which is now a trace of light, an incandescence out of the past which returns to haunt the narrator. Light accompanies many ecstatic passages in Beckett's fiction (the dimming light in *Footfalls* and *Rockaby,* for instance), as well light-in-darkness and light out of darkness. Consider the light art installations of James Turrell, Robert Irwin and Dan Flavin in relation to this extract from *Company*:

...the light was there then. On your back in the dark the light there was then. Sunless cloudless brightness. You step away at break of day and climb to your hiding place on the hillside. A nook in the gorse. East beyond the sea the faint shape of high mountain. You lie in the dark and are back in that light. Straining out from your nest in the gorse with your eyes across the water until they ache. You close them while you count to a hundred. Then open and strain again. Again and again. Till in the end it is there. Palest blue against the pale sky. You like in the dark and are back in that light. Fall asleep in that sunless cloudless light. Sleep till morning light.2

It's as if Beckett's narrator were describing the optical effects of staring at an Agnes Martin, Brice Marden or Robert Ryman canvas.

MINIMAL ART AND PHILOSOPHY

Among philosophers, the Existentialists (Jean-Paul Sartre, Søren Kirkegaard, Albert Camus and Martin Heidegger) were still trendy and hip with Sixties artists (as well as the Existential novelists, such as Knut Hamsun, André Gide, Hermann Hesse and Franz Kafka). Friedrich Nietzsche's influence has never gone out of fashion among the intelligentsia since the early 20th century. The Minimalists read Ludwig Wittgenstein (B, 292); some of Minimalism's key theorists – Ad Reinhardt, Donald Judd, Robert Smithson, Carl Andre – could refer to philosophers knowledgeably (i.e., they understood them). Don't forget the enormous impact of Oriental mysticism (Zen Buddhism, Hinduism, Confucianism, the *I Ching, Tao Te Ching,* and Jiddhu Krishnamurti). And shamanism, and the rediscovery of Native American religion. And the drug culture gurus (Carlos Casteneda. Timothy Leary and Aldous Huxley). And psychoanalysis continued to have an immense influence: Sigmund Freud, C.G. Jung, Alfred Adler, Wilhelm Reich and Jacques Lacan.

In Ludwig Wittgenstein's philosophy one finds the idea that there are limits to expression and language, that one should be humble in the face of the inexpressible or incommunicable. The limits of philosophy for Wittgenstein were bound up with the limits of language. Wittgenstein believed that there were things that could not be said (which he dubbed 'mystical'). There is a limit to the cultural world as there is to the physical world. Value, for instance, was not part of the world for Wittgenstein, because language cannot talk about value. For Wittgenstein, the world as a whole cannot be spoken about, only details or parts of the world can be discussed.1

In his *Tractatus Logico-Philosophicus*, one of the key precursors of Minimal philosophy, Ludwig Wittgenstein stated:

The world is *my* world; this is manifest in the fact that the limits of *language*... mean the limits of *my* world. 2

In the 1965 article "ABC Art", Barbara Rose remarked that '

If Jasper Johns's notebooks seem a parody of Wittgenstein, then Judd's and Morris's sculptures often look like illustrations of that philosopher's propositions. (B, 291)

Oriental philosophy explored notions of nothingness which appealed to the Minimal artists: Tibetan Buddhism spoke of the 'Clear Light of the Void', which has affinities with Yves Klein's empty gallery, or the lighted corridors of Bruce Nauman, or Dan Flavin's vacant spaces lit by white fluorescents, or the spaces altered with scrims, veils and false walls and ceilings of Robert Irwin, Michael Asher and James Turrell. In a sense, all of Turrell's art of skyspaces is all about contemplating the 'Clear Light of the Void' (in Turrell's case, the sky itself). An extract from the *Tibetan Book of the Dead* gives a flavour of this radical, uncompromising experience of nothingness:

O nobly born... listen. Now thou art experiencing the Radiance of the Clear Light of Pure Reality. Recognize it. O nobly-born, thy present intellect, in real nature void, not formed into anything as regards characteristics or color, naturally void, is the very Reality, the All-Good.
Thine own intellect, which is now voidness, yet not to be regarded as of the voidness of nothingness, but as being the intellect itself, unobstructed, shining, thrilling, and blissful, is the very consciousness of the All-good Buddha.
Thine own consciousness, not formed into anything, in reality void, and the intellect, shining and blissful – these two – are inseparable. The union of them is the Dharma-Kaya state of Perfect Enlightenment.
Thine own consciousness, shining, void, and inseparable from the Great Body of Radiance, hath no birth, nor death, and is the Immutable Light – Buddha Amitabha. (1957)

MINIMAL SCALE

The awareness of scale is a function of the comparison made between that constant, one's body size, and the object. Space between the subject and the object is implied in such a comparison.

Robert Morris (1966, 21)

In sculpture, there's quite a concrete relationship between one's size as a person and/or mass as a person and the mass of a piece of sculpture.

Carl Andre (1970, 57)

One of the hallmarks of art made since Word War Two is its massive scale as well as size. For some artists, it has become *de rigeur* to construct at least one or two very big projects, while for others, anything less than colossal just isn't quite the business. Among the thousands of examples of large-scale art in the postwar and contemporary art eras are David Smith's *Wagon I* and his *Cubi* sculptures (huge, weighty, chunky and towering pieces which dominate their surroundings), Christo's wrapped structures and fences 24 miles long, Michael Heizer's *Complex One*, and Tony Smith's black polyhedra. Even medium-sized works, such as Donald Judd's wooden boxes, are sometimes seen as monumental. A critic on the *New York Times* called Judd's 1977 installation at the Heiner Friedrich Gallery a 'majestic and finely measured presence'.1

Donald Judd wrote of the new sculpture of the Sixties that '[t]his scale is one of the most important developments in twentieth century art' (DJ, 200f). The Abstract Expressionists, such as Jackson Pollock, Robert Motherwell and Willem de Kooning, had helped to inaugurate the era of Big Art with their very large canvases, which dwarf the spectator when s/he moves close to them. One can get up close to a Morris Louis or Mark Rothko canvas and be enveloped by it. (Rothko spoke of wanting to achieve a sense of intimacy by using large canvases – intimate contact through large scale. Small pictures, Rothko reckoned, were *outside* your experience, something separate, but large images could be part of the viewer's experience).

Lucy Lippard pointed out that scale is not just a kind of measurement, but

> a sense of scale is also a *sense* proper. Scale is *felt* and cannot be communicated either by photographic reproduction or by description. (1968)

What Lippard's referring to here is the important point that works of art really have to be seen in the flesh in order to experience their full effect.

The colossal 3-D art from the postwar to contemporary era was not made exclusively by male artists (though it has been always associated with them). Patricia Johanson, Rebecca Horn, Mary Miss, Helen Harrison, Donna Dennis, Louise Nevelson and Alice Aycock have made huge works. Helen Escobedo created some enormous concrete and steel sculptures which attempted 'to fuse hard-edge geometric forms with nature's organic manifestations', as she put it. Sculptures such as Escobedo's *Snake* (1982) rise impressively from the earth, celebrating the flux and movement of organic forms. Beverly Pepper's large, curving mirrored slabs of wood buried in sandy beaches (*Sand Dunes*, 1985) might be seen as a type of 'Earth Mother art', art which works harmoniously with the Earth, rather than, as in some male earth art, cutting it, penetrating it, or polluting it.

Male artists have been responsible for many of the celebrated products of contemporary art, the icons of the postwar art scene which have become the academy, the canon (and Minimal artists have been predominantly male). In sculpture, these include: Donald Judd's 'specific objects', the stacks or ladders or blocks of aluminium and tinted Plexiglas that climb gallery walls;[2] Tony Smith's monumental black cubes and tetrahedra with their

thereness, the primacy of presence, not effect;[3] Dan Flavin's mesmeric, flickering fluorescent tubes;[4] Sol LeWitt's Conceptual open white cube systems (mathematics made solid in plywood and aluminium);[5] Richard Serra's huge walls, slabs and props of steel leaning together;[6] and Carl Andre's floorpieces of plates of steel, magnesium, copper and zinc.[7] The new industrial materials were central to Minimalism: Plexiglas (transparent thermoplastic, a.k.a. acrylic glass), and fiberglass (fiber-reinforced polymer, a.k.a. glass-reinforced plastic).

One of the most exciting developments of postwar and contemporary sculpture and art is the installation, the management of a whole space or environment – the floor, walls, ceiling, furnishings, lighting and doorways, as in Rebecca Horn's *Ballet of the Woodpecker*, a room full of mirrors, or Sylvia Stone's *Crystal Palace*. Pretty much all of contemporary art is a kind of installation of one kind or another these days. Artists aren't content any more to demurely hang paintings on walls or peacefully place sculptures on pedestals. Art exhibitions now are typically an art of environments, with TV monitors, computers, cameras, supports, scaffolding, cables, bones, wire mesh and a zillion other items installed everywhere (though video screens are the favourite installation media). At *Nine At Castelli* (1968), Bruce Nauman, Richard Serra, Eva Hesse and Keith Sonnier *et al* deployed a variety of materials, including aluminium, polythene, plastic, water, steel, latex rubber, acid, chicken wire, canvas, neon, cotton, copper, felt and flocking.[8]

In Bruce Glaser's "Questions to Stella and Judd", Donald Judd continually stressed the point that the new (Minimal) art was definitely American and non-European. Time and again Judd stressed that the new art was trying to get away from the European tradition (some of the Abstract Expressionists had said the same thing, although some of them – Mark Rothko and Willem de Kooning, say – seemed less inclined than the Minimalists to ditch Henri Matisse, Kasimir Malevich, Wassily Kandinsky and Piet Mondrian completely). 'It suits me fine if that's all down the drain', Judd said. 'I'm totally uninterested in European art and I think it's over with'.9

The urge to break away from Europe is important (if impossible) in contemporary American (and Minimal) art. It meant a move from modernism to something beyond modernism (later dubbed 'postmodernism'); from Paris, centre of European art, to New York City, centre of international (and American) art from the mid-century onwards; from the Old World to the New World.

It couldn't be wholly achieved, though, as each of the key American artists (Frank Stella, Donald Judd, Ad Reinhardt, Mark Rothko, Andy Warhol, Jeff Koons, Jean-Michel Basquiat, Robert Rauschenberg or whoever) found. The 'new art' of America of the 1950s through 1970s (which's now thirty, forty, fifty years old), was wholly based in European culture, and founded completely on Renaissance tenets. The *space* of American art since the Fifties, for instance, is still basically Renaissance space (as Stella discussed in his *Working Space* series of lectures).

The Minimal painters found inspiration in, or were influenced by, Paul Cézanne, Henri Matisse, Claude Monet, Joan Miro, Pablo Picasso, Paul Gauguin, Piet Mondrian, Wassily Kandinsky, Salvador Dali, Max Ernst and Kasimir Malevich, while the sculptors consciously or unconsciously took up Constantin Brancusi, Auguste Rodin, Naum Gabo, Vladimir Tatlin and Marcel Duchamp. The influence of Mondrian, Malevich and Kandinsky is especially strong among Minimal painters, and it's easy to spot the grid out of Mondrian in Agnes Martin, the exuberant color out of Kandinsky in Jules Olitski or Elizabeth Murray, or the monochrome geometric shapes of Malevich in the Hard Edge painting of Ellsworth Kelly, Frank Stella and Kenneth Noland. (In fact, some Malevich's paintings, made around 1915-16, are extra-ordinarily close to Kelly or Noland).

THE PRESENCE OF THE OBJECT IN MINIMAL ART

Minimalism never finally lets go of the object: it is always ultimately an art of the objects, even if they have new conceptions and new names, like 'unitary objects', or 'specific objects', or 'primary structures', or 'anti-forms'. In Minimal art, the object and its 'objecthood', its 'objectness' or presence, is primary. As William Tucker wrote towards the end of the Sixties: '[i]t is the matter-of-fact 'objectness' of sculpture that has become in recent years its prime feature'.1 The new notion of the object and its 'objecthood' is problematic, theoretically and artistically, partly because the world is full of objects – it is a continuum of objects (as all artists have to acknowledge. And not only is the world full of objects, but millions of them have been produced by earlier generations of artists. There can never be a wholly 'new' or 'pure' object, like a Platonic Ideal Form, an object which could exist without some connection to millions of other objects.

As art critics have pointed out, much of what makes art art or sculpture sculpture or an installation installation is that the object/ artwork/ installation is contextualized, physically as well as æsthetically and psychologically, as a sculpture or artwork or installation. Context is crucial (as the French philosopher Julia Kristeva said), for context carries so much meaning. Thus, a pile of bricks on a building site is... a pile of bricks; ordinary, unremarkable, just another cluster of objects on a planet covered with them. But a pile of bricks in an art gallery is... sculpture. This is what Carl Andre explored with his *Equivalents* series. The *response*, affected by so much of culture, socialization, physical context, education, politics, and so on, makes objects sculptures. As Garth Evans wrote:

> What happens to a sculpture is determined largely by factors outside of itself. The fact of its being thought of as a sculpture is more critical to its existence, its life, than any other facts

about it. This is a fundamental distinction between objects and sculpture. (62)

New objects, then, but not wholly abstracted from humanity or the body. The body is still at the heart of Minimal art, even when it seems as if nothing remains of it. One can see the body written into, say, or Constantin Brancusi's extraordinary egg shapes (a recognizable organicism), but not, perhaps, in the giganticism of Michael Heizer's *Double Negative* or Donald Judd's groups of giant concrete boxes at Marfa in Texas. Yet, even here, the human body is present – the earthwork and the sculpture always relate to the human body. Carl Andre said:

I once described the change in sculpture in the 20th century as moving in its concerns from form to structure and now having a concern with place... I believe now you can make sculpture you can enter. (1978, 31)

Minimal sculptures are not set on pedestals, like Renaissance or Greek sculpture; they sit on the floor, or lean against walls (as in Robert Morris's *Floor Piece*, or Carl Andre's 78 metal tiles in *Twelfth Copper Corner* [1975], or Donald Judd's four hollow cubes in *Untitled* [1969, City Art Museum of St Louis]). The new sculptural space must have 'three, not two co-ordinates' said Robert Morris. 'The ground plane, not the wall, is the necessary support for the maximum awareness of the object'.2

Minimal sculptures exist in the same space, on the same plane (the floor) as the viewer. They suggest a continuity between spectator and object, and a different relationship between the two from that in previous art, which enclosed the art object in a separate place from the observer, in its own cultural space or aura. The new sculptures are, as Robert Morris claimed, in an in-between cultural space, somewhere between being monuments and being ornaments, between being architecture and being jewellry.3 Mel Bochner said (in a review of the important *Primary Structures* show) that for the

Minimal artists art was 'unreal, constructed, invented, predetermined, intellectual, make-believe, objective, contrived, useless'.

Frank Stella searched for sensuality in the notion of the 'working space' of a painting. Stella wrote of the space a painting creates, and how this space can envelop the viewer, sensually:

An effective painting should present its space in such a way as to include both viewer and maker each with his own space intact. It is not that this experience should be literal; it is simply that the sense of space projected by the painting should seem expansive: expansive enough to include the viewing and the creation of that space. (WS, 9)

Art critics were a little confused over what to call the new works by Minimal sculptors (but that didn't stop them coining new terms for the new art). Donald Judd called his sculptures 'specific objects'; Robert Morris used the term 'unitary forms' and 'anti-forms'; 'primary structures', 'structures' and 'object sculptures' were other phrases used.

In "Notes On Sculpture", Robert Morris quoted a famous Q & A session aimed at Tony Smith, *pace* his *Die* sculpture:

Q: Why didn't you make it larger so that it would loom over the observer?
A: I was not making a monument.
Q: Then why didn't you make it smaller so that the observer could see over the top?
A: I was not making an object.4

A good example of the new sense of the sculpted object was Richard Serra's *Splashes* (1968, destroyed), installed at Leo Castelli's New York gallery. With its emphasis on process and 'anti-form', *Splashes* was more Postminimal or Process sculpture, than Minimal art. A sense of the random and immediate was central to *Splashes*, which comprised some lead that Serra splashed and poured along the join of a wall and floor. *Splashes* evoked spontaneity, waste, ephemerality and 'organic' form. It was also a work which couldn't be bought (or sold) or transported, or hung on a wall, or exhibited elsewhere.5 *Splashes* was distinctly a new kind of sculpture – it was *new* 'new sculpture', and a significant departure from the 'new sculpture' that had been heralded by Anthony Caro and David Smith.

■ It didn't look like traditional sculpture, or previous sculpture (it was a splash mark on the wall and floor);

■ it wasn't welded and constructed Cor-Ten steel or cast in bronze or chiselled marble;

■ it wasn't based on a clay model;

■ it didn't arise from sketches or plans; it wasn't figurative;

■ it didn't conform to traditional notions in sculpture of 'beauty', volume, form, illusion and allusion;

■ the form it took was partly haphazard, and not wholly dictated by the artist;

■ it wasn't placed on a pedestal;

■ it could only be experienced in that particular context (it was site-specific);

■ it didn't draw attention to itself (it could easily be overlooked, or mistaken for dirt);

■ it wasn't permanent; and it could not become another commodity in the exchange of objects in the commercial art world.

MINIMAL ART AND CONSTANTIN BRANCUSI

The influence of Constantin Brancusi's sculpture is apparent in much of Minimal (and contemporary) sculpture. Robert Morris, Donald Judd, Scott Burton, Carl Andre and Dan Flavin acknowledged the impact of Brancusi's art (among many other artists of the era and since then). Brancusi was name-checked much more than other modernist sculptors, such as Auguste Rodin, Jean Arp or Henry Moore (though Constructivists, such as Naum Gabo and Vladimir Tatlin, or Pablo Picasso's metal sculpture, are obvious ancestors of Minimal sculpture, plus the machine art of the Futurists, and not forgetting the Dada and Surrealism of Marcel Duchamp and Max Ernst).

Constantin Brancusi's monumental *Endless Column* (1937-38) was singled out by Minimal artists as especially significant. Built from cast iron, *Endless Column* was 96.2 feet high (and 35.4 x 35.4 inches in cross-section), and installed in Tîrgu-Jiu in Romania. Brancusi called it 'a stairway to heaven'.

But also important was the way that Constantin Brancusi photographed his sculptures in his studio, his radical simplification of form, and the way he presented his sculptures in exhibitions. Carl Andre's early work *Last Ladder* (1959) is something (deliberately) like Brancusi's *Endless Column*. The Brancusian ethics, of simplicity, purity, smoothness, interiority and organic form are found in the Minimal sculptors, as well as the Constructivist notion of working with materials in a 'natural' way, so that the material dictates the form one creates with it. 'Each material has its own life,' Brancusi wrote,1 and the 'essence' must be brought out by the artist, as Brancusi said:

> The natural element in sculpture means allegorical thinking, symbol, sacredness or the search for essences hidden in the material and not the photographic reproduction of external appearances.2

Barry Flanagan commented that sculpture works directly with materials:

> The convention of painting has always bothered me. There always seemed to be a *way* of painting. With sculpture, you seemed to be working directly, with materials and with the physical world inventing your own organisations.[3]

Letting the material go part way in dictating the form would become a central tenet of Minimal art, and later art, such as Process art, Serial art, land art, and Postminimalism.

Scott Burton admired Constantin Brancusi's supports for his sculptures, and the furniture, the tables and chairs which Brancusi built. Brancusi was as original in his creation of a new art object as Marcel Duchamp with his readymades or Vladimir Tatlin with his Constructivism, Burton claimed:

> in today's climate Brancusi's embrace of functional objects seems as absolutely contemporary as his invention for our century... of sculpture as *place*.[4]

While some Minimal artists took up the more Romantic, esoteric and spiritual elements in Constantin Brancusi's art (notably Carl Andre, for instance), that aspect of Brancusi didn't interest many Minimalists. Brancusi's pursuit of Platonic Ideal Forms was not for every Minimal artist, but his radical simplification of sculptural forms had a big impact on modern sculpture.

MONOCHROME AND MONOTONOUS: IS MINIMAL ART BORING ART?

Many Minimal artworks are lean, blank, slick, spartan – but leanness or blankness does not necessarily mean unfeelingness, uninterestingness, meaninglessness or valuelessness. This is a problem that Minimal art can generate. Some people thought that Minimal art was boring (and some still think that the Minimal approach in design or architecture or advertizing is dull). Minimal art was only 'cold' or 'boring', said John Perreault in "Minimal Abstracts", because of its 'minimum degree of self-expression' (B, 260) – self-expression being one of the aspects of art that modernist and pre-modernist critics and artists valorize. Of a group of Tony Smith's black plywood sculptures, Perreault said that the

> "Minimal" geometry that Smith employs and his modular use of tetrahedrons are a means to an end, and that end is not severity for its own sake, but severity in the service of poetry and a well-articulated expressiveness. (B, 261)

In Minimal painting and sculpture, surfaces are, typically, smooth, utterly sleek and 'pure'. If one wanted to, a standard Freudian psychoanalytical interpretation of the obsession with cleanliness and purity would relate it to anality and toilet training. It could be seen also as a reaction against action painting and Abstract Expressionism – splattering pigment everywhere like a child, messy, loose art (which Freudians would associate with anal or sphincter art, paint as faeces spread all over, and so on).

'I wanted everything to be on the surface', said Frank Stella (WS, 155). Minimal art seems to have no hidden depths, therefore no subtlety. (No solidity, either – the forms of Donald Judd, David Smith and Robert Morris were hollow). Simplicity is exalted, as is repetition, seriality, process, and flatness, as well as volume and space. The many materials are flattened out and depersonalized, and gestures, so important to certain kinds of painting and sculpture (such as that of Pablo Picasso or Michelangelo Buonarroti), are suppressed. In many cases, Minimal art was machine-made, and erased the touch of the hand completely. Indeed, the flatness of the surfaces, whether in the art of Robert Morris, Donald Judd, Brice Marden, Agnes Martin, Carl Andre, Ronald Bladen or Tony Smith, is crucial. But the alleged 'boringness' of Minimal art becomes a part of the metaphysics of Minimal art.[1] As Donald Judd put it, '[a]rt is something you look at' (B, 164). As Barbara Rose said in "ABC Art", Minimal art was intentionally 'vacant or vacuous' (1965, 62). Andy Warhol remarked: 'I like boring things. I like things to be exactly the same over and over again'.[2] Lucy Lippard commented:

> The exciting thing about… the "cool" artists is their daring challenge of the concepts of boredom, monotony and repetition… their demonstration that intensity does not have to be melodramatic. (1966)

Dreary art for some is exhilarating art for others, just as erotic art for some is pornography for others. Thus, James Mellow wrote that a Donald Judd exhibition was 'one of the most provocative of the season' (1966, 89). Irving Sandler reckoned that the very 'boringness' of Minimal art could be its most interesting aspect. Sandler said that

> in its boredom, [Frank] Stella's painting has affinities to [Ad] Reinhardt's, but… Stella appears to have made it the content of his art – a content so novel and perverse as to be interesting.[3]

Minimal art, opined John Perreault, 'in spite of the polemics, is emotional, but the emotions and the experiences involved are new and unexpected'. As it's made by humans, Minimal art is not robotic and cold, but always human (it cannot be anything else but 'human'). It is just as human as 'Egyptian architecture, Tibetan banners, or Sung paintings', asserted Perreault.[4]

Donald Judd answered the charge, often levelled against Minimal art, of reductionism: '[i]f my work is reductionist it's because it doesn't have the elements that people thought should be there. But it has other elements that I like' (B, 159). Judd's assertion is the common one of artists defending their work (along the lines of 'well, *I* like it'). As Judd stated, while other people may be disappointed after looking for certain things in Minimal art and not finding them, he was satisfied with the elements he included. Minimal art, as Judd explained, challenged audience's expectations. Judd, Robert Morris, Carl Andre, Eva Hesse *et al* were simply not going to deliver what viewers expected to see every time.

Robert Morris commented that art is found 'boring' by those who desire 'specialness', a unique art object unlike any other, the eternal one-off:

> Such work which has the feel and look of openness, extendibility, accessibility, publicness, repeatability, equanimity, directness, immediacy, and has been formed by clear decision rather than groping craft, would seem to have a few social implications, none of which are negative. Such work would undoubtedly be boring to those who long for access to an exclusive specialness, the experience of which reassures their superior perception. (1967, 29)

Minimal artists such as Donald Judd, Carl Andre, Sol LeWitt and Robert Morris explored the notions of 'boringness' and 'interestingness' by taking repetition and reductionism to extremes in artwork after artwork. 'Boring art is interesting art', wrote Frances Colpitt in her excellent book on Minimal art (C, 121). Judd, the chief explicator of Minimal æsthetics, wrote: 'I can't see how any good work can be boring or monotonous in the usual sense of those words', adding: '[a]nd no one has developed an unusual sense of them'.[5]

Clearly, the Minimal artists thought they were making 'interesting' art. Or at least, *they* were interested in it. One can see in Donald Judd's output an artist having a good time exploring the forms, structures and possibilities that interest him. If art's good, it can't be 'boring', said Judd, claiming that 'a work needs only to be interesting'. Bruce Boice glossed Judd's statement that 'all a work needs to be is interesting' thus: 'what was meant is not so much that interest is enough, but that interest is all that is possible'.6 Michael Fried in "Art and Objecthood" said that the 'literalist' art of Judd's type is not so much 'boring' as 'merely interesting'. Whereas, the typical modernist artwork had to have 'conviction', that it could compare with other art, that it had attained a certain level of quality.7

The discussion of terms such as 'interesting', 'boring' and 'value' becomes a quagmire of semantics and the metaphysics of meaning. Language soon fails to describe the kinds of intentions that artists have, and the kinds of responses that critics have to works (or the experience viewers have to art). Robert Mangold said: 'I certainly know whether I'm interested in the work or whether I'm not interested in the work'.8 One might see Minimal art as so 'cool' it's deadening. Yet, despite the profusion of smooth white surfaces, which speak for some of the antiseptic aridity of clinics and hospitals, or the chrome and steel expanses of airport terminals and factories, or the boxes of warehouses, there is much to enjoy in Minimal art.

Certainly to take one Minimal artist, Frank Stella: his art is intense, and not at all humdrum: his *Black Stripe Paintings*, his *Protractor* series, his copper paintings, his *India Birds*, are potent works of art. Works such as *Quathlamba* (1964), *D* (1963) and *Avicenna* (1960), are very powerful paintings. *D*, in particular, is impressive: one of Stella's *Purple Polygons* series, it is a huge (7 feet high and wide) ten-sided polygon, with the centre left empty, as often in Stella's paintings. The exhibition of *Purple Polygons* was called 'boring' and 'monotonous' by some critics.9 But how could paintings such as *D* be termed 'boring'? Just the opposite of boring, one could say.

Viewers might see Robert Ryman's (or Jo

Baer's) white-on-white paintings as unsensual, flat, tedious. No way: Ryman's paintings are very striking. They are painter's paintings. The surfaces themselves are highly poetic, but Ryman also moves towards the state of sculpture, like Stella, with his use of many different materials, from wood to steel, from fibreglass to Plexiglas, from cardboard to copper.

It would be harder to see Sol LeWitt's cuboid, mathematical, conceptual sculpture as sensual (in the conventional sense). LeWitt's angular objects – the wooden frames of cubes painted white – seem to be the antithesis of sensuous, pleasurable art (i.e., a lush landscape by Jean-Antoine Watteau or John Constable, or an Auguste Rodin nude).10 LeWitt's art is all about ideas: the initial idea, the conception, is everything. As Sol LeWitt said:

all of the planning and decisions are made beforehand and the execution is a perfunctory affair. The idea becomes a machine that makes the art. 11

Much of contemporary sculpture since World War Two consists of hard-edged cubes or rectangular slabs. Whether this use of such stark mathematical forms as cubes and rectangles is rational or intuitive, science or passion, it takes a didactic, numerical approach to art to extremes. The idea, Donald Judd remarked, is to simply do 'the next thing'; 'one thing after another'. This is the basis of Serial art (also called Systems art or Process art). It is a strategy that is not called a strategy, a systemless system. To make a work of art, one starts a process, then stops: as Carl Andre put it, '[a]ny work consists in moving from the beginning of an operation to its end' (2000). You pick up a metal tile, place it next to another one, and keep going until you stop. You pick up a brush, make one mark, then another, until you stop. Of Frank Stella's paintings, Judd asserted in "Specific Objects" that the 'order is not rationalistic and underlying, but is simply order, like that of continuity, one thing after another' (1965, 82).

One of Jasper Johns' key statements was:

Take an object
Do something to it
Do something else to it
" " " " "

The formal notions of Minimal art – seriality, succession, progression, repetition, permutation – have been around for a long time. Leonardo da Vinci, one might say, painted the same picture in different ways, often abandoning projects before completion (Leonardo was a classic artist in that respect, having so many projects on the go, his attention flitting from one to another, and unable or unprepared to finish them. Constantin Brancusi said that no work of art is ever finished).

But, whether the 'system' is serial or modular, whether there is progression or simply repetition, the notion of Donald Judd's – of 'doing the next thing' and of 'one thing after another' – explains so much of Minimal art (and subsequent contemporary art). It explains so much of Judd's work, for instance, those 'ladders' or 'stacks' of forms ascending to the ceiling in bronze, aluminium or Plexiglas, and those long lines of curved shapes (crenellations) set eye-height on a wall. It also describes how artists simply go on making work, as variations, or repetitions, or progressions, or just one piece, the same piece, like Mark Rothko with his many canvases that explore different combinations of purple or yellow clouds floating on oceans of red or blue, or Ad Reinhardt's seemingly repetitious but actually methodical explorations of five-foot square black cruciform canvases.

In his important essay "Systematic Painting" (the introduction to the Guggenheim 1966 *Systematic Painting* show), Lawrence Alloway suggested that meaning in the new painting may not be confined to a single painting, but may be a function of a series of paintings.[12] Maybe it took a run of paintings before the full value or meaning or effect of an artist's intentions came across. Certainly, many of the Minimalists (sculptors as well as painters) worked in series, reckoning that only in a run of pieces could all of the possibilities of an idea or approach be worked out.

Minimal (æsth)ethics can produce some extremes of mathematics and seriality. For Michael Fried, the concept of endlessness, of going on (or of having to go on, as Samuel Beckett would say), was central to the notions of interest and objecthood in Sixties literalist art ('literalist' was Fried's term for the kind of Minimal art Donald Judd produced). Endlessness might be 'the experience that most deeply excites literalist sensibility', Fried claimed (1967). For Lawrence Alloway, what made form in Sixties art meaningful was not 'ingenuity or surprise' but 'repetition and extension'.[13] Alloway's view applies equally to painting as well as sculpture.

CONCEPTUAL ART

Minimal art is related to – and a part of, and concurrent with – Conceptual art. The two art movements are closely related and at times (in Hans Haacke or Richard Long or Eva Hesse) indistinguishable. Much of Conceptual art existed (still exists) only in photographs, memories, words and various texts. In traces of different kinds. Works that can be seen and those that are hidden or 'invisible' have the same importance for the Conceptual artist. A work that only the artist knows about can be as significant as one that's on public display. A work that's planned but never made can be as important or valuable as one that's made. A work doesn't need to be made physically, or exhibited. A good concept can be superior to an object. But perhaps the most important legacy that Conceptual art left behind was: art can be anything and anything can be art.

One of the hallmarks of the 'ideal Conceptual work', as artist-critic Mel Bochner offered in an interview, is 'an exact linguistic correlative, that is, it could be described and experienced in its data and it could be infinitely repeatable' (1974, 62). Conceptual art includes plenty of Minimal art, such as Robert Morris's and Hans Haacke's fog and steam pieces, which exist now only as photographs, memories and criticism.

Many artists have spoken of the importance of the *making* of the artwork, its actual construction, with real (and sometimes organic, living) materials. In some artists' output, the material employed also has a symbolic or added meaning (as in Joseph Beuys' *Fettecke* or 'fat corner', a sculpture with powerful autobiographical and semiotic associations). There was an understanding among 1960s art critics that sculpture was more 'real' than painting, that sculpture was 'less illusionistic', as Clement Greenberg put it. 'Sculpture, existing in real space and physically autonomous is *realer* than painting'.[1] These are philosophical issues that artists and critics love to debate *ad infinitum*.

A classic example of Conceptual art was Joseph Kosuth's *One and Three Chairs* (1965, MOMA, New York): a real chair, a photograph of a chair, and the description of a chair from a dictionary were exhibited side by side, an exploration of art as language (concepts, photographs and real objects), and the relation between language (art) and the real world.

A typical exhibition of Conceptual art was held at the Kunsthalle in Bern: Walter de Maria installed a telephone, with a message beside it saying the visitor could talk to him; Richard Long walked in the mountains and recorded his walk in a gallery statement; Jannis Kounellis put bags of grain on a stairway; Michael Heizer created *Berne Depression*, smashing the pavement near the Kunsthalle with a wrecking ball; and Joseph Beuys smeared fat along the walls.

For Clement Greenberg, Minimal art was too Conceptual: in his essay in *American Sculpture in the Sixties*, Greenberg claimed that

> Minimal art remains too much a feat of ideation, and not enough anything else. Its idea remains an idea, something deduced instead of felt and discovered… There is hardly any æsthetic surprise in Minimal Art, only a phenomenal one of the same order as in Novelty Art, which is a one-time surprise. (B, 183-4)

Conceptual art, as well a being art, is also (very often) meta-art, para-art, trans-art, *art about art*, and art that relies on other art to 'exist'. Some forms of Conceptual art exist for a brief moment, then become myth, gossip, photography, words (but all part of discourse or language). Conceptual artists are often much concerned with writing and written texts. A Conceptual art exhibition might feature only written texts on display and photographs. Sixties Conceptual artist Lawrence Weiner produced some of the classic textworks in contemporary art, comprising capitals letters on a wall or in a book (Barbara Kruger, Sophie Calle, John Baldessari, the Art & Language group, Hamish Fulton, Richard Long and Michael Craig-

Martin have also made post-Conceptualist wall textworks).

Maps are also prominent in Conceptual art (and even more so in land art). They constitute a new landscape of the soul, as Robert Smithson wrote in 1968:

A cartography of uninhabitable places seems to be developing – complete with decoy diagrams, abstract grid systems made of stone and tape (Carl Andre and Sol LeWitt), and electronic "mosaic" photomaps from NASA. (1968, 26)

While some Conceptual artworks exist only as photographs, most Process, Serial, ABC, Cool or Minimal art does not need photography to exist (partly because it produces real, physical objects, and many Minimal artists preferred to construct durable objects). Some Conceptual artists must also be photographers; they must make choices about film stock, framing, angles, lenses, lighting and so on. If photographs are to appear in the Conceptual art exhibition, the artist must oversee the journey of the films from development through printing to framing.[2] The Conceptual artist or sculptor must be (or deal with) accomplished photographers. Their work must be high standard, because it is exhibited in high art locations, such as the city gallery, or published in glossy coffee table art books.

In Conceptual art, as in many contemporary art forms, the commentary, the written records, the obsessive documentation, can be just as important as the artwork itself (the artist's journal or work-book becomes a new fetish object – it is placed at the centre of the art school system in Britain, for instance). Often, in Conceptual art, the documentation is the artwork. The artist's life sometimes becomes part of the artwork, or there is a continuity between the artist and the artwork. By contrast, Minimal art is an art of real objects, often with the aura of (auto)biography excised.

When Marcel Duchamp and Kurt Schwitters put 'real' objects into the art gallery, they did so because it seemed a logical thing to do

(Duchamp's *Urinal* (1916) is the original Conceptual artwork. And the fact that the *Fountain* exhibited in museums today is a replica is even better. Ultimately, anyone could have a Duchamp artwork if they possessed a similar urinal. But Duchamp's *Urinal* still held the aura of the artist, who signed it – even if 'R. Mutt' is a joke).

It's the same with Sixties artists: why not have an art made out of found objects, such as stones found on a remote path, or car parts, or household bricks? The use of everyday items in Minimal and Process art ushers in a new sense of the object in art, a new way of looking at art, and a new relationship between viewer and artwork. The 'real' objects and readymades of Marcel Duchamp and Kurt Schwitters were developed by Robert Rausch-enberg and Jasper Johns, among others. As with Rauschenberg's art, the stuck-on objects set alight Johns' paintings; the paintings of Rauschenberg and Johns depart radically from art of 50 or 60 years previously, from the academy and easel paintings of the 19th century. Johns explained why he used real things stuck onto his paintings:

My thinking is perhaps dependent on a realization of a thing as being the real thing... I like what I see to be real, or to be my idea of what is real. And I think I have a kind of resentment against illusion when I can recognize it. Also, a large part of my work has been involved with the painting as object, as real thing in itself. And in the face of that 'tragedy,' so far, my general development... has moved in the direction of using real things as painting. That is to say I find it more interesting to use a real fork as painting than it is to use painting as a real fork. [3]

It is easy to see how Jasper Johns' dictum applies directly to Minimal art; Roberts Smithson and Morris also preferred what they see to be real, to be the object in and of itself. They disliked illusionism and allusiveness (one of the ways Morris erased allusiveness in his art was by titling all his works *Untitled*, the most common title in contemporary art). For Minimal artists, their works don't 'symbolize' or 'represent' things, the world or nature or an idea, they *are* things, the world and nature and ideas. As Johns said: 'I find it more interesting to use a real fork as painting than it is to use painting as a real fork.' Similarly, one can see how, for artists like Alice Aycock, Michelle Stuart and Carl Andre, it's much more interesting to use a brick as a brick rather than as a representation of something else. Smithson's definition of an earthwork applies here: 'instead of putting a work of art on some land, some land is put into a work of art'.4

For Donald Judd, simply working in three dimensions cuts out one of the recurring problems in Sixties art – that of illusion:

Three dimensions are real space. That gets rid of the problem of illusionism and of literal space, space in and around marks and colors – which is riddance of one of the salient and most objectionable relics of European art. The several limits of painting are no longer present. A work can be as powerful as it can be thought to be. Actual space is intrinsically more powerful and specific than paint on a flat surface. (1965)

In "Specific Objects", Donald Judd described his vision of a 'minimal' art, one reduced to its interesting essentials:

A work needs only to be interesting. Most works finally have one quality. In earlier art the complexity was displayed and built the quality. In recent painting the complexity was in the format and the few main shapes... The thing as a whole, its quality as a whole, is what is interesting. The main things are alone and are more intense, clear and powerful. (1965)

Minimal art creates an ambiguous continuity with the world of nature that exists outside the gallery. Sometimes this ambiguity works against the work on show in the gallery space.5

One of the problems Minimal art addressed is the age-old relation between the 'real world' and art, between objects as they are in the everyday world, and objects as they are represented in art. By using 'real' objects, such as Carl Andre with his bricks or Dan Flavin with his fluorescent tubes, Minimal artists aimed to demolish traditional notions of representation and mediation. Of course, there are problems with using objects as objects – Marcel Duchamp with his readymades confronted this problem (but didn't solve it). The problem is partly one of context: because, placed in a museum or art gallery, obviously as items to be carefully studied, everyday forms become art. The articles may not be on pedestals, but they are perceived as art objects. If the viewer is looking at art in a book or a gallery, they are already anchored in a gallery/ art/ æsthetic mode of viewing. Maybe art can only ever be art, or perceived as art, or never *more* than art. (Perhaps the notion that art can be progressive, or utopian, or that it can change the world socially or politically, held by many modernists, is dead).

With its emphasis on the object, Minimal art was (is) seldom ephemeral. It had a definite solidity. It declined to dispense with modernism's unflinching insistence on the object. Much Conceptual art, meanwhile, was (is) transitory. As Lawrence Weiner remarked: '[o]nce you know about a work of mine, you own it. There's no way I can climb into somebody's head and remove it.'6 Thus, much of Conceptual art (and one could also say Minimal art, and all art) exists in that socio-cultural space which is actually inside people's heads (it's called the 'cultural imaginary' in contemporary critical theory). Thus, anyone can 'own' Conceptual art, simply by thinking about it. Once thought about Conceptual art (or any art) can be 'possessed' by the viewer, in Weiner's system. Indeed, some Conceptual art requires the existence of the viewer to make the work work at all. The viewer brings the piece alive (a kind of inverse Werner Heisenberg principle). Like a ghost (or a paranoid celebrity), the artwork has no life unless someone is looking at it or thinking about it.

THE RELIGIOUS ELEMENTS IN MINIMAL ART

It's inevitable that the American form of Minimal art should be sympathetic to Eastern mysticism, because Zen Buddhism, Shinto, Hinduism, yoga, meditation, Transcendental Meditation and Taoism were particularly popular in Sixties culture (and not just on the West Coast – though definitely in California if anywhere on Earth). It was an inexorable development, it seems, from Parisian Existentialism to Californian Zen Buddhism, from Albert Camus and Jean-Paul Sartre to Carlos Casteneda and D.T. Suzuki. Many of the chief precepts of Taoism and Zen Buddhism chime with those of Minimal art. Matsuo Basho, an important Oriental poet (a favourite among counter-cultural writers), wrote that if one wanted to 'learn about the pine', one should 'go to the pine' and study it, leaving behind one's 'subjective preoccupation with yourself'.[1] Makoto Ueda explained what Basho meant: 'learn means to enter into the object, perceive its delicate life and feel its feelings.'[2] These notions of searching for the 'essence' are absolutely in tune with the æsthetics of Carl Andre and Donald Judd.[3]

Like Chinese landscape painting and Zen Buddhist garden design, Minimal art exalted surface (in going no deeper than the surface, in bringing everything up to the top layer). Brice Marden's paintings, like those of Morris Louis, Robert Mangold, Agnes Martin and Robert Ryman, were not concerned with creating 'illusionistic space', with the space of traditional Western post-Renaissance art, but with a new flatness. The painting was a thing-in-itself (of and for itself), to employ a common term of Existential philosophy. Frank Stella asserted the flatness of painting. His famous early statement runs thus:

My painting is based on the fact that only what can be seen there is there. It really is an object...All I want anyone to get out of my paintings, and all I ever get out of them, is the fact that you see the whole idea without any confusion... What you see is what you see.[4]

Frank Stella changed his views on space over his career, but in the early 1960s his view was that the painting became an object (should become an object), and he wished to do away with a dichotomy between the painting as an object and what the paint on its surface depicted.

Any painting is an object [said Stella] and anyone who gets involved enough in this finally has to face up to the objectness of whatever it is that he is doing. He is making a thing.[5]

While painters such as Frank Stella and Kenneth Noland stressed the flatness of Sixties painting, Helen Frankenthaler said that

all totally abstract pictures _ the best ones that really come off – Newman, Pollock, Noland – have tremendous space; perspective space despite the emphasis on flat surface. (1965, 36)

Flatness in painting is necessary, Helen Frankenthaler asserted, if one wanted to have an artwork clear of connotations:

Sentiment and nuance are being squeezed out so that if something is not altogether flatly painted then there might be a hint of edge, *chiaroscuro*, shadow and if one wants just that pure thing these associations get in the way. (1965, 38)

On the other side of the flat, non-relational, non-hierarchical painting camp, there were artists whose aim was to destroy the rigid flatness of painting. One painter who threw anything onto the picture plane was Robert Rauschenberg (see his many 'combine' paintings, mixed media assemblages and extravaganzas). Claes Oldenburg's soft telephones and toilets far outdo Rauschenberg for pure silliness when it came to doing anything with a traditional art form. Oldenburg went much further than Andy Warhol in questioning the holy notion of 'Art' with a capital 'A'. The picture plane, which had been so scrupulously flat throughout the Renaissance (ignoring the embossed and punched gold, and the ornate frames, and the multiple panels), suddenly burst open in art during the 1950s. As Clement Greenberg put it: '[p]ictorial space has lost its "inside" and become all "outside"' (1961, 134).

Of course, some postwar artists asserted the flatness of the picture plane even more fervently: Morris Louis with his stained canvas, Frank Stella with his black stripes done with housepaint direct onto cotton duck, Mark Rothko with his cloud-like shapes, Agnes Martin with her finely pencilled squares, and Sol LeWitt with his spacious wall-drawings.

Robert Morris spoke of 'negative presence', and Ad Reinhardt continually evoked the associations of blackness. Brice Marden made mute, gray blankness the cornerstone of his art. Barbara Rose, in her excellent article "ABC Art" (1965), related the blank, empty and reductive aspect of Minimal art to the renunciation and denial of ascetic mysticism and contemplation. Mediæval mystics such as Meister Eckhart with his tenet of 'from nothingness to nothingness', Jan van Ruysbroeck with his 'superdazzling darkness', and St John of the Cross with his 'Dark Night of the Soul', evoked the sacrality of the void. Rose compared the 'blank consciousness', the 'meaningless tranquillity and anonymity' of Eastern and Western monks and yogis to the inertia and passivity of some Minimal art.

Minimal artists such as Ad Reinhardt and Dan Flavin deliberately evoked mystical or spiritual connotations in their art. Flavin, for example, called his sculptures 'icons', and made works such as *William of Ockham* and *Via Crucis*, light sculptures with conscious allusions to religion. Yves Klein's exhibition *The Void* was also known as *The Specialization of Sensibility From the State of Prime Matter to the State of Stabilized Pictorial Sensibility*. So that his aura could impregnate the gallery space Klein had the walls whitewashed. Minimal art

followed the oft-used tenet of negative mysticism (found in Taoism, Buddhism, and some strains of Christianity) that 'less is more', or as Carl Andre put it, "'minimal' means to me only the greatest economy in attaining the greatest ends'.[6]

The relation between Minimal art and Oriental mysticism, in particular Taoism and Zen Buddhism (the more ascetic mysticisms of the Far East), has been noted by some commentators. Zen Buddhism and Taoism, for instance, speak of the 'here and now', spontaneity, *satori* or enlightenment, intuition, nature, emptiness, change, meditation, and cosmic unity. Many of these qualities can be applied to Minimal art, and are sometimes elucidated by Minimal artists. For example, the experience of viewing Minimal art is not quite Zen *satori*, in the strict definition of *satori* (as spiritual enlightenment), but certainly Minimal artists aim for an 'epiphany' (as James Joyce called the æsthetic shock). With the Minimal object, there are 'no strings attached', i.e., 'what you see is what you see', as Frank Stella put it. One sees the whole thing there, and that is everything one gets. It's all there; there's no digging to a deeper 'meaning', no hidden depths. This instantaneous aspect of Minimal art is a Zen-like notion. *Satori*, too, has affinities with the descriptions of Minimal sculpture that some Minimal artists have given (Robert Morris's objecthood, for example).

The lure of the void is easy to discern in Minimal art, in the sense of emptiness in Donald Judd's and Dan Flavin's art (the sense of void inside and surrounding their art objects), and those wildernesses beloved of Michael Heizer and Walter de Maria (the desert being the ultimate Minimal environment). Emptiness is consciously evoked by painters such as Ad Reinhardt, Brice Marden, Gerhard Richter and Robert Ryman with their all-black, all-gray or all-white canvases. China has a long tradition of landscape painting, and it's not difficult to see the many connections between the contemplative aspects of Chinese landscape painting and monochrome, reductive Minimal art.[7]

Most artists affirm the 'livingness' of their art,

and some say that they *live* their art (few artists promote the life*less*ness of their art). In the act of creation, art is not intellectually discussed or made at a critical distance. Rather, the artist is right in the middle of her/ his art, living it. There is no separation of art and life. Art is a way of mythicizing one's sense of being-in-the-world, a way of making presence visible, tactile, *there*. 'Presentness is grace', wrote Michael Fried in his influential essay "Art and Objecthood" (B, 28). Uncomfortable as they are with notions of 'spirituality' or 'mysticism', some Minimal artists, such as Richard Long, Dan Flavin, Carl Andre and Robert Smithson, are in some ways religious artists.

LIGHT AND SPACE

Go back out, move back, the little fabric vanishes, ascend, it vanishes, all white in the whiteness, descend, go back in. Emptiness, silence, heat, whiteness, wait, the light goes down, all grows dark together, ground, wall, vault, bodies, say twenty seconds, all the greys, the light goes out, all vanishes.

Samuel Beckett, *Imagination Dead Imagine*[1]

Numerous artists have worked with light and lighting; light art has become a whole sub-genre of contemporary art. Some of the Minimalists made light central to their art: James Turrell (with what he calls his 'skyspaces', environments which have openings onto the sky); Robert Irwin (who reworked gallery spaces with scrims, false walls and ceilings); Eric Orr (with his sound and light environments); Dan Flavin (with his famous fluorescent tubes); Bruce Nauman (who built narrow corridors lit by green fluorescents, as well as many neon tubing sculptures); Maria Nordman (who extended studio exteriors); and Nancy Holt (with her environmental sculptures based around celestial events). Other light artists include Douglas Wheeler, Hap Tivey, Susan Kaiser Vogel, Chryssa, Keith Sonnier, Stephen Antonakos, Nicolas Schöffer, Larry Bell, and DeWain Valentine. Sculptors, even the most traditional kind, have to work with light: sculptures are usually meant to be seen (even though sculpture is known as an art of touch).

Some of the artists who made light central to their work in the post-WW2 era were known as Minimal artists (Dan Flavin, Larry Bell and partly Bruce Nauman), while others were more usually categorized as installation or environmental artists rather than Minimalists (James Turrell, Robert Irwin and Eric Orr), although Turrell, Orr and Irwin utilized Minimal principles. Many of the major works of Minimal art, though, have used light as the foundation of the piece. For instance, the mirrored boxes of Donald Judd and Robert Morris, or Larry Bell's decorated glass cubes, or Robert Smithson's *Non-site* sculptures. Some Minimal artists fitted lamps into their works (such as Morris with his half-circle floor sculpture). And many of the Minimal painters also worked directly with light in their monochrome canvases, experimenting with optical effects (Jules Olitski, Agnes Martin), merging into Op Art (Morris Louis, Frank Stella), and the viewer's perception of color and light.

Many artists have taken gallery spaces and reworked them, adding walls or scrims, or drapes, or false ceilings, or doorways, or new windows, or altering the floor with liquids or false floors. The forms of the additions to gallery spaces were often Minimal – smooth, undecorated, rectilinear partitions, doors, walls and scrims to hide, block or enhance spaces. Often these light and sound spaces look like empty gallery rooms: Eric Orr's *Light Space* (1985), Hap Tivey's *Sodium Exchange* (1976), Susan Kaiser Vogel's *Point Conception* (1980), DeWain Valentine's *Curved Wall Spectrum* (1974, acrylic tubes hanging alone from gallery ceilings), Larry Bell's *Leaning Room II* (1988), Bruce Nauman's *Yellow Triangular Room* (1973), Douglas Wheeler's *All Gray Graduating Light* (1976), Maria Nordman's *6/ 21/ 79 One Day Only* (1979), James Turrell's *Second Meeting* (1988), and Robert Irwin's Kansas *Installation* (1979).

The forerunners of these light art spaces included Yves Klein's *Le Vide*, and the modernist light art of László Moholy-Nagy (*Light-Space Modulator*, 1923-30), Naum Gabo (*Kinetic Construction*) and Alexander Rodchenko (*Hanging Construction*, 1920-21). Some artists made the reconstituted gallery interior one of their trademarks, Robert Irwin being prominent among them. Irwin's installations include: *Fractured Light – Partial Scrim Ceiling – Eye-level Wire* (1971), *Acrylic Column* (1970), *Eye-level Room Division* (1973), *Soft Wall* (1973), *Scrim Veil* (1975), *Wall Division – Portal* (1974), *Window Room* (1973), *Black-Line Volume* (1976), *Scrim Veil – Black Rectangle – Natural Light* (1977) and *Untitled*

(Three Triangulated Light Planes) (1979).

One of Robert Irwin's favourite devices is to restructure a museum interior with large semi-transparent scrims and veils, so that visitors aren't sure which is the wall, or the ceiling, or the door, or where the light is coming from (Irwin controls lighting carefully as well as spaces). At first it can seem as if the artist hasn't done much to alter the environment; the visitor isn't sure where the existing room ends and Irwin's art begins; only on closer inspection does the extent of Irwin's interventions in the gallery space become apparent.

In *Silence and the Ion Wind* installation (1980), Eric Orr constructed a series of dark rooms culminating in the *Golden Room* (described as 'an allusive structure for an elusive experience'), a space which was approached through an ion wind.[1] In works such as *Wall Shadow, Sky Lights, Sound Tunnel, Zero Mass, Sunrise, Blood Shadow, The Stone Snake, Prime Matter* and *Blue Void,* Orr deployed sound, light, wind, sand, ice and shadow. For *Prime Matter* (1981), Orr created fog and flames from a twenty foot tall metal column (a larger version was constructed outside the Mitsui Fudosan Building in L.A. in 1991, as a permanent sculpture). Other Orr pieces include firing xenon lasers up into the sky on top of skyscrapers in Long Beach, California (a permanent installation, *Landmark Lumière*, 1991).

Minimal painting was also linked to light art and Op Art, as well as Minimal sculpture. The chief practitioners of Op Art included Bridget Riley, Larry Poons, Piero Dorazio, Victor Vasarely, Richard Anuzkiewicz, Günter Uecker, Jesus Rafael Soto, Carlos Cruz-Dietz and Yacov Agam. As can be seen from the discussion above, Op Art (and its artists) was closely related to light art and light artists (Bruce Nauman, Keith Sonnier, Stephen Antonakos, James Turrell, Dan Flavin) and kinetic sculpture (Otto Piene, László Moholy-Nagy, George Rickey, Kenneth Martin). Some of the key Minimal painters could also be classed as optical artists: Frank Stella, Brice Marden, Ad Reinhardt, Ellsworth Kelly, Kenneth Noland, Robert Ryman and Agnes Martin.

They all experimented with the physiology of the eye and the science of visual perception. The optical effects of a Reinhardt, Stella, Martin or Marden exhibition could be just as intense as any of the Op artists.

The Minimal painters were particularly interested in painterly effects that explored the edges of optical perception: putting two panels of single colors together which were very close in value or tone; creating gradual shifts in color or tone; painting tense color clashes; producing all-black paintings which mixed in colors very subtly; using very large canvases, which took up peri-pheral vision; deploying repetitions of forms which desensitized the viewer; testing the viewer's eyes by offering very little to look at (at first), with patterns or shapes only discernible after lengthy contemplation.

KINETIC SCULPTURE AND MINIMAL ART

Kinetic art is linked to Minimal art, but most Minimal art tended to avoid the flashier, show biz side of art which emphasized optical tricks and puzzles, or motion (although there is a sense of play in the Minimalists, more than might be expected from an artform which has a reputation for being fussy, perfectionist and sombre). And the Minimal painters indulged in optical gimmickry from time to time. When one considers the major Minimal artists, their work tended towards being impassively, implacably static (Donald Judd, Sol LeWitt and Carl Andre, for example). The last thing the classic works of High Minimalism were going to do was move.

Many modern sculptors, though, actively developed movement in sculpture: Marcel Duchamp with his *Rotorelief* (1935), which span, creating a virtual circle; Naum Gabo with his *Kinetic Construction* (1920), with its oscillating rod; Len Lye's magnetized steel *Loop* (1963) and his *Fountain* (1959), which wafts from side to side; Andy Warhol's room full of silver balloon-pillows, which drifted about; or the balloons which Hans Haacke released over Central Park (1967). Minimal artists did explore issues related to movement, such as time, performance, measurement, distance, and location (especially as Minimalism developed into Postminimalism and Process art).

Alexander Calder (1898-1976) has been one of the premier kinetic or 'open form' sculptors, with his instantly recognizable spindly, intricate mobiles – the small metal plates (painted in childlike primary hues, red, blue, green yellow) supported by wire. A sculpture such as *Non-Objective* (1947) is a very complex hanging mobile, which drifts slowly, carving out its own space (and the viewer can affect the shapes the sculpture makes, too, by moving in the same space, and shifting the air). An enormous piece of public sculpture of Calder's, such as *Flamingo* (1974), at the Federal Plaza in the Windy City (where it's surrounded by vast skyscrapers of concrete and glass in the brutal International Style – buildings that're Minimal artworks in themselves), draws on the welded metal sculpture of David Smith and Antony Caro, but is characterized by the sweeping curves Calder favoured.

In upstate New York at the Storm King Art Center there are many very large Alexander Calder sculptures – and with plenty of space around them (they are installed in fields of clipped grass), they can expand in all directions. The greater the scale the more intense does the balance between weight and lightness, between mass and movement, seem.

The mobile is taken for granted now, so obvious does its construction appear. It's as if mobiles *à la* Calder have always been around. One sees mobiles everywhere, with teddy bears, whales, fairies, clowns, stars, moons, trains and Pierrots hanging from them. What is most exciting about Alexander Calder's skeletal mobiles is their motion, or their potential to move. Calder's mobiles drift slowly, each arm moving in a different manner from the others. They are powered by the random, natural energy of the breeze; thus, they could be seen as environmental artworks, because they are dependent for part of their impact on natural forces such as wind, temperature and air pressure. The balancing acts of Calder's mobiles are playful – the sculptures set alight the space around them with their gravity-shaping design and movement (as if in the act of moulding the space around them). Calder does not have a monopoly on thin, spindly sculptures made of steel: David Smith, Hans Uhlmann, Eduardo Chillida, Nancy Graves, Jean Tinguely, Alberto Giacometti and Norbert Kricke all produced sculptures in this manner.

BOXES AND SQUARES

Though circles and curves appear in Minimal art, by the far the most popular geometric shape is the square, the box and the rectangle. Minimal art is an art of right angle corners and hard edges, of large cubes and straight lines. A large proportion of Donald Judd's sculptures were cubes, usually hollow and smooth-sided (and usually not just one, but repeated in variations). David Smith created proto-Minimal sculpture with a cube. Tony Smith and Isamu Noguchi also made important cube sculptures (such as Smith's *Die* [1962], and Noguchi's *Red Cube* [1969, at 140 Broadway, New York]).

One of Tony Smith's boxes was entitled *The Black Box* (1963-65) and seemed to be simply that: a wooden box, painted black, measuring 2.5 by 3 feet. Hans Haacke constructed a *Condensation Cube* (1963-65), a clear acrylic cube with water condensating inside it. Joseph Beuys covered a 39-inch wide box with rubber and tar (*Rubberized Box*, 1957, Darmstadt). Some of Sol LeWitt's works consisted of hundreds of interconnected white cubes (and some were partial cubes, as in the *Semi-Cube Series*, 1974).

Robert Morris made his famous *I-Box* with its capital I letter-shaped door. Morris also built a box which revealed its own construction via a tape recording (*Box With the Sound of Its Own Making*). Jackie Winsor fashioned a wooden cube three feet on each side in *Burnt Piece* (1977-78). Josef Albers painted endless variations on interlocking squares in his *Homage To the Square* series. Richard Artschwager's *Table With Tablecloth* (1964) was a smooth-sided painted wooden box. *Accession II* (1967), by Eva Hesse, was a steel cube filled with rubber tubing. Larry Bell constructed many boxes, such as *Untitled No. 7* (1961) and *Bette and the Giant Jewfish* (1963), glass boxes with patterned, mirrored surfaces. The Christos wrapped up buildings like huge boxes. Most of Robert Ryman's paintings are square, like Albers' (the square was also employed as a central device by Frank Stella, Brice Marden, Jo Baer and Agnes Martin). Ad Reinhardt's most famous works, the *Black Paintings*, were five-foot squares. Robert Smithson used square mirrors set in the landscape; he also put earth and other material in boxes in his *Non-site* sculptures. The basic unit of Carl Andre's floor sculpture is a square slab of metal (Andre rarely uses individual units in his sculptures that aren't cubes or rectangles).

The Minimal cube was hard-edged, flat, precise, a mathematically perfect environment. Boxes are containers, and they can contain whole worlds, as Joseph Cornell demonstrated time and again. Cornell based his entire output around the box (box art, or art-in-a-box, became popular in the 1990s, like exhibitions of artists' books). Often, though, Minimal boxes do not contain anything – except air. The interior of the Minimal box, though, is sometimes visible, either through one wall of the cube being left open, or through (as with Donald Judd) colored Plexiglas. Sometimes the Minimal cube is an open frame, as in the sculptures of Sol LeWitt or Stephen Antonakos. The interior shape, volume, contour, lighting and texture thus becomes a part of the artwork. It alters the response to the sculpture if the viewer knows that the box or sculpture is hollow. The Minimal box cordons off the world, segments it, makes it a manageable size and shape. Irregularities are smoothed out and only the cube's six slick sides remain.

The Minimal box and square and rectangle stood out instantly from other art made in the 1960s, and from the art that preceded it. The black, white and gray cubes were very different from the soft curves of the sculpture of Jean Arp or Auguste Rodin, or Alberto Giacometti's nervous, spindly forms, or the 'organic' forms of Henry Moore and Barbara Hepworth.

MINIMAL CIRCLES

The circle motif is one of the primæval symbols (of eternity, cycles, time, rebirth, organic forms, or the 'feminine' – take your pick). The circle motif is employed in Minimal art, though the cube and rectangle are more obviously linked to Minimalism. Among Minimal artists, Donald Judd, Robert Smithson, Dennis Oppenheim and Robert Morris have used the circle. Judd produced two circular steel bands, 180 inches in diameter, a floor sculpture, as well as a concrete circular 'wall' (though he much preferred slabs, rectangles, cubes and boxes). Morris's *Untitled (2 Half-Circles With Light)* (1966), part of an installation of untitled sculptures at the Dwan Gallery in 1966, was a circle of painted wood, illuminated in the narrow gap between them by a white fluorescent lamp.

Robert Morris fabricated gigantic circular works, such as his *Observatory*, which was a huge earthwork recalling the megalithic structures of ancient times, such as Avebury and Stonehenge stone circles in Britain. Morris's *Labyrinth* was a maze-size sculpture, the kind of maze one finds in theme parks, zoos and country houses, except that *Labyrinth* used the ancient pattern of the Cretan labyrinth. Robert Smithson's *Closed Mirror Square* was like an Aztec ziggurat, while his *Amarillo Ramp* re-called the massive embankments found at British Neolithic earthworks such as Maiden Castle, or Iron Age hill forts such as British Camp on the Malvern Hills.[1] Some artists have produced stone circles which look very much like Stonehenge, such as Nancy Holt's monumental *Stone Enclosure: Rock Rings*. These Minimal sculptures are ambivalently related to ancient monuments, however, as Samuel Wagstaff remarks of Tony Smith's works:

> They are related to early cultures intentionally or through sympathy – menhirs, earth mounds, cairns... [and] to this culture with equal sympathy – smokestacks, gas tanks, dump trucks, poured concrete ramps.[2]

Michael Heizer, Robert Smithson, Robert Morris and Nancy Holt made references to ancient earthworks (Smithson visited some of Britain's prehistoric monuments, for instance). Minimal artists benefit from the allusions to ancient monuments, because the atmosphere and magic of prehistoric stones rubs off on their own work. One could see Smithson's spirals and circles as relating to feminine themes such as time, cycles, phases of the Moon, dance, transformation, ritual, initiation, astronomy, and so on. The circle is also a profound shape for alchemists. As the *Rosarium Philosophorum* has it: 'make a round circle and you will have the stone of the philosophers'.[3]

All of this allusiveness (to history, prehistory, mythology, legend, religion) is after the fact and of no concern whatsoever for Minimal artists such as Donald Judd or Sol LeWitt. It might be OK for Nancy Holt, Richard Long, Robert Smithson, Brice Marden and Carl Andre to talk about about earthworks, prehistoric circles, mythology, places and land-scapes, but it wasn't part of the agenda of Minimal artists such as Judd, LeWitt or Ryman.

PART TWO

PAINTING

#2

MINIMAL PAINTERS

THE ÆSTHETICS OF MINIMAL PAINTING

Minimal paintings, like all paintings, demand that one see them in the flesh, so to speak. The colors, shapes, patterns, forms, canvases, stretchers and scale of the paintings are crucial; one has to see them close up and for real. Minimal paintings are very physical paintings, but this is true also of Berthe Morisot, Gwen John, Artemisa Gentileschi, Diego Velásquez, Cimabue, or any painter one cares to name. The problem of appraising Minimal paintings only from reproductions in books, art magazines or the internet is that they are often abstract, and monochrome, and turn out in print form as little more than a rectangle of blue or gray. A figurative canvas by Albrecht Dürer or Jacopo Tintoretto renders much clearer in reproductions as recognisably a head, a face, a body (even modernist artists like Pablo Picasso or Vincent van Gogh are fairly clear in illustrations). But a Brice Marden or Robert Ryman in reproduction is a rectangle of gray or white which could be a patch of sky, a concrete wall, or a close-up of a car door. But even a full-color reproduction in a big, glossy art book is no real indication of a what a painting is really like. It *seems* to be more 'accurate' than a black-and-white reproduction, but it isn't.

Although Minimal paintings emphasize the frontal aspect, one can walk around the sides and look at them from other directions. Frank Stella's copper and aluminium metallic paint canvases, though apparently 'flat', are complex spatially and physically. They have a depth from the wall (Stella was fond of deep stretchers which raised his canvases a few inches out from the wall. It happened by accident, Stella explained, when he turned some wood on its side). Some of Stella's 1960s copper and aluminium stripe paintings are vast, zigzagging down gallery walls. A painting such as Stella's *Tampa* are a 100-inch high 'X' which, because of its scale (as with Mark Rothko, Morris Louis, Barnett Newman, Franz Kline or Willem de Kooning), towers over the spectator.

Even so, Minimal paintings are not usually domineering in the way that the art of Rothko or Robert Motherwell can be. The very lightness and bright colors of Stella's art dispel the sense of being overwhelmed by the paintings. Stella's art is not oppressive or gloomy at all, but is vivacious, muscular, positive and sometimes joyous.

Confronting Frank Stella's *Black-Stripe Paintings*, the spectator is really surprised by their size. In this they take much from Abstract Expressionism, but the contact between paint and canvas is new. There is no attempt at tonal, sculptural painting in the output of Stella, Morris Louis, Robert Mangold or Jo Baer. The paint touches the canvas in one flood of color. Stella's paintings are not aiming at illusionistic space, at creating illusions of faces, buildings, skies, landscapes. (Stella did, though, move towards the notion of an illustionistic 'working space' in his later painting, those 'maximalist' paintings or 'reliefs'.) Morris Louis, Stella reckons, suggested a new form of pictorial space in painting:

> What is needed is a serious effort at structural inventiveness. What Morris Louis did for a while twenty years ago, following the lead of Barnett Newman, remains more of a promise than a fulfilment. But if his promise were read rightly – if the structural potential of his spatial dynamics were understood and the disjunctive intensity of his color appreciated – his painting could lead to a new beginning… Morris Louis was nearly the last abstract painter to hint at the potential that abstraction might have for creating a full and expansive pictorial space like that of Rubens. (66)

The Sixties was an era which drew attention to the *physicality* and 'objecthood' of artworks. Color was another element in the materiality of an art object. Color was treated in the same physical (cool, detached) way as the other formal aspects of the artwork (size, shape, texture, weight, and so on). For the Post-Painterly Abstract painters (such as Morris Louis, Jules Olitski, Ellsworth Kelly, Richard Diebenkorn and Marcia Hafif), color had a direct sensual effect. The symbolic and icono-logical aspects of color were seen as not as important as haptic physicality.

In "The Plasmic Image", Barnett Newman wrote:

The present painter can be said to work with chaos not only in the sense that he is handling the chaos of the blank picture plane but also in that he is handling the chaos of form. In trying to go beyond the visible and the known world he is working with forms that are unknown even to him. He is therefore engaged in a true act of discovery in the creation of new forms and symbols that will have the living quality of creation.[1]

The (w)holistic quality of Abstract Expressionism was crucial – the instantaneous Zen-like 'all-over effect', as Barnett Newman described it (if it happens at all, it happens all at once). Donald Judd said that this holistic approach was the legacy of Jackson Pollock: this unification was 'the paramount quality and scheme of Abstract Expressionism', and it is central to the art of Frank Stella, Kenneth Noland, John Chamberlain, Mark Rothko and Barnett Newman (1964, 28). In "Specific Objects", Judd wrote that:

it isn't necessary for a work to have a lot of things to look at, to compare, to analyze one by one, to contemplate. The thing as a whole, its qualities as a whole, is what is interesting. (1965)

Jackson Pollock and Abstract Expressionism had to come first before Frank Stella's paintings could blossom. Stella makes many references to Jackson Pollock in *Working Space* (quite right: Pollock towers over modern art, and not only in painting):

we need to use Pollock. We see the potential: in the speed of the moving line, in the encapsulation and entanglement of shallow space, and in the sheer beauty of the painting's literalness, what amounts to the embodiment of its abstraction… We should be able to expand

Pollock's pictorial space and to follow the lead of his paint skeins. Painting desperately needs the literalness, immediacy, freedom, and clarity of the drip paintings. (60)

For Frank Stella, the edge of the painting may be 'hard', as in the Hard Edge painting of the Sixties, but it must enable expansion beyond (compare with Rosalind Krauss's notion of 'expanded field' sculpture):

What painting wants more than anything else is working space – space to grow with and expand into, pictorial space that is capable of direction and movement, pictorial space that encourages unlimited orientation and extension. Painting does not want to be confined by boundaries of edge and surface. (WS, 35)

Clement Greenberg had noted that any painterly mark alters the state of the canvas: '[t]he first mark made on a canvas destroys the literal and utter flatness', he wrote (1961, 106). Jackson Pollock had moved in this direction with his 'non-figurative' skeins of color.[2] But when one comes to the Minimal painters – Brice Marden, Kenneth Noland, Jo Baer and Morris Louis – there is paint brushed (or poured) straight onto the canvas, with no attempts at the usual forms of traditional Renaissance illusion, other than a simple pattern, or all-over monochromy.

When viewers first confront a Minimal painting, and see the bare canvas, it stops them up short. Something is different about Minimal paintings. One doesn't at first notice what it is. One looks closer: yes, one can see raw canvas. This bare canvas is not a sly reference on the painter's part to the manufacture of the painting (though it is that too, especially in canvases, such as Brice Marden's early works, which contain a strip of paint drips along the bottom edge, which refer to the paintings' making). They are not showing the canvas to show the spectator how the painting is made (much as a movie camera can pull back from a scene to show the lights, crew, director and people standing around, or like Robert Morris's *Box*

With the Sound of Its Own Making). Marden, Kenneth Noland, Morris Louis and Frank Stella reveal the canvas for different reasons. The paint on their canvases is not 'representational', in the usual, modernist (Renaissance) sense. It is not paintwork referring to something outside of itself. It is just *there*, it partakes of *thereness* or *dasein*, to use the terms of Zen Buddhism and Existentialism, two important influences on contemporary American art. Tony Smith remarked of his sculptures: 'I'm interested in the thing, not in the effects' (B, 385). *Things*, not effects. This is fundamental. Smith followed this view to the extent that he claimed he was not really interested in the materials, either. 'I wanted *form* to be form made of space and light and not material', he asserted.[3]

Frank Stella has the viewer confront the paint stuck on the bare canvas. A new sort of painting is created. For Sheldon Nodelman, Stella and Kenneth Noland produced a new fusion of paint and canvas, so that 'no contrast' will be 'set up between the image-content and the picture-object' (1967, 75). Finally, a painting will become an object, as Jo Baer wrote:

> The last radical paintings to attend figure-ground problems were Kenneth Noland's circle paintings of about 1960. Painters discarded ground altogether, and paintings became objects altogether. (1967, 6)

Many painters of the 1960s and after employed shaped canvases (they were also dubbed Hard Edge artists). They included Elizabeth Murray, Kenneth Noland, Frank Stella, Ed Meneeley, Dorothea Rockburne, Robert Mangold, Sam Gilliam, David Novros and Richard Tuttle. The rectangular canvas inside a gilt frame had been dispensed with by the Abstract Expressionists (and some painters before them). The complex shapes of 1960s painting added to the interpretation of the paintings as 3-D objects, perhaps sculptures, and not simply frontal-based, illusionistic paintings.

For some critics, Minimal paintings such as Brice Marden's abstract paintings created a response of 'so what?' His paintings were beautiful and sensual (a 'beautiful presence and another and another and another', as one critic put it), but to what end?[4] But beyond the difficulty and restraint of Marden's paintings, there was quite a bit going on. It's the same with other Minimal and Post-Painterly and Process/ Serial art. The closer one looks, the busier and more complex and sensual these works become. What appeared from a distance to be a uniform set of paintings or sculptures turned out to be a collection of individual works, each created with its own set of æsthetic considerations. What Marden, Agnes Martin, Robert Ryman, Donald Judd and Sol LeWitt were doing was exploring art within an apparently narrow or 'minimal' set of æsthetic constraints. When the spectator looked closer, the sense of narrowness and limitation disappeared. The feeling of openness, experimentation and play blossomed.

FRANK STELLA

Frank Stella (b. 1936) knows where he fits into the history of contemporary art: he comes after Barnett Newman and is contemporary with Jasper Johns (b. 1930), Jim Dine (b. 1935) and Sol LeWitt (b. 1928). Stella was happy to be slotted into a post-Mondrian tradition of painting by a critic:

Take, as an example, the first printed criticism of my work, which appeared in the *New Yorker* in 1960. There Robert Coates lamented "how sad it was to see the 23-year-old Frank Stella right back where Mondrian was twenty-five years ago." I realized that this remark was a polite put-down; nevertheless, the thrill it gave me was overpowering. It would have been an honour to be right back where Mondrian was twenty-five years ago, if that had been the case; but even without that possibility, the fact that my name appeared in print in the same sentence with Mondrian's seemed to be an incredible affirmation of personality and ability. It actually took me a while to get over the shock of publicity, the quick glare of history passing over me. (1986, 146)

Frank Stella's paintings command relatively high prices in the art market, though perhaps not as high as Jasper Johns' works. In Frank Stella's 1987 show at Knoedler Gallery in London's Cork Street, the larger pieces were selling for 260,000 dollars. His art was derisorily called 'bank art', the sort big companies buy. Stella has always been successful and popular, it seems. He has not gone out of fashion: his works have been a part of group shows and one-person shows ever since the late Fifties/ early Sixties. His Charles Eliot Norton lectures in 1983-4 were very popular with students.

Frank Stella has carved out a niche in the art world for himself. There are no works quite like Stella's around. There are similar pieces, but Stella's works remain instantly recognisable as Stella's works. The same cannot be said for any number of other artists.

Frank Stella wrote of contemporaries he admired, Barnett Newman and Morris Louis in *Working Space*:

The strength of his [Newman's] painting comes from the ability of the stripes (or, as he liked to call them, "zips") to attach themselves to and into the background. They fit beautifully, zipping the space together. Newman sets up the motion of his figuration counter to the motion of the space supporting it... It may be that what makes Morris Louis's late paintings so appealing is their peculiar Kandinsky-like understanding of Newman. Louis brought a determined looseness to Newman's abstraction that Kandinsky would have applauded. Louis had the opportune sense of contiguous touch that is so necessary to link the moving elements of abstraction. This touch enabled him to exploit separation in a way that modern painting admires but cannot seem to imitate. (1986, 123-125)

At the same time, Frank Stella's art broke with earlier art, as Mel Bochner noted:

Stella's work neatly bypassed most of the traits common to the painting that preceded him. Subsequent art, therefore, did not have to be the same as previous art. (1966, 40)

In *Working Space*, Frank Stella nostalgically re-called his early days in New York, where he arrived as a young would-be artist.

Exciting abstract expressionist painting seemed to be everywhere. I went from gallery to gallery, museum to museum, opening to opening, and then back to my studio to look at my own paint-ing... The painting activity surrounding me held me up physically and emotionally. The painting activity that was flowering everywhere was very open and available... (1986, 153)

Donald Judd often praised Frank Stella. Getting rid of illusion in painting, Judd said, was one of the 'decisive advances' made by Stella and Kenneth Noland.[1] In 1980 Judd said that Stella's painting had been important in the 1960s because it was non-relational and non-anthropo-morphic (F. Colpitt, 69). Stella's new sense of space, Donald

Judd argued,

> makes Abstract Expressionism seem now an inadequate style, makes it appear a compromise with representational art and its meaning. (1964, 28)

For Donald Judd, a Stella painting (referring to one of the aluminium series) was 'something of an object, it is a single thing, not a field with something in it, and it has almost no space' (1963). Sheldon Nodelman concurred with Judd, claiming that Stella and Noland had finally done away with illusionism.[2] Willis Domingo said that Stella solved

> the contradiction in a spatial ambiguity whereby literal and illusionistic space become indistinguishable from one another.[3]

When one looks at Frank Stella's paintings, the intention is that all of the painting is glimpsed all at once. The effect really is like that of Zen Buddhism, and the references to Zen of course were occurring in places such as the Beat poets in New York in the late 1950s, when Stella was starting out as a painter. The Beat poets – Allen Ginsberg, Jack Kerouac, William Burroughs, *et al*, appropriated Oriental philosophy for their own ends. They Americanized it, one might say.

Frank Stella steers clear of such philosophizing, but the all-over, instantaneous effect he desired in painting has much in common with the 'timeless now' of Tao and Zen philosophy. It is other American painters who theorized in the grand fashion, bringing in Oriental mysticism – such as Robert Motherwell and Barnett Newman. In *Working Space*, Frank Stella sticks to theorizing in the Western tradition about æsthetics, making references to the 'great' names of Western painting: Titian, Michelangelo Merisi da Caravaggio, Pablo Picasso, and Peter Rubens.

Frank Stella relates to the Old Masters and historical tradition. Just as Kasimir Malevich made references to the Byzantine ikon tradition and Brice Marden acknowledges Old Masters such as the Spanish painters Francisco de Zurbarán, Diego Velásquez, Édouard Manet and Paul Cézanne, so Stella refers consciously to many former artists. Michael Fried, in a "New York Letter" of 1964, writes that Stella and Barnett Newman are 'historically self-aware' (1964). Stella's acute (art) historical self-awareness came out very clearly in his book *Working Space*.

Frank Stella often talked about the uncertain reaction to the new painting:

> I always get into arguments with people who want to retain the old values in painting – the humanistic values that they... find on the canvas. If you pin them down, they always end up asserting that there is something there besides the paint on the canvas. My painting is based on the fact that only what can be seen there is there... What you see is what you get. ■

Frank Stella was certainly influenced by Jasper Johns, as William Rubin noted:

> Frank was, I think, very interested in Johns' work in his last months at Princeton and immediately after he graduated. Johns' flags would be the pictures we'd have to look to in that sense, because they provided a concept of a picture that would be striped, as these pictures are, and also where the stars are a kind of box, which is not unrelated to the box in the center of *Coney Island*. Johns' pictures interested Frank because of certain repetition, repetition of numbers or letters or stripes of the flag, and Frank saw possibilities in this repetition which Johns himself was not to see.[4]

Jasper Johns' ideas on painting are much more romantic than Stella's: Johns writes of his desires for painting:

> I think that one wants from a painting a sense of life. The final suggestion, the final statement, has to be not a deliberate statement but a helpless statement. It has to be what you can't avoid saying.[5]

The power of Jasper Johns' works comes partly

from his incredible surfaces, which are made of oil and wax or encaustic, spread thickly on the canvas. Paintings such as *White Flag* (1955, collection: the artist), *Highway* (1959, collection: Mrs Leo Castelli, New York), *Scent* (1973-74, collection: Ludwig Aachen) and *Canvas* (1956, collection: the artist) are really exquisite works, so intensely tactile and sumptuous. In Frank Stella's art the sense of surface is not as stridently sensual as in Johns' art. Stella is interested in different things.

Frank Stella was relatively successful early on in his career, like his contemporaries Jasper Johns and Robert Rauschenberg. Of Johns' career, which parallels that of Stella, Peter Fuller wrote:

> In 1958, Alfred Barr cooled his support of Abstract Expressionism, and urged artists to rebel against their elders. Significantly, Barr, too, was involved in the manufacture of Jasper Johns. Until 1958, Johns was an obscure artist who had inserted certain Dadaesque representational components into what was essentially a modified Abstract Expressionist style. That year, he was given a one-man show by Castelli; before it opened, the decision had been taken to put him on the front cover of *Art News* (hitherto a partisan Abstract Expressionist publication). MOMA immediately purchased examples of his work.[6]

William Rubin discussed the relation between Jasper Johns and Frank Stella, and the influence it had on Stella:

> there's a vast difference in sensibilities and in aims, so I don't want to make this relationship too close, but I think Johns also had one other importance. That is, his flag pictures and some of the other images he made were the first paintings in which the field of the pictures is absolutely identical with the motif of the picture: the boundaries of the pictures are identical with the boundaries of the flag. The flag is laid out as a flat pattern on the surface, and although Johns is a representational painter in that sense and Frank became an abstract painter, I think the notion of making the motif identical with the

shape of the field, even though that shape remains rectangular in Johns' flag, lurks somewhere behind what would become the principle of Frank's shaped canvas. And that principle is, if I can define it in its simplest way, essentially that the boundary of the picture is going to be determined by the governing pattern of the surface, and that there will be an absolute reciprocity between the outer shape of the picture, which might be considered simply the outside line of a pattern that operates over the entire surface.[7]

Marcel Duchamp and Kurt Schwitters are usually cited as precursors of Robert Rauschenberg's and Jasper Johns' mixed media explorations. Rauschenberg and Johns rewrote the notion of painting-as-object by sticking objects onto it. Schwitters is often cited as a major exponent of multi-media formalism. Schwitters explained how he came to do it:

> I simply could not see any reason why old streetcar tickets, driftwood, coat checks, wire and wheel parts, buttons, junk from the attic and heaps of refuse should not be used as material for paintings, any less than colors made in a factory.[8]

Frank Stella moved into three dimensions in the 1970s, building his paintings out from the wall, with paintings such as *Warka III* and *Leblon II*.

There are many other contemporary artists who have developed out of Jasper Johns' and Frank Stella's post-Abstract Expressionist painting: among the more successful are painters such as Christopher Le Brun, Thérèse Oulton, Lance Smith, Hughie O'Donoghue, R. B. Kitaj, Jim Dine, Richard Diebenkorn and Anselm Keifer (such as in his *Wayland's Song* (1982), which uses oil, emulsion, straw on photo, on canvas with lead). Painters who seem to have a direct Stellan component include Brice Marden, Sean Scully, Howard Hodgkin and Gerard Richter. The Minimal sculptors – Donald Judd, Robert Morris, Carl Andre – have acknowledged Stella's importance.

Frank Stella employed hard-edged, angular

motifs, shapes such as Vs, Zs, Xs, Hs, Ls, Ts, Us, 'notched Vs', polygons, squares and rectangles. He also used symmetry, an exact symmetry made explicit and bold by his stripes and the shaped stretchers, so that the stripe pattern, writes John Coplans, 'begins at the center and spreads outward by his use of various kinds of symmetry'.9 For Stella, the new sense of symmetry was not sited within an illusionistic space; rather, the use of hard edges, symmetry and the monochrome bands helped to push away illusionistic space:

A symmetrical image or configuration placed on an open ground is not balanced out in the illusionistic space. The solution I arrived at – and there are probably others although I know of only one, color density – forces illusionistic space out of the painting at a constant rate by using a regulated pattern.10

Frank Stella's symmetry, then, is not concerned with 'illusionistic space', as he calls it, the space of traditional Western post-Renaissance art, but with a new flatness. Stella said:

I had to do something about relational painting, i.e. the balancing of the various parts of the painting with and against each other. The obvious answer was symmetry – make it the same all over.11

While painters such as Frank Stella and Ken Noland stressed the flatness of Sixties painting, Helen Frankenthaler said that

all totally abstract pictures – the best ones that really come off – Newman, Pollock, Noland – have tremendous space; perspective space despite the emphasis on flat surface. (1965, 36)

Even when the stretchers are not shaped, as in with the *Black Paintings*, which were (usually) rectangular, the V-shapes still deny illusionistic space. At first, the *Black Paintings* seem to be somewhat 'traditional', as they employ the rectangular shape. Inside the field of the rectangle,

though, Stella paints, directly onto the canvas, stripes of black, in V-shapes and rectangles, as in *Tomlinson Court Park* and *Point of Pines*.

Max Kozloff wrote in 1962 of Jasper Johns' motifs, the flags and targets saying they were

merely so many abstract forms upon which social usage has conferred meaning, but which now, displaced into their new context, cease to function socially. From this tremendous insight alone have sprung the momentum of Pop Art and the huge quantities of abstraction that is emblematic in character.12

The key to Jasper Johns' reworking of formalism and abstraction in the flags, targets, numbers and alphabets was precisely the sensuality of his art. It was the way he so powerfully employed the techniques of the Old Masters, of 'great art', that made his flags and targets so successful. For critics could not see Johns' banal signs culled from popular culture as trivial art, because Johns used one of the key elements in high art, the sensual, heavily impastoed surface. Johns' art could not be dismissed by critics, then as now, because its surface is as sensual and painterly as Rembrandt van Rijn, Diego Velásquez, Édouard Manet or Titian. In *Working Space*, Stella discusses Michelangelo Merisi da Caravaggio's art:

The second miracle of Caravaggio is the miracle of surface. Skin, flesh, and pigment blend into reality. Painting is acknowledged as an act and as a physical fact, but immediately afterward, almost simultaneously, the presence of the human figure is felt as real, touchably there. (1986, 11)

Frank Stella, though he would deny it, also created sensual art objects. Stella often denies any 'emotion' or 'feeling' in his art. It is not about that, he says. For some people, he knows, his art comes across as cold. Brian O'Doherty called Stella 'the Cézanne of nihilism, the master of *ennui*'.13 Donald Kuspit called his art 'authoritarian' and mechanistic (1977, 25). Irving Sandler said that in its boredom, Stella's painting has affinities to Reinhardt's, but… Stella appears to have made it the content of his art – a content so novel and perverse as to be interesting.

It is not Stella's intention to be 'cold' or 'unfeeling'. Stella reckons his *Black Paintings* were as emotional as Mark Rothko's tragic canvases:

> Certainly no one would see the black paintings now as cold and calculating or very logical, but they seemed to seem that way in the context of '59 and '60. They were lean compared with some paintings, but the general look of them, if you really looked, seemed to me to have an awful lot to do with somebody like Rothko in feeling – and no one accused Rothko of being cold and intellectual. [14]

For Donald Judd, 'painterly feeling' was not valid anymore. Painterly feeling did not have to be the only element in art, Judd said. 'It's been fully exploited and I don't see why the painterly relationship exclusively should stand for art'. [15] There does not seem to be much going on in Frank Stella's paintings, as in many Post-Painterly Abstract paintings. But there is, in fact, a lot going on. Stella limits himself to a narrow set of rules. Like Brice Marden, Kenneth Noland, Barnett Newman, Morris Louis and Mark Rothko, Stella sets himself to explore a few configurations of painting. But these things – shape of the canvas, internal organization of the stripes, color of the bands – offer up endless permutations. Painters go over the same simple patterns and set-ups again and again. J.M.W. Turner painted thousands of seascapes – the same basic ocean, framed in the same lower third of the picture, the same mixture of clouds and sun in the sky, and so on, attacking it from thousands of different viewpoints and different locations, from every shoreline of Britain, to France, Switzerland, Italy and Germany. Similarly, Claude Monet painted the same basic picture of a sunlit river time after time.

Like other Sixties artists, Frank Stella explored the endless permutations that a few very simple elements offered up. The results seem to be 'lean', but even in the most minimal of Minimalist works there is sensuality and presence. Samuel Wagstaff notes that the Minimal painting asserts the painting above the painter: the author slips into the background: '[t]here is an attempt to suggest the presence of paint rather than the presence of the painter' (1964, 62). Michael Fried remarked that 'the vital presence of Stella's paintings cannot be understood'. Stella said that he didn't want the heroic gestures and detail of traditional or Abstract Expressionist painting:

> One could stand in front of any Abstract Expressionist work for a long time, and walk back and forth, and inspect the details of the pigment and the inflection and all the painterly brushwork for hours. But I wouldn't particularly want to do that and I also wouldn't ask anyone to do that in front of my paintings. [16]

Certainly Frank Stella's art is intense: his *Black Stripe Paintings*, his *Protractor* series, his copper paintings, and his *India Birds*, are intense examples of art. Works such as *Quath-lamba* (1964), *D* (1963) and *Avicenna* (1960), are very powerful paintings. *D*, in particular, is impressive: one of the *Purple Polygons* series, it is a huge (7 feet high and wide) ten-sided polygon, with the centre left empty, as so often in Stella's paintings. This exhibition of *Purple Polygons* was called 'boring' and 'monotonous' by some critics [17] but how could paintings such as *D* be termed 'boring'? Just the opposite of boring, one could say.

On Frank Stella's stripe, Kenneth Noland commented:

> It's as if Frank works from the outside of the picture in. I'd always felt myself like I was working from the inside of the picture out, and that the shape was a resulting factor rather than a determining factor. [18]

Carl Andre commented on Frank Stella's stripe thus:

Frank Stella has found it necessary to paint stripes. There is nothing else in his painting. Symbols are counters passed among people. Frank Stella's painting is not symbolic. His stripes are the paths of brush on canvas. These paths lead only into painting. (1959, 76)

'I lose sight of the fact that my paintings are on canvas, even though I know I'm painting on canvas, and I just see my paintings', said Frank Stella.[19] In the *Black Stripe Paintings* the space between each stripe is smudged; in the *Dartmouth* and later in the *Protractor* paintings, the bands became more and more clearly defined, so that Stella ended up with a clear width between each area of paint. As with David Hockney, Morris Louis and other painters who worked directly onto canvas, Stella's colors fuse with the support and canvas. The realization that the painting is an object in its own right developed in Stella's æsthetics, until the movement into painting-reliefs and then into sculptural paintings, or painterly sculptures, was quite natural. 'A sculpture is just a painting cut out and stood up somewhere', said Stella.

Frank Stella's stripes or bands are a powerful visual element which firmly anchor his paintings. The relation between the shaped canvas and the stripes makes sure that the painting remains intense. In *Chocorua III* (1966), a bright yellow stripe follows the edge of a complexly shaped canvas, creating a luminous zigzag which partially enclosed an equilateral canvas, which is slotted into the larger canvas. This bold conception is made powerful by Stella's use of the yellow stripe abutting a grey stripe, which encloses the pink centre of the triangle. Stripe and shaped paintings such as *Valpariso Flesh and Green* (1963), are typical of Stella's boldness and simplicity: two triangular stretchers are slotted together: one is orange, the other is green, both triangles are painted in stripes.

In many Frank Stella paintings, the stripes 'radiate out from the center of the canvas towards the edge', wrote William Rubin (1970, 65).

Paintings such as *Gur* (1968) are powerful, relying on a simple geometry – a circle dissected into colored segments – coupled with blinding colors: pink, yellow, light white, orange, black, purple, blue. Stella is very dexterous at handling colors, at putting colors beside each other. His colors are so exuberant partly because of his handling of complimentary colors, the way he sets yellow next to black, or green next to orange.

The all-over evenness of his paintwork enhances the power of his paintings. As he wrote: 'I tried for an evenness, a kind of all-overness, where the intensity remained regular over the entire surface'.[20] But Frank Stella did not want people to stand in front of his admiring his dexterous skill in painting. He was not 'showing off' gesturally. He didn't want attention drawn to the marks he made, but to the painting as a whole. Stella changed his mind, though: in the late 'maximalist' works there is a huge emphasis on gesture and brushwork. Paint is daubed in all manner of gestures on the huge aluminium and steel reliefs. Glitter is stuck onto the surfaces, the paintings beg for a sensual response. 'I don't know how I got into sculpture. I liked its physicality, that's the only reason'.

Frank Stella's supports in the 1980s became increasingly complex, and huge. The Vs, Zs, Xs, Hs, Ls, Ts, Us and polygons of the Sixties dazzle with their simple geometry. Like the Pyramids in Egypt, they are simple shapes, but given a bombastic, decisive, rigorously methodical treatment. The use of monochrome helped to give the huge paintings a pictorial unity. Some of the metallic paintings are vast. The *Protractor* paintings combined circles and rectangles, but it is the colors which one notices first, the complex interlocking arches and circles of colors, reds interweaving and over-lapping with yellow, pink, blue, purple, amber, green, black. Incredible colors, in Stella's *Protractor* series, utterly distinctive, visible from a great distance.

Frank Stella's paintings are full of confidence and assertiveness. They are paintings that know exactly what they are doing. They are full of a drive that one might see as ruthlessness, but is in fact the Sixties ethic of taking an idea to its logical conclusion. Stella loves method, like so many artists. One can follow his thinking as he moves from pattern to pattern, from each configuration of color, shape, support, scale, stripes and space. 'The paintings got sculptural because the forms got more complicated. I've learned to weave in and out'.

In Frank Stella's post-1970s paintings, there is no attempt to smooth over the edges, or to provide a smooth surface to the paint, as with the Sixties *Protractor* paintings. Rather, Stella draws attention to the expressive qualities of his brushwork, as with William de Kooning or Julian Schnabel. The expressiveness of Stella's gestures becomes an important element in the painting. The brush-strokes are not hidden as in Barnett Newman's art, who painted with a small brush in small strokes, building up his layers of paint carefully, so that no brushstrokes showed. Stella, rather, constantly draws attention to his brushstrokes, to the very manufacture of his paintings. Works such as *La Vecchia dell'orto* (1986), *Guadalupe Island* (1979), *Shards II* (1983), *Steller's Albatross* (1976) and *Shama* (1979), open out to reveal their manu-facture.

In the 1960s, Frank Stella used bright colors, like Morris Louis, but kept them neatly bounded within their stripe patterns. The late maximalist works continually refer to the making of paintings. For Stella, the artist is a privileged participant in the making of art: the 'audience' or viewer is always one step away, is always 'after the fact': '[t]he sensation is one that the artist experiences as the first and only necessary viewer' (1986, 127).

MORRIS LOUIS

Morris Louis (1912-1962) was a Colorfield painter, who died of lung cancer age 49 in 1962. Louis studied at the Maryland Institute of Fine and Applied Arts, between 1929 and 1933. In the late 1930s, he lived in New York City for four years, and met artists such as Arshile Gorky, Jack Tworkov, and David Alfaro Siqueiros. He worked for the Works Progress Administration Federal Art Project. He taught in Baltimore (privately) between 1940 and 1948. In 1947 he married Marcella Siegel. By 1952, Louis was living in Washington, D.C., where the art scene included artists such as Anne Truitt, Kenneth Noland, Gene Davis, Tom Downing and Howard Mehring. In the late 1950s (between 1955 and 1957), Louis destroyed many of his paintings.

Among the important exhibitions of Morris Louis' work were the retrospectives in 1986 at New York's MOMA and a touring show at the Hirshhorn in D.C. in 2007-08. Also, shows in Washington in 1976, Boston in 1967, and the Guggenheim in 1963.

Morris Louis's guru was the critic Clement Greenberg. According to Robert Hughes, Louis's paintings were selected and altered by Greenberg; the critic decided 'where to cut off the stripes'.[1] Apart from Greenberg, influences on the develop-ment of Morris Louis's art included the intense coloration of Pierre Bonnard and Henri Matisse. Painters such as Matisse and Pablo Picasso are cited time after time in discussions of Colorfield and Post-Painterly Abstraction, as well as Abstract Expressionism. The other important presence in painting for the Sixties Colorfield painters was Jackson Pollock (and also Mark Rothko and Willem de Kooning). One can see how Pollock's way of approaching the canvas directly inspired Louis.

The other significant presence in Morris Louis's career was Helen Frankenthaler. It was seeing one of Frankenthaler's huge stained canvases (*Mount-ains and Sea*, 1952 and later paintings) that supposedly inspired Louis (and Kenneth Noland), when the artists visited Frankenthaler in Gotham in

1953. He called Frankenthaler's method of stained painting a 'bridge between Pollock and what was possible'.[2] For Clement Greenberg, Louis was reacting against his former Cubism. 'The crucial revelation he got from Pollock and Frankenthaler had to do with facture as much as anything else', Greenberg remarked.[3]

In Morris Louis's works, John Elderfield noted in his 1986 monograph on the artist, color was freed up from 'sculptural modelling', 'but not entirely, because in such a white-infused, close-valued style, shifts of color tend also to read as shifts of tone'.[4] The problem for Louis was that when color is used in abstract painting without any visual motifs it can lose the 'traditional stability and gravity' of painting, can be descriptive more of dusky atmosphere than clean open air'.[5] In his 1987 essay on Jackson Pollock and Louis, Andrew Kagan claimed that Louis learnt from Pollock about 'æsthetic morality, about the necessity of risk, about greatness, seriousness, absoluteness, bigness, and individualism'.[6]

Morris Louis advocated the direct contact with the canvas that characterizes much of Post-Painterly Abstraction. Louis poured paint onto the canvas in creases and twists and folds, to produce deeply saturated furls, blotches and drapes of color, in paintings such as *Alpha-Delta* (1961, Everson Museum of Art, New York), *Saraband* (1959, Guggenheim Museum, New York), *Vav* (1960, Tate Gallery), and *Aleph* (1960, collection: del Amo, Madrid).

Unlike some of the other Sixties and Colorfield painters, Morris Louis sometimes used titles for his paintings which recalled the mythic subjects favoured by the Abstract Expressionists. Louis did not want the process of making the painting to be apparent: he didn't want brushstrokes to be seen. Instead, he folded the canvas and used gravity to stain the canvas. Robert Morris and the Process artists later reversed this tendency, by making the process of making the work one of its most prominent features. Louis wanted the paint to fuse with canvas, so that all sense of illusionism would be avoided. Louis's stained paint was semi-transparent, so the veils of color seemed to float apart from the cotton duck canvas. Louis's aim, according to Clement Greenberg, was to keep the pigment thin enough to prevent a sense of the tactile, so that when the canvas was soaked with paint it becomes 'paint in itself, color in itself'.[7] Louis's veils were held back, color-wise, at the edges: he overlaid grey and brown on his veils of bright color.

Cloaking them outwardly in dignified reserve, he allowed only precisely measured, tantalizing glimpses of the passionate intensity within. He created images not only of great beauty but also of monumental power

wrote Andrew Kagan (139).

Morris Louis's method of pouring paint onto canvas was kept a secret, and, because there is not very much documentation, it is not certain exactly what his methods were. Louis worked in a small room, and it is thought that the fumes from his solvents contributed towards the lung cancer he died from at 49 years old.

Part of Morris Louis's staining technique derived from the particular kind of paint he used: Magna was a synthetic medium (oil-miscible acrylic resin paint) which could be thinned to the consistency of watercolor. Also the Magna paint dried quickly, so that Louis could pour the paint in layers, on top of each other.[8] Paint manufacturer Leonard Bocour supplied Louis with his new acrylic polymer emulsion, in gallon cans ('big tubes for big paintings'). Louis told Bocour that 'part of my thesis is that materials influence form' (ibid.). Louis controlled the absorbency of the paint using thinners, adding turps and resins thinner; later, he abandoned sizing the canvas, so the color could penetrate the weave deeper.

The 'Veils' and 'Unfurleds' were made by attaching the canvas to some scaffolding: Morris Louis poured the paint down the canvas, putting one color on top of another. Some of the overlapping areas produced stunning color effects (as in *Saraband, Beth Chaf, Atomic Crest* or *Longitude*). The floral motifs were achieved by pouring the paint onto the cotton duck from a few different points towards the centre (as in *Point of Tranquillity, Number 99, Spawn* and *Aleph*). The staining technique (in the *Floral* series, for example) related also to Renaissance fresco painting, as well as Impressionism's open color and the example of Henri Matisse's open color (J. Elderfield, 1986). In paintings such as *Beth* (1959-60, Philadelphia Museum of Art), *Point of Tranquility* (1959-60), and *Aleph Series V* (collection: H. Frankenthaler), Louis produced some enormous, incredibly luminous, and very memorable works. *Point of Tranquility, Spawn* (1959-60, London) and *Number 99* (1959-60, Cleveland) were riots of rainbow hues: bright yellows, oranges, reds, greens, and blues, all exploding outwards from the centre of the huge canvas (*Point of Tranquility* is 2.58 by 3.43 yards).

Beth is one of Morris Louis's most radiant paintings, being predominantly red (the vibrancy of the scarlet is only slightly modulated by the introduction of smaller patches of green and blue). *Beth Chaf* (1959, collection: M.L. Brenner) was similarly warm-hued, with only a thick stripe of dark green countering the reds, oranges and browns. In *Aleph Series V* the color saturation reaches a new intensity, with the explosion of rainbow colors being overlaid with layer upon layer of pigment, so that the main central area is stained dark brown by the sheer force of one color on top of another.

In the 'Veils' series, Morris Louis's paintings layered and mixed colors, sometimes not always successfully. The 'Veil' paintings could be overwhelming, being walls of color. In the *Gamma, Sigma, Alpha* and *Omega* paintings of the early Sixties, Louis kept the colors more separated. The centre of the canvas was often left unpainted, resulting in more open and relaxed forms. In *Gamma Iota* (1960, private collection), *Gamma Pu* (1960, private collection), and *Alpha Alpha* (1960, collection: W. Ehrlich), there are fewer stripes of

color than usual (4 on each side), green, blue and black on the right, red, purple and black on the left. In *Alpha Beta* (1960, collection: I.M. Pei) there are only three bands of colors on each side, and the whole color scheme only consists of two hues: green and yellow (thus, on the left and right, the diagonal rivers of color are yellow-green-yellow). In *Alpha Tau* (St Louis Art Museum), Louis left a very wide gap of bare canvas between the diagonal stripes (eleven on each side). *Alpha Lambda* (1961, collection: C. Hendrickson), *Beta Kappa* (1961, National Gallery of Art, Washington), *Beta Lambada* (1960, MOMA, New York) and *Sigma* (1961, private collection) were more typical, employing a bunch of some 13 or 14 diagonal bands, with hot and cool colors complementing each other. Generally, in these *Alpha* diagonal paintings, the colors on each side reflect each other. Not in a simple symmetry; but the orange stripe on the left would be picked up on the right, but in a different place.

Pillars of Hercules (1960, Thyssen-Bornemisza Collection) was part of Morris Louis's 'Column' series, made before he started on his 'Unfurleds' series. The strips of Magna paint are vertical, three or four on each side of the canvas: yellow, violet and two reds on the left, two reds on the right. Other paintings in the 'Column' series, all featuring narrow bands of color grouped together to form a single column, included *Number 11* (1961, private collection), a tight mesh of overlapping colors; *Burning Stain* (1961, University of Nebraska, Lincoln), much softer/ lighter hues; *Number 9* (1961, collection: L. & G. de Menil), closely-packed brightly-hued stripes (greens, yellows, oranges); *Third Element* (1961, MOMA, NY), where blues and greens alternate with reds, yellows and oranges; *Number 33* (1962, private collection) and *Biplane* (1962, collection: T. Wiesel), in which the column is separated by a single band of bare canvas; *Number 2-64* (1962, collection: A. Rock), a simple group of six colors; *Number 19* (1962, collection: D. Mirvish), a narrow group of 8 hues; and *Castor and Pollux* (1962, the Eli and Edythe L. Broad collection), 9 bands of bright colors, framed by an orange stripe each side. Then there were one or two of the 'Columns' series which featured more than one column, such as *Number 1-99* (1962, collection: L. Brenner), which had three columns.

Omega IV (1959-60, private collection) was unusual in Morris Louis's *œuvre*: it had two series of rivers of color interweaving from opposite directions on the canvas; in *Delta Upsilon* (1960, private collection), the group of colors on the right is joined by another group, breaking the usual Louisian sense of symmetry. In *Alpha Eta* (1960, private collection) and *Alpha Epsilon* (1960, Museum of Contemporary Art, Los Angeles), the rivers of color were joined together over a strip of bare canvas.

Morris Louis's *Blue Veil* (1958-59, Fogg Art Museum) was a vast area of mainly blue paint. The edge of the paint stain could be clearly seen around the edge of most of the canvas. Underneath the blue paint Louis had poured variations of violet and green, both colors linked with blue in the traditional color wheel. Yellow was also employed (on the right-hand side) as an under-color The effect was a curtain of blue modulated by green, violets and yellows, which moved in and out of the dominant hue. *Blue Veil* was in musical terms a variation on blue, using the colors that harmonized with blue. The effect recalled the layering technique of Mark Rothko's paintings. In *Blue Veil* the facture of the work is plainly visible: the viewer can take apart the process of making the artwork, so that Louis can almost be glimpsed pouring the acrylics, folding the canvas, manipulating the paint using gravity, allowing one layer to dry, but ensuring another layer is poured on top of one that's still wet.

Blue Veil is one of Morris Louis's most appealing, most mesmeric canvases, in the way that the hues of the pigment shifts as they travel across the picture, the selection of voluptuous colors, the way some colors melt into others, and some retain their form, with harder edges, the balancing of hues (for example, pale blues on the extreme right and left), and the sheer scale of the painting. *Blue Veil*

celebrates the act of painting, so that there's no way it could be said that Painting Was Dead by 1960. In its way, Louis's *Blue Veil* is as vivacious and subtle a celebration of the art of painting as any of the Old Masters. Certainly Louis's method of layering pigment is as technically dazzling as the films of oil paint the Early Netherlandish painters (Jan van Eyck, Rogier van der Weyden, Hans Memling *et al*), where paintings were created by building up successive layers of oil, to produce that glowing inner light. Louis's light may be much more on the surface than Early Flemish art, but just because it doesn't enshrine depth doesn't mean it's no less valuable (Louis's canvases look towards the flatness and surface of postmodern art, where everything happens on the surface, where everything is brought to the front, *à la* Jean Baudrillard and Frederic Jameson).

Another drape work, *Number 1-89* (1959, Des Moines Art Center), was unusual, in being a light-toned and largely monochromatic work, this time in yellow and ochre. *Verdicchio* (1959, collection: J.D. Murchison) was a similarly single-color drape of paint (light green). *Mem* (1959, collection: B. Wright) was in the more familiar Louis hue of orange/ gold.

Tet (1958, Whitney Museum of American Art) was another large *Unfurled* canvas (twelve feet nine inches wide), comprising curtains of blue and green superimposed on yellows and golds. It achieved an impressive wash of pure color, with the canvas cut around the sides just above and around the points where the synthetic polymer soaked into the canvas. In *Untitled* (1959), an unfurled painting, swathes of blended acrylic create a drape of color in this portrait-format picture. In between the large areas of pigment, Morris Louis had left bare canvas.

Kaf (1959-60, collection: Kimiko & John G. Powers, New York) is one of Morris Louis's most fabulous canvases, an 8' 4" by 12' painting in rich, warm reds, oranges, yellows, greens, blues and purples. The unrestrained, opulent colors spread over the surface of the canvas in irregular patterns, outward from the centre, as in other *Unfurleds*, but with darker areas of red and blue in the middle vaguely reminiscent of the vertical stripes.

A series of veils or drapes of the mid-Fifties (*Iris, Salient, Pendulum, Longitude, Atomic Crest, Intrigue*) were much paler, with more of the translucent effects of watercolor technique. These paintings employed washes of pastel hues – pinks, purples, blues, greens – recalling Helen Frankenthaler's paintings. *Intrigue* (1954, collection: J. Slifka, New York) used mainly purples and pinks and reds; *Atomic Crest* (1954, Lannan Foundation) merged similar hues with more blues and greys; in *Salient* (1954, collection: D. Zucker), Morris Louis thinned the pigment considerably, so that towards the base of the canvas the colors were faded; *Longitude* (1954, collection: M.L. Brenner) veered towards the warmer end of the color spectrum, with an irregularly-patterned staining composition; *Iris* (1954, collection: E. Schwartz) and *Pendulum* (1954, collection: H.W. Anderson) moved into the more familiar, darker tones of the later Louis paintings, with a more complex and multi-layered structure.

The 'Bronze Veils' series were large horizontal canvases with swathes of stained paint merging together: *Beth Anin, Earth, Beth Gimel, Beth Kuf, Curtain, Beth Rash, Beth Heh, Beth Nun, Beth Samach, Beth Peh* and *Spark*. They were all in gold, bronze, brown, yellow and ochre colors, with all the color values relatively close, like the tones. Yellow under-painting is allowed to burst out from underneath, to the right, in the otherwise sombre all-over brown of *Beth Gimel* (1958, collection: R. Rowan). In *Beth Samach* (7 ft 5 in by 11 ft 5 in) the greeny-gold on the left merges into orangey-gold, then reddish-gold; then greenish-gold on the right. In *Beth Heh* (collection: G. Gund), there is brown on the left, ochre in the centre and right, with red stains in the middle. In *Beth Ayin*, swathes of brown frame gold and red in the centre. 1959's *Golden Age* (Ulster Museum) was a drape of dark ochre and gold, with yellow, blue and green underpainting. *Loam* (1958, Houston) was a much darker

canvas, with a similar interior composition to *Golden Age*.

Bower (1958, Nationalgalerie, Berlin) was another bronze/ brown painting, but with the luminous reds and greens of the under-staining showing in patches over the surface. In *Beth Rash* (1958-59, collection: J. Lebron) the palette moves towards dark blues and purples, but caught in the same vertically symmetrical composition, with the colors being poured from the top downwards. In *Beth Rash*, some of the colors underneath can be glimpsed in rows at the top of the canvas: purple, orange, turquoise, red, yellow. *Italian Bronze* (1959, collection: S. Hahn) had fused stains bleeding into each other: green, blue, brown, damson, and black.

Where (1960, Smithsonian Institute) was another large (3.33 yards wide) landscape format 'curtain' of color, but this time with no layering or under-painting; each stripe of color was kept separate, with a few inches of bare canvas in between. The stripes ran vertically across the whole of the canvas, from top to bottom. The color choices combined to create an ecstatic piece: yellow, orange, green, blue, lemon, khaki, brown, red, turquoise. *While Series II* (1959-60) was similar to *Where*, but had the vertical stains overlapping in groups. *While Series II* was also framed each side by a very dark blue and black stripe. In *Moving In* (1961, André Emmerich Gallery, NYC), narrow bands of acrylic run in vertical stripes from roughly the same point in this portrait-format canvas. Warm hues predominate: reds, oranges, yellows.

Later, Morris Louis produced a series of paintings consisting of stripes in groups. Louis mounted these either vertically or horizontally. *Horizontal I* (1962, collection: M. Cogan) was a simple group of colors (beige, orange, red, brown, blue, and yellow), clustered in the lower half of the nearly three-yard-wide canvas. *Horizontal III* (1962, private collection) was a landscape-format painting consisting of two groups of bands of colors (yellow, red, green, purple and black). *Horizontal VIII* (1962, private collection) also featured two groups of horizontal bands of color, four above and four below, separated by a layer of empty canvas.

Morris Louis's *Omicron* (1961, private collection) has a large empty V-shaped space at its centre, with the familiar Louis stripes each side, running diagonally from the sides of the canvas to the base. The colors of the right-hand group of diagonals – red, purple – are picked up in the left-hand group. While the 'Columns' inevitably recalled Barnett Newman and his famous zip or stripe, some of Louis's last works evoked the art of Kenneth Noland and Ellsworth Kelly: these pieces (such as *Hot Half*, 1962, private collection and *Equator*, 1962, private collection), featured a band of stripes moving across the canvas diagonally. However, the edge of each band of color was straight, recalling Hard Edge and Colorfield painting.

In *Working Space* Frank Stella wrote of this new painterly/ Post-Painterly/ Colorfield/ Hard Edge abstraction:

The free-unfettered access to abstraction's early roots had a wonderful and powerful effect: close attention to the early masters coupled with a natural, relaxed attitude toward enlarged pictorial scale and gesture made exciting painting. Jack Youngerman, Ellsworth Kelly, and Sam Francis took off in what seemed like a marvellous, yet familiar, vector. Helen Frankenthaler and Friedel Dzubas were reaching new, relaxed, lyrical heights. Morris Louis, Kenneth Noland, and Jules Olitski undertook an exotic trip in search of firstness, while Donald Judd, Larry (now Lawrence) Poons, and I laid the track to literalism. (160)

Here one senses Frank Stella's pride in being a part of 1960s painterly abstraction. With Stella's *Black-Stripe Paintings*, one is really surprised by their size. In this they take much from Abstraction Expressionism, but the contact between paint and canvas is new. There is no attempt at tonal, sculptural painting in the art of Morris Louis and Frank Stella. The paint touches the canvas in one flood of color. Stella's paintings are not aiming at illusionistic space. In contrast, though, Stella

moved towards the notion of an illusionistic 'working space' in his later painting, those 'maximalist' paintings/ 'reliefs'. Morris Louis, Stella reckons, suggested a new form of pictorial space in painting:

What is needed is a serious effort at structural inventiveness. What Morris Louis did for a while twenty years ago, following the lead of Barnett Newman, remains more of a promise than a fulfilment. But if his promise were read rightly – if the structural potential of his spatial dynamics were understood and the disjunctive intensity of his color appreciated – his painting could lead to a new beginning… Morris Louis was nearly the last abstract painter to hint at the potential that abstraction might have for creating a full and expansive pictorial space like that of Rubens. (66)

Morris Louis exploded color, developing it from Wassily Kandinsky and Henri Matisse. Robert Hughes called Louis's paintings 'among the most purely optical ever made in America'.[9] Critics spoke about Louis's art in terms of 'optical', 'retinal', 'opulence', and 'hedonism'. Daniel Wheeler wrote of a 'new retinal beauty of Matissean hedonism and opulence, but pure, luminous, fluid, and incorporeal as never before' (191).

Morris Louis focussed the viewer on his colors: there was simply the color on the canvas, with no references to other things. Yet, of course, Louis's furls, like Frank Stella's black stripes, were also æsthetic structures, which spoke of pictorial illusion. There was a structure to Stella's *Black Stripe Paintings*, as there was to Louis's 'Unfurleds' and drapes of color.

Morris Louis's paintings were not simply paint thrown at a canvas. Similarly, Jackson Pollock's painting were not the result of random splashes, as if someone had set off some grenades in a row of tins of paint on 25 square yards of canvas. Frank Stella liked to use paint 'as good as it was in the can'.[10] Pollock, Louis and Stella planned their paintings carefully. The paintings were imaginative, artistic works, each speaking of the personal touch and gesture of the artist. Although Louis did not use a paintbrush, his gestures were unmistakable. Stella's marks were apparent more in the later works. In Stella's Sixties *Protractor* series, the paint was applied smoothly, as in Brice Marden's monochrome panels. Yet one can see the personal touch in Marden's paintings: he left a gap at the base of his paintings, and allowed drips to form there.

Frank Stella changed his mind about Morris Louis, Kenneth Noland and Helen Frankenthaler, painters with whom he felt were his contemporaries. In 1972, for instance, he said:

What I felt at the time – and I don't feel this now – I felt very strongly that Morris Louis, for example, and Ken Noland and particularly Helen Frankenthaler, in their use of the staining technique, there was identification with the facture and weave and all that, but it still seemed to me basically those stains read quite illusionistically. [11]

Morris Louis's paintings, with their huge splotches of color, are, as Frank Stella says, loose, open works. Louis's paintings are free of figurative imagery and illusions, even though the stripes, furls, columns and curtains and star shapes are all æsthetic constructs. A.J. Carmean commented: '[f]or Morris Louis the staining technique was such a breakthrough'. [12] Like Helen Frankenthaler's paintings, Louis's staining technique allows for an æsthetic freedom which is refreshing after so much tight, close, dry paintwork, as found in, say, the art of Nicolas Poussin and René Magritte. Frank Stella wrote:

It may be that what makes Morris Louis's late paintings so appealing is their peculiar Kandinsky-like understanding of Newman. Louis brought a determined looseness to Newman's abstraction that Kandinsky would have applauded. (125)

It's true, Wassily Kandinsky would have enjoyed

Morris Louis's multicolored explosions, for example, *Point of Tranquillity* (1958, Hirshhorn and Sculpture Garden, Washington, DC), where yellows and oranges predominate, anchored by deep blues and a vivacious green. Frank Stella and Louis are the product of a long tradition in art of broken color: Titian broke up color in his late works; J.M.W. Turner did too; the Impressionists broke up color further; Georges Seurat turned it into dots.

Some critics regarded Morris Louis's paintings are the first properly abstract paintings, because they did not relate to a theme or subject, but existed as themselves. In this sense, Louis went further than Wassily Kandinsky, Kasimir Malevich, Piet Mondrian, Jackson Pollock or Barnett Newman (D. Wheeler, 193). Louis influenced painters such as Frank Stella, Richard Diebenkorn, Jules Olitski, Sam Francis, Sandro Chia, Sigmar Polke, David Salle and Arnulf Rainer (C. Riley, 167).

Critic Peter Fuller, in his grumpy, eccentric way, reckoned that the New York School did not 'influence' British painters in a one-way flow of æsthetic information. After 1958, Fuller said, American painting no longer triumphed over the rest the world. [13] Fuller thought that Patrick Heron influenced the American painters: 'I believe not only that Heron's stripe paintings preceded those of Morris Louis, but also that they are better, much better, in æsthetic terms'. [14] Compared with Heron's late 1950s work, Fuller claims,

there is a dowdy and depressing feel about even the best Morris Louis canvases. With few exceptions, Louis's paintings, today, have the look of last season's used and abused fashions. (ib., 218)

Peter Fuller's negative appraisal of Louis's art is part of his basic anti-American, pro-British philosophy. Instead of spending idiot amounts of money on Louis's canvases, Fuller said, collectors would be better off buying Patrick Herons.

Peter Fuller may be right about the influence of Patrick Heron on Morris Louis, with regard to the colored stripe motif of the latter. But Heron's own stripe paintings – the stripes moving horizontally across a portrait format canvas – look suspiciously like Mark Rothko's late 1940s and early 1950s paintings. Rothko's paintings of the late 1940s, such as *Number 11* (1949, Washington) and *Number 17* (1947, New York), are clearly the ancestors of Heron's late 1950s paintings (such as the Tate Gallery's *Horizontal Stripe Painting* by Heron). And Louis's stripe paintings are far superior to those of Heron.

AD REINHARDT

Ad Reinhardt was born in Buffalo, New York, December 24, 1913, and died August 13, 1967 in New York City. Reinhardt was an Abstract Expressionist whose characteristic works were the five-foot square black canvases with their dim cruciform shapes he made late in his career. Reinhardt was probably the most polemical of the American abstract painters of the 1960s. This extract from one of his "Art-as-Art" pieces is typical:

> No lines or imaginings, no shapes or composings or representings, no visions or sensations or impulses, no symbols or signs or impastos, no decoratings or colorings or picturings, no pleasures or pains, no accidents or readymades, no things, no ideas, no relations, no attributes, no qualities – nothing that is not of 'essence'.[1]

This extract from Ad Reinhardt's unpublished notes is typical, and defines not only his own form of painting, but also that of other 'Northern' painters such as Mark Rothko, Barnett Newman, Christopher Le Brun, Thérèse Oulton, Brice Marden and Anselm Keifer:

> "Northern" preferences for black medium
> "Black," medium of the mind
> Puritan, self-righteous, self-criticism
> Conscience of a bad conscience
> Luminous darkness, true light, evanescence
> "Him that has made the dark his hiding place"
> "Flight of the lone to the alone"
> Perfection, central, cohesive, purifying principle
> Polemic, dogmatic, scriptural (1991, 90)

Ad Reinhardt's writings are sometimes pretentious and portentous, quite different from Barnett Newman's matter-of-fact statements, or Joseph Cornell's wistful, dreamy diaries. Reinhardt's written statements are sometimes brilliantly argumentative, so much so that his art seldom seemed to live up to his polemics. On the other hand, if

Reinhardt's black paintings had not been powerful on their own, they would have severely weakened his artistic statements.

Ad Reinhardt advocated a violent break with everything that had gone on before in the history of art. Reinhardt proposed in "Twelve Rules For a New Academy" (1957) that the modern artist use no texture, no brushwork, no sketching, no forms, no design, no colors, no light, no space, no time, no size, no movement and no object.[2] Reinhardt discarded the 'religious' monicker, and disliked the allusions viewers made to Islam, Christianity, Buddhism and Hinduism when discussing his paintings (even though he wrote about religion more than almost any other contemporary painter). Reinhardt even stated that 'painting really has no relation to any of the religions nor ever has' (1991, 14). This is an extraordinary statement from a well-read artist, for art since earliest times has been associated deeply with religion, and much of the greatest art made in the last hundred thousand years has been in the service of religion.

Before he embarked upon his arduous quest for the Ultimate Black Painting, Ad Reinhardt made some rather mundane abstract art, such as *Abstract Painting, Blue* (1953, Connecticut), *Abstract Painting, White* (1955, private collection), and *Abstract Painting, Red* (1953, Washington). In these paintings, blocks of slightly different hues of one color – red in some, blue in others, then lastly black – made rectilinear shapes. Before the paintings of the 1950s, Reinhardt had produced political cartoons and journalistic sketches aligned with Communist politics. He also participated in demonstrations. marches and picket lines. Robert Hughes called him a '[g]adfly, fanatic, and dandy', who though he was of the same generation as the Abstract Expressionists, he 'had nothing in common with their spirit. He was an aphoristic preacher and a deadly parodist'.[3]

By the late 1950s, Ad Reinhardt developed his art to the reductionist point of no return: the series of black paintings. Reinhardt's black paintings were all called *Abstract Painting, Black*. He dubbed them '[c]lassical black-square uniform five-foot timeless trisected evanescences of the sixties' (1991, 10). Examples of the *Abstract Painting, Black* include *Abstract Painting, Black* (1960-66, National Gallery of Australia, Canberra), *Abstract Painting, Black* (1960-66, Marlborough Gallery, New York), *Abstract Painting, Black* (1960, collection: Arnold Glimcher, New York), and *Abstract Painting, Black* (1960-66, Gilman Paper Company). Each one is different but all are united by the same philosophy. On the back of the Tate Modern, London's *Abstract Painting, Black (no. 5),* Reinhardt wrote 'Reinhardt/ 732 Broadway/ NYC 3' and a plan of the painting, indicating in capitals the red, blue and green colors that were mixed with matt black.

Ad Reinhardt defined the *Abstract Paintings, Black* like this:

> A square (*neutral, shapeless*) canvas, five feet wide, five feet high, as high as a man, as wide as a man's outstretched arms (*not large, not small, sizeless*), trisected (*no composition*), one horizontal form negating one vertical form (*formless, no top, no bottom, directionless*), three (*more or less*) dark (*lightless*) non-contrasting (*colorless*) colors, brushwork brushed out to remove brushwork, a matte, flat, free-hand painted surface (*glossless, textureless, non-linear, no hard edge, no soft edge*)... a pure, abstract, non-objective, timeless, spaceless, changeless, relationless, disinterested painting (1991, 82-83)

They were meant to be formless (but they weren't), lightless (they couldn't be), spaceless (not possible), changeless (they were not) and relationless (they were full of relations, internally, and were related to countless other works of art). Ad Reinhardt's paintings were sensual where he wanted them to be beyond sensuality; they were never completely imageless because Reinhardt insisted on the cruciform shape. Richard Stankiewicz wrote of them: '[t]he extraordinary object, the one with presence, is one which is subjectively and tyrannically there... It is the ultimate realism, this presence'.[4]

I've taken on all the bad terms of the '30s [Reinhardt said]. Like meaningless, useless, imageless – those kinds of words. Words like inhuman, sterile, cold – they became cool.

For all his exaltation of Oriental mystical precepts, his insistence on the radical reductionism of his art, his belief in black as negation ('pure non-being'), his desire to 'push painting beyond its thinkable, seeable, feelable limits', Ad Reinhardt's abstract black paintings were not the last paintings to be made, or that could be made. In his quest for an imageless, relationless, timeless art, Reinhardt was doomed to failure, for despite his insistence on the immateriality of his quest, the painter is always deeply entrenched in the materiality of painting. The difficulty was evoking the void using physical objects. As Barnett Newman said: '[e]mptiness is not that easy. The point is to produce it with paint'.[5] Yves Klein had experimented with notions of emptiness; his exhibition *The Void* was also known as *The Specialization of Sensibility from the State of Prime Matter to the State of Stabilized Pictorial Sensibility*. So that his aura could impregnate the gallery space Klein had the walls whitewashed.

Ad Reinhardt's task of describing the indescribable with the halfway decent means of paint was bound to fail. The quest for delimitation and non-representation was much stronger in Reinhardt than in the art of Mark Rothko or Barnett Newman: Reinhardt kept up with the *Abstract Paintings, Black* for some seven years, from the end of the 1950s to his death in 1967. As David Sylvester put it in a review of Reinhardt's 1964 ICA (London) show:

The extreme thing about Ad Reinhardt, by twentieth-century standards, is not that he's done paintings which are black all over; it's that for ten years all his paintings have been black all over. (1996, 68)

Ad Reinhardt's art did not offer the same pleasures as Abstract Expressionists such as Mark Rothko, Michael Benedikt suggested: no sensuality, no 'sheer pulsation' in Reinhardt's art; instead, Reinhardt's paintings offered a pleasure that was architectural rather than painterly.[6] Instead of offering traditional notions of 'beauty', Reinhardt should be admired as a 'spiritual worker', Benedikt suggested, someone who changed how attitudes are used in art, not just producing a different painterly style (ibid.). Clement Greenberg was dismissive:

Reinhardt has a genuine if small gift for color, but none at all for design or placing. I can see why he let Newman, Rothko, and Still influence him toward close and dark values, but he lost more than he gained by the desperate extreme to which he went, changing from a nice into a trite artist.[7]

For Harold Rosenberg, Ad Reinhardt was 'a drier logician than Rothko', and Rothko would not follow Reinhardt's reductionism to its radical finality (1972). Mark Rothko commented on Reinhardt thus:

The difference between me and Reinhardt is that he's a mystic. By that I mean that his paintings are immaterial. Mine are *here*. Materially. The surfaces, the work of the brush and so on. His are untouchable.[8]

The ironic thing is that Ad Reinhardt's paintings were no more immaterial or 'untouchable' than those of Mark Rothko or Barnett Newman. Furthermore, what people think of Reinhardt also applies to Colorfield and Minimal painting. What is said by critics of Reinhardt's art can apply to Colorfield and Minimal painting, and vice versa.

Ad Reinhardt's lifelong friend, the mystic Thomas Merton, wrote of the disappearance of the self in God, which could apply equally to Reinhardt's black square paintings as a project: '[s]o it is with one who has vanished into God by pure contemplation. God alone is left'.[9] The theologian Paul Tillich said of Reinhardt's work that it depicts the 'non-representational expression of mystic depths of experience.'[10]

Ad Reinhardt's black paintings do mark the end of a certain strain of painting, which might be said to go back to Matthias Grünewald and Early Netherlandish painters such as Rogier van der Weyden. It is a strain of Northern European painting which descends into the shadows (Rembrandt van Rijn, Georges de La Tour, Frans Hals), of which Mark Rothko and Reinhardt can be seen as the last flowering. Other painters did not agree that 'painting was dead', that there was nothing else to do. Jasper Johns remarked that painters continue to work, while Helen Frankenthaler said in 1970: 'I think there's still a lot more to do in abstract painting'.[11]

'The one direction in fine art or abstract art today is in the painting of the same form over and over again', affirmed Ad Reinhardt, justifying making his series of black paintings.[12] There is something deeply obsessive about Reinhardt's late works, as with the late works of Vincent van Gogh or J.M.W. Turner, as if there was something Reinhardt felt he had to get at, somehow, and so he kept working over the form until it offered up its secret knowledge. In this respect, as an alchemical, shamanic quest, Reinhardt's seven-year project of obsessively turning out the square black paintings seemed to be in the hope of reaching some sublime point, some absolute, some infinity or end zone. Reinhardt pursued his ritualistic journey with utter ruthlessness, aided by reams of æsthetic dogma. Art is useless, Reinhardt declared, and 'can only be defined as exclusive, negative, absolute, and timeless'.[13] Reinhardt went further than most by going over the same problem again and again. His passion for pure painting was daunting, but not heroic, nor laudable necessarily.

Making itself is a gesture: thus Ad Reinhardt's painting, like other Minimal works, could not be totally 'non-gestural'. The human touch could not be utterly erased. Reinhardt's paintings aimed at a nothingness that could only ever be conceptual. Franz Kline had made paintings of black brush-strokes on white (such as *Wotan, Untitled* and

Elisabeth) which looked like Chinese ideograms. Kline's world of giant Chinese signs recalled Zen Buddhist art, in which the concept of nothingness is embodied in the term *mu* (in Japanese, *wu*). Reinhardt's *Abstract Paintings, Black* seemed to be moving towards the spiritual state of Zen Buddhist *mu* (in his notebooks Reinhardt spoke of the Zen concept of *wu wei*, or non-action).[14]

In Princeton Art Museum at the university in New Jersey, there's a wonderful display of an Ad Reinhardt painting in the midst some Oriental art. One of Reinhardt's *Abstract Paintings, Black* has been hung in between two Asian statues.

In Sixties painting, the object-in-itself was all. Sixties painting aimed to be non-symbolic, non-relational, and non-objective. In this it shared its aims with mysticism. 'It is the mysticism of non-objective art rather than its forms that shocks', wrote Michael Fingesten (28). For Sixties painters, the emotional content of the painting, as well as the traditional elements, had to go. Frank Stella said '[y]ou want to get rid of things that get you into trouble'.[15] The old techniques – of easel painting, the process of doing preliminary studies, drawing from life, using traditional iconography – was dropped. However, this pursuit of formlessness can be seen as religious in itself; it partakes of a 'cosmic religiosity'.[16]

Ad Reinhardt's project was 'religious' – Reinhardt's esoteric, erudite and eclectic writings refer frequently to Zen, Taoism, Buddhism, the dark night of the soul of Christianity, Rosicrucian occultism, Mother Night, the dark-on-dark of mystics such as Meister Eckhart (who spoke of the 'divine dark'), *The Cloud of Unknowing*, St John of the Cross, and so on. Reinhardt's square black paintings can be seen as equivalents for this kind of religious darkness, which was defined by Reinhardt in countless notes and essays with the terms of Buddhism – 'not this, not that'. Reinhardt spoke about the use of black in the *Bible*, Geoffrey Chaucer, John Milton and William Shakespeare (in *Macbeth, Othello* and *Love's Labour's Lost*); in the black castle and the black knight; the realm of hell and Pluto; the Kaaba, the black cube at Mecca; the black rock in the dome of the rock in Jerusalem; and blackness in the *Tao Te Ching* ('the Tao is dim and dark', says Lao-tzu, while Reinhardt wrote that the 'Tao is through and through mysterious and dark').[17] Reinhardt acknowledged the maternal, 'dark-earth-mother' of night and blackness, and related it to Goddesses such as Diana of Ephesus (1991, 97). He spoke of darkness as regressive, prime matter, 'primordial darkness', the void, a place of rebirth, the subterranean zone, the 'alchemist's lair', lightlessness, 'negative presence', 'melting away', dematerialization, non-being, the 'black monk', 'prince of darkness', 'black-humour, Black-Protestant, black-blasphemy, black-mass, black arts', emptiness, 'Dark-flame, dark-fire, coal, charred wood', and night as 'mother of all things, veil of stars' (1991, 96-98). But it wasn't these myriad connotations and symbolisms associated with black that Reinhardt wanted to explore, but rather 'the idea of black as intellectuality and conventionality'. 'It's the negativeness of black, or darkness particularly, in painting, which interests me', he wrote (1991, 87).

Ad Reinhardt wanted to '[p]ush painting beyond its thinkable, seeable, feelable limits' (1991, 104). 'I'm just making the last paintings anyone can make', he added.[18] Reinhardt was not messing about, he was really serious about making a series of five-foot square black paintings. An ancestor of Reinhardt's black paintings was the occultist Robert Fludd's five by five inch magic square (a black square of religious abstraction made hundreds of years before Reinhardt's canvases).[19] For Reinhardt, black was 'negation' (1991, 87), 'pure non-being' (91), The emphasis on blackness links Reinhardt's paintings to the connotations of the color black: night, chaos, formlessness, creation, madness and mysticism. Black night is also the time of the feminine or maternal realm, but Reinhardt's *Abstract Paintings, Black* depict a cold, lonely and egoless night which aims to eradicate all traces of humanity. Reinhardt appropriated the language of Buddhism, with its perennial emphasis on negation and nothingness, as in the *Heart Sutra* of Buddhism which speaks of 'no body, no mind; no shape, no color, no sound, no smell, no taste, no touch, no concept; no visible world'.[20]

■

Staring into an Ad Reinhardt painting is a curious experience. The black, for a start, is not black, but tinged with red, blue and green. A cruciform structure can be vaguely discerned. The surface is matt yet reflective, inviting absorption but also repelling it. One might evoke the sheen of death in Reinhardt's paintings, but it might also be the no-non-blackness of timelessness (and therefore death/*less*ness). The light Reinhardt's paintings breathe out is steady, dim, gleaming, a 'total light', to use Sidney Tillim's term.[21] The surface of the *Abstract Paintings, Black* is smooth, blemishless, yet also hand-painted. No use of masking tape or spray guns here. The cruciform shape is only faintly visible, but definitely there. Each painting, too, as not exactly the same as the others. The paintings are of varying quality, some of them have become quite scruffy with the passing of time. 'The matt black surface starts to sing: we recognise the vibrations given off by the inexplicably living surfaces of all authentic works of art', remarked David Sylvester (1996, 69).

For some critics, Ad Reinhardt's spacing of blackness went further than almost any other painter. For critics such as Priscilla Colt[22] and Nicholas and Elena Calas,[23] Reinhardt's black paintings had taken purity to extremes. Wassily Kandinsky was not so convinced about black: 'the silence of black is the silence of death', he asserted.[24] For Lawrence Alloway, 'Reinhardt's choice of black was an æsthetic and philosophic choice, an aid in investing 'abstract art with a momentous subject'.[25] Reinhardt wanted to paint everything out in the history of art, to negate it all by painting over it all.[26]

Ad Reinhardt's search for the Ultimate Black Abstract Painting marks the end of one kind of 20th century painterly abstraction. Into the black spacelessness of Reinhardt's five-foot canvases all the abstractions of Cubism, Surrealism, Suprem-aticism, Expressionism and Pure Painting fall, to be eaten up alive. There are other ways past Rein-hardt's end-point of Post-Painterly Abstraction: Brice Marden, Gerhard Richter, Thérèse Oulton, Jasper Johns and Frank Stella have demonstrated that abstract painting can be developed (Marden, for example, went on to paint his *Annunciation Series* of monochrome abstract paintings in the 1970s which took the Virgin Mary's story as its starting-point).

Ad Reinhardt's black paintings mark the end of a particularly masculinist form of abstraction, an absolute reductionism. He never reached his goal.[27] Reinhardt's paintings mark the end of a strain of religious painterly abstraction that began in Byzantine icons and developed into the Renaissance images of Leonardo da Vinci, Michelangelo Buonarroti, Matthias Grünewald and Rogier van der Weyden. Brilliant and necessary though Reinhardt's *reductio ad absurdum* was, it was not the final word in Minimal, Colorfield, Sixties or contemporary painting, nor was it the final pronouncement in religious painting.

BRICE MARDEN

Like artists such as Frank Stella, Carl Andre and Donald Judd, Brice Marden (b. 1938) has always made abstract art. There was no period of early figurative work, as with the Abstract Expression-ists, Mark Rothko, Jackson Pollock, Willem de Kooning and Robert Motherwell. They all drew and painted figurative art, much of it influenced by the Surrealists, before they turned to abstraction in the 1940s and 1950s. Stella and Brice Marden, though, were abstract artists from the beginning (although there are one or two early figurative works by Marden).

Brice Marden's art draws on Abstract Express-ionism, however: he did not reject it as much as did Donald Judd and other Minimal artists. Marden speaks of the relation between himself and the two movements with which he is often associated, Abstract Expressionism and Minimalism:

> Rothko was talking about painting, about death and I was much more interested in that than in Judd's Minimalist æsthetic. Emotions? I wanted to keep that open. Subject matter was no longer valid but I felt my work was much more of a continuation of Abstract Expressionism than a rejection of it. (1992a, 55)

Although Barnett Newman's form of painting seems much more in tune with 1960s Minimalism than Mark Rothko's 'tragic' and 'transcendent' art, Brice Marden came to admire Rothko. In Rothko's mural series (especially in the 'Rothko Chapel' at Houston), Rothko had refined his sense of color and form radically, aligning it with the Christian Passion. Marden visited the Rothko Chapel in 1972, and the solemn, massive panels of color made a deep impression upon him (1992a, 24). Later in the Seventies, Marden created his own series of religious abstract panels, the *Annunciation Series*. Interestingly, while Rothko moved through various phases from pseudo-figuration (in his post-Surrealist period), through the intense subjective expressionism of the radiantly colorful 1950s 'clouds' or 'things', to the radicalization of the dark, sombre, maroon murals series (the Seagram, Harvard and Houston paintings), Marden went the opposite way: beginning very austere and monotone, all in greys, in the 1960s, Marden opened up (like Frank Stella), relaxing into colorful reds, yellows and blues in his multi-canvas paintings of the 1970s, and branching out (literally – he used twigs to draw) into the 'calligraphic drawings/ paintings of the 1980s and 1990s.

For a time, in the late 1960s, Brice Marden and Mark Rothko were both making ascetic grey-on-grey abstract rectangular paintings. Rothko's dual-tone vertical grey rectangles were associated (by critics) with a cosmic, tragic exhaustion – the works presaged Rothko's suicide in February, 1970. Marden's Minimalist grey horizontal rect-angles, meanwhile, were associated with personal depression, alienation from his wife, and the *ennui* of a young artist searching for his voice.

Brice Marden's surfaces take time to open up and reveal themselves. The first perceptions of emptiness and denial of physicality give way to a formal (spiritual) richness and palpable physical presence. The dense planar geometry loses its initial reductive impenetrability, and depth is soon asserted. Denial becomes affirmation, and self-erasure becomes self (and world) glorification. Marden's canvases suggest layering, with colors underneath leaving ghostly traces on the surfaces. Not all art critics saw the underlying colors and gauzes of paint: Scott Burton wrote of Marden's Bykert Gallery show of 1966 that Marden's colors were 'closed', like skin: 'you can't look into them, only at them.'[1]

At the Jewish Museum, where he worked, Brice Marden admired Jasper Johns' work, in retro-spective, in particular Johns' grey paintings, such as *Gray Numbers*. Grey became one of Marden's (and Minimalism's) key colors of the mid-1960s. Robert Rauschenberg's influence on Marden is harder to spot than Johns' quiet intensity: Rausch-enberg is an extraordinarily dynamic artist, whose

work displays an energetic exploration of painterly possibilities. Rauschenberg had, for example, painted all-white paintings years before 1960s Minimalism, Colorfield and Post-Painterly Abstraction (in 1951). Interestingly, one of Marden's jobs when he worked for Rauschenberg was to repaint the white paintings as they yellowed with age.[2]

Brice Marden's sense of color and abstraction draws largely on the Old Masters, the Spanish Golden Age masters, and Northern European painting. Robert Rosenblum, in his influential book *Modern Painting and the Northern Romantic Tradition,* saw Northern European painters as being the precursors of modern abstraction, and the masters of modern abstract art – Piet Mondrian, Wassily Kandinsky, Kasimir Malevich, Paul Klee – are distinctly Northern European figures. Marden sees himself as a Northern painter (M. Poirer, 52), and his paintings, especially the ones of the late 1960s and early 1970s, have the austerity and mystery of Northern European painters such as Caspar David Friedrich, Emil Nolde and Kasimir Malevich. The spiritual dis-course of the modern abstract artists (the affinities with Rudolf Steiner, theosophy, occultism, Rosi-crucianism, Cabbalism, and so on), is a key element in the art of Malevich, Kandinsky, Mondrian and Klee. This European taste for the sublime and mystical was later developed by the Abstract Expressionists (the *Qabbalah* in the work of Barnett Newman, Judæo-Christianity in Mark Rothko, Zen Buddhism in Ad Reinhardt, Robert Motherwell and Franz Kline), and in Brice Marden there is Classical mythology, sacred architecture, the Christian Annunciation, the symbolism of numbers (numerology), alchemy, and so on. While fellow 1960s Minimalists and Colorfield artists rejected such spiritual hankerings (Frank Stella, Donald Judd, Dan Flavin, Robert Morris, Robert Mangold, Richard Serra and Kenneth Noland), Marden embraced them. Other Sixties artists, in their own way, also acknowledged a religious dimension to their work: Carl Andre, David Novros,

Richard Long, Eva Hesse, Ad Reinhardt, Robert Smithson and Morris Louis.

For a long time, Brice Marden's colors were extremely subdued. Though Marden is grouped with Kenneth Noland, Ellsworth Kelly, Jules Olitski and others, Marden's 1960s colors were nowhere near as brilliant and saturated as theirs. Compare a canvas by Olitski, Noland or Kelly with one by Marden and one sees bright greens, radiant yellows and pulsating scarlets in the former, while Marden's canvases sink deep into grey, light brown, beige, and more grey. For Minimal sculptors, grey, white and black were suitably 'neutral' colors which did not scream expressively, as reds and purples had done in Mark Rothko's or Willem de Kooning's paintings. It was years, really – until the mid-Seventies – before Marden used colors as glowing as the Post-Painterly Abstract-ionists.

Brice Marden's paintings, like those of Morris Louis, Robert Mangold, Agnes Martin and Robert Ryman, were not concerned with creating 'illusionistic space', with the space of traditional Western post-Renaissance art, but with a new flatness. On the other side of the flat painting camp, there were artists whose aim was to destroy the rigid flatness of painting. One painter who threw anything onto the picture plane was Robert Rauschenberg (see his many 'combine' paintings, those mixed media extravaganzas). Claes Oldenburg's soft telephones and toilets far outdo Rauschenberg for pure silliness. Oldenburg like Andy Warhol questioned the holy notion of 'Art' with a capital 'A'. The picture plane, which had been so scrupulously flat throughout the Renaiss-ance (ignoring the embossed and punched gold), suddenly burst open in contemporary art. As Clement Greenberg put it: '[p]ictorial space has lost its "inside" and become all "outside"'.[3] Of course, some contemporary artists asserted the flatness of the picture plane even more fervently: Morris Louis with his stained, furled canvas, Frank Stella with his black stripes done with housepaint direct onto cotton duck, Mark Rothko with his cloud-like shapes, Agnes Martin with her finely pencilled squares, and Sol LeWitt with his spacious wall-drawings. Lucio Fontana, though, destroyed the flatness of the canvas in a phallic, penetrative fashion: he slashed the canvas. Fontana explained his seemingly violent, nay, pornographic act thus:

> I want to open up space, create a new dimension for art, tie in at the cosmos as it endlessly expands beyond the confining place of the picture. With my innovation of the hole pierced through the canvas in repetitive perforations, I have not attempted to decorate a surface, but, on the contrary, I have tried to break its dimensional limitations. Beyond the perforations a newly gained freedom of interpretation awaits us, but also, and just as inevitably, the end of art.[4]

Brice Marden employed many of the æsthetics of Minimalism in his paintings: seriality, repetition, symmetry, flatness, abstraction, functionalism and monochromism. In terms of color, Marden's paint-ings of the 1960s and 1970s were sombre, restrained, impenetrable, physical, tactile, sonor-ous. When he uses one color, Marden generally fills the whole painting with it; it's an evenly-spread field of color. When he takes up two colors, Marden establishes the relationship between them very carefully. In the multi-part paintings, the colors and the panels exist on the same plane, which is smooth and flat.[5] Marden modulates his colors so that they seem to inhabit the same tone zone, even though they can seem to be from different color families. Even though each panel contains different colors, the color value is often the same.[6]

A painting such as *Three Deliberate Greys for Jasper Johns* (1970, Ottawa, and spelt 'grey' not 'gray'), is a work that takes much of its power from the relativity of grey tones. In this homage to (and wry look at) Johns, Brice Marden explores the interaction of the tonal value of the ubiquitous 1960s 'neutral' color. It is a tribute to Marden's talent that he could make the painting work. After all, the project of making a painting using only grey, without any figurative or representational elements, entirely in abstraction, could have backfired easily. It is the sort of brief, if given to art students, would have them groaning, dissolving into bouts of apathy and dead-ends. Yet Marden's *Three Deliberate Greys for Jasper Johns* is one of his most successful works, the culmination of his exploration of the neutral color.

From the beginning, Brice Marden acknowledged the emotional power of color. Underneath the monochrome greys and beiges there is an emotional subtext. Marden associated his 1960s grey color, for example, with depression. He was depressed at the time he made some of the paintings. A later pen-and-ink set of drawings was entitled *Suicide Notes* (a series of rectangles, some shadowy, some incomplete, some constructed from webs of lines). Marden wanted the viewer to come away from his paintings changed: to go in expecting something, but to get something else. Marden's Post-Painterly Abstract monochrome paintings hide something underneath, which Marden expressed in terms of color:

Gray was the way I could deal with color at the time. What I liked about it was how you could twist it, how you could make it be gray, and also be red – how you could get two readings out of one thing. (1983)

Clearly the realm Brice Marden was aiming for was quite from different from that of Roy Lichenstein, say, or Judy Pfaff. Of course, it might seem wholly inappropriate to compare Marden's 1960s Minimal project with that of Lichenstein or Pfaff, for he is so different. But then, Marden is different even from those most closely associated with him – Robert Ryman, Agnes Martin, Robert Mangold, Donald Judd and Jules Olitski. Marden is in a world of his own. One can make cultural comparisons, but this is only partially helpful. One only has to compare the subdued grey and pale cobalt panels of Marden with the vivacious, multicolor of Robert Mangold's paintings to see how far Marden was from mainstream Minimalism, Colorfield and Hard Edge painting and most Post-

Painterly Abstraction.

In the early 1970s Brice Marden began to loosen up his palette and introduce much deeper, more saturated colors – and tones. Nature was also more apparent, in series of paintings such as the *Grove Group* and the *Sea Paintings*. The *Sea Paintings* introduced much deeper tones, or rather, much stronger contrasts between one tone and the next. Instead of gentle modulations between one panel and another, Marden was happy to make sudden contrasts and leaps. Thus, in *Red, Yellow, Blue* (1974), the red is very dark, while the yellow, as usual in Marden's art, is light. The result was a sharp leap in tone from the left to the middle panel, which the right hand (blue) panel helps to modulate by its tone, which is mid-way between the red and yellow. Paintings such as *To Corfu, Le Mien* and *Morada*, from the mid-1970s, featured the narrow vertical panels which Marden used so effectively in the *Annunciation Series*. Prints contemporary with the time, such as *Untitled* (1973), also featured vertical columns.

New colors in the Brice Marden *œuvre* (part of his 'red yellow blue' period) appeared in *Morada* (1976, Stedelijk Museum, Amsterdam) and *Le Mien* (1976, Zurich): a dark, damson red, which's followed, in both paintings, by a mid-grey or greyish-blue. In *Morada* there are the usual colors of Marden's Seventies Greek period: olive greens, light greys, and a dark grey. Into this mélange of familiar light/ mid/ dark greys, the damson hue is really surprising. It is, literally, a 'splash' of color – living color, the color of life (blood, anger, passion, fecundity). Imagine this damson-red entering the austere Greek paintings, such as *Lethykos, Moon I* and any of the *Grove Group Paintings*. In *Le Mien* the damson color takes up one of the wide panels on the left, and is echoed by the mid-red in the right-hand narrow panel. Against these sonorous hues, Marden places his olive grove greens and greys. The painting is symmetrical, in terms of color (though not with the perfect symmetry of *Lethykos (for Tonto)*): warm green is set against deep crimson; lighter red is set against light grey.

In the paintings of the late 1960s and early 1970s, Brice Marden's palette warmed up, with mid-earth-browns in *For Pearl*, lemon yellows in *Rodeo* and buttercup yellows in *Range, First Figure (Homage to Courbet)* and *Starter*, and one of Marden's most radiant colors, the orangey-red outer panels of *Pumpkin Plumb*. The outer panels in *For Pearl* (1970, Lannan Foundation, Los Angeles) contain and moderate the warmest color, the earthy brown, with two more restrained hues (a grey-blue on the left, and a sand tint on the right). *Rodeo* (1971, Lannan Foundation) is one of the first of Marden's horizontal format dual color paintings: an expanse of lemon yellow in the upper half; dark slate grey in the lower half. *Untitled* (1971-72, Walker Art Center, Minneapolis) is unusual for Marden at this period: three warm colors, rather than, as is more usual, one warm and two cooler colors. The central band of light orange is modulated and contained by the outer panels of light carmine. The colors in *For Pearl* and *Untitled* are rare in Marden's art of this time.

In *First Figure (Homage to Courbet),* the usual three Brice Marden panels are set on top of each other, unusually, creating a tower of three near-square panels. The colors, crowned with a mustard yellow in the upper panel, are those of Seventies works such as *Summer Table, Range* and *Starter* (yellow plus a light and dark neutral color). *Pumpkin Plumb* (1970/73, collection: Helen Harrington Marden), contains a vivid contrast between the subdued grey of the 1960s monochrome paintings (in the central panel) and the bright orange, a hue which looked towards the primary colors of the *Red, Yellow, Blue* series of the following year (1974). *Summer Table* (1972-73, Whitney Museum, New York) uses the color-configuration of *Range, First Figure (Homage to Courbet)* and *Starter*: a warm yellow panel in amongst two cooler panels. *Summer Table* is clearly a part of the (Greek) landscape works of the first half of the 1970s (the *Grove Group* and *Sea Paintings*). The warm color is at the centre, but the flanking two blues (one pale, one dark) cannot restrain it. The yellow of *Summer Table* is dominant, overwhelming the outer panels. The structure of the three rectangular panels in a horizontal format of *Summer Table* recalls *Point, Range* and the *Moon Series*. The sullen, recalcitrant greys and blues of the 1960s monochromes are left behind decisively with paintings such as *Summer Table, Pumpkin Plumb* and the *Red, Yellow, Blue Series*. With his new, colorful palette, Brice Marden's art gained a new intensity, no longer tied to an introspective, 'depressed' mood.

Miranda (1972, New York) is three panels of closely-valued color in a horizontal format making a 72 by 72 inch square. The allusions to landscape in the upper olive-grey-green, middle mid-blue and lower sand-earth colors are unmistakable. *Blue Painting* (1972, private collection) is also a part of the group of landscape-based works of the early 1970s. *Blue Painting*, like the *Moon, Hera,* and *Red, Yellow, Blue* paintings, is a vertical three-panel configuration. The colors are those of the *Grove Group* and *Sea Paintings* (light and mid-toned blues). In *Blue Painting* Marden explores the sense of narrative and progression (moving from light through mid to dark blue), which became increasingly important (culminating in the *Annunciation Series*).

Two paintings based on Brice Marden's experience in Morocco also employed earthy colors, like *Starter* and *Summer Table*. Both *Moroccan Painting* (1978, New York) and *Helen's Moroccan Painting* (1979, collection: Helen Harrington Marden) set a mid-green against an earth red-brown. In the former work the panels are side by side vertically, in the latter they are set one above the other (this vertical format was another reworking of a format used in the early Seventies). In both the effect is of an exploration of landscape; In this case, a response to the particular landscape of Morocco, with its abundant greenery that grows out of what appears to be nothing but dust and partial desert. Such deep green plants amongst such seemingly arid, barren soil is an astonishment to the traveller used to the lush green of temperate Northern

Europe and North America. Brice Marden's Moroccan panels explore the wonder of the North African landscape, where the dry, apparently lifeless browns of *Hydra* and the early *Untitled* paintings gives way to a luscious, fertile green.

These hues broaden considerably the narrow range of colors Brice Marden had employed in works such as *For Otis, T.K.B., Wax I, Nebraska* and *Decorative Painting*. In those 1960s monochromes, Marden seemed to be working in the rarefied and extreme realm of abstraction occupied by the likes of Ad Reinhardt and late Mark Rothko; with the post-1969 multi-panel paintings, and the new, luminous palette, Marden joined the ranks of Post-Painterly Abstract artists such as Morris Louis, Frank Stella, Kenneth Noland, Richard Diebenkorn and Ellsworth Kelly. Even so, paintings such as *Rodeo, For Pearl, D'après la Marquise de la Solana, Point, Starter* and *Miranda* were still more severe and restrained than anything in the art of Louis, Kelly, Murray or Diebenkorn. In amongst the more colorful works of the 1970s (such as *Starter* and the *Red, Yellow, Blue* series), there were still ascetic greys and near-blues, such as in *Gober* (1971, Spiegel Family Collection). This is a narrow vertical dual-color panel whose two muted greys look straight back to the *Untitleds* of the early 1960s. The first *Hydra* (1972, New York), too, is extremely closed-in and muted, quite unlike the later hymns to the Greek landscape (such as *Thira* and the *Grove Group*). *Shunt* (1972, New York) is also restrained, in *Hydra*-like beiges and greys.

In amongst the many colorful paintings of the first half of the Seventies, then (such as *Pumpkin Plumb, Blue Painting, Starter,* and *For Hera*), Brice Marden was still producing quiet panels in earth, grey, olive and brown hues (*Hydra, Shunt, Gober, Three Deliberate Greys for Jasper Johns* and so on). Even with a subject such as the one-off rock star Patti Smith, Marden produced a piece in subdued light and dark greys (*Star (For Patti Smith)*, 1972/74, private collection).

Brice Marden's *Grove Group* paintings are in the landscape or horizontal format, like other paintings that referred to nature (*Seasons, Summer Table, Winter Painting, Moon I, Thira* and *Gulf*). The thematic dimensions of the *Grove Group* is that they are about, well, olive groves; or, more specifically, they take as their departure point Marden's experience of sitting in olive groves. The olive dominates so much of Greece. Indeed, Lawrence Durrell speaks of the Mediterranean as that area marked out by the olive tree. The shiny, silvery underside of the leaves, and the dark tops of the leaves, the extraordinary twisted trunks and branches, the sound of leaves in the wind, the shelter they offer from the noonday sun, all these aspects and more of olive trees would interest a poetic painter such as Brice Marden. He is a painter who comes across more and more as someone who has spent a long and careful time observing nature. His paintings are born out of lengthy immersions in the natural world. He wrote in his notebooks of the importance of considering nature, and of feeling a part of nature, even though this absorption in nature can be problematic.[7] Nature is the teacher, the inspiration, the starting-point for many of Marden's works.

The *Grove Group* employ 'natural' colors, the blues, greens and greys one finds in the natural world. The *Grove Group* paintings are large – the five paintings are 72 by 108 inches. The series begins with a single-color panel, one of Brice Marden's largest expanses of a single hue (*Grove Group I*, 1973, MOMA, New York). The sheer scale and breadth of *Grove Group I* invites comparisons with Barnett Newman's work, but how subdued Marden's painting is compared to the sonorous ultramarines of Newman's works (*Cathedra*, 1951, for example). The expanse of blue is consuming, especially as, in *Grove Group II*, the soft cobalt on the left is only partially held back by the darker, mid-ultramarine. *Grove Group III* (1973-80, private collection) is in the familiar 1970s Marden horizontal tripartite format (there are two three-panel *Grove Group* paintings, two dual-plane pieces, and one single panel, *Grove Group I*).

Grove Group III, which was reworked in 1980,

does not contain blue, like *Grove Group I* or *Grove Group V*. Instead, Brice Marden concentrates, as in other Greek/ Hydra paintings, such as *Lethykos*, on his beloved greys. A pale greeny-grey begins the three-panel work, with a very light grey in the centre. Harnessing these pale greys is a dark grey in the right-hand panel, bringing the painting down to Earth. *Grove Group V* (1976, Chicago) is a much warmer painting than some of the other *Grove Groups*: a panel (horizontal this time) of a pale sky blue is at the centre of this painting. A simplistic analogy may be the sky (or sea) glimpsed between the green of the olive leaves. In *Grove Group V* Marden reprises the mid-green of *Grove Group I*, which sandwiches the sky blue panel.

In the *Grove Group* paintings the paint reaches right to every edge. There is no strip of canvas kept bare, as in the mid-1960s monochromes. Like subsequent multi-panel paintings of the Seventies, the *Grove Group* paintings are self-contained, they offer a unified sense of space, with none of the relics of gesture that occurred in the single panel canvases of the Sixties with their strip of splashed or runny paint (Marden's paintings, a critic writes, follow the rule that 'a painting contains within itself its *raison d'être*').[8]

Of all Brice Marden's paintings, the *Grove Group* are among his most tranquil and self-absorbed. They have a mute passivity, which one discerns elsewhere – in the *Back Series* or in *Lethykos (For Tonto)* – but the *Grove Group* paintings are not aligned with the emotions of depression and anxiety, which were so much a part of the 1960s monochrome paintings.

The sheer number of Brice Marden's paintings that deal with Greece, or the sea, attest to the significance the Mediterranean country had (and has) for Marden. Hydra, where he has a house, appears in many works (in the early 1970s multi-panel oil and wax paintings, in the 1979 *Hydra Group*, 1987's *Hydra* (Art Institute of Chicago) and again in the *Hydra (Summer 1990) Series* of 'calligraphic' paintings). The *Sea Paintings* were about the sea, as one might expect. Like *To Corfu*,

Towards Brindisi, the three *Hydra* paintings and *Adriatic*, the *Sea Paintings* were part of Marden's response to the way the sky and sea dominate the landscape. Marden had begun to paint vertical format paintings divided into light and dark halves with *Gober* (1971, New York) and *Urdan* (1970-1). The upper-lower format of the *Sea Paintings*, as with the *Hydra Paintings* of 1972, derives from Marden's response to the experience of staring at the sea on the voyages he made between Greece's beautiful islands.

Lawrence Durrell eulogized Greece many times, in his novels and poetry. This is a stanza from 'On Ithaca Standing':

Tread softly, for here you stand
On miracle ground, boy.
A breath would cloud this water of glass,
Honey, bush, berry and swallow.
This rock, then, is more pastoral, than
Arcadia is, Illyria was. (CP, 111)

And from 'Limits: Mykonos Windmills':

The pure form, then, must be the blue silence
And the archaic shape of whiteness posed
On blueness utterly bemused, a sort of coyness
Which garners the wind of the four quarters.
(*The Mediterranean Shore*, 144)

This picture painted in 'The Anecdotes' of Rhodes is another typical Durrellian scene: the languor, the boats, the cicadas, the figs, and Spring:

Anonymous hand, record one afternoon,
In May, some time before the fig-leaf:
Boats lying idle in the sky, a town
Thrown as on a screen of watered silk,
Lying on its side, reddish and soluble,
A sheet of glass leading down into the sea...

In Greece, one cannot help but be impressed by the sheer hardness and purity of the horizon line, where sky meets water: it is this pure line that bisects not only the *Sea Paintings*, but also many prints of the same period. The obviousness of the *Sea Paintings* does not detract from their power. There is an upper panel in one color and tone, which is clearly related to the sky, but poetically, and a lower half which is the sea. Sometimes the upper half is lighter, as the sky often is over the sea, as in the London *Sea Painting*. This is not a rule, however: it is the *relationship* between the two panels that interests the artist. In the second Saatchi *Sea Painting*, for example, the tones and hues are very close. Hardly anything differentiates them, except that one lies above the other. As he sailed over the Adriatic and other parts of the Mediterranean, Marden would have seen many lighting changes, many different hues of blue. Sometimes the sea and sky are very close, color-wise, so that one cannot differentiate between the two, and sometimes the horizon is very misty: this is what the second *Sea Painting* depicts.

The prints related to the *Sea Paintings*, *Adriatics*, are also about the different weights and densities of the sea and sky: sometimes close, sometimes far apart. The first three of the *Adriatics* prints echo the format of the *Sea Paintings* – an upper and lower half relates to ocean and air. In these prints, the contrast between the top and bottom rectangle is very strong, even though Marden modulated the contrast with foul-biting, wiping the plates and drawing on the prints. A lithograph of 1969, *Gulf* was a horizontal format image divided into two halves. The upper half is very dark, the lower half is mid-grey. *Gulf* relates directly, Marden said, to the view out of Robert Rauschenberg's window at his house in the Gulf of Mexico, at Captiva Island. The bottom edge of both rectangular blocks of color is left roughly hewn, in keeping with Marden's practice in the 1960s canvases.

Number One (1983-84, Whitney Museum, New York) is another of the large, multi-panel *Thira*-type paintings Brice Marden was working on during 1983-84 (such as the *Elements Series*, *Green (Earth)*, and others). With its twelve panels (as with *Green (Earth)*), *Number One* is nearly as complicated, structurally, as the 18-panel *Thira*.

Number One is among the darkest of the *Thira* era paintings, with over half (seven) of the panels very dark tonally (in blacks and ultramarines). The reds, too, are severe, especially those in the right-hand *tau* shape. Two central panels, though, stave off the darkness that threatens to consume *Number One*: the mid-red and yellow of the central uprights of the *tau* crosses in the centre of the left-hand groups of panels. Although these paintings are 'aggressive', as Marden accepted, he did not let them become wholly consumed by darkness. Actually, the *Thira* paintings are amongst his brightest works. Only one painting appears relentlessly 'negative' or 'depressed', in the old, 1960s Marden sense, and that is *Green (Earth)*. But even this painting is actually (partly) about the fecund powers of the Earth, its dark soil and green plants.

The post and lintel multi-panel format of *Thira*, *Numbers One* and *Two*, the *Elements Series*, *Coda*, *Green (Earth)* and other paintings proved to be loose enough for any number of serial variations. Brice Marden could vary the hues and tones *ad infinitum*, it seemed. The severe shapes of the rectangular panels was a rigorous framework to hold down the explorations of color and tone. *Elements II* (1981-82, Stedelijk Museum) is just one *tau* cross shape, composed of four panels. The colors relate to Marden's alchemical concept of the four elements (fire, air, earth, water): blue, earth-brown, dark green and mustard yellow. Though alchemically-allusive, these hues in *Elements II* are kept firmly earthbound, closely tied to colors found in the natural world. The shape of the *tau*-cross is emphasized by Marden placing the two warmer colors (ochre and yellow) on either side of the viridian panel which forms the upright of the cross. *Elements I* has three vertical panels (red, blue, yellow) capped by a horizontal green (earth) panel. The colors in *Elements IV* (1983-84, New York) are the vivid, near-primary colors of the *Red, Yellow, Blue Series*: the red, yellow and blue appear twice, but modulated each time. On the left is a mid-red, which is repeated but lightened a little in the fourth panel from the left. In amongst the bright primary colors in *Elements IV* there are the colors of the *Thira*-type paintings: dark blues and olive greens. The presence of these darker, earthier colors moves *Elements IV* on from the more joyful exchanges in the *Red, Yellow, Blue Series*.

Brice Marden's influence continues to be seen in contemporary painters, and his works have remained some of the most enduring and valuable productions of the Minimal and 1970s period. Marden's art, however, transcends its origins in Minimalism, and takes its place among the richest artworks of the contemporary era.

ROBERT RYMAN

As I worked and developed the painting, I found that I was eliminating a lot. I would put the color down, then paint over the color, trying to get down to a few crucial elements. It was like erasing something to put white over it.

Robert Ryman[1]

Ad Reinhardt painted black-on-black squares (though Robert Rauschenberg had painted all-black paintings before Reinhardt). Jasper Johns' use of gray, and Reinhardt's and Rauschenberg's use of black influenced other monochrome painters, such as Brice Marden, Frank Stella and Robert Ryman.[2] Ryman (b. 1930) explored the sensuality of surfaces via really sumptuous white squares. Ryman delved into the mysticality of white-on-white, as Kasimir Malevich had done.[3]

I would say that Rothko had an important influence on me [acknowledged Ryman]. There was also Matisse, particularly, and Cézanne. What interested me in Matisse was not so much what he was painting but how he was doing it. It was his sureness, the way he put the paint down... He was so sure, it was so immediate. (R. Ryman, 1983)

Robert Ryman said that Mark Rothko was the first artist to see the painting as an æsthetic object; Ryman said he wanted to emphasize the object-hood of a painting by using paint: 'I wanted to make a painting getting the paint across. That's really what a painting is basically about' (1971).

A cursory glance at Robert Ryman's paintings would see nothing but white squares of various sizes (typically 60 or 72 inches square). Looking closer, however, one saw that Ryman was metic-ulously and vigorously exploring the relationships between color and support, between shape and color, between objectification and illusion, and between abstraction and figuration. Far from being all the same monotonous white-on-white, Ryman's paintings were all individual. Each one had its own specifications of frame size, support (aluminium, canvas, plastic, wood, fibreglass). There were clips around the edge of some paintings, while others were bolted to the wall.

Paintings of Robert Ryman's such as *Depart7ment* (1981, oil on aluminium, 60 x 60 in, collection: Rhona J. Hoffman, Chicago), *Untitled,* a small painting by postwar standards (53.5 inches square), or the very small *Untitled* of 1961 (12 inches square), display a sense of the tactile to rival Jasper Johns. Ryman's art, like Johns' art, is founded largely on the sensuality of paint, of surfaces, of the eroticism of texture. One comes back to this again and again in art criticism, this sensualism of surface. As Lynda Nead writes of Kenneth Clark:

Clark reads brush marks and lines as though they are part of a symbolic language of sensual impulses, telling traces of sexual desire.4

Robert Ryman's use of white was not to hide the painting's manufacture under a cloak of blankness. The white, rather, emphasized the painting's structure and sensuality. Ryman used white 'in order to make other things in the painting visible, color for instance'.5 The use of white unified the formal aspects of the painting, so the artwork was read as a whole. Aspects of the piece, from surface texture to the support, became interpreted as a totality. White was useful in painting, Ryman explained, because it didn't 'interfere.' It was a

neutral color that allows for a clarification in painting. It makes other aspects of painting visible that would not be so clear with the use of other colors. (ib., 16)

By limiting himself to one color, Robert Ryman, like Brice Marden and Ad Reinhardt, freed himself up for an exploration of different formal aspects. There was nothing limiting about Ryman's concentration on the color white (which is all colors, optically). In Ryman's case, the formal

exploration included moving through a range of media, for Ryman painted in white on many kinds of material: canvas, linen, cotton, wood, paper, steel, copper, aluminium, mylar, fibreglass, Plexiglass, cardboard. He painted with different sorts of media: oil, baked enamel, paper, vinyl acetate emulsion, and so on. As Ryman said, typically of so many contemporary artists: '[t]here is never a question of what to paint, but only how to paint'.6

It didn't matter that most of Ryman's paintings were white. A Robert Ryman exhibition, too, was not at all 'boring'. Indeed, there was a sense of greatness in his painting to rival the masters of contemporary art, such as Mark Rothko. Ryman demonstrated that by limiting oneself in one respect, an unlimited realm would be opened up for exploration. A Robert Ryman show is thus also a display of how to paint, how paint can be used on a variety of media. Different sorts of paint – oil, enamel, emulsion – produce different sorts of effects. Go into any household superstore these days and one can see just how subtle variations there are of white and cream. Ryman showed that even when one limits art to a very narrow set of attributes, infinite variations are still possible. Ryman showed that there isn't just one kind of white. Painters have always known this, but Ryman's concentration on white made it obvious.

Instead of being cool, detached or unemotional (which one might expect from such a Minimal project of painting nothing but white paintings), Ryman's art was highly emotive. 'What is interesting about his work,' wrote Arthur Danto in "The Historical Museum of Monochrome Art", 'is the degree to which, for all its blank whiteness, it reflects the times through which the artist lived' (1997, 169). In the Fifties, Ryman's work reflected the gestural, pigment-rich of Abstract Expressionism; in the Sixties, Ryman became a Minimalist and materialist, and the paintings become 'surface, support, and pigment and nothing more' (ib., 169). In the Eighties and Nineties the works become sculptural, incorporating plastic, waxpaper, bolts and fasteners.

Some of Robert Ryman's white paintings of 1960-61 fill the entire surface with scumbled and impastoed white oil paint. Though severe they are also beautiful, and, in a way, traditional. The white paintings of the late 1970s and 1980s introduced add-ons such as aluminium clips of fasteners which became part of the painting. Attention was thus drawn to the borders of the work, as with the Hard Edge painters, and artists such as Frank Stella, Morris Louis and Jo Baer. The aluminium fasteners drew attention to the painting as object, as something physical to be attached to a gallery wall. The primacy of illusion inside the painting was shattered. The painting had to be considered in its entirety, not simply as something upon which paint was arranged to suggest something outside of itself (a painting of a sky, a tree, a person). Paintings such as *Dominion* (1979), *Courier* (1982), *Director* (1983) and *Report* (1983, all Saatchi Collection, London), were internally smoothly painted in all-over white. The interesting things seemed to be happening around the edges: prominent aluminium clips in *Dominion*; large fasteners in *Courier* as well as the use of oil and enamelac on fibreglass; the same media in *Director*, but with a narrow stripe of a cream hue across the centre of the painting; and a square of fibreglass with the mount being visible in *Report.*

Art critics wondered whether Robert Ryman's all-white squares represented the 'end of painting', as with Ad Reinhardt's black squares.[7] Arthur Danto mused whether Ryman's white squares could been seen as the beginning something new in art, in the way that Giotto stood at the beginning of the Renaissance (1997, 155). Ryman's work can be seen as the end of narrative, modernist art, or as part of a postmodern, pluralist art, where painting is one element in amongst installation art, photography, video art, earthworks, performances and so on (ib., 171).

AGNES MARTIN

Agnes Martin (1912-2004) is an archetypal Minimalist, Cool or Post-Painterly Abstract painter. Her paintings, in which 'nothing seems to happen', to use a Samuel Beckettian phrase, are deeply poetic. As with Robert Ryman's white paintings (which are more like Martin's than most), there was a lot happening in Martin's paintings. From a distance, Martin's paintings looked like off-white squares with hardly anything done to them. When one looked closer, one saw different grids, and different ways of marking the grid (gold leaf, pencil, ink). Sometimes the grid was very tight and compact, with a tiny rectangle being described; sometimes there was a web of horizontal lines, widely spaced; sometimes the white was attenuated by a faint pink or grey or cream between each set of horizontal bands.

Agnes Martin's paintings are, like Robert Ryman's and Ad Reinhardt's paintings, flat squares in a human-scale (often five or six foot square, for instance). They have poetic titles: *Mountain II* (1966, collection: R. Solomon, New York), *Drift of Summer* (1965, Saatchi Collection, London), *Graystone* (1981), *Song* (1982) and *Night Sea* (1963, Saatchi Collection, London).

Agnes Martin's white paintings are not all they seem at first, as with Frank Stella's *Black Stripe Paintings* and Robert Ryman's work. *Night Sea* is, unusually in Martin's œuvre, a light blue, hinting at nature, at skies and seas. It is painted in oil and gold leaf. The variations that Martin makes within her basic format are many: sometimes the grid is packed tightly, as in *Drift of Summer* and *Stone,* but lightly drawn, so the painting remains mainly white all over. In *Night Sea* the rectangles are much larger, so that the spaces between the blue paint is visible from a distance. In *Untitled No. 8* (private collection) the grid becomes vertical stripes forming a salmon-pink row of bands. In *Untitled No. 12* (1977, Pace Gallery) the pencil and india ink lines define small vertical rectangles on a six-foot square canvas. In the series of paintings entitled *Untitled* (*Untitled I, Untitled II, Untitled II* and so on up to *Untitled XII* and beyond [made in 1979, Saatchi Collection, London]), the graphite marks (on linen) do not describe rectangles but bands of horizontal lines. *Untitled No. 9* (1980) is a series of repeating vertical bands of pale, nearly ephemeral colors (pink, yellow and blue).

Beauty and happiness and life are all the same and they are pervasive, unattached and abstract and they are our only concern. They are im- measurable, completely lacking in substance. They are perfect and sublime. This is the subject matter of art.

Agnes Martin's painterly reductionism seems austere, but in fact poeticizes the world, as with the art of Robert Ryman or Brice Marden. Agnes Martin's paintings, according to Barbara Rose,

require a degree of concentration so intense from the viewer that, like Ad Reinhardt's black paintings, they are oases of quiet in a tumultuous, over-stimulated environment.[1]

Rather than being aligned with the polemical Minimal artists, such as Donald Judd and Robert Morris, Martin is more usefully associated with the Abstract Expressionist painters most often linked with the Colorfield and Minimal painters (that is, Barnett Newman and Mark Rothko).

In Agnes Martin's art, subject matter was crucial. This alone distances her work from painters such as Morris Louis and Frank Stella, who insisted on the thing-in-itself, the ubiquitous 'what you see is what you get' principle of much of Minimal (and 1960s) art. Martin's art, meanwhile, emphasized poetry and evoked nature.

In "The Untroubled Mind", Agnes Martin wrote

My work is anti-nature
The four storey mountain
You will not think form, space, line, contour
Just a suggestion of nature gives weight
light and heavy

light like a feather
you get light enough and you levitate.
When I say it's alive, it's inspired
alive
inspiration and life are equivalents and they
come from outside (1973, 17)

Agnes Martin says that inspiration is 'moments of happiness', which are always around us. 'Inspiration is there all the time for everyone whose mind is not clouded over with thoughts whether they realize it or not'.[2] Martin's inspiration is thus an æsthetic and ontological openness, a state of awareness which some artists cultivate or hope to induce in others. Inspiration, Martin says, is always waiting for the untroubled mind. As children seem to be more untroubled than adults, they have more inspiration, and thus sensibility, says Martin. Instead of parents trying to 'educate' their children in social issues or traditional education, Martin reckons that 'the awakening to their sensibility is the most important thing' (1973, 24).

My paintings are not about what is seen. They are about what is known forever in the mind.

Once she had discovered the basic format of her work – the white square canvas upon which a screen of small rectangular shapes were drawn – Agnes Martin proceeded to explore, as with Robert Ryman, the possibilities of such a reduced configuration. The use of small rectangles or the grid was distinctly Minimalist, but the use Martin made of it pointed towards a lyricism and spirit- uality Minimalism seldom consciously courted. Critics such as Thomas Hess and Daniel Wheeler could not help associating Martin's art with the New Mexico desert where she lived – linking the sparseness and grandeur of the desert with Martin's ascetic, pared-away but often beautiful art. Oh, and the famous and exquisite New Mexico light: if you've been in New Mexico (or Colorado or Arizona or California), you'll appreciate the quality of light there, and the Big Skies).

RICHARD DIEBENKORN

Like many painters of the second half of the 20th century, Richard Diebenkorn (1922-93) started out in figurative art and moved into abstraction. Artists who helped influence Diebenkorn included Edward Hopper, Paul Cézanne, Henri Matisse, Pablo Picasso and Pierre Bonnard, as well as Willem de Kooning, Robert Motherwell, Arnold Gottlieb, Clyfford Still and Mark Rothko.

Richard Diebenkorn's most celebrated work was the *Ocean Park* series of paintings, named after an area in Santa Monica. In 1966 Diebenkorn moved from the East coast to L.A. and used Sam Francis's studio in Ocean Park.

Prior to the *Ocean Park* series, Richard Diebenkorn had painted hundreds of figurative works: Hopperesque landscapes of Middle America; Bonnard-like female nudes; and not a few pictures of open windows or doorways, recalling a favourite motif of Matisse. The seeds of the great *Ocean Park* series can be seen in Diebenkorn's early and mid-period works, however. There is not such a sudden leap between figuration and abstraction. Many of Diebenkorn's landscapes contain large rectangular areas of flat color – blues, yellows, white – the palette later used in many of the *Ocean Park* paintings. One can see, in the canvases of the mid to late Sixties such as *Recollections of a Visit to Leningrad* (1965, San Francisco), *Window* (1967, Stanford University Museum of Art), *Cityscape* (1963, California), and *Interior With Doorway* (1962, Pennsylvania Academy of the Fine Arts), the elements that became the æsthetic basis of the *Ocean Park* series: the areas of flat color, the light tones, the use of horizontals and verticals, the foundation in an appreciation of landscape.

The first *Ocean Park* paintings, such as *Ocean Park No. 16* (1968, Milwaukee Art Museum), *Ocean Park No. 21* (1969, New York) and *Ocean Park No. 39* (1971, New York), predominantly consisted of areas of monochrome organized on a vertical grid, with sometimes a band of diagonal lines of color in the middle section of the composition (as in *Ocean Park No. 9* [1968, Los Angeles], *Ocean Park No. 40* [1971, private collection] and *Ocean Park No. 27* [1970, Brooklyn Museum]).

The *Ocean Park* paintings are large abstract canvases which relate to the Californian coastline: the clear Pacific light, the white of gables, the sloping hills descending into the sea. Diebenkorn's abstract canvases took as their departure point the view of the sea, roads, fences, pier and sky that Diebenkorn could see framed in his large transom windows.

The *Ocean Park* paintings (such as *Ocean Park No. 60* (1973, Buffalo), *Ocean Park No. 30* (Metropolitan Museum) and *Ocean Park No. 78* (1975, Honolulu)), are large, spacious works, serene, clear. They are both gestural in the Abstract Expressionist manner and filled with substantial areas of Minimalist monochrome.

Ocean Park No. 60 was one of the bluest in the series of Richard Diebenkorn's paintings, as if this painting was devoted almost entirely to the ocean. Large areas of *Ocean Park No. 60* were painted in the same cerulean blue hue, with all the fiddly bits occurring around the edge. Similar blue-dominated paintings included *Ocean Park No. 79* (1975, Philadelphia), *Ocean Park No. 115* (1979, Museum of Modern Art), *Ocean Park No. 125* (1980, Whitney Museum), *Ocean Park No. 128* (1984, New York) and *Ocean Park No. 129* (1984, private collection). As with so many of the *Ocean Park* paintings, *Ocean Park No. 60*'s composition set the lines and panels of different colors along the top and right-hand edge of the canvas. There were red and black lines suggesting architectural structures in *Ocean Park No. 60* and others, such as *Ocean Park No. 83* (1975, Washington) and *Ocean Park No. 87* (1975, Virginia), with cream and yellow pigment put into the rectangles the lines made. Only in those rectilinear spaces did Diebenkorn allow a departure from the generally consistent monochrome passages of the main part of the painting.

In many *Ocean Park* paintings a sizeable proportion of the canvas is taken up by one block of color. Some of the *Ocean Park* paintings are in pale hues, which sometimes look pastel (pale blue, green, yellow, cream) – for example, *Ocean Park No. 114* (1979, California). Some are primarily cream and yellow, such as *Ocean Park No. 48* (1971, California), *Ocean Park No. 91* (1976, California), *Ocean Park No. 95* (1976, San Francisco), *Ocean Park No. 96* (1977, Guggenheim Museum), *Ocean Park No. 100* (1977, California), *Ocean Park No. 118* (1980, Miami), *Ocean Park No. 123* (1980, California) and *Ocean Park No. 131* (1985, California), some were predominantly deep blue, such as *Ocean Park No. 92* (1976, private collection) and *Ocean Park No. 137* (1985, Los Angeles), some were mostly dark green (*Ocean Park No. 111*, 1978, Hirshhorn Museum, Washington), while others used large areas of mid-green and mid-blue, such as *Ocean Park No. 45* (1971, Art Institute of Chicago), *Ocean Park No. 105* (1978, private collection), *Ocean Park No. 66* (1973, Albright-Knox Art Gallery) and *Ocean Park No. 140* (1985, Los Angeles).

Unusually, canvases such as *Ocean Park No. 70* (1974, Des Moines Art Center, Iowa), were mainly red and pink. Paintings such as *Ocean Park No. 63* (1973, private collection), *Ocean Park No. 49* (1972, Los Angeles County Museum of Art), *Ocean Park No. 43* (1971, San Francisco) and *Ocean Park No. 64* (1973, Carnegie Museum of Art, Pittsburgh) consisted of large areas of flat white. A painting such as *Ocean Park No. 107* (1978, Oakland Museum) layered green, yellow, grey, pink, dark blue and red above a large pastel blue rectangle. They are often light, airy paintings, with few dark tones. The *Ocean Park* series exhibit echoes of the Minimal grid: the paintings are sometimes divided into rectilinear blocks of color by black lines, which are sometimes painted over. But the square pattern of the grid is still visible.

The force and impact of the *Ocean Park* series derives partly from the sheer number of canvases, from the Conceptual and Serial art notion of doing one thing then another. 'Do it again', repeat and repeat: how many impressive contemporary works of art have we seen that comprise essentially of nothing more than one element replicated endlessly? You take something than replicate it. A floor tile, repeated… a painted stripe, repeated over a canvas… a metallic box, repeated, up a wall…

On their own, each the *Ocean Park* painting is impressive, but when you view the series as a whole, it contains much more power (however, the paintings are scattered all over the planet: *Ocean Park* is not a group of paintings in one place, like Barnett Newman's *Stations of the Cross* in Washington, DC, or Mark Rothko's *Rothko Chapel* works).

ROBERT MANGOLD

Robert Mangold (b. 1937) explored color and architecture in his multi-panelled paintings which often contain a unifying element of drawing (in *Four Color Frame Painting no.1* [collection: Martin Sklar, New York], for example). Mangold's multi-part canvases have much in common with the art of Brice Marden, Ellsworth Kelly and Frank Stella. Mangold used monochromy (but much more saturated hues than Marden or Ryman), occasionally complex interior architecture, and produced 'walls' or 'areas' of paint.

Manilla Area (1966), *Red Wall* (1965), and *1/2 Blue-Gray Curved Area* (1967) are typical of Robert Mangold's shaped canvases of the mid-Sixties. Mangold also ventured into curved shaped canvases, instantly recognizable as Mangold's work: the *W Series* (1968), for instance. Mangold later developed a series of monochrome canvases with thin lines described simple geometric shapes inside: a circle in *Distorted Square/ Circle (Blue-Green)* (1971) and *Distorted Square/ Circle (Red)* (1971, London), squares inside circles in *Untitled (Blue-Violet)* (1973, London), squares inside a shaped triangular canvas in *Three Squares Within Triangle (Wine Red)* (1976, London), and rectangles and rhomboids in *Painting For Three Walls (Blue, Yellow, Brown)* (1979).

In the series of four-part panel paintings (*4 Color Frame Paintings,* 1983), Robert Mangold deployed canvases of different sizes, each painted in a different monochrome (red, yellow, green, pink, brown). Each panel was mounted on the wall abutting each other, and an ellipse painted in black pencil was inscribed across the four panels. A later group of paintings, the *Attic Series* (1990-91), featured ellipses and figure 8's drawn in pencil on complexly-shaped monochrome canvases (such as *Attic Series XIV,* 1991). In the *Curved Plane/ Figure* series of the mid-Nineties, Mangold was still producing monochrome, curved canvases as he had done at the height of Minimalism in the 1960s.

And he was still drawing ellipses in pencil on top of them (as in *Curved Plane/ Figure IV (Double Panel),* 1995).

ELLSWORTH KELLY

Like Kenneth Noland, Richard Diebenkorn and Frank Stella, Ellsworth Kelly's paintings were instantly recognizable as his own. Kelly (born in 1923) moved through a number of different styles, as many young artists do, before arriving at a kind of lyrical Hard Edge painting embodied in works such as *Yellow-Blue* (1963, Des Moines Art Center), *White-Dark Blue* (1962, London), *Blue, Red, Green* (1962-63, Metropolitan Museum, New York) and *Red Blue Green* (1962, La Jolla Museum of Contemporary Art). The latter was made at Coenties Slip, where Kelly shared studios with Jack Youngerman, Agnes Martin, and James Rosenquist.

Ellsworth Kelly's art was marked by brilliant coloration and a harmonious organization of color and shape. Like Brice Marden, Robert Mangold and David Novros, Kelly made multi-panel paintings in which each panel was given a single all-over color. Kelly said he wasn't influenced by the Abstract Expressionists (whom he had seen in 1954), but by Egyptian, Oriental and Byzantine art, by French Romanesque architecture, and Vincent van Gogh, Paul Cézanne, Claude Monet, Paul Klee, Pablo Picasso, Max Beckmann and Henri Matisse.[1] Kelly's *Spectrum* series (such as *Blue Green Yellow Orange Red* [1966, Guggenheim Museum]) were brighter than any of Marden's monochrome paintings.

Ellsworth Kelly expressed a view in his "Notes of 1969" article that was common to many of the Sixties painters: '[t]he form of my painting is the content'. It was not the brushmarks that interested Kelly in his paintings, so much as 'the "presence" of the panels themselves'. It was in 1949 that Kelly started to make objects rather than paintings.

> Instead of making a picture that was an interpretation of a thing seen, or a picture of invented content, I found an object and "presented" it as itself alone.[2]

This encapsulates the fundamental break between traditional art and postwar and contemporary art.

The 1999 Harvard University Art Museum show of early drawings, like the later show at the Tate Gallery in Blighty, demonstrate how immensely creative Kelly's art was, and how he has been overlooked for too long. In *The Early Drawings, 1948-1955*, Kelly's sense of joy in the exploration of painterly abstraction is palpable: especially fine are the mysterious two-color works (such as *Study For a White and Black Painting*, 1955), and the white-on-white studies (*Study For a White Relief*, 1953).

Although Ellsworth Kelly is still not the most well-known contemporary artist – mention his name and I'm sure many people, even dedicated art lovers, won't know who you mean – his art is completely distinctive. In an era (1960s-1970s) when 100s of artists, it seems, were churning out smooth, rectilinear, monochrome works – boxes, canvases, slabs, repeated objects – Kelly's art still stands out as something wholly his own. And that's no mean feat.

Walk into a gallery or museum today, and you can recognize Ellsworth Kelly's art instantly. There's a superb display of Kelly's Serial repetitions on the wall of the Metropolitan Museum of Art in Gotham, for instance (*Spectrum V*, 1969). It's a group of vertical format paintings which run thru the color spectrum, and it's immediately seen as a Kelly work. And in the atrium of Chicago's Art Institute, there are giant Kelly slabs high on the wall, with his stamp all over them (*Chicago Panels*, 1989-99).

You take a form, reduce it and compress it to its most fundamental essence, and somehow it increases the æsthetic impact; then you add those distinctive 1960s primary and secondary colors, and the works bounce off the white walls of galleries and museums.

GERHARD RICHTER

Gerhard Richter (b. 1932) is renowned as an influential figurative and abstract painter, a painter of representations such as the softly smeared *Annunciations After Titian* (1973), a series of meta-paintings, paintings about paintings, which explored Renaissance art in terms of post-modernism.

The art of Gerhard Richter is not wholly (or nearly wholly) abstract. Eighties paintings by Richter such as *Untitled (531-4)* and *Group of Trees (628-1),* are near-abstract pieces, consisting of thick brush-strokes, in the Willem de Kooning or Howard Hodgkin manner. The more abstract painting, *Untitled*, still retains notions of representation: it has a 'background' space to the foreground shapes which is a light blue, something like the smooth, clear skies of Yves Tanguy.

The series of *Gray Paintings* (1967-76) were archetypal Minimal pieces: groups of gray monochrome canvases which aimed, Gerhard Richter said, to 'clarify nothingness'. Richter explained that he selected gray as a point of departure because he 'did not know what I should paint or what there might be to paint' (the Samuel Beckett position again).[1] Gray was something of a 'non-color', indifferent, 'the epitome of non-statement', and 'suitable for illustrating "nothing"'. Richter's *Gray Paintings* represent another example of The End of Painting (*pace* Ad Reinhardt's *Black Paintings, Abstract*, or Robert Rauschenberg's white and black painting). Richter was very conscious of being an inheritor of the vast, rich history of painting, and wanting to measure himself against it, as well as investigate it and draw upon it.[2]

Photography is one of Gerhard Richter's recurring concerns. Many of his paintings have been based on photos, but Richter's use of photography is much more complicated than that (though those paintings from photographs are beautiful enough on their own). Richter's photographic paintings combine plenty of theoretical and philosophical explorations with sensual, visual magic. They work on many levels, and seem designed to delight people who still think postmodernism is important. (That is, Richter's art is tailor-made for art history students or for art critics for whom terms like 'postmodernism' and 'Baudrillardian' and 'hyper-reality' still hold some weight).

Aligned to photography is Gerhard Richter's exploration of monochromism, so that many of his paintings begin with a black-and-white photograph, reproducing its black-and-white æsthetic make-up (though not in the same way as Andy Warhol). Richter has also gone far into Minimalism's beloved area of grey art, of exploring multiple shades of grey.

Later pieces by Gerhard Richter developed his striking technique of smearing paint wet-in-wet, which, combined with employing vivid hues, lend his works an appealing sensuality and impact. Richter builds on the Colorfield art of the 1960s and 1970s (particularly the Washington school) — by Gene Davis, Morris Louis and Kenneth Noland — and takes it even further in areas of pure optical pleasure. Richter's smeared abstractions are works which refer to nothing but themselves, and they create the means and ways by which they are to be consumed. The æsthetic and painterly force of these paintings is undeniable.

Gerhard Richter is also an artist, I think, who demonstrates for all to see that painting is not dead, but vibrantly alive. The *energy* coming off the walls in Richter's art is so strong. You can't ignore it. This man knows what he's doing, and he does it so well — indeed, he does it better, more skilfully and more flamboyantly than almost any other of his contemporaries.

If you are losing your faith in contemporary painting, go straight to Gerhard Richter: he will restore it, he will make you realize why you loved painting in the first place.

Gerhard Richter is thus another 'painter's painter' (like Jasper Johns, Robert Rauschenberg or Brice Marden), and that's another reason why

Richter is popular with artists and critics. Richter's art is also meta-art, art about art, an on-going conversation between the artist and the history of art. And Richter shows, decisively (once again), that painting isn't dead.

OTHER MINIMAL PAINTERS

Other painters who exhibited Minimal mannerisms include: Kenneth Noland, Jack Bush, Jules Olitski, Paul Mogensen, Jeremy Moon, Max Bill, Edward Avedisian, William Anastasi, Ross Bleckner, Oliver Mosset, Allan McCollum, Sherrie Levine, Richard Prince, Phillip Taafe, Elizabeth Murray, Jo Baer, John Hoyland, Ralph Humphrey, Ed Meneeley, Alexander Liberman, Dorothea Rockburne, Jake Berthot, Lucio Fontana, Robert Barry, Fred Sandback, Gotthard Graubner, Günter Uecker, Dean Fleming, Jim Dine, Al Held, Larry Poons, James Bishop, Allan D'Arcangelo, Jennifer Bartlett, Sam Gilliam, Mark Lammert, Cy Twombly, Niele Toroni, Peter Halley, David Novros, Alan Charlton, Bob Law, Peter Joseph, John Walker, Bridget Riley, Sally Drummond and Helen Frankenthaler.

SAM GILLIAM (b. 1933) created complexly shaped 'paintings' (such as *Like Today*, 1985, Monique Knowlton Gallery, New York) which, gleefully smash the primacy of the traditional rectangle in painting. Some of Gilliam's distinctive works are canvases hung in loose shapes on the wall, not stretched on a wooden frame, rather like multi-colored versions of the felt works of Robert Morris.

Both **ALEXANDER LIBERMAN** and **AL HELD** produced post-Mondrian, post-Pollock Hard Edge paintings, such as Liberman's *Omega VI* (Princeton) or Held's *Taxi Cab* series in the late Fifties (probably his most celebrated work). Hard edge art was also to the fore in **JACK YOUNGERMAN**'s paintings (Youngerman was part of a social group which included Ellsworth Kelly, and his paintings, such as *Black, Yellow, Red* [1964, Finch College Museum of Art, New York] show affinities with Kelly). Not strictly a Minimal painter (more known for his abstract and semi-figurative art), **CY TWOMBLY** employed some of Minimalism's principles (such as the formal gestures towards monochromy – in Twombly's case, that usually meant white [as in *Hero and Leander*, 1981-84, Galerie Karsten Greve, Cologne]).

In *2V Dwan 2* (1965-66), **DEAN FLEMING** joined three canvases and painted in acrylic a sheared band across them. **ROBERT BARRY** produced a series of small monochrome paintings in the 1960s, experimenting with unpainted canvass, the edges of the painting, and the invisible, negative spaces between paintings (as in *4 Red Squares*, 1967).

LARRY POONS (b. 1937) developed an Op Art format consisting of a monochrome canvas with small disc-shaped blobs of paint dotted across the surface (the 'jumping beans' were carefully situated in relation to each other). In *Rosewood* (1966, William Rubin Collection) these discs were mainly pink, orange and pale green on a dull yellow ground. In Poons' *Untitled* (1966, Whitney Museum of American Art), blue, green, pink and orange impastoed dots floating disembodied on a pale green ground. As with Jules Olitski, Ken Noland, Helen Frankenthaler and Morris Louis, Larry Poons' paintings stressed the sensory thrill of opticality. Like Bridget Riley's or Richard Anuzkiewicz's paintings, Poons' works revelled in creating retinal after-images. (And Poons' bright dots led directly to the substandard imitations by British pseudo-artist Damien Hirst).

LUCIO FONTANA (1899-1968) was a Conceptual and assemblage artist whose most famous works were the canvases which the artist slit or slashed with nails and awls (such as *Spatial Concept/ Waiting* [1959, Trieste] or *Spatial Concept* [1965, Fashion Concepts, New York]). Fontana employed the monochromy of Minimalism in these pieces (red, white). **PIERO MANZONI** , art trickster (or genius?), was famous for canning his own faeces (*Merde d'artista*, 1961) and 'signing' real people as works of art. But Manzoni also produced white monochrome paintings, the *Achromes* series (such

as *Achrome*, 1958, London), which aimed to go beyond pictorialism, expressivity and represent-ation.

JULES OLITSKI (b. 1922) devoted himself to formalist abstract paintings that employed Minimal æsthetics (such as the use of large areas of monochrome) with opulent color (as in *Green Goes Around* [1967, private collection], or the rich reds in *Feast* [1965, collection: Catherine Zimmerman]). Olitski is more usually categorized as a Post-Painterly Abstractionist, or Colorfield painter, than a Minimalist. Many of his canvases explore closely-valued hues, as in *(Twice) Disarmed* (1968, Metropolitan Museum, NYC), pinks, roses, lilacs modulate softly across the width of the painting (it's 212 inches wide), with a vestige of submerged layers or under-painting on the left. Most of *High a Yellow* (1967, Whitney Museum of American Art) is monochrome yellow, spreading throughout a 7' 8.5" x 12' 6" canvas, with remnants of under-painting visible around the upper righthand edges (red, green, mustard).

The emphasis on optical effects in Jules Olitski's art, with affinities to Mark Rothko and Morris Louis in particular, are obvious: this is painting as a pure sensory experience, in which colors and abstract forms seem intended to act on the body and the senses immediately. The relations to anything representational are vague and ambiguous. As with Brice Marden's art, Olitski's device of leaving the edges of the paintings worked around with other colors and forms emphasized aspects of the manufacture of the work, and also added some elements of solidity or reference for the central expanses of single colors.

Canadian **JACK BUSH** (1909-77) went through the roster of 20th century art styles (Cubism, Expressionism, Abstract Expressionism) before making Colorfield paintings that consisted of his 'sash and fringe' motif: rows of brilliant colors were set beside a neutral-hued vertical ground (as in *Tall Spread*, 1966, National Gallery of Canada).

Op Art or optical art of the Sixties had its ancestors in artists such as Josef Albers and Victor Vassarely. Apart from Vassarely, the chief practitioners of 1960s Op Art included Bridget Riley, Larry Poons, Yaacov Agam, Enrico Castellani, Günter Uecker, Jesús Raphael Soto, François Morellet, Piero Dorazio and Richard Anuzkiewiscz.

Linked to Op art and optical art are kinetic art, and light art, where machines or devices move to create optical effects, or neons and lamps are employed, or, as in the art of James Turrell, the sky itself. It's easy to see how expanses of the sky, or the lighting effects of Dan Flavin, the neons of Bruce Nauman and Nam June Paik, have equivalences with Minimal painting.

The German painter **GOTTHARD GRAUBNER** (b. 1930) developed the all-overness of Abstract Expressionism and did away with geometric motifs altogether. Graubner's paintings consist of areas of color which merge like mist, as if Mark Rothko's 'cloud-like' images had been dissolved in fog (as in *Blue-Rose Colour-Space*, 1961-62, Kunstmuseum, Düsseldorf). Graubner's art evoked a spaceless meditative zone, which Graubner enhanced at times by placing fabric on top of paintings made with foam rubber on canvas.

One of **GÜNTER UECKER** 's (b. 1930) styles was distinctly Minimalist, austere monochrome canvases (in black, white and gray), which explored the materiality of the painting-as-object: some of Uecker's paintings were reliefs using nails (*Painting Nailed Over* [1957, collection: the artist] and *Informal Structure* [1957, Staatliche Museen zu Berlin]), others mixed oil and silver leaf, as in *Silver Spiral* (1957, collection: the artist), some recalled the textured white panels of Robert Ryman (*Vertical Structure White*, 1958, collection: the artist), and some were classic Minimal pieces (half of a painting in white, the other half in black), recalling Ellsworth Kelly and Brice Marden (*Black-White*, 1956-57, collection: the artist).

RALPH HUMPREY (1932-90) was one of the earlier Minimal painters, whose monochrome canvases (such as *Atlanta* [1958] and *Olympia* [1959]) were precursors of Brice Marden and Robert Mangold (who admired Humphrey). Like Jo Baer, Robert Ryman and Agnes Martin, Humphrey explored the formal possibilities of all-over white in pieces such as *Rio* (1965) and *Camden* (1965). The edges of the painting become the zone of interest, the central area being all white.

ELIZABETH MURRAY (1940-2007) was one of many (post) Sixties artists who used multiple panels or 3-D paintings, in the manner of Frank Stella and Robert Mangold. Murray produced marvellous shaped panels, such as her *Simple Meaning* (1982, collection: Jerry & Emily Spiegel, New York) and *Fire Cup* (1982, Paula Cooper Gallery, New York). Murray's *1, 2, 3* (1984, private collection) was a complicated shaped abstract canvas using three layers. *1, 2, 3* was lushly painted in blues, greens, yellows and purples.[1] You will come across Murray's works in many museums and galleries around the world (mostly in the U.S.A., inevitably), and while Murray's isn't as celebrated as many of the other Colorfield and Post-Painterly Abstract artists, her work is always impressive, particularly in the realm of the shaped canvas.

There's a kind of miracle involved with paint [Murray wrote]. It's just this stuff in a tube... you squeeze out. It's this physical thing, yet you use it as a transforming agent.

A 1981 painting such as *Painter's Progress* (MOMA, New York) – an apt title – comprised no less than nineteen separate panels, with the abstract patterns on the canvas leaping over the irregular gaps between the panels. Murray remarked:

I was imagining a whole thing – dropped or fallen and then shattered – on the ground, in the air, or perhaps in the body or mind. The image inside is trying to form the pieces whole again.2

Painter's Progress was about shattering a picture into fragments and putting them together again – not only physically and formally, but also imaginatively.

DOROTHEA ROCKBURNE also developed the Hard Edge shaped canvas, as in her *Noli Me Tangere* (1976, New York), with its internal geometry of triangles and squares. **ED MEN-EELEY**'s shaped canvases recalled Noland's and Kelly's, with stripes bordering the shapes (as in *Untitled*), as do **JEREMY MOON**'s shaped pictures (such as *Blue Rose*, 1967, Tate, London).

One of **JAKE BERTHOT**'s formal techniques was to put two canvases side by side, inhabited by rectilinear forms, hints at architecture and horizons, and allusions to Romanticism, produced with a return to traditional methods of painting, as in *Walken's Ridge* (1975-76, MOMA, New York). In *Belfast* (1981) Berthot's shadowy rectangular forms and lines recall Diebenkorn's *Ocean Park* series, though the coloration (dark blues and blacks, with patches of red and white) are much darker than Diebenkorn's.

NIELE TORONI's trademark was to paint all of his pictures using the same means, as the title given to his works shows: *Imprints of a No. 50 Brush Repeated At Regular Intervals* (1967). Toroni explores the materiality and cultural value of painting. Even a poet like **HENRI MICHAUX** produced paintings along Minimal lines (his india ink paintings).

RICHARD TUTTLE (b. 1941) produced shaped canvases for a time, such as *Tan Octagon* (1967, London), made from dyed cloth, and *8th Paper Octagonal* (1970, London). Tuttle's artworks were somewhere between paintings and sculptures, as with so many of the 1960s artists. Tuttle's *Canvas Dark Blue* (1967, private collection, NYC) cut the canvas in an irregular, consciously non-geometric shape, with a roughly rectangular hole in the middle, and pinned the painted result on a wall.

The speciality of **DAVID NOVROS** (b. 1941), a Minimal painter much less well-known than Brice Marden or Frank Stella, was complex shaped canvases painted in monochrome with vinyl and acrylic lacquer. Typical examples include the L-shaped canvases that constitute 1965's *Untitled* (6 by 8 feet), 1968's *Untitled* (Los Angeles) and *Untitled* (1968-69). Novros also employed fibreglass as a basis for his paintings, rather than canvases or linen, to achieve a smooth look, and make the paintings more like an object.

ALAN CHARLTON followed the strictly monochrome route of Ad Reinhardt and Alexander Rodchenko, producing panels of different shades of gray. Victor Burgin and Mel Ramsden had also experimented with the *reductio ad absurdum* of monochrome art. **MILTON RESNICK**'s *Elephant* (1979, New York) was a field of impastoed gray, on a large, 209 inch wide canvas, recalling Brice Marden's gray Sixties panels. Britons **PETER JOSEPH** and **BOB LAW** made Postminimalist paintings; Law had an exhibition of all-black canvases at the Whitechapel in 1977.

Color was central to many of the Post-Painterly Abstract painters such as Kenneth Noland, Jules Olitski, Joseph Albers and others. **HELEN FRANK-ENTHALER** (b. 1928) was one of the best of the bunch. Only a few of the Minimal painters (such as Frank Stella and Ken Noland) allowed themselves colors as lush as those of painters such as Frankenthaler or Ellsworth Kelly. Frankenthaler rejoiced in the exuberance of pure color. See, for example, her *Movable Blue* (1973, Louisville) and *Nature Abhors a Vacuum* (1973, Andre Emmerich Gallery, New York).

JENNIFER BARTLETT (b. 1941) shared something of Helen Frankenthaler's love of opulent coloration, as her *Falcon Avenue, Seaside Walk,*

Dwight Street, Jarvis Street, Greene Street (1976) (Whitney Museum of American Art) revealed. Barlett also utilized the Minimalists' penchant for seriality and repetition, as well as the small square panel.

Some of **JO BAER**'s (b. 1929) paintings consist of large areas of white, with a narrow band of color around the very edges of the canvas (as in *Sidebare (Lavender White)* [1972, Australia], *Untitled* [1963], and *Untitled (Red Wrap-Around)* [1969]). This format recalls Morris Louis's stripes, where the major, central section of the painting is either white or bare canvas, color being relegated to the periphery of the spectator's vision. As with the art of Frank Stella and Robert Ryman, the really interesting area of a Jo Baer painting was the edge. Baer also typically painted a band of black on the outside edge of the canvases, enclosing a narrow band of color (as in *Untitled (White Square Lavender)*, 1964-74). In Baer's later paintings, the side edges of the painting as well as the front edges become important (as in *Untitled (Double Bar Diptych – Green and Red)* [1968], and *Untitled (Red Wrap-Around)*). Baer defined her style of painting as having no ambiguity, no hierarchy, no illusion, no space, no time.[3]

The 'Neo-Geo' artists, the East Village artists of the early 1980s, influenced by Jean Baudrillard and his concept of *simulcra* and surfaces (Peter Halley, Ashley Bickerton, Meyer Vaisman, Jeff Koons and Haim Steinbach), produced postmodern, hybrid, ironic, Neo-Conceptual art, which sometimes developed and parodied Minimal, Colorfield and Post-Painterly Abstraction. **PETER HALLEY**'S paintings, for example – *Asynchronous Terminal* (1989) and *Nirvana* (1992) – drew on Joseph Alber's squares, Sixties Day-Glo colors, computer diagrams, comics, and the large scale of the New York School.

SEAN SCULLY's (b. 1945) art is Postminimal, post-Abstract Expressionist, and in love with the history of modern painting (its emphasis on materiality, on rectilinear forms, on luscious brushwork and surfaces, on color, on single motifs repeated endlessly through countless paintings). Scully's use of the grid, or vertical stripe motifs, also directly recall painters such as Barnett Newman, Frank Stella, Kenneth Noland and Agnes Martin. One could also discern Henri Matisse, David Bomberg, Piet Mondrian, and the Minimalists in Scully's shaped canvases.

Sean Scully's trademark was big, blocky canvases daubed with wide bands of textured color, usually with a smaller section of canvas that was inserted parallel to (or sometimes above) the picture plane (as in *To Want* [1985, Walker Art Center, Minneapolis]).

Sean Scully painted thickly in horizontal and vertical stripes. His subject was the way the stripe was painted. 'The stripe is neutral and boring and that makes the stripe receptive to interpretation', Scully said. The variations in the way the stripes were painted were intended to make different sorts of paintings.

ROSS BLECKNER (b. 1949) made Hans Hofmann-like Neo-Op paintings, all energy and light (*Cage* [1986], *Fallen Object* [1987], and *The Oceans* [1984]). Bleckner's is an art of dim phosphorescences glowing out of dark monochromy (*God Won't Come* [1983] and *Delaware* [1983, both private collection]), or vague, antiquated motifs (leaves, snowflakes, mono-grams), as in *Fallen Summer* (1988, private collection).

PHILIP TAAFE (b. 1955) parodied Barnett Newman's zip in his *Abraham and Isaac* (1986, a Newmanesque title), turning the revered stripe into a decorative twisted cord (a motif that also evoked Henri Matisse, who used Hermès silk scarves). **ANTONI TÀPIES** (b. 1923) might count as another precursor of Minimal painting; like the Minimalists, Tàpies acknowledged that he was 'obsessed with materiality' (as a glance at any of his major paintings would show: for instance, *Black Form On*

Gray Square, 1960, or *Black With Two Lozenges*, 1963).

BLINKY PALERMO (1943-77) was also influenced by Minimal painting, as well as Conceptual art and performance art, as in his *Textile Picture 18* (1968, Stuttgart) and *Softspeaker* (1965, Frankfurt). Palmero's 1960s paintings were typically made using colored fabrics (as in *Fabric Painting, Pink-Orange-Black*, 1968). Some of Palermo's paintings (*Fabric Painting*, 1969, private collection) were archetypal Minimal works, echoing Brice Marden and Ellsworth Kelly with bands of monochrome (though in painted fabric). Later, Palermo produced installations of wall drawings (Hamburg, 1975).

LUDWIG SANDER produced monochrome post-Mondrian explorations of grids (such as *Chincoteague II* [1961, New York]). **WILLIAM ANASTASI** turned in monochrome Minimal paintings as part of his *œuvre* (as in *North Wall, Dwan Main Gallery* [1967]). **DAVID HOCKNEY**, though associated with Pop Art, used Minimal means at times. In his most famous painting, *The Splash* (1966), he employed large areas of unbroken single colors, reminiscent of Robert Mangold or Ellsworth Kelly (Tom Wesselmann was another Pop artist with a similar painting technique of flat, opaque color).

PAUL MOGENSEN explored mathematics, geometry, systems, proportions, and formulas in his paintings, such as *Standard* (1966) and *Untitled* (1967). Mogensen's *Copperopolis* (1965-78) took a series of sixteen monochrome canvases in diminishing sizes as the paintings moved from left to right. Some of **LARRY ZOX**'S paintings recall the Hard Edge canvases of Ellsworth Kelly or Kenneth Noland. Zox produced paintings with the chevron and trapeze designs favoured by Noland and Frank Stella (as in *Tyeen*, 1966).

PART THREE

SCULPTURE

#3

MINIMAL SCULPTORS

DONALD JUDD

Donald Judd's is the Minimalists' Minimalist; he is the quintessential Minimal artist, and probably the most important Minimal artist. Judd's art is absolutely at the centre of Minimalism (in theory, in practice, and socially, and in the art world), and it is also representative of most of the manifestations and phases of Minimal art.

The works of Donald Judd (1928-1994) at first seemed to be firmly fixed in a monotonous, monochrome rectilinear view of the world. It seemed to be an arid, vacuous world of boxes and more boxes. Looking closer, the viewer saw that there was a great sense of play and humour at work in the choice of materials (sometimes wood, sometimes steel, or aluminium, or glass, or copper, or lacquer, or Plexiglas). Sometimes Judd's serial boxes were open, and the spectator could see inside them; at other times, Judd placed colored Plexiglas over the end, and the interior was hidden or vaguely discernible; the boxes were usually constructed from heavy materials, such as steel, but they were hollow; they hung on walls as if lightweight, but were also very solid and heavy. Sometimes the boxes were sprayed with Harley Davidson motorbike lacquer and enamel, so they'd be bright green, or red (red was a favourite color in Judd's early pieces). Using Plexiglas meant the colors would deepen across the row of boxes. Judd initially worked in wood, but later moved into metal, employing professionals to complete his designs.

The emphasis on hollowness meant there was nothing to hide; there was mystery, but no deliberate mystification on the part of the artist. Donald Judd's wall-mounted objects did not require a base; they seemed to float in space. They were unitary, modular: there was no single unit that stood out from the others. The gaps between each object was also regular. Hierarchy was avoided.

Although they looked like rows of boxes at first, there was in fact a lot going in Donald Judd's works. Robert Hughes, in *American Visions*, defined Judd's work as the product of 'esthetic fanaticism' and uncompromising reductionism:

> Judd was the doyen of "high" Minimal art: inorganic materials (steel, tin, colored plastic, aluminium), blatantly artificial colors (Harley-Davidson red lacquer was a particular favourite), geometric rigidity (but without the Utopian overtones of earlier geometric abstraction), industrial process, and, in its refusal of touch, an address to the eye alone. (1997, 563-4)

Donald Judd's theorizing on art and Minimalism was influential in Sixties art (his famous articles included "Specific Objects" and "Local History"; he was one of the most learned of Minimal artists: he had a BA in philosophy and an MA in art history, at Columbia University).

Most of Donald Judd's works are entitled *Untitled* (it's a little confusing discussing Judd's works, because most of them are called *Untitled*, as with other 1960s artists, such as Robert Morris and Bruce Nauman, and 100s of other artists). The *Untitled* of 1965 (Saatchi Collection) is nothing more than a galvanized iron box on its own, 6 by 27 by 24 inches. Both *Untitled* (1965, London) and *Untitled* (1966, collection: J.W. Froehlich) are slightly larger boxes (20 by 48 by 34 inches) but this time with clear Plexiglas sides, and steel panels at each end. A 1968 box (*Untitled*, Whitney Museum of American Art) employs stainless steel and Plexiglas to create a hollow, floor-standing box, but the configuration is quite different – now the box has another box inside it, of steel.

Donald Judd's *Untitled* of 1963 (A & W. Hokin) is a painted wood box with a semi-circular groove along the top of it which utterly alters the regularity of the hollow box. Inside the sculpture is a series of regular vertical divisions. Other *Untitleds* of 1963 (also painted red) fit an aluminium tube along the groove (collection: Philip Johnson), or a half-pipe. In *Untitled* (1964), a small wooden box, painted red, was fitted with brass grooves along its top; an

Untitled of 1964 (Helman Collection, New York) was very similar, though with iron, and painted yellow. Even within these apparently narrow formal limitations (each box is a similar size, painted red, made from wood), Judd is able to complete a wide variety of configurations.

You could give Donald Judd the narrowest set of parameters or limits you could imagine (about form, shape, pattern, scale, material, etc), and I bet he would discover all sorts of ways of introducing variations. His sense of invention is simply remarkable. Just when you thought no other possibilities could exist with boxes and panels and simple curves, Judd will uncover more.

An *Untitled* of 1965 is more recognizably a Donald Judd work: four hollow aluminium boxes are arranged on a wall at eye level, all the same size (34 inches on each side). Two sides of the boxes are glass, so the row of four boxes can be looked through from each end. 1964's *Untitled* was a hollow steel ring (93 by 78 inches) placed on the gallery floor.

An assemblage of iron pipes by Donald Judd – *Untitled (For Dave Shackman)* (1964), which could easily be mistaken for scaffolding – still appears radical today ('radical' but not 'uncompromising'; perhaps 'self-assured' or 'completely confident' are better terms). It's recognizably a modernist art object, and a sculpture, but it's peculiar, mysterious. It hints at some obscure function (is it a support for a theatrical stage?, a try-out for a children's playground?, a left-over from a building site?, a cage?). It has the implacable 'thingness' (Rainer Maria Rilke's 'kunst-ding') of much of Minimal sculpture. Its presence is undeniable, but its purpose is unfathomable.

In *Untitled* (1970), aluminium blocks were attached to a hollow four-inch tube, resulting in a long, narrow wall-piece. The blocks decreased in width along the tube, from left to right (Judd took up the form and experimented with it over a series of works).

In *Untitled* (1976-77, Los Angeles), Donald Judd did a Carl Andre, and crafted a floor-piece comprising ten stainless steel blocks, laid in two rows of five on the floor. Steel perforated with small circular holes was the material (unpainted) for another low floor-piece (*Untitled*, 1965), ten feet long and shaped in the form of a low wedge.

The wooden box in *Untitled* (1976, private collection) was small (five feet long), and seemed just another Minimal box, except that it had a sloping lid, which ran down from a corner to the bottom of the box. The diagonal plane within a box soon became one of Donald Judd's trademarks, absolutely his own, and explored in numerous sculptures. A copper box like *Untitled* (1981, London) is typical: it's hollow, backed with blue Plexiglas, and relatively small (35 inches wide, 19 inches high). But it's mounted on the wall, and has a slab of copper inside it, tilted slightly. Not only is it no ordinary box, it is a box like no other Minimal (or any) art: it's a Donald Judd box.

Some of the wall boxes are huge (particularly the later ones): the *Untitled* of 1981 at the Saatchi Collection, made from plywood, recall the works of Louis Nevelson. It takes up a gigantic space (some 927 inches along one wall). 1974's *Untitled* (collection: the artist) also reaches across a whole room (again using wood), from wall to wall, a large, rectilinear presence in the room. In *Untitled* (1973), six giant hollow wooden structures (basically cubes with sheared sides) dominate the gallery space (in the National Gallery of Canada in Ottawa they have been installed opposite 1973's *Untitled*, a series of six plywood box spaces, set in a row.)

Other familiar Donald Judd works include the horizontal wall-mounted 'crenellations'. These are generally small wood, steel or iron sculptures in which rounded or rectilinear blocks protrude from a slab of metal fixed to the wall (for instance, *Untitled* [1965, Minneapolis], *Untitled* [1964, Doris Thistlewood], and *Untitled* [1967, London]). Typically, the hemi-cylindrical crenellations are painted in monochrome lacquer, red or green or silver. Some of Judd's wall-mounted crenellations are large – the *Untitled* of 1973-75, for example, is over six feet wide. Typically there were four protuberances in the crenellations (as in *Untitled*, 1974, collection: M. Rea), but sometimes six (as in *Untitled*, 1967, private collection). 1965's *Untitled* (St Louis Art Museum), in satiny red lacquer, was one of the larger, longer pieces, with ten protuberances (but they decreased in width from left to right).

Other wall-mounted boxes include an *Untitled* of 1975, featuring six open rectangular boxes made from plywood. *Untitled* (1966) comprised four identical steel and Plexiglas hollow boxes, mounted in a row on a wall. *Untitled* (1968, Milwaukee Art Museum) employed amber-hued Plexiglas inside shiny steel boxes. Blue tempered glass was utilized for the side panels of 1985's *Untitled* (Saatchi Collection), enabling the spectator to stand at the side of the wall sculpture and look through the hollow boxes. In *Untitled* (1966, Norton Simon Museum of Art, Pasadena), four galvanized iron cubes (40 inches on each side) were placed in a row on the floor, and connected by a square hollow aluminium rod, painted with blue lacquer.

In *Untitled* (1982, collection: A. & G. Verna), three boxes of aluminium with purple Plexiglas backing were mounted side-by-side on a wall, each with variations on diagonal inserts. A 1976 installation in Berne (*Bern Piece No. 3*) was an enormous hollow plywood box, with a lid raised a few inches above the top. Around the walls of Leo Castelli's gallery in 1974, Judd placed large iron panels, five feet high, and protruding 8 inches into the room.

In 1986's *Untitled*, six units of Douglas fir wood and orange Plexiglas were mounted on the wall, designed to explore the permutations of inner leaves which were so much a feature of Donald Judd's later art. On the top row of three boxes, one box has a single sloped panel, the second has one diagonal and one right angle panel, and the third, logically, has one diagonal and two right angle panels. Judd also applied these experiments with the interior of his boxes in his wall stacks (as in *Untitled* [1986, collection: J. Chiat], and *Untitled* [1984, Whitney Museum of American Art]).

In the 1980s, Donald Judd developed another signature form, the small rectangular open metal box, painted in bright hues (red, yellow, green, blue, orange). Each box was a hollow shape (against with hints of industrial machinery), bolted together to form groups, and mounted on the wall (*Untitled* [1985], and *Untitled* [1984, collection: D.S. Cramer]), or sometimes gathered together to create free-standing sculptures.

Some of Donald Judd's wall sculptures were mounted vertically, usually rising high above the spectator, like ladders, stacks, towers or steps (such as the *Untitled* of 1978, and *Untitled*, 1990). The wall-mounted stacks or ladders, perhaps Judd's signature form, could be large: one *Untitled* of 1969 forms a tower of steel and Plexiglas that looms over the spectator, as does another *Untitled* of 1969 (in the Hirshhorn Museum and Sculpture Garden in Washington), and a 1966 *Untitled* (private collection).

The ladders or stacks were typically constructed from identical boxes, which were repeated to form a stack or ladder. Each box typically had metal sides (painted in black, or red, or green), with Plexiglas forming the top and bottom sides. The rear side of the boxes was flush with the wall. Sometimes the boxes were fabricated entirely from metal, left bare (as in *Untitled* [1968, collection: G. Locksley & G. Shea], and *Untitled* [1978, Indiana University Art Museum, Bloomington]). Sometimes they were all metal, but painted (as in *Untitled* [1967, Helman Collection, New York]). Very often the Plexiglas was utilized for the upper and lower sides (as in *Untitled* [1969, Hirshhorn Museum and Sculpture Garden] and *Untitled* [1980, collection: F.C. Golding]). Aluminium was a favourite metal for the stacks, but Judd also used steel and brass. The ladders or stacks were usually grouped in even numbers: 10, 8, 6, for instance.

Two floor-standing boxes in the Saatchi Collection (London) are archetypal Donald Judd works: made from anodized aluminium and copper, these are largish boxes (the 1969 one is 33 by 68 by 48 inches and the 1973 box is 36 by 60 by 60 inches). They have sides of colored Plexiglas.

Untitled (1969, St Louis Art Museum) comprised four aluminium hollow cubes with Plexiglas interiors. The 1977 *Untitled* is a row of four large steel and nickel boxes, each about five feet square. What's clear here is that the space around the units and in between them is important. Donald Judd's boxes are areas of calm and regularity in amongst the chaos of the real world.

In a big floor-standing piece, *Untitled* (1966), a group of 8 rectangular open frames, made out of aluminium and painted turquoise, were placed in a close-knit row. It was a form Donald Judd returned to a number of times (as in *Untitled* [1966, Whitney Museum of American Art], and *Untitled* [1980, Foundation Daniel Templon, Paris]).

Untitled (1968) was another large installation of floor-standing boxes – this time eight steel units four feet on each side. Three rows of galvanized iron boxes comprised another large installation (*Untitled*, 1969), each box far deeper than usual (pushing out six feet from the wall).

In the middle of L.A. there's a striking Donald Judd piece (*Untitled For Leo Castelli*, 1977), giant concrete open boxes, in the Sculpture Garden of the Los Angeles County Museum of Art, which I've seen many times. It's part of a typical modern art museum Sculpture Garden, so that it stands next Alexander Calder, Auguste Rodin, Anthony Caro, Alice Aycock and Henry Moore.

To see a host of Donald Judd's works at one time in place is a treat: the retrospective at London's Tate Modern in 2004, for example, was an extraordinary exhibit by any standards, taking in the whole of Judd's career. Play, experiment, exploration, tests, meanderings, refinements, it was all here. The London show demonstrated just how inventive Judd was, how imaginative, how even within a narrow set of parameters his art was bursting with life. It's the opposite of boring, or lifeless, or repressed art: rather, Judd's art came across as deeply poetic, and deeply emotional.

It's true that some Minimal art can appear somewhat forbidding and impenetrable, pushing the spectator away. But what came thru in the 2004 exhibit was how full of feeling Donald Judd's art is, and how vitally significant Judd's art is for contemporary art.

Many of Donald Judd's finest Minimal works are housed in his permanent installation in Marfa, Texas. Like many artists before and since, Judd was attracted to the South-West of the U.S.A. Judd's Chinati Foundation at Marfa constitutes the culmination of Minimal art, and its greatest achievement. Pretty much the whole history of Minimal art is represented at Marfa.

Marfa was a former military base (Fort Russell), which Donald Judd redesigned. He installed his sculptures in the artillery sheds and the fields, as well as creating exhibition spaces for other artists' work. He designed a huge amount of furniture, fittings, structures and interiors at the Chinati Foundation, including tables, desks, beds, chairs, pergolas, pools, yards, walls, a library, a labyrinth of adobe walls, and the artists' compound.

One of the main works at Marfa is the epic *Untitled* (1980-86), one hundred large (41 x 51 x 72 inch) mill-aluminium boxes, each one apparently the same, yet each one different (some were open at the side, some on top; many had the signature Donald Judd diagonal and right angle panels). The field of boxes was funded by the Dia Art Foundation, and made by the Lippincott Foundry, New Haven. The 1981 *Untitled* was a row of enormous hollow concrete boxes, separated into groups, and installed in the fields near the artillery sheds. Each module was eight feet high, with some eight feet wide and some 16 feet wide. This was Juddian Minimal box permutation on a grand scale.

When you consider the whole of Donald Judd's work, and the depth and insight of his theories and writings, you have one of the most valuable of modern artists. It's not only what Judd's art achieved in itself – though that is as significant as any great artist's work (including any Renaissance master) – it's what Judd's *œuvre* *suggests* and hints at and points towards. Judd's art maps out – like the art of Robert Smithson or Andy Warhol – so many possibilities, so many avenues, so many projects that can be pursued. And for future art, that is invaluable.

TONY SMITH

Tony Smith (1912-1980) was revered as one of the key sculptors of the era, and an important forerunner as well as practitioner of Minimal æsthetics. Smith's *Die* (1962) became one of the icons of Minimal art, along with Donald Judd's Marfa installations, Ron Bladen's *X* and Frank Stella's *Black Paintings*. Smith's most celebrated pieces tended to be large, imposing, blocky sculptures, usually based around the cube (*Die,* and *The Black Box* [1963-65]), the square column, and L-shapes (*Night*, 1966). The *Wandering Rocks* group (1967, Milan) explored irregular polyhedra forms, painted black. *Cigarette* (1961) was a big public sculpture in Smith's familiar black bulky tetrahedra form. *Black Triangle* (1966) was a mighty plywood inverted triangle. Of an installation of Smith's sculptures at Bryant Park, Harold Rosenberg described how they appeared to be weighty and solid, but were hollow; they seemed 'intangibly alien' in the setting of the park, they were big, but not huge or overwhelming; and they appeared to be somewhat incomplete and looked as if they were seeking completion.[1]

Tony Smith's *Smoke* (1967) was an enormous installation at the *Scale As Content* show in Washington, DC (where Ronald Bladen's *X* was also exhibited). The basis of *Smoke* was something Robert Smithson would approve of: tetrahedron shapes recalling crystal molecules. It became a well-loved fixture in the basement of the Los Angeles County Museum of Art, where you walk thru it like the legs of a giant black spider. There are also examples of Smith's cubes in Washington, outside the modern art wing of the National Gallery of Art. Even though some of Smith's art is a black box, it's instantly recognizable as by Smith.

Tony Smith liked to show his black sculptures in low-light conditions, such as dusk, with the windows of his studio covered with canvas. In that dim light, Smith likened his sculptures to prehistoric monuments such as Stonehenge:

In my studio they remind me of Stonehenge. I like dawn or dusk light. Since there is nothing else in the room, I think that if light is subdued a little, it has more of the archaic or prehistoric look that I prefer. (B, 380)

CARL ANDRE

Carl Andre's biography is often cited in accounts of his art. Here are some snippets: for a time Andre (b. 1935) worked in Frank Stella's studio in Manhattan (they were students together at Andover). Stella influenced Andre's way of making sculpture: Andre often stayed with Stella in the early years. When Andre was working on a large log, Stella told him that unworked the wood could be sculpture too. Andre considered what Stella had said, and thereafter used materials in an untouched state, 'using them as 'cuts' in the space that surrounds them, shaping the space itself'.[1] In 2000, Andre acknowledged that Stella and photographer Hollis Frampton 'had an incalculable influence on my formation as a sculptor and poet and were the most stimulating audience imaginable for my emerging work'.[2]

The most infamous incident in Carl Andre's biography was the death of artist Ana Mendieta, his lover at the time, when she fell from a building in New York City in 1985.

Carl Andre worked on the railways, as a freight conductor and brakeman from 1960 to 1964 (in Newark, at the Pennsylvania Railroad), and this is used by art critics to explain Carl Andre's use of modules and units which join together to form a work (even though systems and seriality was common in Minimal sculpture of the time). Like Sol LeWitt and Donald Judd, Andre takes one unit and multiplied them until he had a line or a square, or a post and lintel, or a tower. In Andre's art, only one type of unit is used in each work: bricks, metal plates and tiles, blocks of wood. Each work is made for the specific site or gallery. Simple rectilinear patterns, such as grids and rows, are favoured. No glues are used, but simple joints. Gravity is one of the key means of construction (as with Richard Serra): i.e., objects are placed on the floor, or on top of each other, without bolts, nails, glue. The question of height is thus rarely introduced in Andre's sculpture.[3]

Before working on the railroad, Carl Andre was 'a wood-carving disciple of Brancusi', as he confessed, carving chunks out of wood beams. For a long time the shadow of Constantin Brancusi lay over Andre's art; an early work, such as *Last Ladder* (1959, London), consciously evoked *Endless Column* with its series of repeated cuts into the wood. *Chalice* (1959, destroyed) out-Brancusied Brancusi, with a wooden totem pole that could easily be one of Brancusi's pedestals.

When Carl Andre came to explain his floor-standing works, such as *Lever*, a line of firebricks, he said he was

> putting Brancusi's *Endless Column* on the ground instead of in the sky... Most sculpture is priapic with the male organ in the air. In my work, Priapus is down on the floor. The engaged position is to run along the earth. (in ib., 104)

It's typical for Carl Andre to speak of sculpture in terms of phalluses. Andre has spoken in interviews that the best creative work is erotic. In a 1970 radio discussion (with Lucy Lippard, Douglas Huebler, Dan Graham and Jan Dibbets on WBAI FM – why don't they have radio shows like that anymore?), Andre said desires, not ideas, were important.

> I have very few ideas, but I have strong desires... I agree with Dr Guillotine that all ideas are the same except in execution... You can't cut off desires except painfully.[4]

Nature was also crucial for Carl Andre: he said he disliked Conceptual art because it was cut off from nature (ibid.). He said his art 'has never been conceptual in any way' (1984). It was about real things, the actuality of the materials:

> The materiality, the presence of the work of sculpture in the world, essentially independent of any single individual, but rather the residue of many individuals and the dream, the experience of the sea, the trees and the stones – I'm interested in that kind of essential thing'.[5]

'I will try to have in my work only what is necessary to it', Carl Andre said (1984). While he was in New Hampshire in 1965, canoeing on a lake, Andre (apparently) realized that sculpture ought to be level, like water. After this, most of his sculpture was floor-standing and flat. Spectators are invited to walk on his sculptures, offering a new relation with the work. As well as sculpture, Andre also wrote poetry.

Carl Andre, like Donald Judd and Robert Morris, was one of the key theorists of Minimal art, and has many pertinent things to say about sculpture. Andre's mid-1960s summary of the history of sculpture defined his own approach to art (and land art):

> The course of development
> Sculpture as form
> Sculpture as structure
> Sculpture as place.[6]

Carl Andre did not make boxes in the usual Minimal manner. Andre's sculptures were modular in the sense that one piece could be removed and put somewhere else without altering the whole (Andre's 'anaxial symmetry'). Lines of bricks or floor squares made from plates of metal were typical Andre works.

Carl Andre's use of materials was not 'poetic' or 'spiritual' in the usual sense of the words. In works such as *Cedar Piece* (1959, Basel), *Pyre* (1971, S. & C. Gilman), *Herm* (1976, Guggenheim), *Stile* (1975) and *Well*, which were made out of wood, Andre was using materials as themselves, but 'not to evoke nature'.[7] Andre did not intend his materials to refer to other things, to be allusive in the art historical or lyrical sense. His Styrofoam planks were not alluding to marble, as some viewers mistakenly thought.[8] *Herm*, though, recalled the ancient Greek statues to the god Hermes, which were set on top of pillars beside roads. The ancient phallic statues sometimes included genitals, which chimes with Andre's erotic view of art.

Carl Andre's *Element* series (noted above)

consisted of wood-carved beams that recalled Constantin Brancusi's art. In *Redan* (1970, Toronto), thick, short blocks of wood were interlocked to form a three foot zigzag wall. *Furrow* (1981) plays with a form employed by many Minimal artists – the post and lintel (Andre has used it a few times). As in *Redan*, *Stile*, *Lever* and many of Andre's wooden sculptures, in *Furrow*, short, squat pieces of wood were used, as individual units that were arranged by the artist to produce the final form of an interlocking post and lintel. For a 1965 installation at Tibor de Nagy Gallery (NYC), Andre built a *Crib*, *Compound* and *Coin* from styrofoam planks. As Andre put it, '[m]y Constructivism is the generation of overall design by the multiplication of the qualities of the individual constituent elements'. Andre found that it was better if the wood in his sculptures was not carved. Therefore he stopped trying to 'improve it in any way'.[9] The wood in his sculpture is untreated, unpolished, unvarnished – very different, in short, from most wood in high art.

Artist and critic Mel Bochner identified the characteristics of Carl Andre's art as:

(1) strictly modular;

(2) use of materials (wood, cement, bricks, steel) which spoke of 'density, rigidity, opacity, uniformity';

(3) only one kind of unit is used in each work;

(4) the typical geometric shape favoured by Andre is the grid, and sometimes the row or line.[10]

Carl Andre's notion of the 'dematerialization' of sculpture was central to his art, and also to much sculpture of the time. When they were not being exhibited, Andre's sculptures simply disappeared. They were not objects on permanent display, but were made specially for each occasion and space. Some of Andre's works outside of shows exist as ideas, photographs, descriptions, memories, and so on, but not as actual works. This emphasis on the materiality and dematerialization of his works led Andre to regard his art as non-spiritual. He said:

My work is atheistic, materialistic, and communistic. It's atheistic because it's without transcendent form, without spiritual or intellectual quality. Materialistic because it's made out of its own materials without pretension to other materials. And communistic because the form is equally accessible to all men. (B, 107)

This is a humble, self-effacing view of his own art. His art was materialistic, Carl Andre said, because it does not pretend to be anything else other than itself. However, at other times (in interviews, for example), Andre comes across as a warmly Romantic artist. It is this aspect of his art that annoyed people when London's Tate Gallery bought, with public money, one of his piles of bricks in 1976 (Andre made a humorous collage of the public responses to this work). Andre's *Equivalents* were 'floor-hugging' sculptures first shown in 1966.

The form of *Equivalent* (a low oblong shape) and the material of the work (brick) seemed available to anyone who visited a household store and bought a few hundred bricks and arranged them in a certain way (the most common snipe at contemporary art is: 'anyone could do that!'). Yet Carl Andre's art is of course not as simple as that, and not as easy to produce as that.

Carl Andre's works seem to be slight, almost insubstantial, but, simultaneously, 'their matter-of-factness that makes them in a multiple sense *present*'.[11] If an object is put in a gallery and displayed in a certain way, the viewer sees the object as art (and a particular kind of Western, bourgeois art, the sort of art that is exhibited in Western, bourgeois galleries). Andre explored the relation between real and represented objects with his controversial pile of bricks. The sculpture was 'controversial' because the general public (whoever they are) perceived, via the media, that Andre had simply stuck some bricks into a gallery. Or rather, that taxpayers' money had been used to purchase Andre's bricks. A pile of bricks on a building site is... a pile of bricks. A pile of bricks in an art gallery is… sculpture. Context is everything here. This is what Carl Andre explored, whether consciously or not: the *response*, affected by so much of culture, socialization, physical context, education, and so on, makes objects sculptures. People make art. A leaf simply exists, but if someone puts it in a gallery or an art book, it becomes art (as well as remaining a leaf). If people think something is art, then it's art, as Donald Judd said.

Carl Andre also produced coils of bands of copper, in spirals, or ribbons, which were placed on the gallery floor (as in *Copper Ribbon*, 1969, and *Glarus Copper Galaxy*, 1995). *Runs* and *Rods* (1971) ran metal and rubber strips along a gallery floor (in this case, the Dwan Gallery). *Spill (Scatter Piece)* (1966) comprised 800 little plastic blocks spilt on the gallery floor. In these works, it was partly haphazard how the coils or blocks arranged themselves in the gallery.

The most distinctive (and sensual) of Carl Andre's works are probably the metallic floor-pieces. Andre's floor sculptures bring out the tactile, visual, material qualities of copper, aluminium and zinc (in, for instance, *5 x 20 Altstadt Rectangle* [1967], and *144 Aluminium Square* [1967]). *8006 Mönchengladbach Square* (1968) comprised 36 identical squares of hot-rolled steel.

Carl Andre's *37 Pieces of Work* (memorably installed in the rotunda of the Guggenheim in 1970) is a good example of Minimalist æsthetic permutations taken to extremes. *37 Pieces of Work* is a 432-inch wide 'floor-hugging' square, in which the colors of the copper, aluminium, lead, steel, zinc and magnesium are to the fore. The colors in *37 Pieces of Work* range from deep bronzes and reds through gold, silver and dark grays. It is a sculpture that is typical of Andre's art, as David Bourdon pointed out in *Carl Andre: Sculpture, 1959-1977*:

Taken as a whole *37 Pieces of Work* consists of 1,296 plates, 216 each of aluminium, copper,

steel, magnesium, lead and zinc. Each metal appears alone in individual six-foot square plains. Then alternates with another, checkerboard fashion, in every possible permutation. Since each of the six metals in the large piece was laid out in the alphabetical order of its chemical symbol, alternating successively with the others, there are two versions of each combination.[12]

Many of Carl Andre's floor-pieces are similar (*Twelfth Copper Corner*, 1975, *Brooklyn Field*, 1966, Belgium, *8 Cuts*, 1967, Switzerland): the spectator is aware of the material first and foremost: the color, mass, weight, size, texture and condition of the metals. Andre's *Steel-Magnesium Plain* (1969, private collection) was a floor-piece of 36 plates of metal which appeared as a chess board (the darker metal interspersed with a lighter metal). In *Copper-Aluminium Plain* (1969, A & W. Hokin), the shiny blue-gray sheen of the aluminium slabs contrasts vividly with the warm coppery hues.

The floor-piece works, with their shiny or dull surfaces of copper, zinc, steel or aluminium, can be extremely sensuous, even as impressive as the classic examples of sculpture, such as the statues of Antonine Canova, Auguste Rodin or Gianlorenzo Bernini. Andre's *Sixteenth Copper Cardinal* (sixteen square copper slabs) is a work that could be described as luscious. Spectators are used to marble and stone being beautiful, and also certain metals – bronze, silver and gold in particular have been central to sculpture for millennia. Why not zinc and copper, too? Carl Andre, like other Minimal sculptors, introduces the viewer to the sensuality of copper, bronze and zinc shaped into nothing more than… a simple shape, like a slab, put on the floor. Andre's slabs are not 'narrative' or anthropomorphic; they do not 'depict' animals or gods or people; but they are no less beautiful, as objects in their own right. 'The shape *is* the object: at any rate, what secures the wholeness of the object is the singleness of the shape', wrote Michael Fried (1967).

Unlike some sculptors who started out using wood (because it was cheap and malleable) then moved on to metal (when they had more money, and could afford professionals to weld and forge it – and transport it), Carl Andre continued to use wood throughout his career. A group of fifty-four three foot high wooden beams was placed on the gallery floor in a grid in *Flanders Field* (1978).

Carl Andre's magnet pieces, which preceded the metal squares, also hugged the floor, so much so that the third dimension was nearly expunged (as, for instance, in *Field*, 1966, produced by tightly packed ceramic magnets). The floor-pieces neatly rid the sculptor of dealing with pedestals. They became 'place-markers'.[13] They have no space, according to one critic, they have 'no appearance of inside or center. Rather they seem to be co-extensive with the very floor on which the viewer stands'.[14] Place, not space or sky, became what mattered for Andre.

Carl Andre made one of his floor-pieces of slabs of metal deliberately so it would be altered by being outside. It was called *Small Weathering Piece* (1971), and contained a large number of metals (large for an Andre sculpture): lead, zinc, aluminium, copper, steel and magnesium. The large number of metals meant that the different ways or rates they weathered was part of the sculpture.

Carl Andre's floor-pieces are viewer-friendly, too: the viewer is invited to (or allowed to) walk over them. Like Donald Judd and Tony Smith, Andre wanted his sculptures to be seen from a variety of viewpoints. Instead of a single vantage point (the Renaissance monoscopic, perspectival viewpoint), one could have a number of angles. Andre compared viewing his sculptures to walking on roads: '[t]hey cause you to make your way along them or around them or to move...over them' (1970, 57).

Carl Andre's *Stone Field* was one of his site-specific works of the 1970s, consisting of 26 very large glacial boulders. It was an imposing piece, introducing the irregular, organic shapes of nature into the haphazard geometry of the city. Andre installed a line of hay bales, placed end to end, in a field in Vermont (*Joint*, 1968, 183 units, Windham College, Putney, VT). It was a line like Richard Long's rows of stones, or Tony Cragg's floor and wall spreads.

Into the 1990s and after, Carl Andre was mining pretty much the same seam of metal tile floor-pieces, wooden planks, and small stacks that he had developed early in the 1960s. Andre's works of the 1990s included the gentle ellipses of wooden planks on the floor in *Angellipse* and *Angelimb* (1995), and small cubes of lead and copper (*1Cu8Pb None* and *Pb Cu*, 1995).

In 2008 I saw a show by Carl Andre in Gotham at Paula Cooper Gallery (*Western Red Cedar*, 2008), which might've come right out of the 1960s, as if nothing had changed in forty-plus years: large, blocky chunks of wood placed together in cuboid forms. One unit... multiple combinations. Set on the gallery floor, as usual. *Western Red Cedar* was beautiful – rectilinear, methodical yet also intuitive, and probably too spare for some tastes; but the sensuality was undeniable.

'I feel emotionally connected to his work,' Eva Hesse remarked of Carl Andre's art. 'It does something to my insides. His metal plates were the concentration camp for me'.[15] A pretty extreme statement – but Hesse often made extreme statements.

One of Carl Andre's most intriguing theoretical statements was this: 'my ideal piece of sculpture is a road'.[16] This applies not only to Andre's lines of bricks or hay bales, but to Christo's *Running Fence*, and to other contemporary artworks. A sculpture as a never-ending process, the same but different at each point. Andre's notion of the ultimate artwork as a road has a parallel with the famous anecdote of Tony Smith who, when driving along the New Jersey turnpike, was impressed by the

dark pavements moving through the landscape of the flats, rimmed in the distance, but punctuated by stacks, towers, fumes, and colored lights.[17]

Something in such a long stretch of empty road, as with airstrips (and, more dubiously, a drill ground at Nuremberg) impressed Smith, who wrote '[i]t seemed that there had been a reality there that had not had any expression in art' (ibid.). Roads are not 'art', not wholly functional either – they have an aura or mystery which Smith tried to explain. 'I view art as something vast', said Smith, arguing for an art of grand, public gestures.[18] Roads, in the Tony Smith view, are also for and about labour and functionality.

The road, for the Minimal or Process artist, in the Carl Andre manner, embodies materially the sense of a sequence or process. One unit (the foot or brick or slab of tarmac or concrete) is placed next to another, forming a road. Artists such as Andre (and Sol LeWitt and Donald Judd) did exactly the same, putting one unit next to another, creating a line or sequence of units.

The road also may have no obvious end (no goal): endlessness was crucial to Minimal (and Process, Serial, Systems and Conceptual art). Many artists emphasize art that goes on and on. Christo's fence, for example, goes on and on for 26 miles. One imagines that Christo would love a fence that could run across a whole country, or, even better, a whole continent. Similarly, Richard Long's walks could extend far beyond their limits, and the modular art of Donald Judd, Robert Morris and Sol LeWitt could expand indefinitely, once the basic pattern has been established. The seriality or endless process of art was identified by Judd as the idea of 'one thing after another'.[19] Carl Andre's concept of the road as the ideal artwork fits in with this urge towards endless process and seriality. The road motif also fits in well with stereotypical American culture, with its love of the 'open road' (Walt Whitman), road movies (*Easy Rider, Natural Born Killers, Duel, Thelma and Louise, Wild at Heart*), the frontier spirit (in Westerns), and in hippy and beatnik culture (Jack Kerouac's *On the Road*, Allen Ginsberg and the 'dharma bums' who drift around from state to state).

ROBERT MORRIS

Robert Morris (b. 1931) has become viewed by art critics as one of the two or three most important Minimal artists. That's partly due to his writings as well as his art. Critics always love an artist who can write: it makes it easier for critics to write about their work, because they can quote the artist, and the artist has already done the difficult work of distilling their art into words. However, as commentators on art have to recognize, there is always something that escapes being put into words in art, even if it is a Conceptual or Post-minimal piece that consists solely of words.

Robert Morris was one of the most eloquent theorists of Minimal (and 1960s) sculpture (along with Robert Smithson, Donald Judd and Carl Andre). Morris had, like Judd and plenty of other sculptors, started out in painting, but moved on to sculpture (Judd's dissatisfaction with painting has been well-documented, not least by Judd himself). Morris studied at Kansas City Art Institute, California School of Fine Arts and Hunter College, New York. In San Francisco in 1961 he worked with the dancer Anna Halprin. Morris was known for his performance art and dance pieces as well as Minimal sculpture. He was part of the Fluxus school, alongside Yoko Ono, Simone Forte, Walter de Maria and Henry Flynt. One can see how Morris was part of many of the chief art movements of the Sixties and after and, like so many artists of the time, he was not fixed in one kind of art-making (sculpture), but took in performance art, dance, body art, installation art and Conceptual art.

Robert Morris published many artistic state-ments. The most famous was probably the articles published in *Artforum* entitled "Notes on Sculpt-ure" (much anthologized). For Morris, one of the things that was new about 1960s sculpture was the object's relationship with the viewer. Before then, Morris argued, the viewer related to the object as something separate, existing on a pedestal, in a different cultural space. The new æsthetic put the viewer into the same space as the object.

> One is more aware than before [observed Morris] that he himself is establishing relationships as he apprehends the object from various positions and under varying conditions of light and spatial context.[1]

This is a crucial concept in Minimal art, which is nearly always viewed in a continuous space between the object and the viewer.

Robert Morris's concept of the object (what Michael Fried called 'objecthood') was central to his notion of sculpture, of what sculpture could be. 'Morris wants to achieve presence through object-hood, which requires a certain largeness of scale, rather than through size alone', wrote Fried (1967). Just as important as the object itself was the sense of space around it, the spatial context in which it was displayed (this was something that Constantin Brancusi had been concerned about). Morris wanted to emphasize that 'things are in a space with oneself', rather than the notion that 'one is in a space surrounded by things' (ib., 127). The whole context of the object in its space ('the entire situation', as Morris put it) was important to Morris's notion of the new sculpture. One might say the new, 1960s sculpture was about the 'thing in itself' (a notion borrowed from Existential philosophy), but also about the 'thing in its space'. For Morris in his Minimal art phase, sculpture should be 'massive, indivisible, tactile, and stable'.[2] Later, when Morris had embraced Process, anti-form and Postminimal art, he spoke of

> Random piling, loose stacking, hanging give passing form to the material. Chance is accepted and indeterminacy is implied as replacing will result in another combination.[3]

Here's an extract from "Notes On Sculpture" which offers a taste of Robert Morris's theoretical musings on the 'new sculpture':

Simplicity of shape does not necessarily equate with simplicity of experience. Unitary forms do not reduce relationships. They order them. If the predominant, hieratic nature of unitary form functions as a constant, all those particularizing relations of scale, proportion, etc, are not thereby canceled. Rather they are bound more cohesively and indivisibly together. The magnification of this single most important sculptural value – shape – together with greater unification and integration of every other essential sculptural value makes, on the one hand, the multi-part, inflected formats of past sculpture extraneous, and on the other, establishes both a new limit and a new freedom for sculpture. (B, 228)

Although Robert Morris denied being an 'environmental' artist, the context was important to his art.[4] For one critic, Morris's sculpture 'redirect[s] the entire environmental experience'.[5] Referring to Donald Judd's "Specific Objects" article, Morris said he did not separate the two, he did not think that something must be either an object or an environment.[6] As he moved towards Postminimalism (and Process, assemblage and Serial art), Morris advocated doing away with a figure-ground relationship; instead, heterogeneous 'stuff' should be used, an 'accumulation of things or stuff' he said in "Notes on Sculpture" (4, 51). Hence Morris's move towards filling gallery spaces with heaps of materials, wood, metal, felt, wire – just 'stuff'. Critic John Perreault remarked:

Robert Morris is the genius of negative presence and the perversity of odd proportions that are subliminal in their aggressiveness. Works of art can in some sense he defined as those man-made objects that are designed solely to call attention to themselves. In this age of bombast, chatter, and random activity, that which does not move and that which is silent is often that which compels our attention and stimulates our awareness most effectively. Donald Judd, too, appears to have this "anti-art," pro-silence bias, and his works, although scrupulously elegant, are a well-formulated attack on "artistic" cliche. (1995, 259)

Robert Morris's Minimal sculptures were often simple polyhedrons, such as cubes, circles, ovals and beams. They were modular and serial. 'Unitary Objects' or 'Unitary Forms' he termed them, recalling Donald Judd's 'Specific Objects'. They appeared at first to be 'simple' in form; as with Judd's sculptures, Morris's did not seem to be hiding anything. They were all on the surface. Yet just because they appeared simple did not mean that their effects were simple: 'simplicity of shape does not necessarily equate with simplicity of experience', wrote Morris,[7] and Minimal art proved him right.

Robert Morris's art was by turns ironic, blank, unambiguously clear and frustratingly amorphous. Morris made 'things' and 'stuff'. Morris's *Battered Cubes* (1965/ 88, Margo Leaven Gallery, Los Angeles) were four boxes of painted steel that were set near each other. Each unit had a gently sloping outside face. *Two Columns* (1961) was a classic Minimal piece: two rectilinear structures in painted aluminium, very sparse and clean and reduced to the bare essentials. The most reductive type of Minimal sculpture – a plain, unadorned wooden box – was the subject (and object) of *Untitled* (1966, Milan).

Untitled (L-Beams, 1965, Whitney Museum of American Art) was another archetypal Minimal sculpture (and one of Robert Morris's best-known Minimal works), a group of L-shaped blocks of stainless steel. Similar blocks of rectilinear structures, in a 1964 installation, were hung from the ceiling, laid on the floor, and leant against the wall. In *Corner Piece* (1964, Milan), a painted plywood triangle (six feet on a side), was placed in the corner of a gallery. In *Untitled (Stadium)* (1967, Guggenheim), steel units were arranged into the shape of a stadium.

Mirrored Cubes, an installation piece at the Green Gallery in Gotham in 1965, explored the space of the gallery, and the viewer's relation with the work, because the viewer was reflected in the sculpture. (Mirrors were a favourite material in 1960s art; Robert Smithson used them as a central device in his *Non-site* pieces. Donald Judd produced a shiny brass box [1970, Chicago] which acted as a mirror. Gerhard Richter built *Four Panels of Glass* [1967], pivoted in metal frames. And Larry Bell constructed mirrored glass cubes).

Robert Morris's Unitary Objects were made in materials such as wood, concrete, wire mesh, aluminium and granite. Morris also fabricated felt works which could not be arranged the same way each time, which determinedly refused to be locked into the Minimal æsthetic of straight edges and regularity. The felt was partly haphazard, relying on gravity, but it was also stiff enough to stay roughly where it was put by the artist. It was not final, not permanent, but malleable. *Continuous Project Altered Daily,* made at Leo Castelli's gallery in Gotham in 1969, was typical of Morris's ideas and sculpture at the time: different materials were re-arranged by the artist over the course of 3 weeks. The felt, cotton, mirror, wood, copper, rubber, nickel and aluminium materials of Morris's floor spreads looked towards Italian Arte Povera.

Robert Morris also came up with some stranger concepts for sculpted and environmental works. His 'mobile' mausoleum was among his craziest: in an aluminium tunnel 3 miles long a coffin made from iron and suspended from pulleys would be moved from time to time. An attendant would shift the coffin using a magnet. By the entrance to the tube would be swooning maidens in marble, carved in the style of Antonio Canova.8 'If something is still capable of moving, is it dead?' Morris wondered.9 In *Pace and Progress*, Morris made a work by walking a horse back and forth over a piece of grass until a path had been worn. The action of walking the horse rubbed down the grass.

Some of Robert Morris's output was of a highly ephemeral nature, looking towards environmental and land art, such as his 'steam pieces' (*Untitled*, 1968-69 and 1974), which were made out of doors on a patch of grass (four steam vents were placed at the corners of a square). How the work turned out was dependent upon physical properties such as humidity, air pressure, wind speed and direction, and temperature. Clouds of steam drifted over the grass.10

Another well-known sculpture by Robert Morris was 1961's *Box With the Sound of Its Own Making*. The sculpture was precisely what the title said: inside the box was a tape lasting 3 hours which replayed the sound of the box being constructed. The past history of the box and the processes which went towards its construction became available to the viewer – a new way of displaying self-reflexivity. Morris's *Box With the Sound of Its Own Making* combined the personal touch valued by modernism (the sound of the carpentry and hand saw, and a hand-made object), an emphasis on the process of manufacture, important for Sixties art, an element of performance art, and the use of technology (the tape recorder), valued by Pop Art. *Box With the Sound of Its Own Making* was also a kind of Conceptual art, and it was also the primary structure of Minimal art, the cube. For Frank Stella, the artist is a privileged participant in the making of art: the 'audience' or viewer is always one step away, is always 'after the fact': '[t]he sensation is one that the artist experiences as the first and only necessary viewer' (1986, 127).

Another Robert Morris box – *I-Box* (1962) – was a jokey comment on Sixties art, on Constructivism and Minimalism. Morris's *I-Box* featured an I-shaped door which revealed a photo of Morris in the nude, smiling. The Duchampian quality of Morris's *I-Box* recalled those paintings of Jasper Johns' which included bits of human anatomy (an arm, a pair of testicles) in amongst otherwise abstract forms. The *I-Box* also recalled Johns' painting/ sculpture *Target* which put male genitals in a little niche above the target.

Robert Morris's *Untitled* (1968, MOMA, New York) was a pile of cotton waste and mirrors. The mirrors were seen sticking up in the cotton (a large sculpture, it covered an area 22 x 17 feet of the gallery). An *Untitled* of 1969 comprised little trees in soil set in rectangular boxes of steel; above the trees hung fluorescent 'grow' lamps. These works interfused the human or 'artificial' (the lamps and mirrors) with the 'natural' or organic (the cotton and trees).

A number of Robert Morris's works were what appeared to be piles of concrete and wool, large oblong blocks piled up on top of each other. Morris produced both indoor and outdoor versions of these sprawls of oblong blocks. Sometimes they looked like the stacks of timber at a lumber yard on the outskirts of a town, or the detritus that's thrown into heaps beside sidings at railroad stations.

One of Robert Morris's largest commissions was the *Grand Rapids Project*, in Michigan (1973-74), consisting of huge ramps leading up to a plateau. Another big Morris sitework was created in King County, Washington (1979), a series of oval terraces recalling Iron Age hillforts. In 1975 Morris wrote "Aligned with Nazca", an article in one of the key magazines of the period (*Artforum*) which related earthwork art with ancient art such as the Nazca lines in Peru. However, such connections with ancient art had already been made by artists and critics of land art.

Robert Morris's later works included further felt sculptures, where an element of randomness and chance dictated how the felt strips would hang (the felt was often hung on a wall). Each installation would be different. Some of the later felt pieces used thick felt (such as in *Untitled 1996*, collection: the artist). Another work entitled *Untitled 1996* (collection: the artist) was modelled, the felt being draped symmetrically over a pole. *Untitled 1996* recalled a human figure.[12] Morris's wall drawings were made by the artist covering his hands with graphite and dabbing them on the wall blindfolded. The large areas of smeared graphite (in *Blind Time IV*, 1991, for example) recall Richard Long's mud wall drawings.

Robert Morris preferred not to give titles to many of his works. Instead, he employed the most common title for modern art: *Untitled* (also favoured by Donald Judd, Ad Reinhardt and Robert Rauschenberg, among many others). He explained:

I think that the reason I don't title them is that I don't think the work is about allusions. And I think titles always are. And I think the work is very much about *that* thing there in space, quite literally. And titles seem to me to have some allusion to what the thing isn't, and that's why I avoid titles.[11]

DAN FLAVIN

Like Carl Andre's bricks or Eva Hesse's strands of rope, Dan Flavin's fluorescent lamps were made by people in factories. They are mass-produced household and commercial objects, not special or unique, like an original oil painting. At first glance, it seems as if Flavin (1933-1996) has simply bought a few fluorescent lamps and set them on a gallery wall. Flavin's art seems to be founded on an act of Minimal literalism as infamous as Carl Andre placing some house bricks in a line and selling it to a gallery. Flavin's art draws attention to its operation: 'you are always aware of the fluorescents as running', remarked Kenneth Baker (1988, 100).

Dan Flavin's art is part of long tradition in contemporary art which explores lighting (electrical and natural) in particular environments. As soon as different types of lighting were invented, artists started to experiment with them. Neon lamps, for example, have been a favourite with sculptors (such as Bruce Nauman and Stephen Antonakos) as with theatre and film designers, not to mention the denizens of cities such as Hong Kong or Las Vegas, which are aglow at night with neon.

Mel Bochner described Dan Flavin's light art as activating the space of a gallery, or including the space of the interior within the compass of the light sculptures. The emptiness became part of the sculpture. 'Flavin "fills" the space in direct proportion to his illumination of it', Bochner commented.[1]

Some of Dan Flavin's sculptures consist of nothing more than a strip light leaning against a wall (*Untitled*, 1976, Saatchi Collection), or a white fluorescent light mounted on a wall (*Diagonal of May 25, 1963* [Saatchi Collection], and *Untitled* [1963, private collection]). This latter early work was described in Flavin's notebook as 'the diagonal of personal ecstasy'. *'Monument' For V. Tatlin* (in a number of versions: 1964, Dia Center for the Arts; 1966, London; 1968, private collection; and 1969,

Minneapolis), was Flavin's *hommage* to the Russian Constructivist artist.

In *Untitled* (1969), Dan Flavin stretched white fluorescent lamps end-to-end along a wall. 1963's *Alternate Diagonals (To Donald Judd)* set four smaller fluorescent tubes at the end of a single, longer lamp. *Red and Green Alternatives (To Sonia)* (1964) was a straightforward work of four fluorescent tubes, two short, two long. *Puerto Rican Light (To Jeanie Blake)* (1965, private collection) sandwiched a shorter white fluorescent tube between longer red and yellow ones. *Pink and Gold* (1968) comprised two colors of fluorescents, grouped vertically along a wall. Four different colored lamps were placed side by side in *Untitled (To Agrati)* (1964, London). In *Untitled (To Jan and Ron Greenberg)* (1972-73), Flavin experimented with square clusters of lamps, tightly packed in parallel. *Untitled (To a Man, George McGovern)* (1972) was a corner piece utilizing circular white fluorescents, grouped into a triangular form 122 inches high. Another corner work, *Untitled (To the 'Innovator' Wheeling)* (1968, Dwan Gallery), used four fluorescents to create an open square, with the upright tubes facing towards the wall (Flavin often explored light that was reflected, light that faced away from the viewer). *Greens Crossing Greens (To Piet Mondrian Who Lacked Green)* (1966) was a curious installation comprising two lines of white strip lights in square white shades. In two sizes, the lamps were placed end-to-end, to produce two lines, one crossing above the other.

> I can take the ordinary lamp out of use and into a magic that touches ancient mysteries [Dan Flavin asserted]. And yet it is still a lamp that burns to death like any other of its kind. In time, the whole electrical system will pass into inactive history. My lamps will no longer be operative, but it is must be remembered that they once gave light. (B, 295)

Dan Flavin's Duchampian, post-Constructivist art of fluorescent lamps was in fact linked by the artist to spirituality, to the ability of light to transform a space, to light as a religious power. This is not something that might strike the viewer coming to Flavin's art afresh, that these ready-made fluorescent tubes are associated by the artist to the idea of light as a mystical presence. Some of Flavin's early works had distinctly religious connotations: *Icon V (Coran's Broadway Flesh)* (1962, Heiner Friedrich, New York), or *The Nominal Three (to William of Ockham)* (1963, Giuseppe Panza di Biumo-Varese), for example, which was an arrangement of six fluorescent tubes standing in three groups (of one, two and three lamps). Red fluorescent tubes were employed to dramatic effect in *Monument 4 Those Who Have Been Killed In Ambush (To P.K. Who Reminded Me About Death)* (1966), exhibited at the *Primary Structures* show in Gotham. For British sculptor Peter Hutchinson, the elegance of Flavin's sculptures, 'the elongation and exaggeration combine with a pseudo-religiosity that escapes being Gothic because of its utter coldness and lack of detail'.[2]

Dan Flavin had an important first one-man show in 1964 (at the Green Gallery in NYC). One of his most significant shows was at the Guggenheim in 1992, where he took over the famous central rotunda with light installations, including a giant pink tower of fluorescents: *Untitled (To Tracy, To Celebrate the Love of a Lifetime*, 1992). Another big commission was the Munich subway installation (1998), an underground space that Flavin designed to be lit by his familiar colored fluorescent lamps. One of the most impressive of Flavin's important commissions was the lighting design of the S. Maria Annunciata in Chiesa Rossa in Milan, made in 1996 via sponsorship from Dia Center for the Arts and Fondazione Prada. Flavin provided blue, gold, pink, green and ultraviolet light for the modern Italian church.

'Flavin turns gallery space into gallery time', commented Robert Smithson (1979, 10). Sometimes Dan Flavin's luminism was an art of unexpected beauty – especially when Flavin set different colored fluorescent lamps next to each other, as in *A Primary Structure* (1964, collection: the artist). Pale blue, red and yellow illumination merged on the wall, casting a ghostly light around the room.

LAWRENCE WEINER

Lawrence Weiner's (b. 1942) solution to making sculpture was that a sculpture on a plinth has to be 'translated' into language by the spectator, so that people can understand it (i.e., it is always a cultural object). Sculpture is language, and words are language, therefore, Weiner reckoned, words can be sculpture:

> when you see a piece of wood lying on the ground with a piece of stone on top of it, you must translate that in your own head into language. What I try to do is present language itself as a key to what sculpture is about... It is a presentation of a piece of sculpture in language.[1]

Lawrence Weiner produced sculptures comprising capital letters in short phrases which are about a viewer's relationship with an object. The words are a means or the expression of a relationship with something.

WITH RELATION TO THE VARIOUS MANNERS OF USE
FOR/ OF VARIOUS THINGS.

This is a 1974 Weiner text piece. Other Weiner textworks include this one, a 1979 installation:

MANY COLORED OBJECTS
PLACED SIDE BY SIDE
TO FORM A ROW OF
MANY COLORED OBJECTS

And this one, exhibited at Leo Castelli's gallery in 1974:

UP ON (IN) THE AIR
DOWN ON [IN] THE GROUND
BEING WITHIN THE CONTEXT OF [A]
REACTION

BEING WITHIN THE CONTEXT OF
REACTION.
UP ON (IN) THE AIR

DOWN ON [IN] THE GROUND

One Quart Exterior Green... (1995) is a typical Lawrence Weiner artwork: bold black lettering on a gallery wall:

ONE QUART EXTERIOR GREEN INDUSTRIAL ENAMEL THROWN ON A BRICK WALL

When you see an exhibition of Lawrence Weiner's works, the effect is much the stronger, as at the retrospective I saw in Los Angeles in 2008. Everywhere you look there are walls of texts, some in different colors and different fonts, some painted, some printed, but it's all words, words on white walls.

Richard Long commented that '[t]he discovery [Weiner] made that art does not necessarily have to be made, that was a great breakthrough'.[2] Weiner is right, of course: words alone can be sculpture: poets have long known that language is an *experience*, not simply abstractions or concepts. Language really does affect people, physiologically as well psycho-socio-politically – otherwise why would they spend so much time consuming language? For example, people in some countries consume 20-30 hours of broadcasting per week – that's over a day and a half spent consuming television and radio per week (or, to put it another way, the cultural imaginary of the global entertainment industry dominates the daily lives of a large proportion of Earth's population).

Lawrence Weiner's words on a gallery wall don't seem at first to be 'art'. They are not sensual and graspable, like a marble statue. Yet those words, whether photocopied on cheap paper or printed by high quality typography on deluxe paper, or stencilled on a gallery wall, are art; they are communication, language, even sculpture.

SOL LEWITT

For those detractors who found Minimal art too cold, or abstract, or mathematical, an art of soulless numbers and brutal, even fascistic geometry, which fatally ignored the organic and natural worlds, the art of Sol LeWitt (1928-2007) was a good target. LeWitt's serial, systematic, mathematical and Conceptual kind of Minimal art was precisely the sort of art that advocates of traditional modernist sculpture couldn't bear. True, it *was* mathematical, it was based on series of numbers, on permutations and variations of number systems, it was eternally abstract, it was an art of straight lines and cold, white forms. It wasn't difficult to characterize LeWitt's art as too unreal, too dry and clinical.

But critics such as Robert Rosenblum claimed that Conceptual art could be 'awesome'. Of Sol LeWitt's art, Rosenblum wrote that it

> elicits... an immediate awe that... has to be translated by the same feeble words – beautiful, elegant, exhilarating – that we use to register similar experiences with earlier art.[1]

Sol LeWitt explained his view thus:

> I wouldn't say that I wanted to like uninteresting things or to dislike interesting things. I think that's one way that you measure your response, if it interests you. 'Interests' means that it somehow makes a bridge between you and it, you and the object, you and the art object. If it hits home, it means that it's of interest.[2]

For Sol LeWitt, the idea was everything: rather than a Minimalist, LeWitt was much more a Conceptual artist. The making of the art became a 'perfunctory affair'.[3] Objects didn't concern him so much as the idea for the work. Such a disregard for the object would inevitably turn off followers of more traditional art; they simply could not learn to like an art comprised solely of ideas. LeWitt espoused some of Conceptualism's and Process

art's anti-art æsthetics: LeWitt deliberately deployed materials that were not 'sexy'.

Sol LeWitt's basic format was an open modular cube, mathematical variations on the cube made from aluminium or wood, and painted in the Minimalists' favourite color, white (such as *Open Modular Cube* [1966, Art Gallery of Ontario, Toronto] or *47 Three-Part Variations on Three Different Kinds of Cubes* [1967/ 74, Allen Memorial Art Museum, Oberlin College] or *Modular Wall Piece With Cube* [1965]).

Sol LeWitt explored the permutations cubes could possess set beside each other. It wasn't even the cube itself that interested him, so much as the permutations it could undergo. *Modular Piece (Double Cube)* (1966) was a tall (108-inch high) open steel frame comprised of interlocking cubes. In *Untitled* (1966), a five foot cube was composed of smaller cubes (36 on each side). *Floor Structure, Black* (1965) comprised five cubes side by side. *Five Modular Structures (Sequential Permutation On the Number Five,* 1972), was a group of five free-standing wooden groups of open cubes, each structure illustrating, as the title suggested, a permutation on the number 5.

A large floor-standing work, *Serial Project No. 1 (ABCD)* (1966), was an elaborate exploration of the mathematical permutations of the cube, mounted on a grid. It looked more like a scientific experiment, or a mathematician's demonstration of a problem in 3-D geometry than an artwork. One of Sol LeWitt's largest indoor sculptures of this time was *Series A*, exhibited at the Dwan Gallery in 1967. In it, the now-familiar floor grid housed big aluminium open frames, painted white again, but in a much larger scale than usual. Permutations within *Series A* included cubes within cubes (*Series A #8*), and open columns inside cubes (*Series A #9*).

1, 2, 3 (1978) was another extensive open-form construction, built from aluminium. *All Variations of Incomplete Open Cubes* (1974) was precisely that: 122 white wooden cubes mounted on a grid, displaying the possible permutations of a cube that didn't have the final side (Sol LeWitt was fond of partial as well as whole forms). In some works, LeWitt constructed large versions of single incomplete cubes (as in the *Incomplete Open Cube* series [1974]).

Sol LeWitt continued to construct his complex framework sculptures of cubes into the Eighties and after (such as *13/ 11*, 1985). LeWitt also began to experiment with more irregular forms, introducing diagonals, trapezes and rhomboids (as in *Complex Form No. 8*, 1988, and *Complex Form*, 1978-80). Enormous installations such as *New Structure* (1995) were built from breeze blocks in square walls and towers.

If you saw a Sol LeWitt exhibition, a more persuasive case was made for the beauty of mathematics and permutations that he was exploring – at a show at Storm King Art Center in 2008, for instance. The best galleries and museums devote a whole room to an artist, if they have enough works. LeWitt certainly benefits from that approach to display, rather than the odd, isolated piece.

Viewing a Sol LeWitt sculpture was like looking at a model which illustrated a philosophical experiment with mathematical permutations. There were in Sol LeWitt's sculptures no figures, no shapely curves of nude women, no animals, no organic forms, no trees or plants, no landscapes, no heroic men or homoerotic male nudes.

Some of Sol LeWitt's most impressive works were his huge wall drawings (such as *Wall Drawing: Part 1 with 10,000 Lines 6" Long* [1971, private collection], and *Wall Drawing No. 1, Drawing Series II 14 (A & B)* [1968]). Some of them were achieved in pencil, or chalk, drawn directly on the wall, in grids and systems. They were deliberately anonymous, detached works (with the correct instructions, anyone could make them, like Richard Long's stone circles; both Long and LeWitt included instructions for reproducing their works in galleries).

All Combinations of Arcs From Corners and Sides: Straight, Not-Straight and Broken Lines (1975) was installed in white chalk on black walls in the Museum of Modern Art, NYC. *Wall Drawing No. 90* (1971, London) is a typical Sol LeWitt wall drawing, using different colored pencils on a white wall. Some of the pencil marks tended to be quite faint, the close-packed grids over white recalled the pale graphite grids of Agnes Martin (as in *Wall Drawing No. 1*, 1968). LeWitt also fabricated installations of wall drawings, so that every wall in a gallery was taken up with multiple overlapping diagonal lines in colored crayon (as in *Wall Drawing No. 273*, 1975, Saatchi Collection, London).

RICHARD SERRA

The most distinctive formal innovation of Richard Serra (b. 1939) was to lean huge pieces of metal together, as in *2-2-1 To Dicke and Tina* (1969, destroyed), and *One Ton Prop (House of Cards)* (1968-69, London), one of Serra's most well-known works (*One Ton Prop* is representative of Serra's æsthetic principles and practical methods). *Circuit* (1972) comprised four plates of steel leaning outwards into the gallery, diagonally, so they formed that favourite Minimal motif, the 'X'. 1969's *Corner Prop* (Gilman Paper Company Collection, New York), featured a small box (25-inch square) supported precariously by a 6 foot pole, in a corner. *Corner Prop No. 8* (1983, London) used the two walls in a corner to lean the upper slab of metal against, as it sat on a second plate. *Kitty Hawk* (1983, London) extended the upper plate of a corner prop to a length of 168 inches. Balanced right on the end of a smaller lower sheet of metal, the sculpture suggested an aeroplane shape.

Richard Serra's prop pieces took up Minimal form and Minimal materiality, and combined that with a sense of spontaneity, improvization, and arbitrariness. They used one of the strongest forces in the cosmos – gravity – as their foundation. They explored paradoxes – that an object so large and heavy could also be so precarious. And puzzles – that an art object could be supported by nothing more sophisticated or sturdy than leaning against a wall, or propped up in a corner.

Lead pours and splashes formed in the wall-floor space were exhibited as *Castings* (1969) in the *Anti-Illusion* show at the Whitney Museum of American Art, and *Splashes* (1968, destroyed). *Belts* (1966-67, Guggenheim Museum), with its 11 vulcanized rubber belts hanging from a wall in a row (entangled with neon tubing), recalled Robert Morris's felt sculptures.

Some of Richard Serra's props and slabs were very large (*Pulitzer Piece*, 1970-71, contains Cor-Ten sheets 60, 55 and 47 feet long). *Schunnemunk Fork* (1981) was another outdoor leaning piece, this time disappearing at one end into a hillside (this's the one at Storm King Art Center in upstate New York. There's a terrific Serra slab in the grounds of UCLA in Bel-Air (*T.E.U.C.L.A.,* 2006, UCLA Sculpture Garden). The ground floor of the new Broad galleries at LACMA on Wilshire Boulevard in L.A. has some colossal-scale Serras. They're so big it looks as if they were installed first and the building was constructed around them. They are so large the visitor is soon engulfed by them: gigantic curving walls of thick steel which's now rusting into orange and brown tower over the viewer as you walk around and inside them.

Richard Serra's most famous work, *Tilted Arc* (1981), a 12 foot high curved Cor-Ten steel wall, was installed at the Federal plaza in Gotham – it was (in)famous partly because locals complained about it, and it was eventually removed by the federal government.

HANS HAACKE

The German artist Hans Haacke (b. 1936) is more usually linked with Arte Povera, Conceptual and Process art, than Minimal art. He is definitely not one of the core Minimalists, like Robert Morris, Dan Flavin or Donald Judd. But Haacke employed Minimal means, as well as some of the forms and materials favoured by Minimalists. Many of Haacke's early works explored natural or organic systems. Later, Haacke moved on to social, economic and political systems (what Haacke called 'real-time systems'). Such political or ideological concerns would take Haacke far from Minimal art (though his presentation techniques still relied on Minimal principles). One of Haacke's tenets was 'the simpler the better'.

Condensation Cube (1963-65) was a combination of Minimal form and Process or environmental content: it employed the classic Minimal form, a Plexiglas cube (a yard on each side), with water inside which condensed on the clear sides of the box, an exploration of process. 'It is changing freely, bound only by statistical limits', remarked Haacke of his 'Weather Box'.

Grass Grows (1966 and 1969) was a mound of soil with grass growing out of it. Hans Haacke later fashioned a row of beans growing along string suspended at an angle, in soil mounted on glass on the gallery floor (*Directed Growth*, 1972), and in tropical plants growing on a circular area of soil, *Rye in the Tropics* (1972). While the artwork was clearly a manifestation of environmental art, the form Haacke chose, of rows and repetition, was that of Minimalism.

In *Sky Line* (1967), Hans Haacke released white helium balloons over Central Park (Andy Warhol had released balloons in a gallery in a famous exhibition). Haacke commented that

in spite of my environmental and monumental thinking I am still fascinated by the nearly magic, self-contained quality of objects. My

water levels, waves and condensation boxes are unthinkable without this physical separation from their surroundings.[1]

Many of Hans Haacke's most compelling artworks were made to explore the ephemeral qualities of ice, snow, fog, steam, smoke and water (as with Robert Morris). The presentation of these process pieces drew on Minimal principles. *Fog, Flooding, Erosion* (1969) used a sprinkler system to turn a Seattle lawn into mud. *Spray of Ithaca: Falls Freezing and Melting On Rope* (1969) and *Fog Dripping From or Freezing On Exposed Surfaces* (1971) explored water and fog freezing on waterfalls and trees. One of Haacke's air and wind constructions comprised a fan blowing a seven by seven foot chiffon sail hung parallel to the gallery floor. Haacke had proposals for monumental-sized windmills and sails, all naturally powered by the winds (Haacke preferred to use unmechanical sources of energy).

In *Rhine-Water Purification Plant* (1972), the subject was the process of purifying polluted river water. Via a series of acrylic containers, filters, hoses and pools, the spectator could follow the purification of the contaminated Krefeld sewage water. The final destination of the water flow was a square pool containing goldfish. *Rhine-Water Purification Plant* recalled the 3-D displays in science and natural history museums that explained the processes of nature and science (some non-art museums have taken up Minimal design in their exhibitions, but the Minimal approach has a drawback when a lot of complex information about science, geography, history or technology has to be communicated to the punter).

In Hans Haacke's piece *Ten Turtles Set Free* (1970), the animals were released in a forest near St Paul-de-Vence (France), a symbolic gesture about humanity's relationship with the natural world and its inhabitants. Haacke photographed seagulls feeding on bread scattered on a lake in *Live Airborne System* (1965/ 68).

Hans Haacke later considered economic

systems in works such as *Shapolsky et al, Manhattan Real Estate Holdings, a Real-Time Social System* (1971). For the *Information* show at Gotham's Museum of Modern Art (in 1971), Haacke exhibited a poll about Governor Rockefeller running for election, inviting visitors to vote. Haacke took on cultural institutions such as museums, landlords, and politicians such as President Reagan and British PM, Margaret Thatcher. On a few occasions Haacke's proposals were negated by the author-ities of the Guggenheim, Wallraf-Richartz and Metropolitan museums, with works and shows being cancelled as a result. Other artists (such as Daniel Buren) protested in support of Haacke.

Hans Haacke has also engaged with Germany's fascist history – in, for instance, his monument *Und ihr habt doch gesiegt* (1988) in Graz, and a piece about the U.S.A. invasion of Grenada (*Isolation Box*, 1983-84), which replicated the wooden boxes used by the America military for prisoners. In Haacke's *Germania*, the whole floor of the German pavilion at the 1993 Venice Biennale was smashed up. It was one of the recurring criticisms of Minimal art that it didn't engage much with the social, the political, and the ideological, and that it was a capitalist art, an art of materialism and commodification. While many Minimal artists were deliberately a-political, others, like Haacke and Dan Flavin, addressed socio-political issues.

EVA HESSE

Eva Hesse, who died at the age of 34 in 1970, is one of the most compelling Minimal, Conceptual and Process artists. Hesse was part of the group that included Carl Andre, Robert Ryman, Sol LeWitt and Mel Bochner. She worked in series, like other Process and Minimal artists. She called her repetit-ions 'sequels' and 'schemas'. Her artworks have an immediate, challenging impact. They hang from ceilings, in rows, made of rubber, latex, cloth, wire and fibreglass, evoking organic forms in ambiv-alent, sensual ways.[1] Pieces such as *Ingeminate* (1965, London) offer up a mysterious affirmation of life in the form of two coils of cord connected by a long piece of surgical hose.

Several (1965, London) comprised a bunch of rubbery, tubular forms hanging from a nail on a wall. *Hang Up* (1965-66, Art Institute, Chicago) was a wooden frame (painted gray) with a length of cord emerging from holes in the frame, looping onto the floor, and back into the frame. In *Addendum* (1967) a row of lengths of cord extend from small domes attached to the wall on a wooden plank 119 inches long. In *Ishtar* (1965, collection F. & R.B. Lynn, New Jersey), the black cords extend from twenty domes now arranged in two vertical rows of ten. *Schema* (1967, Philadelphia) is a grid of small latex hemispheres laid on a sheet of latex. In *Continent* (1969, National Gallery of Australia), 8 panels of cheesecloth encased in latex hung from the ceiling.

A big piece by Eva Hesse, *Extended Expansion* (1969, Guggenheim Museum), also employed latex over cheesecloth, creating a series of panels propped up by fibreglass poles. *Repetition 19, III* (1969, MOMA, New York) comprised 20-inch high tubes of fibreglass, each one irregular and individ-ual, mysterious beakers or vessels. Hundreds of rubber washers were stuck to a small, low table that Sol LeWitt had given Hesse in *Washer Table* (1967).

Sans II (1968, London) was a dozen rectangular

'compartments' made from fibre-glass which hinted at some obscure systematization of flesh and organic form. In *Untitled* (1970, Iowa) four roughly rectangular forms were mounted on the gallery wall, in fibreglass and latex, with two lengthy, spindly ropes emerging from the flat rectangles and trailing onto the floor (a work which wound down to the gallery floor was a favourite motif of Eva Hesse's, which seemed to connect the space of the wall sculpture to the viewer's space). In *Untitled (Rope Piece)* (1970, Whitney Museum of American Art), latex and rope hung irregularly, entangled, from the ceiling. 1968's *Area* (Wexner Center For the Arts) comprised a rectangular section of latex-covered cloth pinned on the wall and allowed to run across the floor.

Eva Hesse wrote: '[i]f I can name the content...it's the total absurdity of life'.[2] As Anna Chave noted, Hesse's forms resemble abstract 'breasts, clitorises, vaginas, fetuses, uteruses, fallopian tubes', articulating a new feminine sexual subjectivity, utilizing the female, not the male gaze.[3] In a 1968 statement, Hesse said, sounding like Ad Reinhardt:

I remember I wanted to get to non-art, non connotive, non anthropomorphic, non geometric, non, nothing, everything, but of another kind, vision, sort. From a total other reference point. Is it possible? I have learned anything is possible.[4]

Sometimes loosely hanging, finding their own form, at other times Eva Hesse's sculptures were bound with wire, as if 'making psychic models', as Robert Smithson said.[5] For Hesse, as for many artists, art and life were not separate things, but part of a continuum. Hesse said she didn't keep them apart: 'art is a total thing. A total person giving a contribution. It is an essence, a soul... in my inner soul art and life are inseparable'.[6]

ANNE TRUITT

Anne Truitt (1921-2004) constructed some archetypal Minimal sculptures, such as her *Southern Elegy* (1962), a smooth, abstract form in cool black. Some of Truitt's rectilinear slabs, like free-standing partitions or walls (built from painted wood), appeared as 3-D versions of the paintings of Brice Marden or Robert Mangold (for instance, *Valley Forge* [1963], and *Knight's Heritage* [1973]). Truitt even divided the sculptures into areas of single colors, very like Marden's canvases. Some of Truitt's Minimal works were blocky, irregular forms in painted steel (such as 1964's *Spring, Solstice* and *Here*).

In her Seventies journal, Anne Truitt spoke of the intimate relationship artists can have with their works. They can regard them as their children or lovers, emanations from the secret self:

When I conceive a new sculpture, there is a magical period in which we seem to fall in love with one another. This explains to me why, when I was in Yaddo and deprived of my large pieces, I felt lonely with the same quality of loneliness I would feel for a missing lover. This mutual exchange is one of exploration on my part, and, it seems to me, on the sculpture's also. Its life is its own. I receive it. And after the sculpture stands free, finished, I have the feeling of "oh, it was *you*," akin to the feeling with which I always recognized my babies when I saw them, having made their acquaintance before their birth.[1]

Like Carl Andre, John McCracken and other Minimal artists, Anne Truitt continued to make works in the 1990s that were very similar to pieces she'd made at the height of Minimalism in the 1960s. An installation in Baltimore in 1992, for instance, isn't radically different from similar shows Truitt produced in the mid-1960s. The same rectangular columns standing on the gallery floor, the same monochrome paint jobs.

Some of Anne Truitt's distinctive art comprises blocky, rectilinear columns in primary or pastel hues reminiscent in form of Barnett Newman's *Broken Obelisk* (1963-67), such as the *Parva* series (1974 onwards) An Anne Truitt exhibition's like a group of skyscraper models, blank, windowless, standing silently like sentinels in the gallery.

LOUISE NEVELSON, BARBARA HEPWORTH, REBECCA HORN, JACKIE WINSOR

Among the many important postwar and contemporary women sculptors, artists such as Mary Miss, Nancy Holt, Alice Aycock, Louise Nevelson and Barbara Kruger relate directly to Minimal art.[1] **LOUISE NEVELSON** (1899-1988) produced huge structures which were like post-Cubist or post-Constructionist altarpieces full of objects, articles made of wood, all painted in one color, black, white or gold, presented frontally, like reliefs: chair legs, railings, and door knobs (in, for instance, *Dawn's Wedding Chapel II*, 1959, Whitney Museum of American Art). Nevelson sculptures resembled magical cupboards, vertical inventories of dreams, built from boxes stacked on top of each other. The rectilinear containers and the use of the box form were among Nevelson's links with Minimalism.

REBECCA HORN 's (b. 1944) sculptures were based like on natural forms, movement, dance, time and environments. Horn was known more as Process, Conceptual and performance sculptor, than a straight-ahead Minimalist, but she shared the same penchant for radical reduction of the Minimal sculptors, the same emphasis on materiality, and the Arte Povera deployment of everyday objects. Horn's wonderful *Peacock Machine* (1982) was an exuberant activator of space, one of those pieces that aimed for the essence of a natural form (like Constantin Brancusi's animal sculptures): a peacock's magnificent tail.[2] It was Brancusi's task to strip away the detritus that had accumulated around sculpture, Henry Moore said, and to give the spectator the pure, simple shape. What Brancusi did was 'to concentrate on very simple shapes, to keep his sculpture, as it were, one-cylindered, to refine and polish a single shape to a degree almost too precious.'[3] This is what many contemporary sculptors have done, keeping their shapes simple and purified: David Nash, Richard Serra and Carl

Andre.

Rebecca Horn demonstrates a wicked sense of humour, however, which's lacking in much of Minimal art: her big show at the Tate Gallery in Britain in 2005 was full of kinetic machinery which explored the themes of violence, transgression and desire.

BARBARA HEPWORTH 's (1903-1975) bio-morphic forms, as with Constantin Brancusi's, hover between subjectivity and objectivity, between natural form and formal abstraction (as in her *Two Forms*, 1933, for example). Certainly not a Minimalist, Hepworth did employ some of the æsthetics of 1960s art, such as seriality, reduction to essence, polished surfaces, and abstract forms. Like Brancusi, Hepworth maintained that she always returned to nature, and took her inspiration from nature. For her, nature meant the Cornish landscape, and the human body.

'We return always to the human form – the human form in landscape', she said. Her sculpture stems from emotion and expression, from feeling: 'I rarely draw what I see – I draw what I feel in my body'.[4] Hepworth's distinctive forms, with their smooth curves and openings, are more obviously sensual objects than the more severe Minimal sculpture.

JACKIE WINSOR (b. 1941) took up the cube as one of her major forms, like the Minimal artists, but she made her cubes from 'natural' materials, such as twine and wood (for instance, hemp and wood in *Plywood Square*, 1973, National Gallery of Australia). Winsor's cubes take the Minimal cube only as a starting-point, because her series of cubes are explorations of the mysteries of being. Winsor also employed the Minimalist grid (*Bound Grid*, 1971-72, private collection), but constructed it from irregular tree trunks. Some of Winsor's works change or decay: the wood and concrete cube in *Burnt Piece* (1977-78) burnt away, alchemically, when the artist fired its interior. As with the land artists, Winsor said: 'I was unable to see how the piece would look until the moment of completion'.[5] In *Exploded Piece* (1980-82), Winsor blew up one of her solid cubes with dynamite (inside it Winsor packed layers of paint, gold lea and plaster).

OTHER MINIMAL SCULPTORS

RONALD BLADEN 's *X* (1967) was one of the stars of the Minimal era, and the huge *The X* (it was 24¹/₂ feet wide) was subsequently reproduced many times in books on Sixties art. *X* was bold, monochrome (black), and blissfully (some would say aggressively) self-contained. Bladen (1918-88) also constructed other giant simple geometrically shaped sculptures, such as his *Black Triangle* [1966], *3 Elements* [1965], and *Kama Sutra* [1977], some 28 feet high. Some of ROBERT DURAN 's sculptures were archetypal Minimal works, such as his low floor-hugging masonite blocks (*Untitled*, 1966-67, Bykert Gallery, New York), recalling the art of Robert Morris and Carl Andre. RICHARD VAN BUREN 's sculptures were equally classic Minimal pieces: floor-standing sculptures constructed in plywood and covered with fibreglass in blocky, geometric forms (for instance, *Untitled*, 1967).

In MICHAEL BOLUS 's (b. 1934) sculptures (such as his 1966 installation at the Kornblee Gallery and *11th Sculpture*, 1963), archetypal Minimal tenets predominate; aluminium materials (painted), floor-standing works (no pedestals), repetition, and simple geometric forms. It's the same with MICHAEL STEINER , another lesser-known Minimal artist, like Bolus. Steiner's sculptures, such as his installation at the Dwan Gallery in 1966, exhibit the same smooth, industrial, rectilinear forms (again in aluminium, one of the favourite media of Minimal sculptors).

ROBERT GROSVENOR (b. 1937) was another less well-known but significant Minimalist sculptor. Some of his works appear even less artless than Carl Andre's untreated wood pieces: Grosvenor's *Untitled* (1974, Paula Cooper Gallery) was a plank of wood on the gallery floor, unadorned (and with one end snapped off). It could have been hiked from a lumber yard to the gallery and placed on the floor, with nothing else added to it. SCOTT

BURTON (1939-89) drew on Minimalism (Donald Judd, Tony Smith, Richard Artschwager) to create rectilinear floor-standing sculptures such as the granite *Two-Part Chairs' Obtuse Angle* (1983-84, Walker Art Center, Minneapolis) and *Two-Cube Table* (1985-86, Max Protech Gallery). Burton's inspiration derived partly from Constantin Brancusi, one of the gods of Minimal æsthetics.

JOHN McCRACKEN (1934-2011) was a Californian sculptor who made Minimal slabs or 'planks' from wood or fibreglass, which were halfway between paintings and sculptures (or neither one nor the other), which he leant against walls (such as *Blue Plank* [1966], *Untitled (Red Plank)* [1966], and *Untitled (Dk Blue)* [1970]). McCracken saw his unitary slabs as 'meditation devices'. At times McCracken's works looked like Barnett Newman's zips, or Richard Serra's leaning sculptures (*Untitled*, 1967, Saatchi Collection). When they were freestanding (*Untitled* [1966, Los Angeles County Museum]; and *Sagittarius* [1988, private collection]), McCracken's sculptures evoked the mysterious, alien obelisk in *2,0001: A Space Odyssey*, perhaps the key Minimal film of the era. But McCracken painted his slabs in bright, Pop Art colors, not the monochromes associated with Minimal art (gray, white and black): the bright *Blue Post and Lintel* (1965), for instance. McCracken was still making his mysterious mono-chrome sculptures into the 1990s (such as *One* [1997], and *Hill* [1997]).

BRUCE NAUMAN (b. 1941) is associated with Minimal art (though, like most good artists, he defies categorization: there's performance art, body art, Conceptual art, Process art, Arte Povera, assemblage and installation art in his output, among other art movements). Nauman became a deity among modern artists, often cited by younger artists as an inspiration (as with Joseph Beuys or Salvador Dali). Nauman's also one of those artists, like Andy Warhol or Yves Klein, whose works have been prototypes or influences on a range of art movements. One can see how a variety of art movements seem to develop from Nauman's œuvre.

Green Light Corridor (1970, Guggenheim, New York) is a typical Bruce Nauman lightwork: a narrow 12-yard corridor is created between two tall flats (higher than average human height), and lit by white fluorescent tubes above (inside the corridor) in a room suffused with green lamps. The idea was to enclose the visitor in a narrow, claustrophobic space and limit their perception.[1] In *Neon Templates of the Left Half of My Body Taken At Ten-inch Intervals* (1966, New York), green neon tubes were mounted on the wall in a vertical series relating to the artist's body. (Nauman was very fond of neon: the typical Nauman neon piece comprised short ironic phrases in different colored neon: the words 'desire' and 'hope', as in *Human/ Need/ Desire* [1983, MOMA, New York]).

STEPHEN ANTONAKOS (b. 1926) was another artist who utilized neon tubing as a fundamental material for his sculptures. The parallel lines forming shapes recalled Dan Flavin (as in *Red Neon Wall To Floor* [1966] and *Orange Vertical Floor Neon* [1966]), but the forms Antonakos developed were much more complex than Flavin's.

JANNIS KOUNELLIS (b.1936), known primarily as an Arte Povera sculptor and Conceptual artist, also produced Minimalist pieces, such as his *Untitled* (1986), a multi-media piece (metal, copper tubing, india ink, paper) which appears like a Robert Rauschenberg assemblage-as-painting (the propane tank that's attached to the sculpture suggests that this is no ordinary triptych. **MICHELANGELO PISTOLETTO** , another of the chief Arte Povera artists, developed some of the principles of Minimalism in his art.

DANIEL BUREN 's (b. 1938) most famous works were Conceptual, Postminimal additions to existing public spaces in the form of stripes (such as adding striped paper to 200 billboards in Paris in 1968). In another series of stripe installations (continuing into the mid-1970s), Buren stuck rows of striped paper from a gallery entrance and out onto the street, to the end of the gallery building. In the Guggenheim Museum in 1971 Buren hung an enormous version of his striped motif in the atrium, a 20 by 10 yard piece of canvas (*Visible Recto Verso Painting*). Buren's Postminimal stripes have become favourites in contemporary art history criticism, and are frequently cited (Buren's installation at the Palais-Royal in Paris [1985-86] has been reproduced in many books).

When bright, primary colors are employed in sculpture, as in the grand scale of Minimal sculpture, such as on **ISAMU NOGUCHI** 's (1904-88) huge *Red Cube* (1969), the result has a formal purity that borders on the child-like. The bold, sunny colors, when combined with the simplicity, self-assurance and exactness of basic geometric shapes such as cubes, or spheres, cones or pyramids, manifests in High Minimalism. Noguchi's *Marble Garden* (1960-64, Yale University) is another example of classic Minimalism, with its geometric forms set in a plain of white marble. Like the garden Noguchi designed for the UNESCO building (1956-58), it draws on the austere Minimalism of Japanese gardens, the placement of semi-organic forms amidst (apparently) empty spaces.

JUDY CHICAGO (b. 1939) produced Minimal cylinders, cubes and columns (*Rainbow Pickets* [1965], and *Ten Part Cylinders* [1966]), before moving onto the feminist pieces of the Seventies which made her famous among feminist artists (for instance, *The Dinner Table*, 1974-79). **LARRY BELL** (b. 1939) exhibited a series of glass cubes (15-inches square) on Plexiglas stands in *Untitled Cubes*, an installation at the Pace Gallery in Manhattan in 1965. Later, in the 1990s, Bell constructed larger free-standing sculptures of sheets of tinted, intersecting glass (such as in *6 x 8 x 4* [1996, Los Angeles], and *Made For Arolsen*

[1992, Germany]). Bell's sculptures took up the Minimalists' love of large, rectangular polished, reflective surfaces (such as Robert Morris's mirrored cubes, or Gerhard Richter's paintings so glossy they act as mirrors).

LUCAS SAMARAS 's (b. 1936) *Mirrored Room* (1966, Albright-Knox Gallery, Buffalo) is a Minimal space of square mirrors, reflecting the spectator *ad infinitum* in the ceiling, floor and walls. Robert Morris and Donald Judd had constructed mirrored cubes. Lucas Samaras's works deliberately subverted the eroticism of sculpture by furnishing his sculptures and assemblages with pins, nails, razor blades, knives and scissors, as in his vicious *Book 4*, which is stuffed with knives, nails and razor blades. It's an art of sadomasochism, fetishized pain. For Samaras, as for so many (male) artists from Dante Alighieri through the Marquis de Sade to Georges Bataille and William Burroughs, sex (pleasure) is intermixed with death. Or, as Samaras put it: 'I cannot separate beauty from pain.'2

GEORGE SUGARMAN 's (1912-99) sculptures were flowing sculptures, twisting, entwined shapes painted in the Minimal colors of red, white, green and yellow. Sugarman created a series of objects, interlinked spatially and thematically, set end to end. Sugarman's seemingly disparate collections of objects were united in part by his use of color. Taking his cue from Stuart Davis, Sugarman used color spatially. In Sugarman's art, the flat color – all-over red, or yellow, or green – tended to suppress the irregularity of his peculiar shapes (in, for example, *Bardana*, 1962-63, Zurich).

RICHARD ARTSCHWAGER (b. 1923) was another important Minimal sculptor, who produced archetypal Minimal pieces with smooth, rectilinear forms (such as *Table With Pink Tablecloth*, 1964, Chicago). Artschwager's *Chair* (1966) reduced the idea of a chair (or 'chairness') down to two rectangular forms, covered in cheesy smoky

formica. **MAYA LIN'** s (b. 1959) *Vietnam Veterans' Memorial* (1982), in sombre black granite, is also distinctly Minimal in design (it comprised two walls commemorating 58,000 Americans with their names inscribed on the stone). Lin went on to construct further memorials in a similar vein.

Among **JOEL SHAPIRO** 's (b. 1941) Minimalesque sculptures were small, irregular polyhedra, mysterious, implacable containers, such as *Untitled* (1980, New York), which's only 12 inches long, or *Untitled* (1973-74), only six and a half inches long. Shapiro's wooden sculpture *Untitled* (1980) was a more recognizable example of abstract art, reminiscent of Anthony Caro or David Smith.

CLAES OLDENBURG (b. 1929), like Andy Warhol or Yves Klein, exists in a category all of his own. One can detect the influence of assemblages, readymades, Pop Art, Process art, Serial art, Conceptual art and Minimal art on Oldenburg's output, but he's not confined to any of those categories. His soft sculptural blow-ups of pop culture paraphernalia are like no one else's work – before or since. I can't tell if it's garbage or genius. It just isn't that interesting for me – whereas a Donald Judd box, which seems to be nuttin' more than a bit of steel and Plexiglas, is infinitely inspiring. Oldenburg, like Judd or Warhol, has his adherents and his detractors, each of which can elaborate persuasive arguments for or against his art. Is it gimmicky, trashy and inconsequential? Or is it a rigorous, ironic exposé of late consumer capitalism?

PHILLIP KING 's (b. 1934) sculptures of the Sixties were signature works of the era in British art and the 'new sculpture' (for instance, his *Rosebud* [1962, MOMA, New York] and *Genghis Khan* [1963, Tate Gallery]), smooth, semi-organic fibreglass forms. Like the Minimalists, King employed bright monochromy, such as the orange and green painted blocks in *Call* (1967, Juda

Rowan Gallery, London). British artist **WILLIAM TURNBULL** took up Minimalism and single colors, partly inspired by seeing Mark Rothko's work in the late 1950s (as in *No. 1*, 1962, London). **WILLIAM TUCKER** created Minimal, restrained sculptures in the Sixties (such as *Series A* [1968, London], and *Memphis* [1966, London]), before moving on to more expressive, 'organic' forms. Another Brit, **TIM SCOTT**, also employed Minimalist principles in his sculptures of the 1960s (such as *Quinquereme*, 1966, London).

ANISH KAPOOR (b. 1954) also drew on the formal invention of Minimal art in his semi-organic sculptures. Kapoor's best known works are probably the biomoprhic, floor-standing pieces which were covered with bright colored powder, as in *Half* (1984, Barbara Gladstone Gallery, New York), and *1000 Names* (1981, Lissom Gallery, London). In some of Kapoor's sculptures, the dusted colors, which cover the sculpture and also the floor area at the foot of the work, threaten to overwhelm the forms. **SHIRAZEH HOUSHIARY**'s sculptures include smooth, semi-organic pieces that recall the sleek sweep of Phillip King's Sixties fibreglass works (for instance, *Himma*, 1985, Lissom Gallery, London).

NICHOLAS POPE (b. 1949), another Brit, has also crafted some Minimal sculpture, such as his 1976 installation in London, and *Roundle Pile* (1979). Pope has produced many outdoor works, which are part of the British land art tradition (such as *The Arch* [1985], *Three Wilderness Stones* [1980], and *Five Amorphous Shapes*), large sculptures using stone and wood in individual, irregular, natural forms. Sculptor **RICHARD DEACON** (b. 1949), more commonly viewed as an artist somewhere between abstraction and figuration, whose sculptures draw on organic forms (he's known for his 'eyes' and 'ears', giant frames loosely inspired by body parts), also displays some Minimal qualities (his 1978 Brixton installation, for instance, exhibits the pared-down abstraction of 1960s Minimalism).

No study of Minimal art would be complete with mentioning **YVES KLEIN** (1928-62). He has been cited through the course of this book, more for what he suggested than actually produced. One of the art world's favourite pranksters (fellow Sixties art tricksters included Joseph Beuys, Andy Warhol and Piero Manzoni), Klein is known primarily as a Conceptual artist. His best known work is probably the 1960 performance piece *Anthropometries* (naked women covered in blue paint imprinting their bodies on canvas accompanied by a string orchestra). His oft-reproduced photographic *The Leap Into the Void* (which he faked, of course) is a close second. But two Kleinisms are significant for Minimal art: Klein's painting *Blue Monochrome* (1962) – painted in IKB (International Klein Blue), of course – was an important early Minimal work, conceptually and formally. And his exhibition *Le Vide* (1958) also helped to lay the philosophical groundwork for Minimalism.

ANDY WARHOL (19278-87), like Yves Klein and Joseph Beuys, towers over art of the 1960s and the following decades. Like many artists of the epoch, Warhol can be placed with the painters or the sculptors, or Conceptual artists, or installation, 3-D artists. But he is more commonly known as a Pop artist than as a Minimalist. Art history has tended to cite Warhol's sculpture of the Brillo pad boxes (*Brillo Boxes (Soap Pads)*, 1964) as an example of Warhol's Minimal phase (i.e., flatness, rectilinearity, repetition).

Andy Warhol's art exhibits many of the qualities of Minimalism: working in series, repetition, flatness and frontality, bright primary colors, paintings-as-objects, early postmodernity, emphasis on materiality, on the fabrication of the work, and on mundaneity.

#4

MINIMAL ART
AND LAND ART

THE ECONOMICS OF MINIMAL ART AND LAND ART

Some Minimal and land art can be very expensive to produce (let alone to buy). It is expensive moving tons of earth around (Robert Smithson), or making rows of metal and concrete cubes (Donald Judd), and even flying over potential land art sites is costly. Taking a motorbike out into the desert and drawing lines with it is one thing (as Michael Heizer did), but making a 40 mile 18 foot high fence (à la Christo) is another. Large-scale Minimal and land art requires patrons, sponsors, co-ordination with galleries, lawyers, public administrators, helpers and industry. The costliness of large-scale art may explain why much of it is American.[1] Big Art requires investment with no immediate return (or no return at all).[2] It's easy to view Beverly Pepper's *Venezia Blu*, or Christo's wrapped buildings or Walter de Maria's $500,000 *Vertical Earth Kilometer* as expensive, pointless art. This sort of large-scale Minimal work may be an art of excessive cost and excessive waste, but then, art has been full of crazy amounts of money for ages. What about Christo's wrappings? They cost more than the G.N.P. of small countries, for sure, but, as Christo says, he pays for it himself, with money made from selling smaller works. Christo's *Running Fence* cost $2.5 million; *The Umbrellas* in Japan and California, cost $26,000,000. Christo says his art 'has to do with things that are very simple'.[3] This definition can also apply to other land and Minimal artists; they, too, transform ordinary things.

When these transformations of the ordinary cost so much (and require 200 rock climbers, as Christo's covering of the Reichstag in Berlin needed), then commentators wonder about the 'importance' of such artistic productions. There is something not too wasteful about Bruce Nauman photographing himself as a fountain, or Sol LeWitt drawing lines on a wall. But there's something cynical and obscene, perhaps, about Michael Heizer or Walter de Maria carving great gashes in the American desert, or Christo making artworks that cost 26 million dollars yet only last for two weeks.[4] When artists spend such vast amounts of money on art, it's no wonder some people find this obscene. How can one 'justify' a $26,000,000 Christo wrapping?

MINIMAL ART AND NATURE

Some Minimal artists seem to have affinities with Romantic art and Romantic artists (as with contemporary artists such as Mark Rothko, Barnett Newman, Jasper Johns, Robert Rauschenberg and Gerhard Richter). Minimal artists such as Donald Judd, Carl Andre and Robert Smithson express some of the marks of Romanticism. Examples of the 'Minimal Sublime' (*pace* Robert Rosenblum's coining of the term 'Abstract Sublime' to describe Barnett Newman's and Mark Rothko's paintings), might include the snow and stone circles made in the wildernesses of Scotland, Nepal and Peru of Richard Long; the stone circles of Nancy Holt; Christo's islands surrounded with pink poly-propylene; Carl Andre's clusters of glacial rocks; and of course Robert Smithson's *Spiral Jetty*.

Minimal artists use some of the same emotional, cultural elements as nature writers and Romantic poets, such as the emphasis on the human relationship with nature. Whatever the Minimal artist makes, it is the *feeling* the work generates that is important (but this's beyond the artist's control). As Clement Greenberg, the foremost critic of postwar art in America, wrote: '[a]rt is a matter strictly of experience, not of principles', a statement which chimes with the views of many artists, for whom experience is primary.[1] Art critic Christopher Hussey defined 7 aspects of the sublime, derived from Edmund Burke: obscurity (physical and intellectual); power; privations (such as darkness, solitude, silence); vastness (vertical or horizontal); infinity; succession; and uniformity (the last two suggest limitless progression.[2] These tenets can be applied to land art, especially that of Michael Heizer, Walter de Maria, Robert Smithson *et al*, and large-scale Minimal art.

The Minimal artwork is a physical thing (unlike many Conceptual works) that is meant to affect people. When Walter de Maria filled a gallery with soil, the sensual aspects of the work (smell/ taste/ touch/ sight/ sound) were crucial. Minimalism

won't let go of the art object, it must always be an object of some kind, and thus always partly modernist and traditional.

The sheer *scale* of some Minimal artworks can of itself be visceral (for example, Sol LeWitt's installations, Dan Flavin's Guggenheim installation, or Ronald Bladen's *X*). No one could deny that what's impressive about some of Donald Judd's larger sculptures is simply their size. The sense of scale has a sensual or erotic component: there is eroticism in Jannis Kounellis' *Cotton Sculpture* (1967), a mass of cotton stuffed into a large steel container – a sculpture of contrasts between the softness of the cotton and the rigidity of the steel, or Robert Morris's felt sculptures, or Jackie Winsor's *Burnt Piece*, a cube made with concrete, wire and burnt wood. Tony Cragg has spoken of having 'an erotic response to the external world', something which, it seems, all artists have, or have to have, to be truly great artists.[3]

Sculptors such as Constantin Brancusi, Bill Woodrow and Carl Andre have spoken of the importance of materials in their work, how they learn from their materials, and 'follow' their materials. Tony Cragg spoke of 'works in which I learnt from the materials'.[4] A stone is not merely a stone for an artist: it has its own essence, its own form and presence.[5]

Artists, Minimal artists included, have a special, fetishistic relation with their materials: they are not simply bits of matter to be wielded in a particular way. They are treated with respect; Minimal artists are no different from most artists in fetishizing their materials, and Minimalism has often been called a materialist movement. Each Minimal artist has their favourite media; Donald Judd with Plexiglas, wood, steel and Harley D. lacquer, Dan Flavin with fluorescent tubes, Frank Stella with household paints and aluminium, Brice Marden with oil and encaustic, Andy Warhol with screenprint ink, Carl Andre with timber and metals, and so on.

Artists such as Wolfgang Laib, Vito Acconci, Jeff Koons, Jenny Holzer, Lothar Baumgarten, Hermann de Vries and Anya Gallaccio use living plants in their sculptures, and their work thus (usually) has a direct, sensual impact. Wolfgang Laib dusted the Earth with pollen, to form an enormous square layer of brilliant yellow. The delicacy and potency of the sculpture is immediately apparent. This is the sort of sculpture that exerts a synæsthetic power over the gallery goer: the pollen affects not only the visual sense with its incandescent hues, but also affects smell, taste and touch.[6]

> I believe that the impossible, the invisible and visions can become reality if one really wants to make the effort,

said Laib.[7] Anya Gallaccio made large installations using flowers: thousands of red roses in *Red On Green* (1992), 101 sunflowers in *Preserve Sunflower* (1991) and 1,600 zinnias in *Untitled* (1992). Gallaccio's flower-pieces emphasized beauty and decay, sensuality and death.

Plenty of Minimal artists use natural materials, or material they find in existing 'natural' locations. Dennis Oppenheim, Hans Haacke, Andy Goldsworthy and Robert Morris have used steam, fog, water and snow, for instance. Robert Smithson employed lakes, landfills, stone and water. Walter de Maria's *Earth Room* was both an installation and land art, both sculpture and 'natural' (soil comprised the material in the piece). And although Minimal art is routinely described as an art of manmade media – glass, hot-rolled steel, mirrors, aluminium, Plexiglas and synthetic paints being favourite materials – it used wood just as much. Carl Andre favoured cedar, for instance, and major Minimal works by Judd, Morris, LeWitt and many others were made with wood.

BRITISH MINIMAL ART AND THE BRITISH LANDSCAPE TRADITION

The British landscape and the British art tradition are important influences on British Minimal art and British sculpture, as well as American Minimal art. Landscape art in Britain is bound up with notions of Romanticism, and the landscape in Albion has had a distinctive influence on British painting and sculpture, including British Minimal art. For critic Robert Rosenblum, the Abstract Expressionists (in particular Mark Rothko) were the last in a long line of Romantic artists. Speaking of his book *The Northern Romantic Tradition*, Rosenblum said:

> were I to write a supplementary chapter to it – I stopped with Rothko and Abstract Expressionism – I would probably include earthworks of the late 60s and 70s. Those seem in some way to be the last gasp of that tradition of trying to find some sort of connection with the Great Beyond or the Void. (1988, 7)

Certainly, in the works of British sculptors who display Minimal art influences (such as Tony Cragg, Hamish Fulton, Shirazeh Houshiary, Anish Kapoor, Richard Long, Bill Woodrow, Barry Flanagan, Anthony Caro and William Tucker), one can see the elements of British Romanticism and British landscape art (as well as the Neo-Romanticism of the 1930s and 1940s). It was Carl Andre who noted, quite rightly, that the British landscape was 'one vast earthwork'.[1]

Aspects of the British landscape and Romantic tradition include (1) the tradition of the pastoral and Arcadian; (2) the sublime; (3) infinity; (4) nostalgia; (5) mythology; (6) soul; (7) magic; (8) nature; and (9) the Gothic. One can trace a path back from British (and American) 1960s artists, including many Minimal artists, to British Romantic poetry (the anarchic idealism of Percy Bysshe Shelley, the luscious sensuality of John Keats, the epic nature poetry of William Wordsworth, the angelic visions of William Blake and the synæsthetic poesie of Samuel Taylor Coleridge); to British Romantic painters (J.M.W. Turner above all, and John Constable, Thomas Girtin, John Sell Cotman and Richard Wilson).

MINIMAL ART AND SCULPTURE IN GREAT BRITAIN

Sixties British sculpture, including its Minimal practitioners, was connected with American Minimal art and Conceptual Art; with New Realism; with Italian Arte Povera; with the art schools (St Martin's, Slade, RCA, Chelsea); with teachers and modernists such as Anthony Caro, Philip King, Hans Haacke, Lawrence Weiner, Joseph Beuys and Henry Moore.

The new British sculpture (the 'New Generation' sculptors were part of this) was loved and loathed passionately (it was 'new' in the 1960s, but has been supplanted by countless 'new' New Art Movements since). Critic Peter Fuller targetted Bill Woodrow's work as an example of what he hated most in (postmodern) New Art.[1] Fuller loved artists who make 'beautiful' things, things that may be difficult or challenging, but which are also 'beautiful' (J.M.W. Turner, Paul Nash, Maggie Hambling and Eric Gill). But Bill Woodrow's sculpture, like Tony Cragg, Jean-Luc Vilmouth and David Mach, destroyed the traditional notions of the 'beauty' of an art object. Stable (modernist) notions of 'purity' or 'meaning' in art are refuted by sculptors such as Tony Cragg, David Mach, Bill Woodrow *et al* (sometimes called 'post-industrial' artists). The 'new' sculpture in the U.K., particularly the post-industrial, postmodern type, created anxieties about authorship, originality, expressiveness, value and meaning. For the new sculptors of the post-1960s period, it didn't matter if there is no 'craft skill' used in sculpture as long as there were some other things going on in it. Richard Long claimed his photographs were not made with great skill, but it doesn't affect the value they have as artworks. Similarly, Andy Warhol showed an artist didn't have to be as skilled as a Leonardo or Raphael to be able to produce 'great art'. One needed to be a good publicist, good with mass mechanical production techniques, good at organizing other people, good with spin, soundbites, glamour.

Tony Cragg (b. 1949), one of the most potent of the post-industrial artists, who drew on Arte Povera's materiality and Minimal principles, was known for his imaginative usage of found objects (such as the colored spreads of items arranged in lines on the floor, as his *New Stones – Newton's Tones* [1978, Arts Council], *Five Objects, Five Colours* [1980, Paris], and *New Stones* [1982]). Cragg's sculptures were re-arrangements of all manner of objects, each given the same status, in a non-hierarchical fashion, laid out on the floor. The forms Cragg employed are Minimalist: lines, rows, circles, stacks. Cragg's 1980 sculpture *Black and White Stack* contains bicycle tyres, tin cans, car radiator grills, the side of a child's cot and an ironing board.

The sculptures of Tony Cragg, Bill Woodrow and David Mach and others, are not simply sensual modernist objects but ironic, postmodernist commentaries on the social and political uses of commodities. In the sculpture of Cragg, Mach and Woodrow, familiar consumer durables and industrial materials are represented in an ironic, metaphoric and parodying manner.[2] The British sculptors who trawl the dumpsters and junkyards in urban landscapes (Cragg, Woodrow, Mach, Nash, Nicholas Pope, Anthony Gormley), make ironic comments on scavenging and ecological recycling. Cragg was not interested, he said, 'in romanticizing an epoch in the distant past', but questioning the massive amount of commodity consumption in a late capitalist epoch.[3]

The humour, scepticism, pathos and irony in the art of Cragg, Woodrow, Mach, Gormley *et al* made their post-Conceptualist, post-industrial sculpture automatically disruptive. They evaded categorization. It is this sense of shifting meanings and ambiguity in constant flux that makes much of the 1960s 'new sculpture' and late modernist work in Albion suspect for some critics, because the work won't *keep still*. It won't be nailed down as an object of High Modernism, such as a family group in bronze by Henry Moore or an Auguste Rodin

nude statue in marble.

One can understand the anger that much of postmodern, Minimal, Conceptual or post-Conceptual art engenders. Walking into one of the big, white-walled brightly-lit modern gallery spaces in the world's larger cities (they are wholly Minimal spaces, and they're dubbed 'white cubes' these days – a wholly Minimal term), the art lover is often confronted by a series of baffling photographs, or 'found objects' placed in a line against a wall, or photocopies of hotel receipts. A glass of water is called an oak tree. Someone following someone else on the street at random is art. Someone having their clothes cut off is art. The remains of a snow-ball melted on paper is art. A small white wooden box on the floor is art.

Some of these contemporary art shows seem full of worthless, everyday objects, things anyone can find. There seems to be nothing *special* about the objects in Tony Cragg's *New Stones,* or Bill Woodrow's dumpster works, or Lawrence Weiner's printed 'wall statements', or the deconstructionist projects of the Art and Language group. How many times has that most common complaint of 'modern' art been heard: *anyone could do that!* Yes, it does seem, at first, as if 'anyone could make' Andy Warhol's screenprints, Tim Head's displays of vibrators and tape recorders or Donald Judd's rows of metal cubes. But it is such a simplistic view, revealing such a narrow understanding of what art is, what it does, and how and why it is produced.

Postmodern, post-Conceptual and Postminimal art ignites many important questions, such as: how does one know about the 'authenticity' or 'originality' of something when it is mediated by the mass media? How does one know something is 'the real thing', when all one knows of it is through images and sounds on the web, radio, television and the press? Does it matter if the 'original' artwork is fake when the mediated product has such 'truth'? Is an artwork that consists of photographs that refer to an artwork that exists elsewhere (such as Lawrence Weiner's printed words 'wall statement' *Sometimes Found*), as 'authentic' as a bronze sculpture by Donatello? Is the artwork that is an 'idea' as sensual or compelling as one made out of marble or oil paint? Minimal art, Conceptual art and the 'new' British sculpture, with its scavenged objects and seemingly 'ordinary' items displayed on the floor, disrupts modernist/ traditional notions of 'beauty', 'purity', 'tradition', 'objecthood', 'presence', 'value' and 'meaning'.

CHANGE, CYCLES, SEASONS

Some action/ performance/ Conceptual artworks had a built-in impermanence, such as in Allan Kaprow's 1967 *Fluids*, large structures made from blocks of ice, which were left to melt, or in Robert Morris's steam works which were blown away by the wind. Barry Flanagan's *Hole in the Sea* (1967-70) was a cylinder embedded in a beach: Flanagan filmed the water covering the hole as the tide came in. Vito Acconci took photographs while he jumped up and down (*Jump*, 1969), the results are a series of blurred Kodak Instamatic images.

An installation by Paul Kos, *The Sound of Ice Melting* (1970, San Francisco), had blocks of ice surrounded by a cluster of microphones on stands. In *Unroll Your Skin/ Stone* (1971), Giuseppe Penone photographed himself placing a stone into a river (he had engraved his fingerprints on the stone). Hans Haacke produced impermanent works, such as ice freezing around an element, or setting turtles free to roam.[1] Haacke wrote of an artwork which would be as majestic and as transient as birds gathering in the sky:

> I would like to lure 1,000 seagulls to a certain spot (in the air) by some delicious food so as to construct an air sculpture from this combined mass.

Jan Dibbets photographed the light, sky and buildings outside the Van Abbemuseum in Eindhoven in a Conceptual art piece, and displayed the changing light seen through a window in a series of photographs (*The Shortest Day At the Van Abbemuseum*, 1970). All of these pieces celebrated ephemerality, decay and change.

In "Natural Phenomena as Public Monuments" (1968), land artist Alan Sonfist suggested building 'museums of air' in cities, which would

> recapture the smells of earth, trees and vegetation different seasons and at different historical times, so that people would be able to

experience what has been lost. (1978)

Alan Sonfist also suggested monumentalizing the natural world with sounds: '[c]ontinuous loops of natural sounds at the natural level of volume can be placed on historic sites' (ibid.).

#5

MINIMAL ARTISTS
AND LAND ARTISTS

ROBERT SMITHSON

Robert Smithson (1938-1973) rivalled Donald Judd, Robert Morris and Carl Andre as the most significant theorist and essayist among the Minimal artists. Smithson, like Judd, Andy Warhol, Yves Klein and Joseph Beuys, has become deified in the art world. His work has far out-stripped its origins in land/ earth/ site art. Smithson has been elevated to the top level of American artists, alongside Jackson Pollock, Mark Rothko, Edward Hopper, Warhol and Judd.

Three essays have become key manifestos of Robert Smithson's theories. In "The Crystal Land", Smithson discussed a journey he had made with Donald Judd to a quarry. Smithson wasn't only interested in geology and time, but also in astronomy, philosophy, and speculative literature (such as Jorge Luis Borges, Samuel Beckett and science fiction). In the essay, Smithson talked about the sense of decay in the quarry, the elements of entropy which would feature in his own work ('cracked broken shattered earth, of fragmentation, corrosion, decomposition, dis-inte-gration, rock crisis, debris slides, mud flow avalanche' [RS, 20]). In the second article, 1966's "Entropy and the New Monuments", Smithson wrote of the important Minimal show *Primary Structures* at the Jewish Museum (one of the major Minimal shows).

Robert Smithson's themes were entropy in art and the natural world. He utilized the science of crystals and minerals as paradigms of the 'new art'. As a child, Smithson had collected crystals and rocks. For the artist, crystallography offered 'a way of dealing with nature without falling into the old trap of the biological metaphor' (R. Hobbs, 12). No wonder, then, that when Smithson saw Donald Judd's pink plastic boxes he compared them to 'giant crystals from another planet' (RS, 19). Few others saw Judd's sculptures in quite the same way, though.

Robert Smithson's *Alogon No. 2* (1966) was a work that explored crystallography: a series of 10 steel groups of cuboid structures. (The dissolution of crystals also provided Smithson with another analogy for his theory of natural entropy.) The third article of Smithsonian æsthetics – "A Sediment-ation of the Mind: Earth Projects" (1968) – concerned notions of time and place. Smithson praised artists such as Walter de Maria, Carl Andre, Michael Heizer, Dennis Oppenheim, Tony Smith and Douglas Huebler, rather than the more tradit-ional sculptors, such as Anthony Caro, artists who still upheld the old-fashioned ideas of beauty, Smithson claimed (RS, 85).

Science fiction literature also appealed to Robert Smithson (sci-fi was more popular in the Sixties than it had ever been, especially in the United States). The poetic elements of Smithson's art can be regarded as a continuum, which runs between the industrial wastelands he trekked to for his 'non-site' sculptures and the bleak, alien worlds of Robert Heinlein, Phillip K. Dick, Frank Herbert and Arthur C. Clarke; between chaos theory and New Physics and the exploration of science in post-modern science fiction; between the forms of crystals and Minimal sculptures, and so on.

Robert Smithson's glorification of desolate post-industrial, post-civilized sites was echoed in the speculative texts of writers who evoked post-apocalyptic worlds. J.G. Ballard, for example, wrote of post-technological deserts and decrepid town-scapes (in *The Drought*, *Vermilion Sands*, *High-Rise* and *Low-Flying Aircraft*). And Brian Aldiss had a novel entitled *Earthworks*, a disaster scenario based on a shortage of soil around the world.

In the essay "Tour of the Monuments of Passaic" (which's itself a sci-fi sort of title), Robert Smithson discussed

great pipes, sand boxes, bridges with wooden sidewalks, all standing for the irreversibility of eternity. Under the dead light of the Passaic afternoon, the desert becomes a land of infinite disintegration and forgetfulness. (RS, 56)

This sort of imagery is echoed in William

Burroughs, J.G. Ballard, Tom Disch and other speculative fiction writers.

Carl Andre, Walter de Maria, Michael Heizer, Dennis Oppenheim and Tony Smith were for Robert Smithson 'the more compelling artists today, who were concerned with 'Place' or 'Site''.[1] Smithson, like Andre, was impressed by Smith's vision of the mysterious aspects of a dark unfinished road; Smithson called Smith 'the agent of endlessness'. Smith's æsthetic became part of Smithson's view of art as a complete 'site', not simply an æsthetic of sculptural objects.

Robert Smithson was not inspired by ancient religious sculpture, by burial mounds for example, so much as by decayed industrial sites. He visited some in the mid-1960s that were 'in some way disrupted or pulverized'. He said he was looking for a 'denaturalization rather than built up scenic beauty.'[2] Smithson explained he was concerned, like many land (and contemporary) artists with the thing in itself, not its image, its effect, its critical significance:

I am for an art that takes into account the direct effect of the elements as they exist from day to day apart from representation. (RS, 133)

Robert Smithson's theory of the 'non-site' was based on 'absence, a very ponderous, weighty absence'.[3] Smithson's proposal was for a theory of an interplay between absence and presence, in which the 'non-site' and 'site' are both interacting. In the 'non-site' work, presence and absence exist simultaneously.

The land or ground from the Site is placed in the art (Non-Site) rather than the art is placed on the ground. The Non-Site is a container within another container – the room [Smithson said]. (RS, 115).

In another place, Robert Smithson wrote:

In a sense my nonsites are rooms within rooms. Recovery from the outer fringes brings one back to the central point... The scale between indoors and outdoors, and how the two are impossible to bridge... What you are really confronted with in a non-site is the absence of the site. It is a contraction rather than an expansion of scale. One is confronted with a very ponderous, weighty absence... There is this dialectic between inner and outer, closed and open, center and peripheral.[4]

Robert Smithson proposed a schema for 'non-site' art in his essay "Dialectic of Site and Non-Site". It looked like this:

Site	Non-Site
1. Open limits	Closed limits
2. A series of points	An array of Matter
3. Outer coordinates	Inner coordinates
4. Subtraction	Addition
5. Indeterminate certainty	Determinate uncertainty
6. Scattered information	Contained information
7. Reflection	Mirror
8. Edge	Center
9. Some place (physical)	No place (abstract)
10. Many	One (RS, 115)

Robert Smithson's 'non-site' works were permanent works, for display in a gallery. *Mirror Displacements* (1968), for instance, consisted of placing some mirrors in different settings and photographing them before moving them someplace else (*Mirror Displacements* was documented in Smithson's *Artforum* article "Incidents of Mirror Travel in the Yucatan"). Sometimes Smithson placed soil on top of the mirrors, to dirty them up, to sabotage 'the perfect reflections of the sky'. Smithson liked dirt, gravel, sand, sludge and sediment – substances that were indeterminate, malleable. Land and Conceptual artists often sabotaged the clinical nature of much of art – putting soil (Walter de Maria) or horses (Jannis Kounellis) in the pristine, white gallery space (some of the Minimal artists, such as Robert Morris, would also venture into this Postminimal territory).

Robert Smithson's other projects of this period

included putting raw, natural materials into Minimalist spaces, creating a tension or dialectic between 'site and non-site', as he called it. *Ziggurat Mirror* was completed by the use of mirrors. The sculpture needed the mirrors to work properly. Employing the mirrors to create repetition, Smithson drew attention to the delimited nature of the sculpture: with the correct use of mirrors, an artwork could be extended infinitely. Endless repetition was central to Minimal and 1960s art (Andy Warhol, Sol LeWitt, Carl Andre, Robert Morris, Donald Judd, Frank Stella and others took a simple unit and endlessly repeated it).

Before he made his most famous work *Spiral Jetty*, Robert Smithson had already been considering the scientific notions of rotation and equilibrium. *Gyrostasis* (1968) was a 75 x 57 x 40 inch painted steel structure based on the spiral form. Smithson explained that *Gyrostasis*, as the title implied, was about how rotating bodies maintain their equilibrium.

> The work is a standing triangulated spiral. When I made the sculpture I was thinking of mapping procedures that refer to the planet Earth. (RS, 37)

Robert Smithson's *Spiral Jetty* is a 'monumental' earthwork, though the use of the spiral motif has connotations with the ancient symbols of eternity, immortality, cycles, and the Goddess.[5] Of his *Spiral Jetty*, Smithson wrote:

> As I looked at the site, it reverberated out to the horizons only to suggest an immobile cyclone while flickering light made the entire landscape appear to quake. A dormant earthquake spread into an immense roundness. From that gyrating space emerged the possibility of the Spiral Jetty. No idea, no concepts, no systems, no structures, no abstractions could hold themselves together in the actuality of that phenomenological evidence.[6]

Robert Smithson was impressed by the charact-

eristics of the Great Salt Lake location – the pinkish mud, the faintly violet water surrounded by limestone hills, and the 'crushing light' of the sun. He had been reading about salt lakes in Bolivia, where bacteria turned the water red to match the color of the flamingos. Smithson found out that the Utah salt lakes were red and pink due to algæ and mineral waste. Smithson and his wife – Nancy Holt – surveyed the area and chose a lake at Rozel Point in Utah, which had a number of cracks in the mud under the shallow water. Smithson started construction in April, 1970, excavating 6,650 tons. *Spiral Jetty* was built from rocks, water, mud and precipitated salt crystals. It was 1,500 ft long and 15 ft wide. Smithson was aided financially by Virginia Dwan and the Ace Gallery of Vancouver. As with many other projects of the time, a film was made of the construction of *Spiral Jetty*. Smithson related the work to spiral nebulæ, to salt crystals and microscopic organisms. Smithson thought in terms of eons of time, and mused on how entropy would overtake the site.[7]

Robert Smithson used one of the primary forms of land art, the circle, in many works, combining it with ideas taken from science (such as *Gyrostasis*, which, said Smithson, 'refers to a branch of physics that deals with rotating bodies' [ib., 37]). Smithson was not adverse to religious feelings about art: when he visited the site of his *Spiral Jetty*, in the Utah salt flats, he experienced a feeling of 'a rotary that enclosed itself in an immense roundness' (ib., 111). The two elements – rational, mathematical, scientific precision and intuitive, emotional, religious feeling – are two of the chief characteristics of land art. On the one hand, land artists talked about measurements, practical details, materials, maps and spatial data. On the other hand, they hinted at religious awe, spiritual feelings, prehistoric art and the influx of the numinous into modern art.

Robert Smithson also identified his *Spiral Jetty* with a mythic whirlpool that sprang up from a tunnel connected to the Pacific Ocean. His *Spiral Jetty* was an 'immobile cyclone', it spiralled inwards from the outside: the track leaves the shore and twists round and round to the centre. *Spiral Jetty* was also linked with notions of decay in nature. In "A Sedimentation of the Mind: Earth Projects", Smithson had written '[e]very object, if it is art, is charged with the rush of time, even though it is static' (RS, 90). Ironically, Smithson's *Spiral Jetty* was itself subject to natural entropy: the water level rose and *Spiral Jetty* was submerged under water. It was ironic too that Smithson died in a plane crash while he was flying over and inspecting a site in Texas. (Smithson's death at a young age may be much more of a loss to the art world than the early deaths of Piero Manzoni, Yves Klein, or Jean-Michel Basquiat).

Robert Smithson's 1971 *Broken Circle* was another large earthwork, like *Spiral Jetty,* using circular motifs that was set adjacent to the land and extended out into a lake. Smithson chose a quarry site near Emmen, Holland. Again, the site had an interesting geological aspect, which was in keeping with Smithson's love of rocks and minerals. Glacial action had formed unusual layers of soil. Unlike *Spiral Jetty*, which is submerged for part of the year, *Broken Circle* remains pretty much the same (it is maintained by local funds). It is a 140 foot circle comprising one half of soil and one half of water, with a twelve foot wide canal cutting around the earth section of the circle, forming a semi-circle. At the centre of *Broken Circle* is a very large glacial boulder. It was supposedly one of the largest in the Netherlands. Significantly, Smithson allowed nothing at the centre of *Spiral Jetty*: the spectator walked round the inward-turning spiral to find nothing. Smithson was exasperated by the prehistoric stone at the centre of his *Broken Circle*, but he let this 'accidental center' stay there, commenting 'it became a dark spot of exasperation, a geological gangrene on the sandy expanse'.[8] Smithson also produced works by pouring stuff down slopes: *Glue Pour* (1970) the contents of a drum or glue were poured down the slope in a quarry. *Ashphalt Run-down* (1969) did the same thing on a slightly larger scale.

Robert Smithson's last major work, before his untimely death in 1973, was *Amarillo Ramp* (1973), one of many land artworks conceived as an observation structure. Nancy Holt worked with one of the major American sculptors of the era, Richard Serra, to complete Smithson's plans. *Amarillo Ramp,* 15 miles North-West of Amarillo in the Texas Panhandle, is a huge inclined ramp or road, made from quarried rocks. The summit of *Amarillo Ramp* is a viewing point.[9]

Taken together, Robert Smithson's three large-scale earthworks, *Spiral Jetty, Broken Circle* and *Amarillo Ramp,* all revolve around circular or spiral motifs, a sense of temporality, of decay and transience, each uses primitive, mythic forms and gestures in a monumental manner. Two of them are set in wilderness spaces, where the marks of humanity are at their weakest. Yet each earthwork of course speaks acutely of the mark of humanity upon the Earth, and a very particular kind of mark: that of late 20th century American art-making.

MICHAEL HEIZER

Michael Heizer (b. 1944) has become known as the land artist who made some of land art's biggest artworks, along with Christo and Robert Smithson.[1] For some (such as feminist and left-liberal detractors), this kind of land art is among the most arrogant, phallic and patriarchal of postwar and contemporary production.[2] In *Double Negative* (1969-70), Heizer's most famous work, he carved two gigantic chunks out of the earth. For nay-sayers, Heizer's intervention was a gigantic 'violation' of the planet, in ecological or green terms.[3] According to the artist, *Double Negative* was 'the smallest piece I've done in relation to the size of the site'.[4] 240,000 tons of soil were excavated from the Mormon Mesa site in Nevada with bulldozers. The cuts are a kind of ramp, sloping down 50 feet through the cliff of the canyon; there's a corresponding cut in a nearby part of the canyon. The spectator can walk down the slopes. The overall dimensions of *Double Negative* are 1,500 x 42 feet. Heizer is very much concerned with *scale*, as well as other formal characteristics of a work. He has said that '[m]an will never really create anything large in relation to the world'.[5]

Michael Heizer's *Double Negative* is a widely celebrated example of land art – it vies with Robert Smithson's *Spiral Jetty* as the most famous example of land art. The photographs of it have been reproduced in many art history books. *Double Negative* appeals to 1960s culture's notions of Zen Buddhism, Existentialism, negativity and empti-ness (and nowadays, post-New Age landscape art). The point about *Double Negative* was its sense of symmetry and relationship, the one cut reflecting the other across the Nevada canyon. Some viewers saw Heizer's enterprise as combining the subliminity and grandeur of Abstract Expression-ism with the emblematic forms of Minimalism. American earthworks art rejuvenated the myth of the sublime West.[6] Mary Miss was not convinced.

When she looked at the work of Michael Heizer or Robert Smithson, 'there's always been an aspect which impedes my relating to it... It's like a mark on the earth' (1981, 6-7).

With his father, Michael Heizer went on archæo-logical digs as a child. He started out with the ambition to be a painter (like so many artists), which he studied in San Francisco. His first earth-work was made in 1967. He accompanied Robert Smithson on geological expeditions. Heizer collab-orated with Smithson and Nancy Holt in 1968 on a Super-8 film, *Mono-Lake*. (Heizer had invited Holt and Smithson to his parents' house at Lake Tahoe).

Michael Heizer's *Complex One* (1972) was a huge bunker-like mass of earth built with the aid of two assistants in Nevada. It was 23.5 feet high and 140 feet long. Each end of the hill had a cut-off triangle of reinforced concrete which resembled giant book-ends. Suspended above the work were cantilevered concrete beams.

> *Complex One* is a magnificent spectacle. Even its minatory look, suggesting a bunker, seems proper to the site – the edge of the Nevada nuclear proving-ground.

remarked Robert Hughes.[7] The forms Heizer employed in *Complex One* (and in the sequels he built) were Minimal. *Complex One* was a pretty large piece of art, as was *Double Negative*, but Heizer's *Effigy Tumuli* (1983) was even bigger, stretching over an area a mile by a mile and a half.

Michael Heizer's other works include gouging huge holes in the ground and putting great chunks of rock in them, like dinosaur nests in the desert. *Nine Nevada Depressions* (1968) comprised 5 cuts in the Blackrock desert, each one 12 feet long in an area 50 by 50 feet. *Munich Depression* (1969) was another cut, a line 15 feet deep. Heizer's motorbike earthwork, made at Mono Lake, was entitled *Circular Surface Displacement*.

DENNIS OPPENHEIM

One of the most interesting of American Conceptual and land artists is Dennis Oppenheim (1938-2011), an artist who has produced an challenging and inspiring range of work.[1] Oppenheim's land art was an extension of his Conceptual art and his sculpture (or his Conceptual artworks were re-enacted in the landscape). Oppenheim often employed Minimal principles. Reducing a work down to geometric forms was one of Oppenheim's characteristics: his favoured device was the circle (unusually among most of the Minimalists).

A typical land art piece by Dennis Oppenheim was 1968's *Annual Rings*, a group of concentric circles that straddled the border between Canada and North America. It was constructed with snow. One of the recurring motifs in Oppenheim's art was the border zone, margins and thresholds in time and space. Oppenheim 'drew' a number of snow works with a snowmobile (much as Walter de Maria and Michael Heizer 'drew' in the desert with vehicles): *One Hour Run* (1968) was a continuous track made in the snow in Maine. For *Time Line*, a work which explored the different time zones, two tracks (side by side) were carved in the snow between Fort Kent, Maine and Clair, New Brunswick, Canada, in 1968. Oppenheim's *Negative Board* (1968) was a dark cut in the snow and ice in Maine.

Mountain. Accumulation Cut (1969) was made at Cornell University: a 100 foot long cut in the ice, running away from a waterfall. Dennis Oppenheim took the floor outline of gallery 4 of the Andrew Dickson White Museum of Art (also at Cornell), and sketched it into the snow and ice outside in 1969. Another *Gallery Transplant*, as Oppenheim called them (also created in 1969), transferred the floor plan of a gallery in Amsterdam's Stedelijk Museum to a snowy hillside in New Jersey.

1973's *Whirlpool Eye of Storm* was an ephemeral piece of land art in the Hans Haacke vein: a jet trail created in the sky by a plane flying above the desert at El Mirage Dry Lake in California. *Directed Seeding* (1969) parodied Action Painting by harvesting a wheat field (Pollock goes rural). Dennis Oppenheim cut a giant version of the Minimalists' 'X' in a field in the Netherlands in *Cancelled Crop* (1969), and kept the grain, as if he were preventing the material he'd cultivated for his art from becoming the raw material for other (illusionistic) art: 'isolating this grain from further processing becomes like stopping raw pigment from becoming an illusionistic force on canvas'.[2] Another 'X' was laid onto the landscape at El Mirage Dry Lake out of asphalt primer (covering an area 610 yards square), entitled *Relocated Burial Ground* (1978). (The 'X' shape, as Lucy Lippard noted, was a favourite motif with male land artists – Chris Burden, Richard Long and Robert Smithson also created 'Xs' – as it was with Minimalists like Ronald Bladen).[3]

Many of Dennis Oppenheim's artworks are conceptual pieces in the tradition of Sixties Conceptual art. That is, many are works made to be exhibited in galleries, on walls. They comprise photographs, drawings and maps, with Oppenheim's typewritten captions and explanations: *Three Downward Blows* (1977), *Salt Flat* (1969), *Boundary Split* (1968), and *Negative Board* (1968). Maps were central to Oppenheim's art.[4] One of Oppenheim's specialities was to impose human-made geometries, symbols and ideas onto the landscape: to transpose map contours, for instance, or the rings of a tree trunk onto snow (in *Annual Rings*), or the International Date Line in snow (*Time Pocket*). Robert Smithson remarked that Oppenheim was 'transforming a terrestrial site into a map'.[5] Generally, Oppenheim tended to enlarge symbols or ideas or images, and recreate them on a colossal scale in the landscape.

In *Time Pocket* (1968), Dennis Oppenheim 'drew' the International Date Line with a diesel-powered skidder in snow in Maine. In *Boundary Split* (1968), Oppenheim carved lines perpendicular to the Time Boundary between Canada and the U.S.A. *Star Skid* (1977) was Oppenheim's proposal for a series of concrete and glass stars that would look from the air as if they had landed on Earth and skidded to a halt.

Dennis Oppenheim created a 'salt flat' in New York City, with a thousand pounds of salt in *Salt Flat* (1969). The rectangle of salt was recreated in the sea in the Bahamas, and in the Salt Lake Desert. In *Directed Harvest* (1969), Oppenheim carved up fields of crops.6 Oppenheim set off underground explosions in *Three Downward Blows (Knuckle Marks)* in Montana in 1977. For *Ground Mutations – Shoe Prints* (1969), Oppenheim created shoe print works over the course of three Winter months (by wearing shoes with a 1/4 inch groove cut in the sole and heel): 'I was connecting the patterns of thousands of individuals... My thoughts were filled with marching diagrams'.

Speaking in 1970, Dennis Oppenheim remarked that art was now 'more concerned with the location of material and with speculation' (i.e., locations or ideas). Now, art was meant to be visited (location) or 'abstracted from a photograph' (conceptualized).7 Oppenheim moved towards a kind of art that would be discovered or visited by the spectator, rather than 'made' in the old, traditional manner (this was part of the 'dematerialization' of the art object in Sixties art). Oppenheim moved away from the idea of the special, unique art object (still valorized by Minimal sculptors), towards found objects, and utilizing existing sites (a move towards Postminimalism, going beyond Minimalism).

Dennis Oppenheim was replacing objects with locations. The *Site Markers* series (1967) comprised posts in locations which were documented with texts, maps and photos. The maps and photos explained where the posts were situated, so that the location, rather than the object, became the centre of the piece. As Oppenheim pointed out, the *Site Markers* works were intended to be about the sites themselves, rather than the manipulation or replication of an object: 'beginning with the site-markers started in a sense a journey: art is travel' (ibid.).

One of Dennis Oppenheim's more Conceptual pieces (*Sound Enclosed Land Area*, 1969) comprised four tape recorders buried in cages in Paris enclosing an area 500 by 800 yards. Each machine played a tape loop which had voice repeating its position (North, South, East or West). *Contour Lines Scribed in Swamp Grass* (1968) transposed contour lines on a map in two different locations (a swamp and a mountain). The use of aluminium filings poured onto grass in concentric circles recalled Richard Long's stone circles.

The contours of Dennis Oppenheim's own thumbprints were the basis for *Identity Stretch* (1970-75), where a truck sprayed white paint on the ground, using the thumb-print (which Oppenheim had elongated) as a guide, within a grid. In 1970 Oppenheim created a performance piece, entitled *Parallel Stress*, made between a collapsed concrete pier and a wall at Manhattan and Brooklyn bridges. Oppenheim stretched his body between the wall and the pier, echoing the New York bridges nearby. The same body position was recreated at an abandoned sump in Long Island.

In later works, Dennis Oppenheim moved into Jean Tinguely mode, constructing whole rooms full of post-industrial, multi-media structures which were part-Conceptual, part-assemblage, part-kinetic and part-installation. In the *Fireworks* series of these sculptures, Oppenheim built sculptures from butane gas, rockets, flares, ramps, and metal supports, creating fires, explosions, flying sparks and smoke (as in *Launching Structure No. 2: An Armature For Projection*, 1982, Bonlow Gallery, New York).

JAMES TURRELL

James Turrell's *Roden Crater Project* – 'sky-spaces', tunnels, observatories and chambers in an extinct volcano near Flagstaff, Arizona – is one of the biggest works of land and environmental art. Begun in 1974, it was funded by many different sources and administered by the Skystone Foundation.[1] The first stage of Turrell's on-going *Roden Crater* project involved bull-dozing 200,000 cubic yards of earth from the volcano's rim, 'so as to shape the sky'. Turrell (b. 1943) planned tunnels, pools and viewing chambers at *Roden Crater*. Clouds were projected onto the floor during the day in some of the spaces at *Roden Crater*, and at night the spaces were linked to the procession of the equinoxes. Celestial events were the basis of many of the spaces that Turrell planned to construct at *Roden Crater*. The full moons, solstices, equinoxes, the movement of the sun, or just being able to view the stars and some planets. The connection with the heavens was important for Turrell: most of his works have openings onto the sky, and the relationship with the sky is the centre-piece of the works. In short, it's important for Turrell to see the stars.

The *Roden Crater* work was about the relation-ship between the viewer and the elements, in particular the sky, celestial events, and light. The environment was a volcano, relating to geological time.

> The work I do intensifies the experience of light by isolating it and occluding all other light. Each space essentially looks to a different portion of sky and accepts a limited number of events. [Turrell explained] (1995, 67)

Thus, each space at *Roden Crater* was designed to highlight some celestial event. The subject of some spaces was the vaulting of the sky, and the curvature of the Earth. Some were about daily events, such as sunrises and sunsets, or the movement of the stars.

The North section of *Roden Crater* is about looking North, the North Star, the rotation of the Earth, changing light, and includes a seat for viewing Polaris. The Eastern space is for witnessing sunrise, and a 'skyspace' overhead. *Bath Space* projects a magnified image of the sky above onto a white sand floor, using a water bath above a large sphere as a lens. The *Sun and Moon Room* was constructed around the furthest South moonset, the furthest North sunrise and the Summer solstice. *Tso Kiva* is a hemispherical space in the centre of the volcano, for observing light, shadows, shapes and the horizon. The *South Space* is an astronomical observatory and star chart. The *West Space*, as one would expect, is for the sunset, and the 'twilight arch', the projection of the Earth's shadow into the atmosphere at nightfall.

The creative goal, as James Turrell saw it, was not to impose his own vision or æsthetics on the visitor to *Riden Crater* or his other skyspaces, but to encourage the spectator to experience things for themselves. Turrell wanted to create the situation or environment in which the observer could have their own experience. The aims were common in art of the 1960s and 1970s: Minimal art also aimed for similar sorts of new relationships between the art object and the spectator. As Turrell said in 1987, the goal was not to turn an experience into art, but 'to set up a situation to which I take you and let you see. It becomes your experience... not taking from nature as much as placing you in contact with it'.[2] Turrell regarded his art as a 'seeing aid', in order to show the observer some-thing that was already there but that they might not have noticed. Turrell said he was influenced by painters such as Mark Rothko, Claude Monet and Paul Cézanne, who explored light.

The fundamental material in James Turrell's art was not the usual stuff of land art, or sculpture, or Minimal art, but light itself. Although Turrell was reshaping a vast hunk of earth – a volcano, no less – he was actually working something as weightless and apparently insubstantial as light.

He called it 'light in the space itself'. That is, he needed the space in which light could be experienced. Like Dan Flavin and Robert Irwin, Turrell wanted to use light as a thing-in-itself, which had presence, a life of its own even, just as the sculptor used a physical object which had presence. The way that Turrell achieved this, he said, was by setting limits on the space in which light manifested itself: 'I give light thingness by putting limits on it in a formal manner. I do not create an object, only objectified perception' (1995, 65).

What James Turrell was attempting was to create or define new spaces in which spectators could perceive the subject (and simultaneously the object) of his works – which was light itself (as well as celestial events). It was important also for Turrell that the viewer was able to enter those spaces physically, not virtually, not at one or two removes. It was an art therefore, that was not trying to create illusions or artificial scenarios or a record of the artwork. Turrell called it 'non-vicarious seeing':

The subject of my work is your nonvicarious seeing. You are not looking at a record of my seeing. (1995, 64).

James Turrell wanted to place the viewer right into the artwork, to have them able to walk into and around the work, and to have an experience of the piece for themselves.

Many of James Turrell's artworks were about working with not just light, but with the sky. The archetypal Turrell space was an enclosed area (a 'skyspace') which had an opening above onto the sky. Turrell spoke of the vaulting of the sky, how the sky looked when the viewer was standing up, or sitting down, or lying down. As the *Tibetan Book of the Dead* puts it:

O nobly-born, when thy body and mind were separating, thou must have experienced a glimpse of the Pure Truth, subtle, sparkling, bright, dazzling, glorious, and radiantly

awesome, in appearance like a mirage moving across a landscape in spring-time in one continuous stream of vibrations. (1957)

Some of James Turrell's 'skyspaces' – indoor rooms or spaces which are open to the sky above, and the opening is often quite large, so the rooms appear like courtyards – include *Spaces That Sees* (1992) in Jerusalem, *Heavy Water* (1992, Poitier) and *Rayzor* (1991, London). The latter's essentially an empty blue room (or it seems so at first, until the viewer realizes that the room *is* full of something: light). The skyspaces were designed along Minimal lines: very sparse furnishings, monochrome walls, floors and ceilings, and no interior decoration. The veils, scrims, false walls and ceilings were all crafted like Minimal sculptures – smooth, sleek, unadorned and unfussy.

James Turrell has also constructed pools of water which combine water and light: in these works, part-swimming pool, part-artwork, at *Roden Crater*, and in Poitier, France, the viewer is invited to dive under the water to reach a space beyond which's open to the sky. The historian of religions Mircea Eliade reckoned that the sky was the first symbol of transcendence, and remains the primary emblem of the sacred, of spirituality, flight, ascension and revelation. The sky is heaven, where the gods live.

I believe, personally, that it is through consideration of the sky's immensity that man is led to a revelation of transcendence, of the sacred.[3]

James Turrell emphasized the spiritual aspects of light in his land art:

I am interested in light because of my interest in our spiritual nature and the things that empower us. My art deals with light itself, the bearer of revelation, but as revelation itself. (1995, 64)

The kind of effect that James Turrell was after in his light sculptures he compared to staring into a fire, a kind of meditation or day-dreaming (before television there was the fire for staring at – was it Jan Dibbets or Joseph Kosuth who placed a fire inside a TV set in a gallery? In the 1973 film *Day For Night,* François Truffaut remarks that before TV there was the fireplace). Turrell encouraged the viewer to sit or lie down in his installations and contemplate light itself, and the effects of light in a particular space. Thus, the spaces that Turrell constructed were furnished with viewing platforms, or benches, or places to lie down and look up at the sky. Situating the spectator in relation to the subject of the artwork (light itself) was Turrell's goal. (Turrell skyspaces have affinities with Op Art and those Minimal artists who explored the limits of visual perception, like Ad Reinhardt or Brice Marden).

As well as drifting off by looking at a fire, James Turrell also often spoke of the experience of flying in a plane and rising into new zones of light, different kinds of light. Turrell evoked the curvature of the Earth when seen from a plane (and how, at a certain height above the Earth, between 600 and 3,000 feet, the Earth seems to curve the wrong way). The Roden volcano was chosen partly because of its relation at that particular place in the Painted Desert to the curvature of the Earth. The low mound of the volcano and its relation to the curvature of the Earth and the sky above had the right mixture of components that Turrell was seeking.

NANCY HOLT

Nancy Holt (b. 1938) worked with Robert Smithson on his non-site projects, including the famous *Spiral Jetty* and *Amarillo Ramp* (Holt had married Smithson in 1963). Holt's art, with its large, heavy landscaping gestures (such as her *Dark Star Park*), is comparable in scope, intent and principles with the male land artists (i.e., it's not only the guys who get to churn up the earth with diggers and trucks). The globes and pools of water in *Dark Star Park*, though, are traditional 'feminine' volumes, but here they're given a new, monumental turn.

Nancy Holt's art, like James Turrell's, concerns the movements of the heavens. Her sculptures focus the viewer on the motions of the earth, moon, sun and stars. It's an art that's always constructing conceptual and physical links between the surface of the Earth and the distant stars. Holt's art is concerned with the notion of time, in particular with geological time, the relation between time and the Earth. Slow-moving time, but time with the force of shifting continents or birthing new islands. Holt was impressed by the desert when she visited it in the late 1960s with Robert Smithson and Michael Heizer.

> Time is not just a mental concept or a mathematical abstraction in the desert. The rocks in the distance are ageless; they have been deposited in layers over hundreds of thousands of years. Time takes on a physical presence.[1]

Nancy Holt has said she was interested in 'conjuring up a sense of time that is longer than the built-in obsolescence we have all around us' (a reference to the intense commodification of the 1960s – especially prevalent in the America of the 1960s). Hence she utilized durable materials, such as steel and rocks. Using enduring materials is not about vanity (wanting one's works to last forever), but rather because Holt aimed to create a sense of time that extends beyond the human lifespan.[2] While many Minimal artists developed into Postminimal and Process artists, delighting in materials with a built-in obsolescence or a fleeting temporality, Holt wanted to utilize materials that would endure, as rocks or stars do.

While working on Robert Smithson's enormous *Amarillo Ramp* after his death in a plane crash, Nancy Holt developed the idea for the gigantic *Sun Tunnels*, her signature work. It comprised 18 foot long concrete pipes that were 9 feet high, with many holes punched in the side, to allow light to enter.[3] Holt searched for a suitable site – a desert floor surrounded by low hills (being open to the heavens was a prime consideration). The site she eventually selected (and bought) was in the Great Basin Desert of Utah. *Sun Tunnels* (which was completed by 1976) had holes in the side of each concrete tube 7, 8, 9 and 10 inches diameter, which corresponded with star constellations (Capricorn, Draco, Columba and Perseus), as with *Hydra's Head*. The pipes were set about 32° North and South of true East and West, aligned with the rising and setting of the sun at the Summer and Winter solstices. During the day the sun shines into the sculpture and creates points of light on the bottom of the tunnels that move as the sun moves. The moon also shines through the holes by night.

Sun Tunnels linked the movements of celestial objects and the viewer on Earth. It is truly celestial art, as archaic in its goals as an early Renaissance fresco which paints spiky star-shapes on a blue background to suggest the heavens, or the stone observatories of ancient peoples. Nancy Holt recalled that she had had the idea for *Sun Tunnels* while being out in the desert and watching the sun rising and setting. The flat desert area evoked 'a sense of being on this planet, rotating in space, in universal time' (1977). *Sun Tunnels* is a deliberately cosmological piece of land art, employing a simple Minimal geometric volume, the cylinder. 'I wanted to bring the vast space desert back to human scale', Holt commented (1977).[4]

Nancy Holt's *Hydra's Head* (1975) also concerned the relation between the heavens and earth, between people and stars. Next to the Niagara River at Art Park, Lewiston, New York, Holt sank six concrete tubes into the ground. Each 3 ft pipe was filled with water, so they formed circular mirrors flush with the ground (all that could be seen of the pipes was the circular disc at the end, rather like Walter de Maria's *Vertical Earth Kilometer*).[5] *Hydra's Head* combined the presence and noise of the rushing Niagara River nearby with the reflections of the sky, stars and moon. Holt's concrete pipe sculptures used the prime symbol of change and all things cosmic, the circle. The *Sun Tunnels* were like enormous telescopes or astrolabes (their scale was a crucial component in their make-up), while *Hydra's Head* evoked six fallen stars, the circles of water reflecting the sky and stars. In Holt's sculpture, light was the linking element – the sky reflected in mirror-like water, or light shining through apertures.

Nancy Holt's romantic evocations of stellar, cosmological themes in concrete and soil flourished again with *Stone Enclosure: Rock Rings* (1977-78), constructed at Western Washington University Bellingham. Holt's *Stone Enclosure* directly recalled, even emulated, prehistoric stone circles, in particular Stonehenge. *Stone Enclosure* makes the connections with ancient astronomy and stone circle building explicit, not slyly implied, as in much of land art. Holt was clear that she was dealing with the ancient astronomical realities of weather, seasons, cycles, stars and time.

Nancy Holt's *Annual Ring* (1980-81), installed at Saginaw, Michigan, was a large dome of steel bars, 14 feet in diameter, with Holt's customary circular holes, recalling an astronomer's observatory, and a children's climbing apparatus in a play area. Another work, *30 Below* (1980), a tower with arches facing the points of the compass, was positioned around the North Star. The still point in the heavens, the Pole Star, was also one of the keys to *Stone Enclosure*, which, Holt said, related to a true North, a dead centre.[6] The Pole Star was a favourite with land artists who wanted to deal with celestial events.

ALICE AYCOCK

Alice Aycock (b. 1946) is far less 'Minimal' than Nancy Holt or Michael Heizer, or most other land artists. That's how it seems at first, but a closer contemplation of Aycock's art reveals many Minimal aspects (in the materials, and the forms, and the insistence on the object). Aycock's installations and artworks are much more ambiguous and deliberately problematic than, say, Holt's or Carl Andre's works. Indeed, Aycock actively encouraged disquiet, unease, and even fear in the responses she was looking for with her sculptures. Unlike many artists, Aycock was definitely much concerned with the spectators' reaction to her art, and strove to create particular feelings in her viewers.

Alice Aycock's works had titles such as *The Machine That Makes the World* (1979), *A Theory of Universal Causality* (1983) and *How to Catch and Manufacture Ghosts* (1979). No *'Untitled'* for Alice Aycock: she liked a long, elaborate (some would say pretentious) title for a work. Aycock's sculpture explored the rationality of machines and techno-logy, and the irrationality of ghosts and magic (H. Risatti, 37). One might also say the irrationality of machines, the ghosts in machines, the machine as mysterious force, machines with their own agency.

Many of Alice Aycock's installations and sculpt-ures involve underground spaces, subterranean passages and rooms, and lightless corridors. In 1972 she constructed a series of underground spaces in *Low Building Made with Dirt Roof (For Mary)* in Pennsylvania. The spectator entered the 20 by 12 foot work through a doorway thirty inches high. The work was experienced by crawling through it. Aycock's intention was to evoke an experience of claustrophia, of being in a cellar. (While Aycock's sculptures might disturb some people, and others wouldn't – or couldn't – crawl through them, others, such as young children, might love them and treat them as another play area. Indeed, the design of some contemporary

playgrounds often includes tunnels or pipes).

Alice Aycock's 1972 *Maze* had direct parallels with the observatories and labyrinths of Robert Morris, Nancy Holt, Julia Barton and Michael Dan Archer (to name a few of the many land artists who have made mazes – even Donald Judd constructed an adobe maze at Marfa). The *Maze* Aycock built consisted of five concentric wooden rings, each six feet high, forming a 12-sided labyrinth. Essentially it was a fence maze, the kind that can be seen at theme parks, zoos and country houses. However, Aycock's New Kingston, Pennsylvania *Maze* is intended to be a labyrinth of the ancient (Cretan) type: a structure in which one is meant to get lost. Aycock stated that she wanted 'to create a moment of absolute panic – when the only thing that mattered was to get out.'[1] Aycock's intentions, then, are quite different from, say, Nancy Holt's, who wishes to infuse a sense of celestial contemplation, or Carl Andre's, who wants viewers to consider the arrangements of metal tiles on the floor. Aycock wants viewers to be confused, even frightened, by her subterranean passage and maze. Aycock did not want the viewer to be able to get out of her labyrinth easily.[2] Aycock said the maze was not thought of as a whole (as a pattern viewed safely from above), but as a 'sequence of body/ eye movements from position to position' (1975).

Alice Aycock has spoken of the relations between her art and her own childhood dreams and fears. Her works recreate disturbing moments from her childhood, such as when she was trapped in a revolving barrel at an amusement park. Aycock's works deal with such moments of fear, confusion, strangeness and risk. Aycock is thus unusual among 1960s and 1970s artists in that she actively encouraged a biographical basis for, or interpretation of, her work. While many Minimal artists preferred to erase many of the marks of the artist in the work, Aycock was happy to have connections made between her own life and her sculpture.

1974's *Walled-Trench/ Earth Platform/ Center*

Pit was a series of three concentric walls Alice Aycock built from concrete blocks. A platform of earth was made between the inner two walls: it was possible for visitors to jump onto this platform over the outer pit. Only when the spectator is standing on the inner platform does another aspect of *Walled-Trench/ Earth Platform/ Center Pit* become visible: a tunnel which leads into a dark inner chamber.

Alice Aycock's *A Simple Network of Underground Walls and Tunnels* (1975) was made in a corn field at Far Hills, New Jersey. It consisted of 6 square wells in two rows of three excavated out of a 20 by 50 foot area. Two of the wells had 7 foot ladders that enabled the spectator to climb down and explore the dark connecting tunnels. Some of the wells were capped, others were open. The effect was a series of spaces that recalled 'ominous historical precedents, caves, catacombs, dungeons and beehive tombs', wrote Roberta Smith (1975, 68). As well as caves and dungeons, the subterranean spaces might also evoke passage graves, or the entrances to burial mounds, or ritual *fogous* (found in Cornwall). It might have a positive aspect – the womb, or Plato's cave, or somewhere to shelter, or rebirth from the Earth, or soil and growth – or a negative one: death, coffins and graves, burial, claustrophobia, entrapment, a descent with no return.

The fear and fantasy elements in Alice Aycock's land and site work found a new level of ambiguity in her 1976 *Circular Building with Narrow Ledge for Walking*. Again, the spectator was invited to explore this artwork physically (and psychologically). *Circular Building with Narrow Ledge for Walking* was a round structure thirteen feet high. Inside the well were three concentric ledges, only 8 inches wide. The wall went 7 feet into the ground, and was 'no more perilous or threatening than a treacherous cliff', the artist said, reassuringly.3 Again, the spectator was invited to investigate the work by climbing a ladder outside the building, then edging their way along the ledges. Indeed, the only way to fully appreciate *Circular Building with*

Narrow Ledge for Walking, as with Aycock's other works, was to experience it directly. With Aycock's bewildering and unsettling catacombs and mazes one had to move 'one's body through them', a process which also involved descending back through time and memory.4

Confronted with the subterranean passage or the *Circular Building with Narrow Ledge for Walking,* it is soon apparent to the spectator that one is not dealing simply with an art object to be admired for its formal characteristics alone (from a safe distance). Alice Aycock wants the spectator to become physically involved in the sculpture: the physical actions of climbing and scrabbling over and through the sculpture trigger an exploration of one's own physiology, psychology and memory. The physicality of the body as a tool for exploration in Aycock's works soon becomes a pretext or an inspiration for an exploration of personal psychology. Visitors are invited to risk themselves in exploring her works. Her land art offers seductive as well as potentially dangerous spaces. Aycock wants the spectator to enter, but then confronts her/ him with a door that opens onto a wall, or a tiny passage to crawl through, or a ledge over a precipice, or a pit to vault over. Such devices go straight back to childhood, to acts of dare and bravado (such as walking along a high brick wall, egged on by other children).

MARY MISS

Among Mary Miss's early works was a 'water-line', involving Miss suspending a double knot of hemp rope a hundred feet over a dry riverbed in Colorado (at Fountain Creek). Every twenty feet there were lines of rope hanging down. Miss threw fifteen foot long wooden stakes into the water at War's Island (in New York). The stakes were weighted down with rocks.

In the middle of a wood in Connecticut in 1974 Mary Miss made *Sunken Pool*: one of her more well-known pieces, it was a circular wooden structure, 10 feet tall, and filled with one foot of water in a galvanized steel interior. *Sunken Pool* was sunken because Miss set it in a hole three feet deep and twenty feet across. The spectator was invited to explore Miss's *Sunken Pool* physically (as with the site work of Michael Heizer, Alice Aycock and Robert Smithson). They could step into the water, or climb up the outer part of the wooden structure and look over the top. Like Aycock's underground caverns, Miss's *Sunken Pool* was secretive, hidden away in a dense wood, with tall wooden sides. It seemed to speak, like Aycock's works, of childhood memories and half-remembered spaces.

1978's *Perimeters/ Pavilion/ Decoys* was constructed by Mary Miss in Roslyn, New York, in a field that was part of the ground at Nassau County Museum. *Perimeters/ Pavilion/ Decoys* consisted of three wooden towers, which looked like tree houses with four platforms on stilts, two mounds of earth, and an underground space that can be accessed by a ladder. The wooden towers were not for climbing on, but for viewing (the tallest was 18 x 10 x 10 feet). The subterranean atrium was for exploring through. It was a 16 ft2 pit with a seven foot hole acting as an entrance: visitors climbed down a ladder to explore different underground spaces, some had wooden, others had soil walls. *Perimeters/ Pavilion/ Decoys* was related (by the artist) to Pueblo Indian structures, Pompeiian and Mexican courtyards, and Mesopotamian brick complexes. The site explored the physical and psychological aspects of 'inside/ outside, above/ below, light/ dark, open/ closed, nature/ artifice'.[1] Miss's works are often large, spreading over a wide area of ground. In Illinois she created a 5-acre scale work.[2]

WALTER DE MARIA

Walter de Maria (b. 1935) combined Conceptual art, Minimal art, assemblages, and land art (and moved into Postminimalism). A dramatic land art gesture was the four and a half mile-long six foot wide cut that de Maria made in the desert in Nevada with a bull-dozer.[1] After the four and a half mile bull-dozer square cut in the Earth, de Maria made a chalk drawing in the desert (he worked with Michael Heizer on some art projects, including the cuts and lines in the desert).

The ultimate example of the grandiose fusion of Conceptual art with land art (the idea and the object) must be *Vertical Earth Kilometer*. It cost $500,000. A one kilometre brass rod was sunk into the planet. Nothing can be seen of the brass rod except a brass disc on the ground, two inches in diameter. The rest of the work remains practically invisible. The making of Walter de Maria's work was perhaps far more interesting than the artwork itself (it involved plenty of people, heavy machinery, and weeks of labour). In a way, it's the ultimate art statement/ non-statement. *Vertical Earth Kilometer* neatly (extravagantly) melds two æsthetic movements prevalent in the Sixties: Conceptual art and Minimal art (there's nothing to see of this half million dollar sculpture except a two-inch brass disc).[2] In 1979 de Maria exhibited *The Broken Kilometer* (a related piece): 500 brass rods each two yards long in a New York gallery, placed in long rows on the floor.

Walter de Maria started out as a musician rather than, like many artists, as a painter or sculptor (he played drums with the Velvet Underground). One of his early ideas (1962) for an earthwork was a mile-long pair of walls that would be 12 feet high and 12 feet apart. De Maria said that 'when you walk between, you can look up and see the sky'.[3] (Bruce Nauman made corridors one of his main motifs in the 1960s, while James Turrell, Michael Asher and Robert Irwin, among others, constructed spaces like corridors).

Walter de Maria's *Earth Room* was a gallery full of dark earth made in 1968 in Munich and later in New York (*The New York Earth Room*, SoHo Gallery, 1977). Again, it was a fairly simple idea, but the carrying out involved shifting heavy material. In this case, dirt. *Earth Room* consisted of 125 tons of soil, taking up 3,600 square feet, 22 inches deep. This was a vivid (and aromatic) example of bringing the outside inside, one of land art's key projects. The contrasts were immediate, between the flat, clean, white, controlled gallery space and the 1,600 ft3 of uneven, 'dirty', dark, organic soil. Critic Roberta Smith said it was a 'shock' to see the soil taking up the interior space usually reserved for things such as furniture and people. 'The dirt carried its own absence, was somehow a living substance' (1978, 104). Although categorized as a piece of environmental art, *Earth Room* was also Conceptual and Minimal.

You can see a recreation of the *Earth Room*, and also the *Broken Kilometer*, in downtown New York City, at the DIA centres, for free. If you haven't seen them, you must go: these are very large artworks in the heart of Gotham, classic Minimal and Sixties and Seventies artworks. You don't walk around them, but view them from a single vantage point. The *Earth Room* is very impressive: it takes up the whole floor of a building.

Bed of Spikes (1969) was called 'a piece of Dadaist Sadism' by Harold Rosenberg (1972, 36). *Bed of Spikes*, an installation at the Dwan Gallery that recalled some of Lucas Samaras's S/M allusive sculptures, comprised 153 metal spikes set in five planks on the floor. (Spectators were asked to sign a release that exempted the gallery for being responsible for any accidents on viewing the installation). *Bed of Spikes* looked forward to *Lightning Field*.

One of the main critics of Minimal art, Kenneth Baker, called Walter de Maria's most famous work, the *Lightning Field,* the 'grandest Minimalist work of the 1970s' and 'the closest thing to a masterpiece to come out of Minimalism' (1988, 125-7). De Maria's first *Lightning Field* was sited

40 miles from Flagstaff in Arizona, consisting of 2-inch diameter steel poles (the same diameter as *Vertical Earth Kilometer*), 18 feet tall, 30 feet apart, in five rows of seven. The second, larger *Lightning Field* was a grid of 400 stainless steel poles, each about 20 feet high, 16 along the width, 25 along the length, set in the New Mexico desert.[4] The poles were sunk in concrete, one foot below ground, able to withstand winds of 110 mph.

The site was chosen for its flatness, isolation and lightning activity. During May-September there are about 60 days when thunder and lightning can be seen from *Lightning Field*.[5] The poles in *Lightning Field* stand alone, about 220 feet apart. Nothing remains on the ground of the work needed to put them there. The tips of the poles define a plane in space parallel to sea level: the length of each pole varied according to the contours of the landscape. The *Lightning Field* was an exact, mathematically-precise human site laid onto nature, where the poles are tiny mirrors which mark out and calibrate the landscape. The site looks like a scientific or industrial project – like a radio telescope site, say, or a technological experiment, or a military communications centre, while the poles themselves recall Constantin Brancusi's *Birds in Space*, and his *Endless Column*.[6] *Lightning Field* was spectacular, with masculine and phallic connotations (lightning is related in traditional symbolism to male creativity, sperm, fire, power and shamanism).[7]

Walter de Maria's *Lightning Field* attracts lightning, and a storm is one of the most spectacular phenomena in nature.[8] May to September is the season of the great storms in the area, sometimes 'two or three a week cross this field of poles' (H. Smagula, 290).

There have been other artists have worked with lightning, clouds and storms. Peter Hutchinson, one of the more interesting Postminimal/ Process sculptors, made a cloud piece (*Dissolving Clouds*, 1970) using Hatha yoga meditation techniques, trying to dissolve clouds through thought (a very late Sixties notion). The work consisted of a sequence of six photographs of clouds. Justin Holland too used lightning in artworks; he collaborated with Westinghouse Electric, making humanmade lightning, and 'seeded' clouds to produce storms. Alice Aycock also made a *Cloud Piece* (1971), photographs of cumulus clouds which melted after a few minutes. Joseph Beuys produced a startling piece entitled *Lightning*: a gigantic chunk of bronze, narrow at the top, splaying out towards the bottom, as if he was trying to make manifest the bolt of energy leaping down to the Earth.

CHRISTO

Perhaps the most famous of land artists (along with Robert Smithson), and certainly the land artist with the biggest international profile at the moment is Christo (b. 1935). He and his wife Jeanne-Claude (1935-2009) make vast public interventions, based around Christo's signature motif, the Wrap: plastic-covered buildings (Reichstag), wrapped bridges (Pont Neuf) or drapes hanging across valleys (Colorado). Christo's art is not 'invisible' like Walter de Maria's kilometre-long brass rod which only reveals a brass disc on the ground. Christo's art is very public, often running foul of politicians and pressure groups. It doesn't take place, like much of land art, in wilderness spots far away from cities and towns and the general public. Rather, Christo's art occurs right in the middle of cities such as Paris, Berlin and Rome.

Christo was born in 1935, in Bulgaria. One of Christo's early activities (while a student) involved tidying up the Orient Express railway route through Bulgaria by covering old farm machinery and haystacks with tarpaulin (in the dark days of Communism). In Prague Christo studied set design, and one of his mid-1960s works in New York was making replicas of shopfronts, like a stage set, but the windows were covered with cloth or paper. In his early works, Christo wrapped up small items such as books, bottles, tins and boxes. Other Assemblages or *empaquetages* (i.e., Assemblages as packages) included nude models, cars, chairs and motorbikes.

Christo's most famous Assemblage, though, was on a larger scale: *Wall of Oil Barrels – Iron Curtain* (1962), his first major work. This was a pile of barrels stacked across (and blocking) one of Paris's oldest streets, Rue Visconti. *Wall of Oil Barrels – Iron Curtain* parodied the Berlin Wall, which had recently been constructed. The sculpture annoyed the locals, and Christo's large-scale works have been upsetting residents ever since (and there's often a moment when detractors

find out they quite like Christo's wrappings, sometimes when the work is taken down).

Christo's first large-scale wrapping was to cover the Museum of Contemporary Art in the Windy City with 10,000 ft^2 of brown tarpaulin. Christo's wrapping of the museum made it the focus of attention in the neighbourhood – some people hadn't realized the museum was there until it had been wrapped. The museum's director reckoned Christo had parodied 'all the associations a museum evokes: a mausoleum, a repository for precious contents, an intent to wrap up all of art history'.[1] Inside the museum was the *Wrapped Floor*, consisting of 2,000 ft^2 of rented drop cloths.

In 1969 Christo wrapped a mile-long section of the Australian coastline. The use of open weave cloth (1 million square feet) meant that wildlife would not be affected (objectors routinely cite ecology and wildlife as a reason for blocking Christo's projects). *Wrapped Coast* (at Little Bay near Sydney) stayed up for 4 weeks. It was a dramatic land art gesture, difficult to ignore. *Valley Curtain* (1972), at Rifle Pass in Colorado, did not last so long. It was blown down. The huge bright orange drape hung across the valley, providing a passageway as well as a visual block to what was beyond.[2] The use of orange, as with the pink in *Surrounded Islands*, gave *Valley Curtain* a new æsthetic, more attuned to lush coloration of Henri Matisse and Claude Monet, quite a departure from the dull brown tarpaulin of the *Wrapped Museum*.

Many of Christo's large-scale wrappings have taken place next to water: *Running Fence* plunged into the sea; *Wrapped Coast* was submerged by the tides; *Surrounded Islands* floated on the ocean; *Pont-Neuf* stretched over the River Seine. *Surrounded Islands* (1980-83) was one of Christo's largest works. Not a wrapping this time, but still involving masses of fabric (6 million feet^2 of it). With a budget of $3.5 million (and 4 engineers, 2 ornithologists, a marine biologist, 2 attorneys and 430 helpers), Christo surrounded 11 little islands for 2 weeks in May, 1983. The choice of brilliant pink meant the enclosed islands stood out vividly against the green sea at Biscayne Bay in Florida. The pink-enclosed islands looked like flowers floating on the sea, recalling the Japanese Buddhist ceremony of setting flowers afloat. Or, more in tune with Western art history, evoking Claude Monet's *Waterlilies*.

Running Fence (1972-76) consisted of 2,050 18-foot panels of white nylon attached to steel poles, running across Marin and Sonoma counties and twelve roads in California. As with Christo's other mammoth projects, there was much opposition to *Running Fence*.[3] When it was taken down, nothing remained of it in the area: the holes were filled in, and bare parts of soil were reseeded. As with other Christo projects, when it was taken away some locals were dismayed: the work had helped them realize the beauty of the area. Christo said his art was

about displacement. Basically even today I am a displaced person. And this is why I make art that does not last. Of course, it will stay for ever in the minds of people.[4]

Christo here espouses the fundamental Romanticism in land art: that it will live on in the memories of people. Christo's large-scale projects – *Running Fence*, *Surrounded Islands*, *Wrapped Coast* – are spectacular works, part of the land art tradition which moves towards the sublime in landscape art (which resurfaced in the Abstract Expressionism of Mark Rothko, Barnett Newman and Robert Motherwell). There is a 'Minimal Sublime', too – in Tony Smith's black sculptures, Donald Judd's Marfa installations, and Richard Long's and Carl Andre's larger floor-standing sculpture.

The ocean end of *Running Fence* was particularly impressive: at Bodega Bay the *Fence* extended gracefully into the Pacific, 558 feet, descending from a height of 18 feet on land to two feet at the section which was anchored to the bottom of the sea. Christo's grand projects are expensive: *Running Fence* cost over $3 million, *Surrounded Islands* cost $3.5 million, *The*

Umbrellas in Japan and California cost $26,000,000, and *Wrapped Reichstag* (1995) nearly double that. Denigrators of Christo's work have noted the expense of the projects, but Christo pays for them himself, by selling photos, drawings, collages, models, lithographs, plans and other works, and by collaborating with industry.

RICHARD LONG

Richard Long (b. 1945) considered his art to be partly Minimal as well as environmental, and Conceptual. Long has become known mainly as an environmental or land artist and sculptor. But Minimal philosophy informs much of Long's output. Long often exhibited with the Minimal artists, and was friends with some of them (such as Carl Andre and Lawrence Weiner).

Richard Long employed Minimal forms throughout his artistic career: the circles, lines, rows, ellipses and arcs are very much Minimal forms. The materials Long used drew on Arte Povera (mud, stone, wood, bark, bones, grass). The art of the walk, which Long perfected to become the ultimate artist-as-walker (drifter, nomad, traveller), was based on Conceptual and Process lines: the *idea* of the walk was critical. Long walked in imaginary circles or straight lines (sometimes he meandered, or walked slow, but usually quite fast). He followed routes planned beforehand on maps. The walk itself was the sculpture, the artwork. The work could be as long as the walk. The emphasis was on making the walk itself, the experience of actually walking.

Like the Minimal artists, Richard Long was much concerned with seriality, processes, mapping, permutations and variations. Long was very fond of numbers and number systems, and of measuring his walks: he walked so many miles for so many hours on such and such a day, for instance. His walkworks record the everyday events of a walk, as well as the number systems and measurements. Long made walks based on number systems. Many of his walks are repetitions of the same basic idea, just as the Minimalists would take one format and reproduce it many different ways. In fact, as a walker, Long was in love with repetition, because a walk is basically one step then another... then another. The walk's basic unit is the step. Similarly, Minimal artists like Carl Andre constructed larger works from simple, small units (the metal tile).

Richard Long's 1967 walkwork *A Line Made By Walking* is routinely cited in art criticism as Long's first major work, but let's use another early piece to illustrate Long's æsthetics. In *A 2 1/2 Mile Walk Sculpture* (1969), Long documented how he walked along parallel 55 yard lines four times. The first time, he walked 32 times back and forth, travelling a mile; the second time, 24 times, going 3/4 mile, the third time, 16 times (= 1/2 mile), and the fourth time, 8 times (= 1/4 mile). As well as the text explaining the walk sculpture, there was a photograph of the grass and lines Long walked, and a diagram of the lines.

This work contains all of the key elements of Richard Long's art: there's a photograph, written text, and a diagram. Each of those three media are vital in Long's *œuvre*. The work was exhibited as a wall piece. The work originated with a performance, made by the artist, alone, with no witnesses (although not in the wilderness spots he became famous for – India, Peru, Iceland, the Sahara. Even though it's not Ladakh, it's still on grass, without people, houses, roads, factories, telephone lines, trash, etc, cluttering up the picture). It was Conceptual: the work was planned beforehand, then executed. It involved measurement, time, distance, speed, and direction, all ingredients which Long would experiment with throughout his artistic career. It was Process or Serial art: it involved repetition. It had a simple geometry and form: straight lines. And the work was primarily a *walk*: the walking was the single most important aspect of the work: walking is the experience upon which all of Long's art is founded. The first significant work he made as an international artist was a walk, and a walk will very likely be his last ever artwork.

OTHER LAND AND INSTALLATION ARTISTS

The field of land and installation art is vast (as pretty much any international art these days is an installation of some kind, it seems). Here are a few further artists who have taken up Minimal or Postminimal devices in making environmental or installation art.

At a quarry in upstate New York **WILLIAM BENNETT** created a *Wedge (Stone Boat)* (1976), an 80 foot long smooth-sided channel in the limestone. Recalling Wolfgang Laib's pollen floorpieces, **SHELAGH WAKELY** covered the marble floor of the British School at Rome with a layer of tumeric spice (*Curcuma sul Travertino*, 1991). **ANTHONY GORMLEY** covered the entire area of a gallery floor in his *Field* installation (1991) with over 35,000 small humanoid figures (but Gormley's most famous piece, for which he will always be remembered, was *The Angel of the North*, a semi-abstract figure – based on Gormley's own body – which looked back to the proto-Minimal metal sculpture of Anthony Caro). In **RUDOLF STINGEL** 's untitled floor-piece (New York), the entire gallery area was covered with a thick shagpile orange carpet.

BARBARA KRUGER covered the floor, walls and ceilings with giant slogans in her customary black, red and white colors in her 1991 installation in New York. Kruger's art is archetypical installation art, but it does draw on the Minimal principles of monochromy (black, white and red are favoured in most of Kruger's pieces), as well as reductionism. For *Post and Beam* (Cologne, 1991), **SIMON UNGER** made a mirror image of the ceiling of the gallery on the floor, complete with lighting and beams (a development, perhaps, of Robert Irwin's Minimal interventions). **GIOVANNI ANSELMO** used stone like painted canvases, mounting thin slabs of granite on a Paris gallery wall like paintings (*Meeting of Two Works*, 1990).

Some installation artists used liquid to cover the floor area of a gallery: in **GLEN ONWIN** 's alchemical installations in Halifax (1991), water, wax and black brine were poured into a large concrete pool. **RICHARD WILSON** 's *20/50* (1987) was a steel pool of sump oil with a walkway in the middle of it. **PER BARCLAY** also used pools of oil: in *Old Boathouse* (1990) an oil pool was set in a Norwegian boathouse beside the sea; in *The Jaguar's Cage* (1991), made at Turin Zoo, a large oil pool was set behind bars. **EVE LARAMEE** spread a rectangular mound of cobalt glass on the gallery floor in her *Requiem For a Blue Fluid* (1991). These interventions in the gallery which produce pools or cover the floor are related to the Minimalists' use of mirrors and flat surfaces, and also the light artists.

In *Monumental Ikebana* (1990), **HIROSHI TESHIGAHARA** made a giant arched path from bamboo in a gallery space. For **VONG PHAEPHANIT** 's bamboo installation (*What Falls to the Ground Cannot Be Eaten*, 1991), a forest of bamboo sticks was hung from the ceiling of the London gallery, approached through a monumental black doorway.

JAMES PIERCE created a series of earthworks at Pratt Farm in central Maine in the 1970s: there was a triangular turf maze; a small earth *Observatory*; a *Serpent* made from large rocks; a *Stone Ship*; a *Burial Mound*; a stone *Altar* (in the shape of male genitals); and different figures made from grass and soil: *Earthwoman* and *Suntreeman*. **HERBERT BAYER** created earthworks which directly evoked prehistoric structures: Bayer's *Earth Mound* (1955) in Aspen, Colorado, contained the familiar motifs of ancient religions and cultures: a circular rampart enclosing a small mound; a standing stone and a hollow were placed beside the mound. In Kent, Washington, Bayer built a series of earthworks (*Mill Creek Canyon Earthworks*, 1979-82) which featured circular ramparts, circular moats, mounds surmounted by walkways, and circular ramparts split by a path.

#6

MINIMAL ART TODAY

What about the influence and legacy of Minimal art? Well, the basic 'minimal' look (a term so vague it can mean anything really) is an enduring look. At the superficial level of visuals (i.e., ignoring ideology, politics and the social), Minimalism is everywhere, thirty, forty years after its development in the 1960s. Take cinema. One of the great Minimal films, made at the time of High Minimalism, was the sci-fi thriller *THX-1138* (1971). To visualize the totalitarian, dehumanizing future, George Lucas and art director Michael Haller opted for white-on-white rectilinear spaces, steel and white walls. And people were simply letters and numbers. Thirty years later, in the futuristic thriller *Minority Report* ([2002], again about a man on the run from the authorities), directed by Lucas's pal Steven Spielberg in 2002, the Minimal look was employed again. This time, it was enhanced with cool grays and pale blues, but it was still a recognizably 'minimal' *mise-en-scène*.

The art movie embraced 1960s Minimalism: obvious examples would be the cinema of Michelangelo Antonioni and Alain Resnais, and also Yasujiro Ozu and Kenji Mizoguchi (one also thinks of Ingmar Bergman, Luis Buñuel, Marco Ferreri, Andrei Tarkovsky and Roman Polanski in connection with Minimalism). Antonioni (in movies such as *The Passenger, L'Avventura* and *Identification of a Woman*) and Resnais (in of course *Last Year At Marienbad*), celebrated empty spaces and scenes in which not much happened at all in a style familiar from Minimalism (Andy Warhol became the king of this kind of un-happening cinema). Jean-Luc Godard's cinema featured numerous images of flattened spaces with Pop Art coloration and imagery (like the Minimalists, Godard favoured bold, saturated colors, such as reds and blues and yellows). *Avant garde* movies also explored Minimalism, where reductionism is taken to extremes – *Wavelength* (Michael Snow, 1967) is the classic example: a forty-minute, s---l---o---w zoom into a wall and a postcard in a New York loft. Once seen, never forgotten!

Probably *the* Minimal movie is *2001: A Space Odyssey* (1968), designed and shot at the height of Minimalism (1965-68). White spaces, rectilinear and curved interior design, fluorescent lighting, primary colors, Minimal materials (plastic, chrome, steel. fibreglass), and even a lightshow culled from light art and rock shows in the Stargate sequence. And the design of the monolith is supremely Minimal, recalling the paintings and sculptures of John McCracken, Ellsworth Kelly, Robert Morris and Anne Truitt.

Apple computers were designed around Minimal lines (and used similar cool blues and grays). The Minimal look is popular in technology, such as hi-fi (just an on-off button, and a volume control). Modern TV sets have controls hidden away, so they don't spoil the clean lines. Swedish cheapo furniture giant IKEA produces modular, rectilinear cupboards, chairs, tables and the like, some of which are so similar to Donald Judd's sculptures, the Judd estate should sue IKEA.

Magazine publishing has used Minimalism since the 1950s (and the 'style' mags of the Eighties made it one of their core looks). In amongst the mountain of junk mail that pours through doors in hundreds of countries there will be plenty of advertizing that employs a Minimal style. Plenty of photographers continue to explore Minimal æsthetics, including Thomas Joshua Cooper, Hiroshi Sugimoto, Vija Celmins, Uta Barth and Geneviève Cadieux (Alfred Stieglitz, the 'father' of American photography, was an early art photographer who approached Minimalism in his *Equivalents* series, which included photographs of clouds). Architecture embraced Minimalism (Philip Johnson, Marcel Breuer, James Stirling, I.M. Pei, Richard Meier and Louis I. Kahn, to cite some of the obvious architects who produced buildings in a Minimal style. Frank Gehry has developed a funky Minimal style, such as in the Walt Disney Concert Hall in downtown L.A.).

The typical Western art gallery is basically a white cube, with Minimal furniture and fittings. It's a very different look from the crowded museums of the Victorian era, when walls were covered with art from floor to ceiling, and the art fought for attention with the decoration of the building (the plaster-work, the colors, the wallpaper, the hangings, the drapes). But the contemporary art gallery is a very spartan affair (at least in the public viewing areas). A museum such as Tate Modern in London bases its whole graphic style, its advertizing, its signage, its presentation and curating on the Minimal look – partly because museum director Nicholas Serota is a big fan of the Minimal approach (and has written a book on Brice Marden, and edited one on Donald Judd, among others). Even the display cases for sculptures in contemporary galleries are basically the Minimal clear plastic cube (in museums with older furnishings, the display cases and shelves are typically decorated with carved wood and many decorative elements, but the modern art gallery prefers a simple clear box atop an unadorned wooden plinth painted white).

One could go and on listing places where Minimal art's influence endures.

One of the common criticisms of Minimal art was that it was too much concerned with materi-ality, with formal issues, and not enough with content, with subjectivity, or with self-expression. It didn't seem to be 'about' anything other than itself (but that was the whole point, the Minimalists retorted).

Another recurring criticism was that Minimal art was a cold, unsensual art. Another was that it was dull, boring, mundane art. Another common critic-ism was that Minimal was reductive and negative. Fascistic art was another opinion: Minimal art was totalitarian, it was authoritarian. It was all or nothing.

Minimal art was in love with objects and materials and commodities for some critics. It enshrined the object above everything else, and didn't leave any room for more important things, such as political and social issues. For left-liberals, Minimal art was an art of late capitalism, an art which celebrated the intense commodification of the post-WW2 era, an art for the consumer society.

Minimal art for the nay-sayers avoided politics, and had nothing to say about history or memory. The same criticism were often levelled at post-modern art (for some critics, Minimal art was part of postmodern art). Minimal art was thus dang-erous and wilfully ignorant, because it avoided all of the really significant issues facing people in the world today.

ILLUSTRATIONS

Illustrations include some influences and
inspirations on Minimal art and artists, followed by
examples of Minimal art in popular culture.

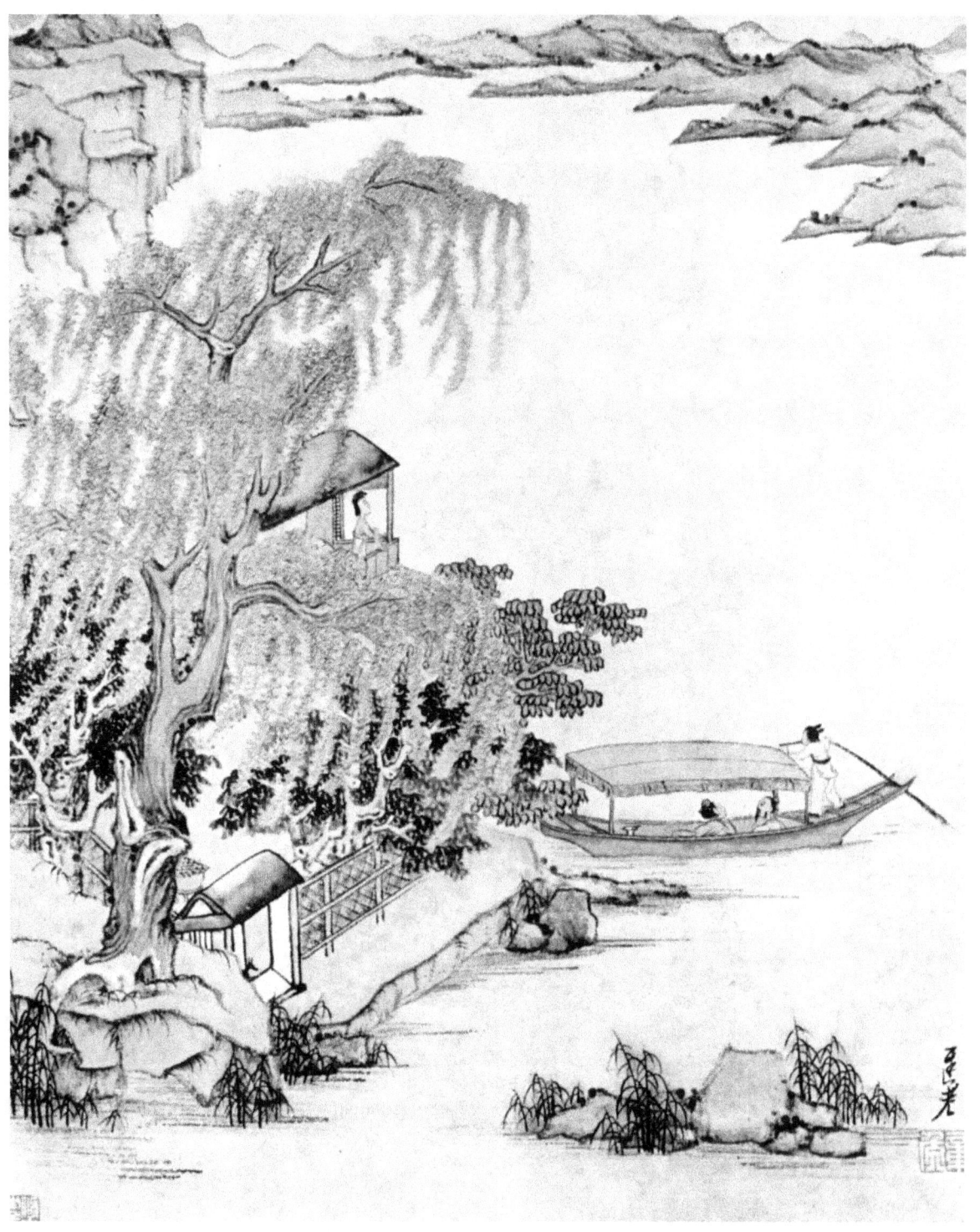

Chinese Landscape, Ming Dynasty, 1630-1650

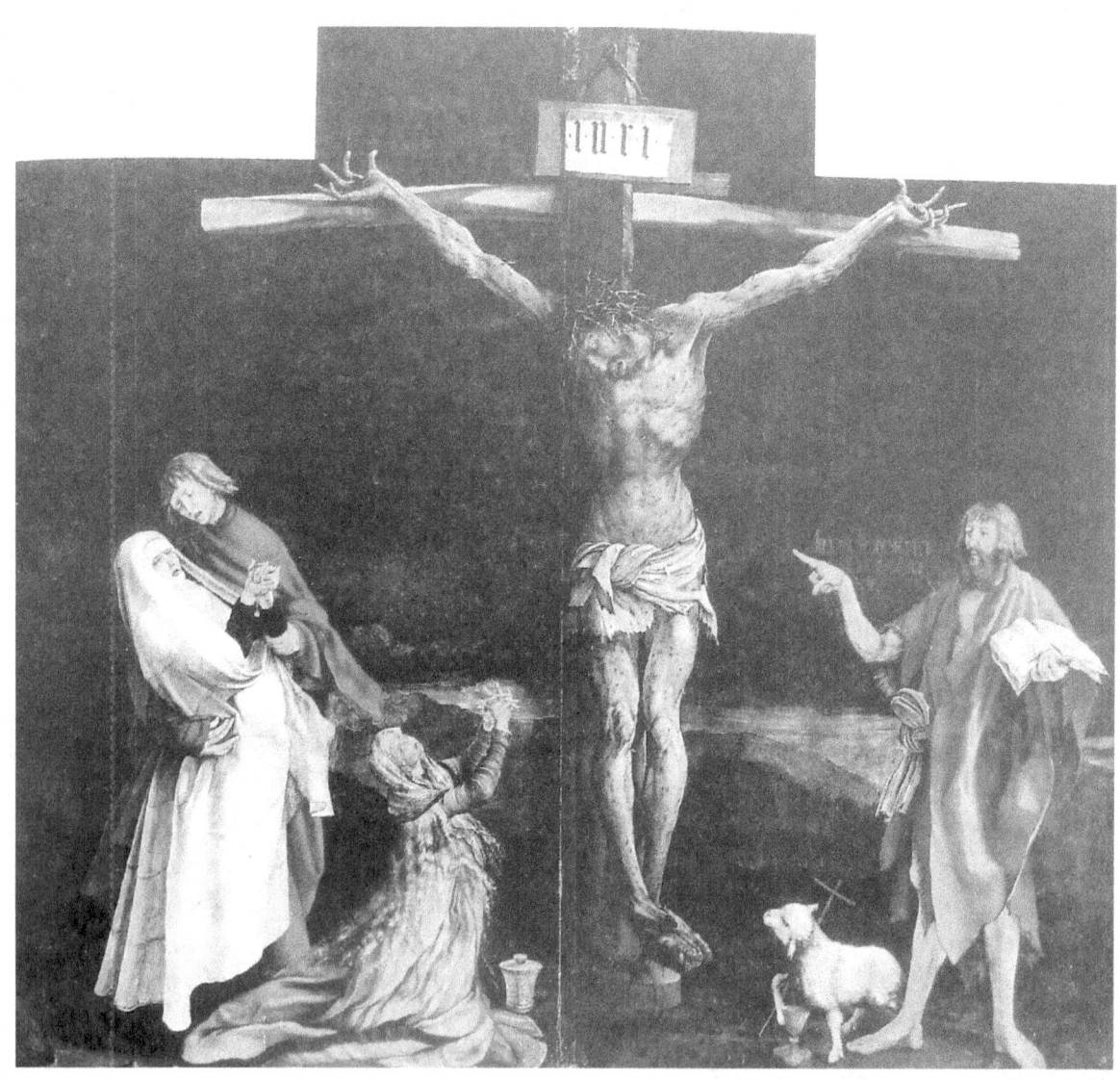

Matthias Grünewald, Crucifixion, Isenheim Altarpiece

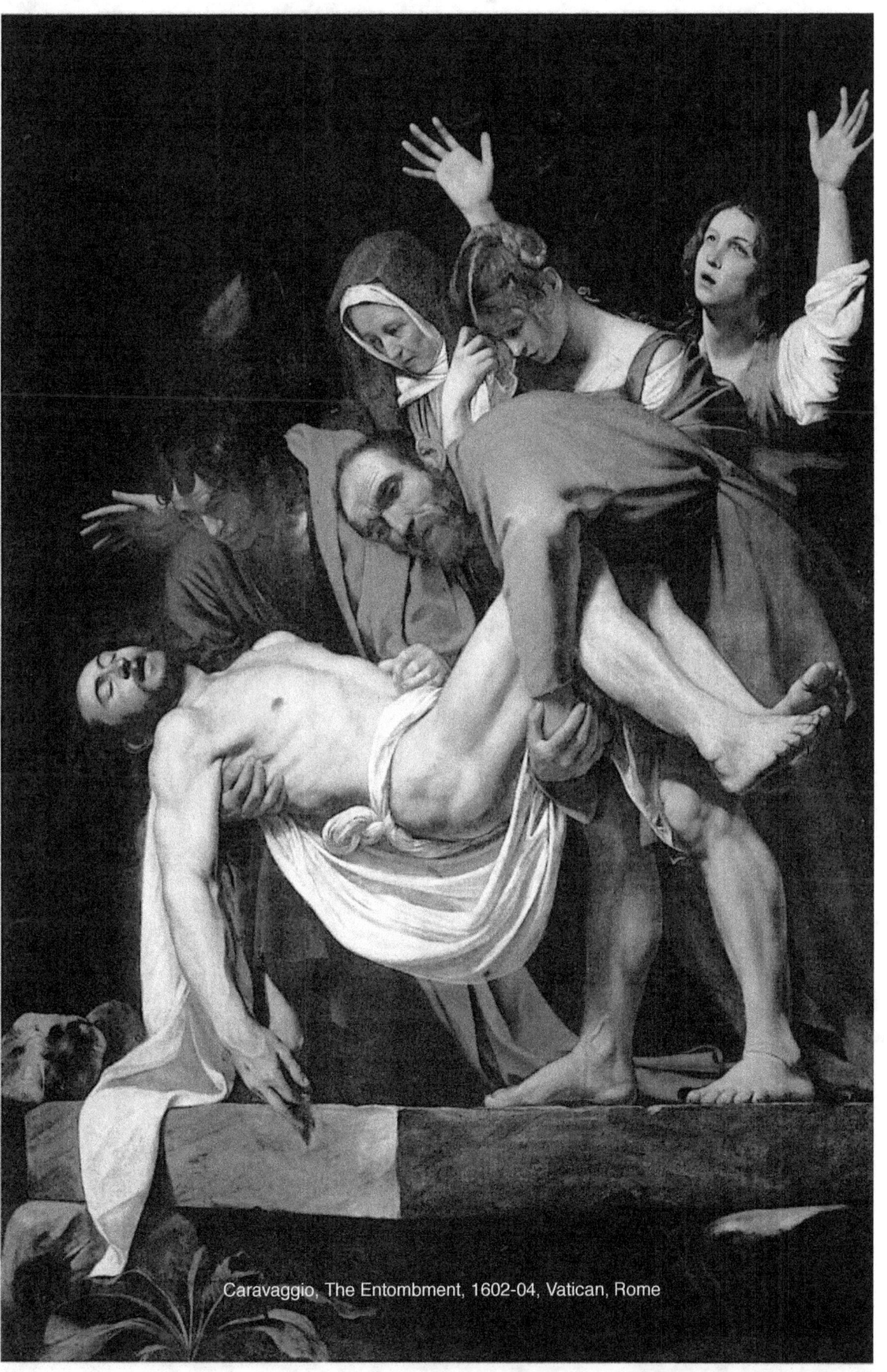

Caravaggio, The Entombment, 1602-04, Vatican, Rome

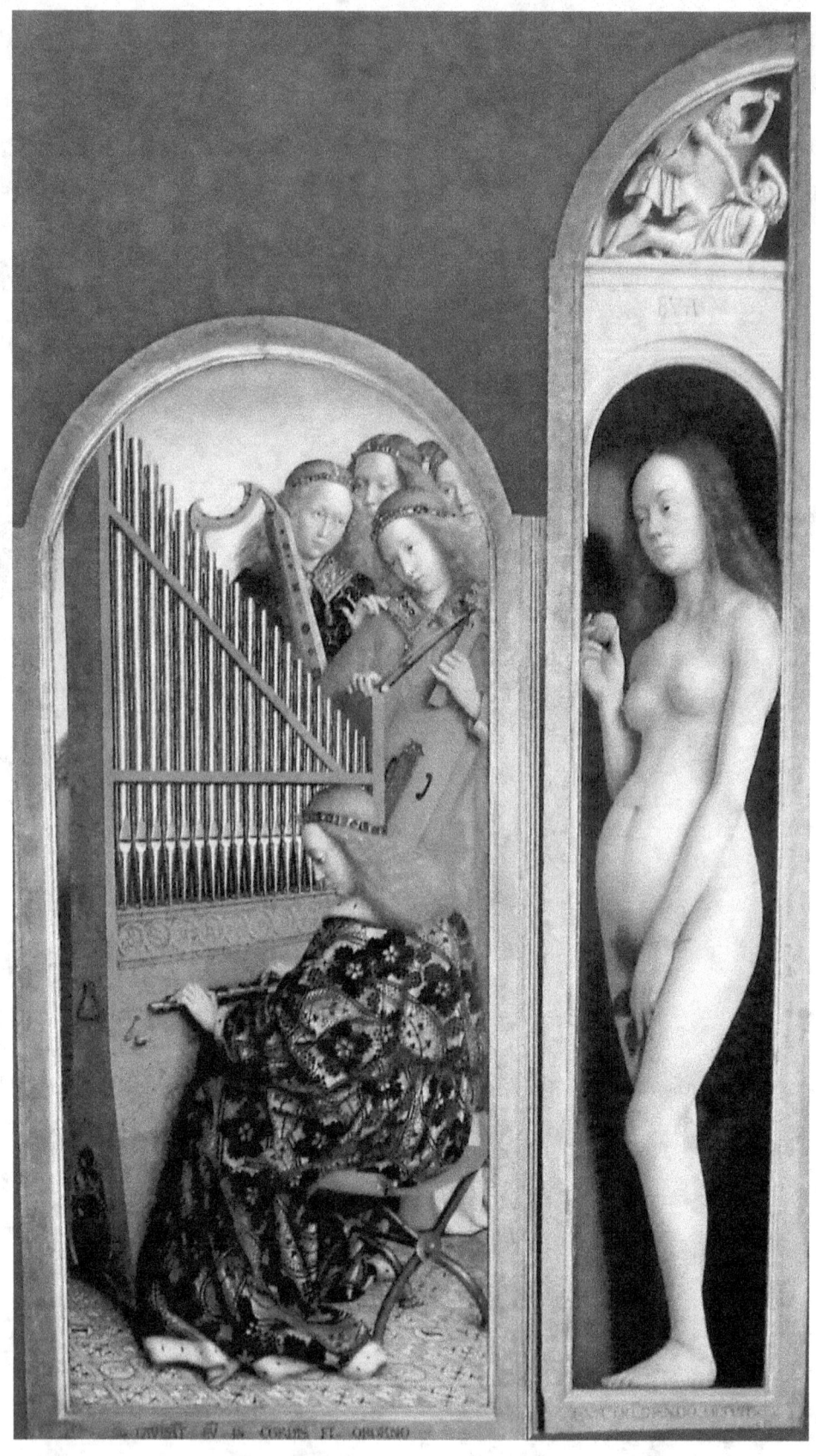

Jan van Eyck, The Ghent Altarpiece, wing

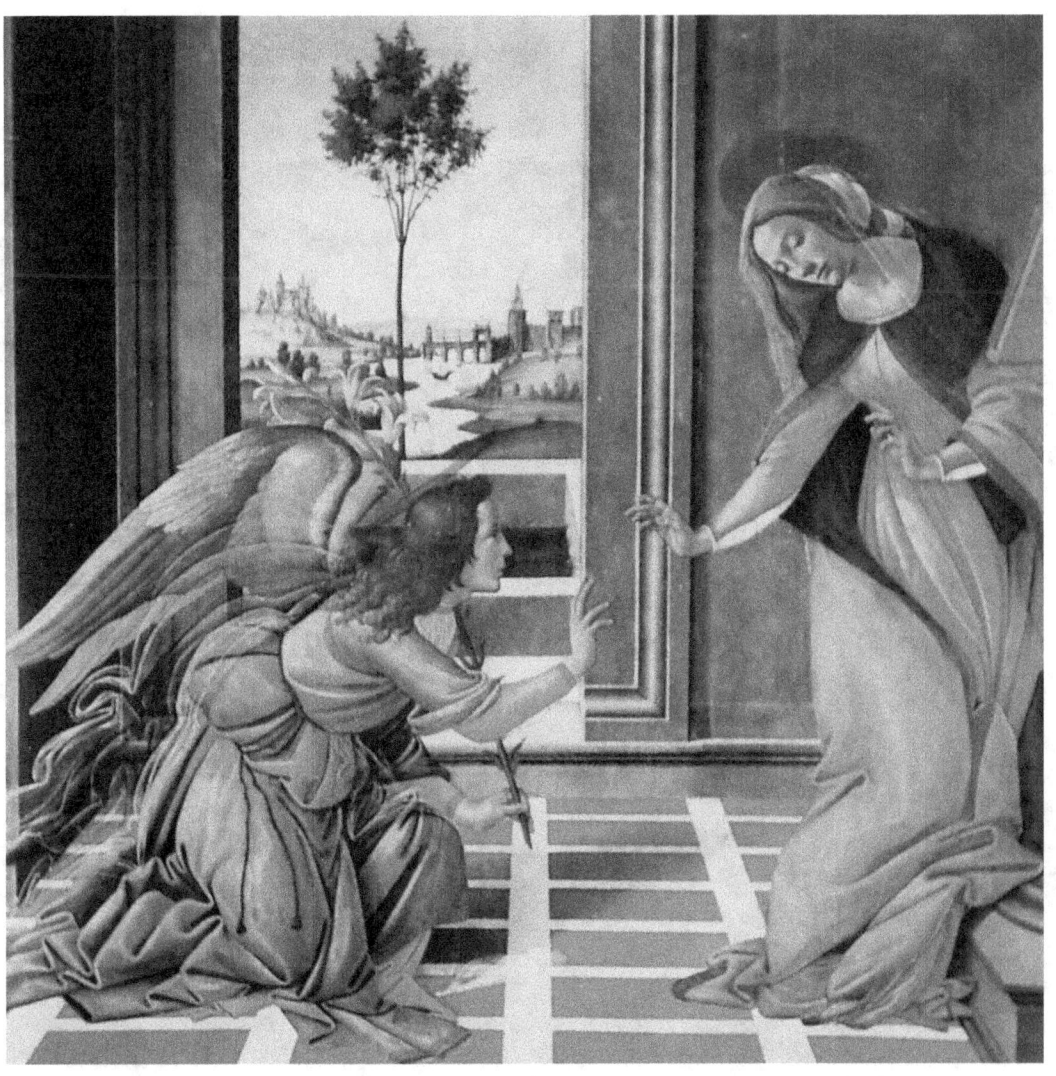

Sandro Botticelli, The Annunciation, Uffizi Gallery, Florence

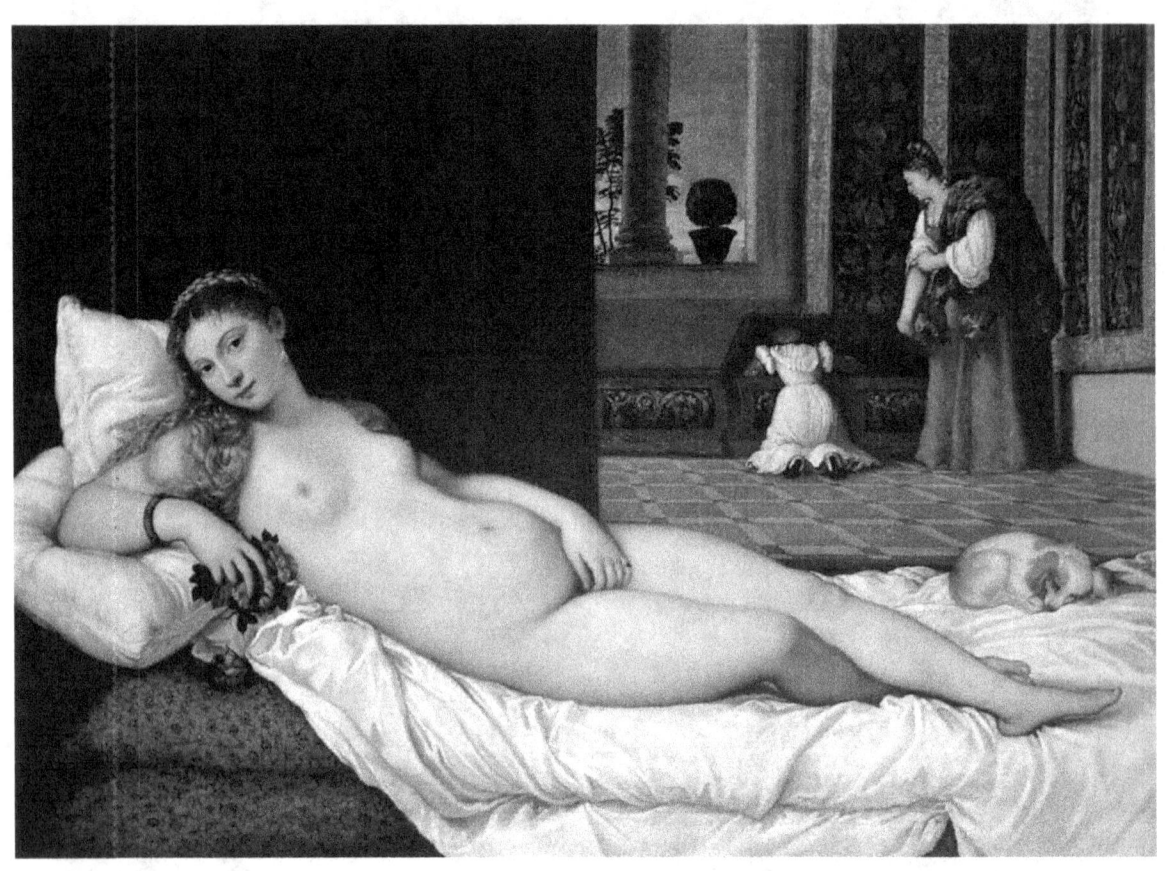

Titian, The Venus of Urbino, 1538, Uffizi, Florence

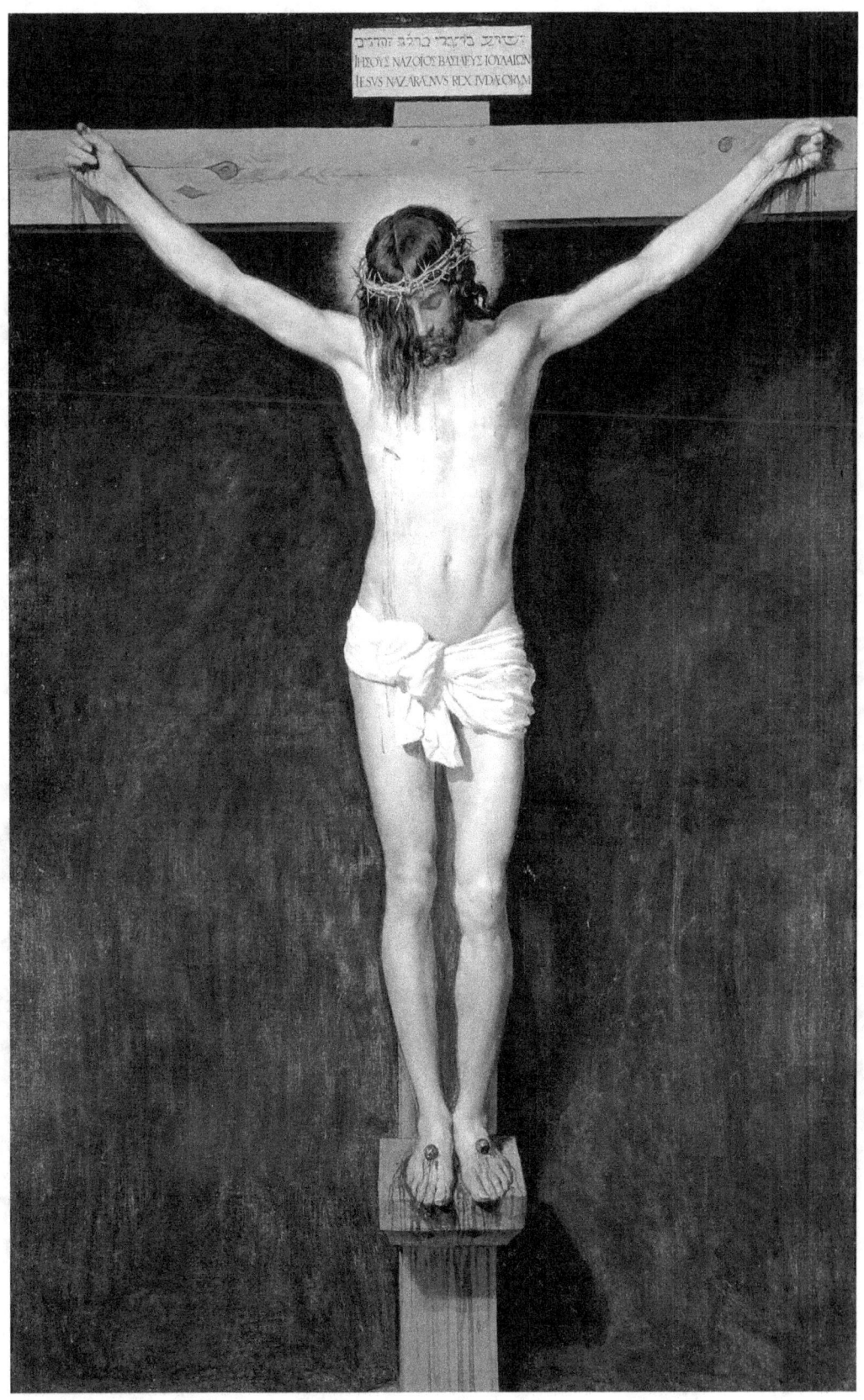

Diego Velásquez, Christ Crucified, 1632, Prado, Madrid

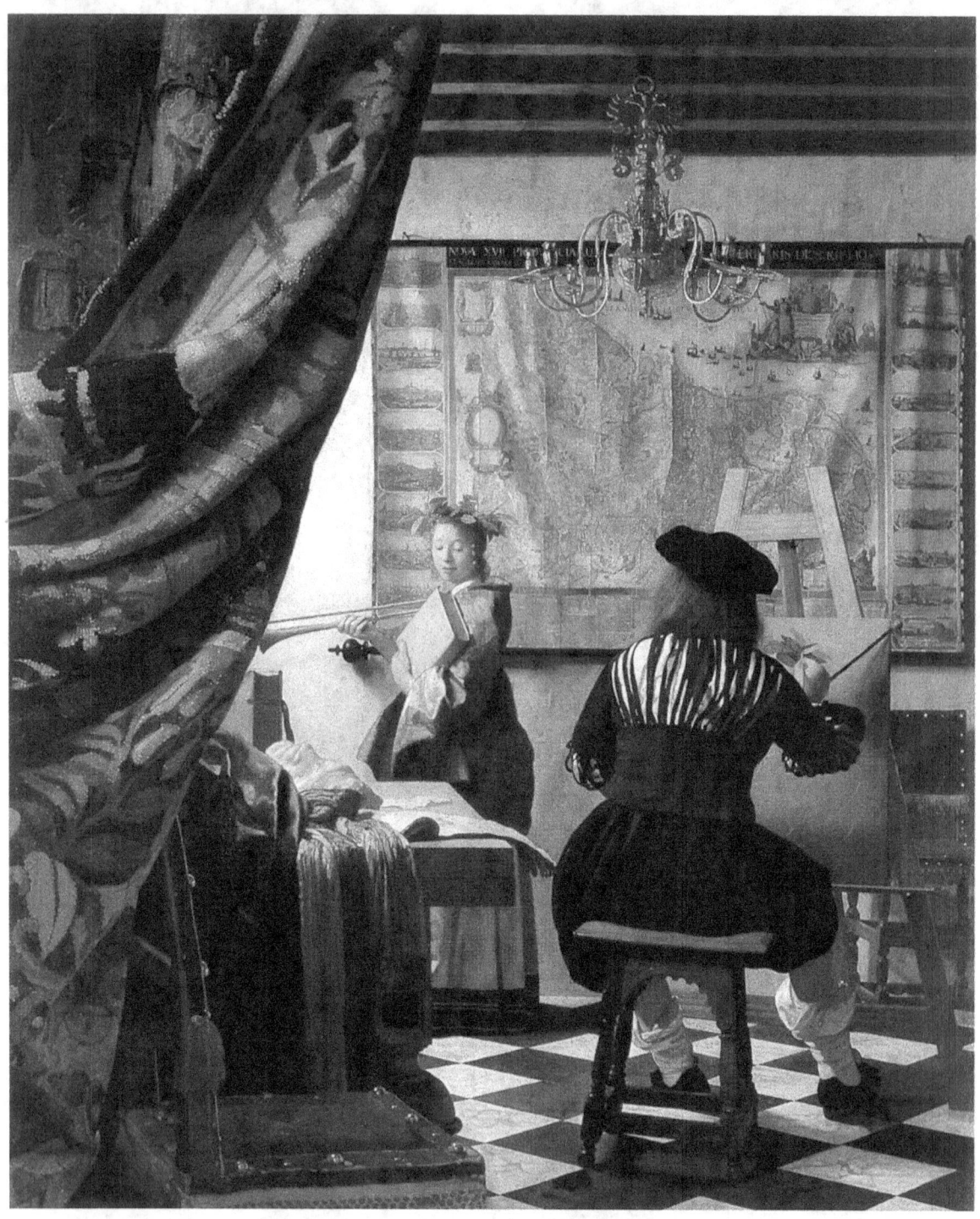

Jan Vermeer, The Allegory of Painting, 1666-67,Kunsthistoriches Museum, Vienna

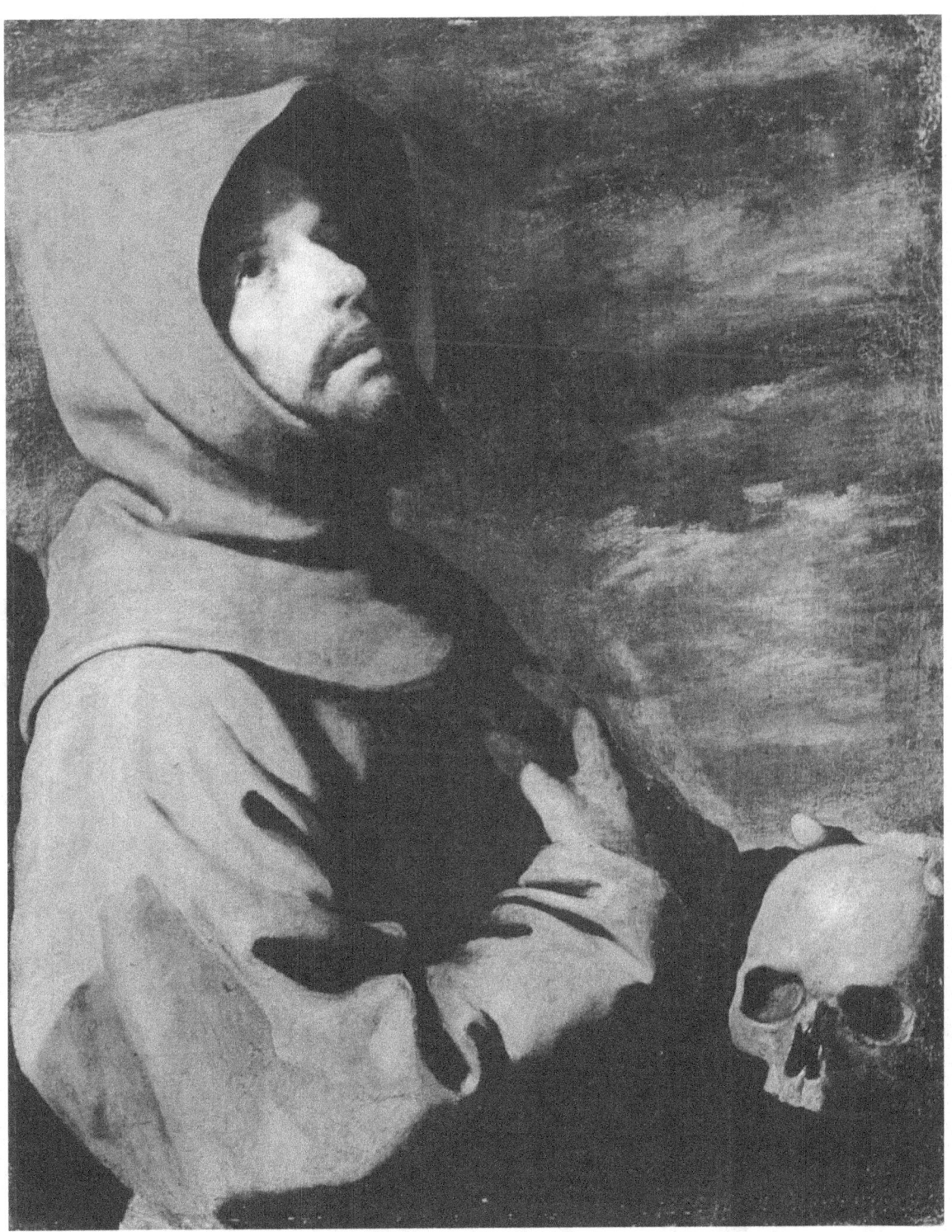

Francisco de Zurbarán, St Francis, Munich

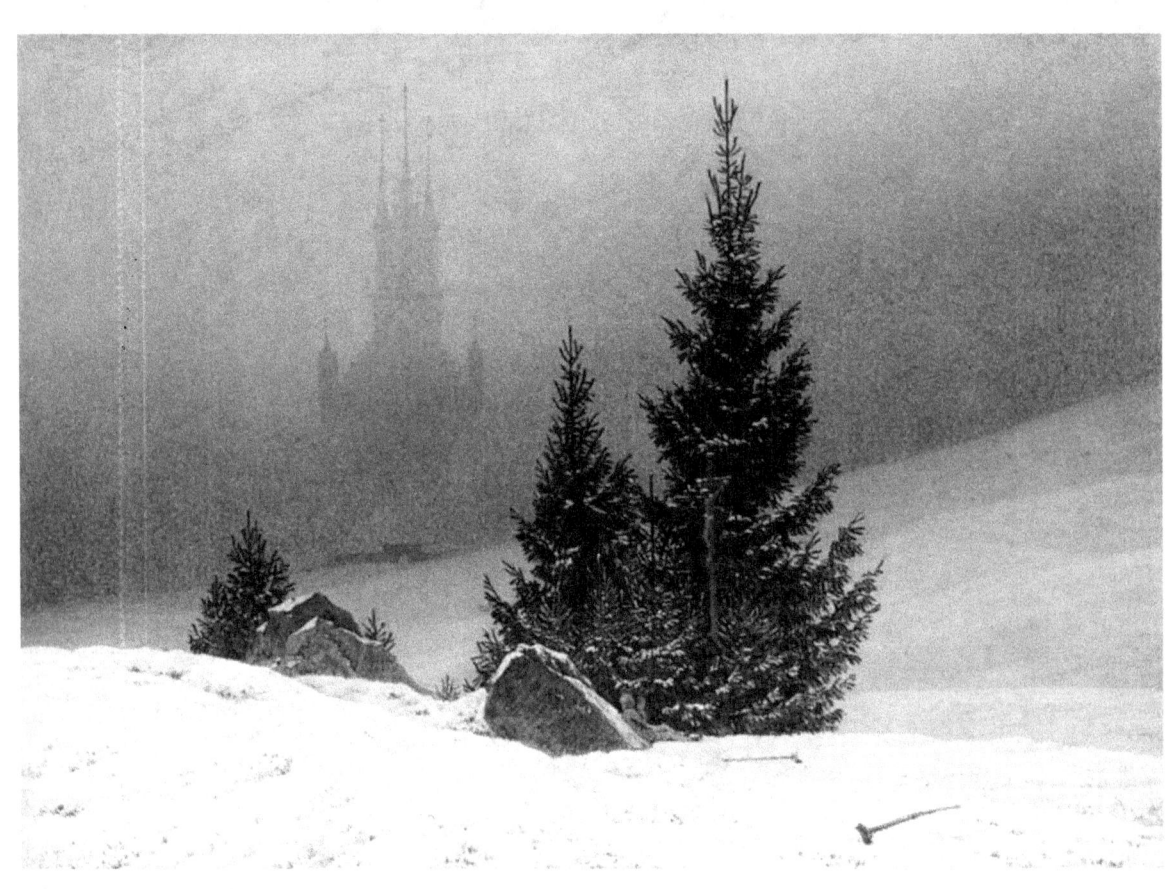

Casper David Friedrich, Winter Landscape, 1811, National Gallery, London

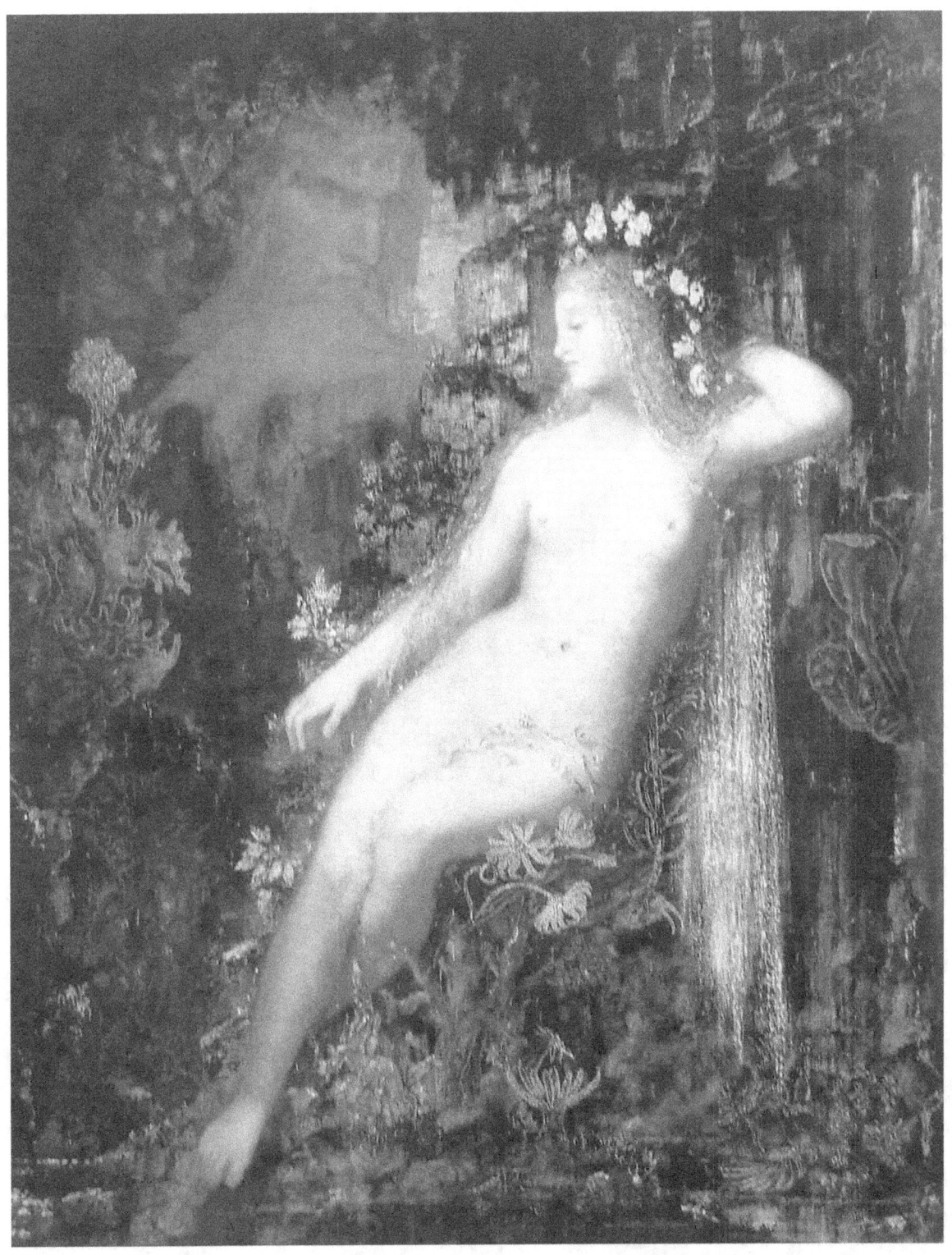

Gustave Moreau, Galatea, 1880

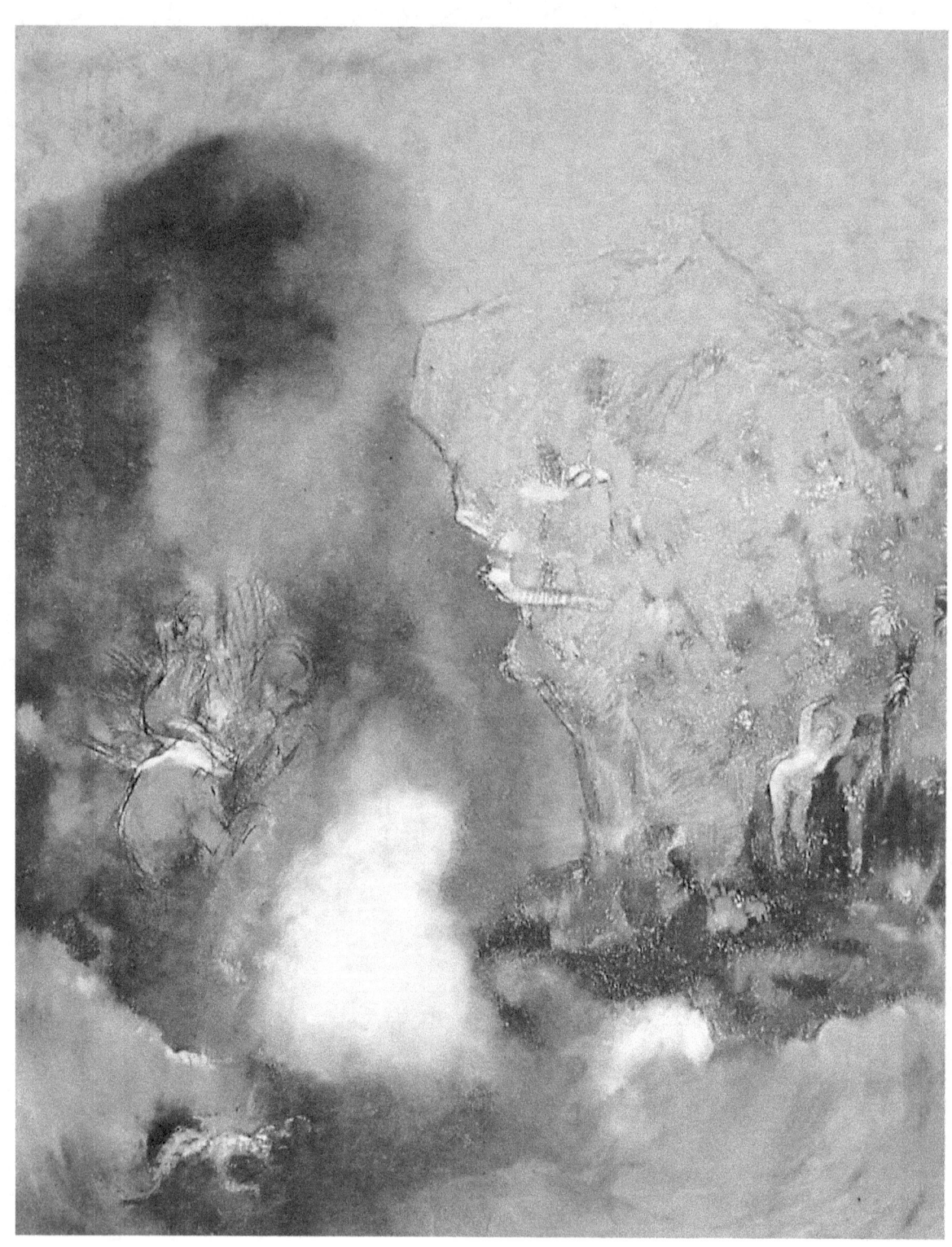

Odilon Redon, Roger and Angelica, c. 1910,
Museum of Modern Art, New York

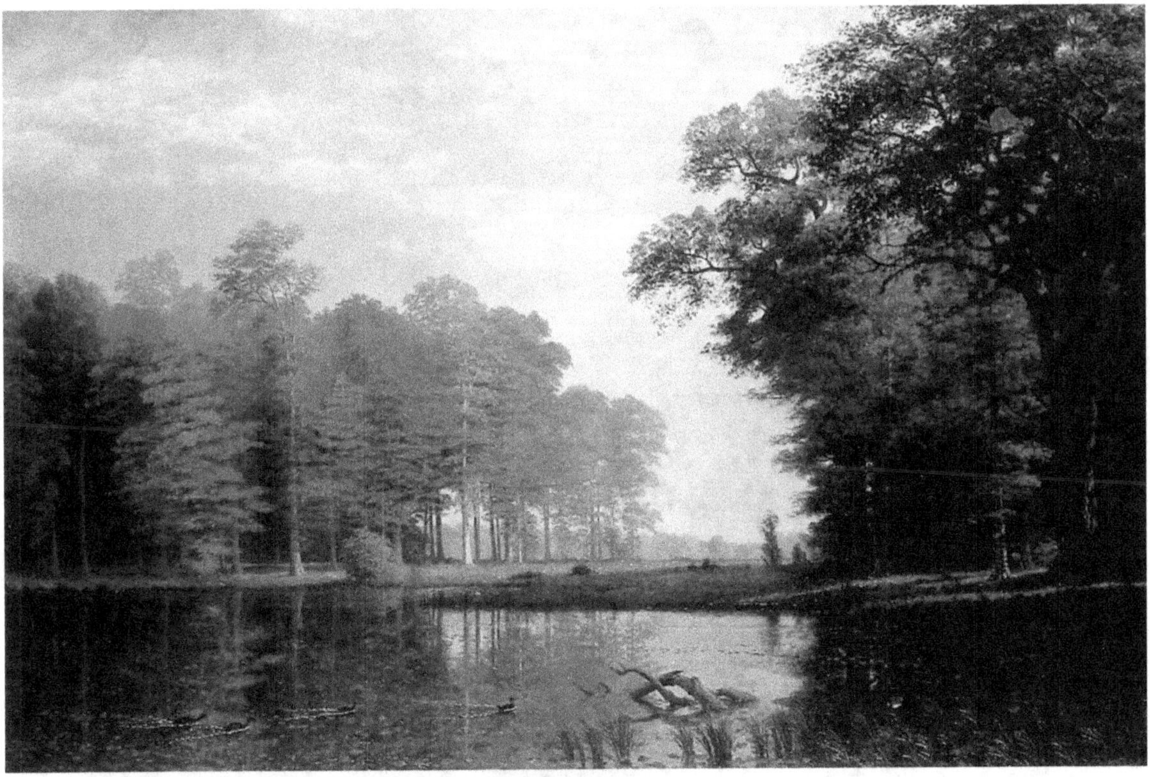

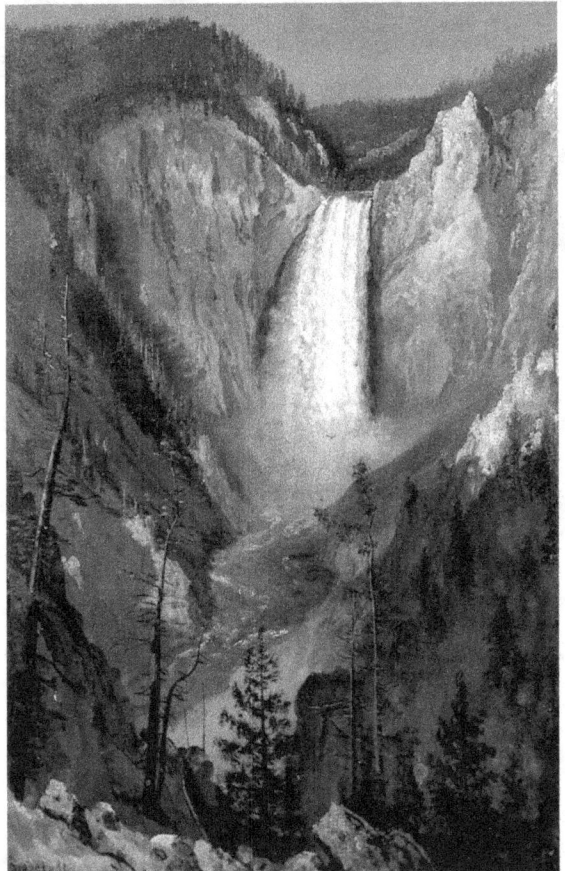

Albert Bierstadt,
Autumn Woods (above), and
Lower Yellowstone Falls (left).

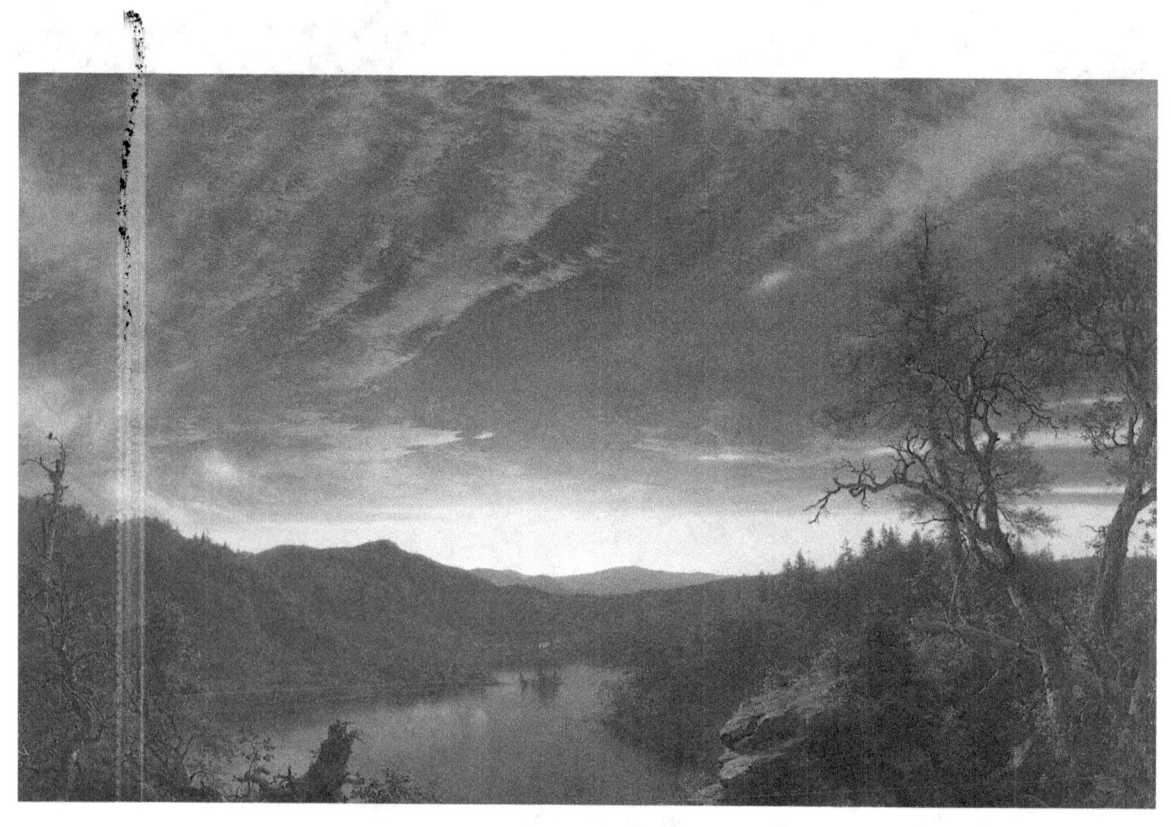

Frederic Edwin Church, Twilight In the Wildnerness, 1860,
Cleveland Museum of Art

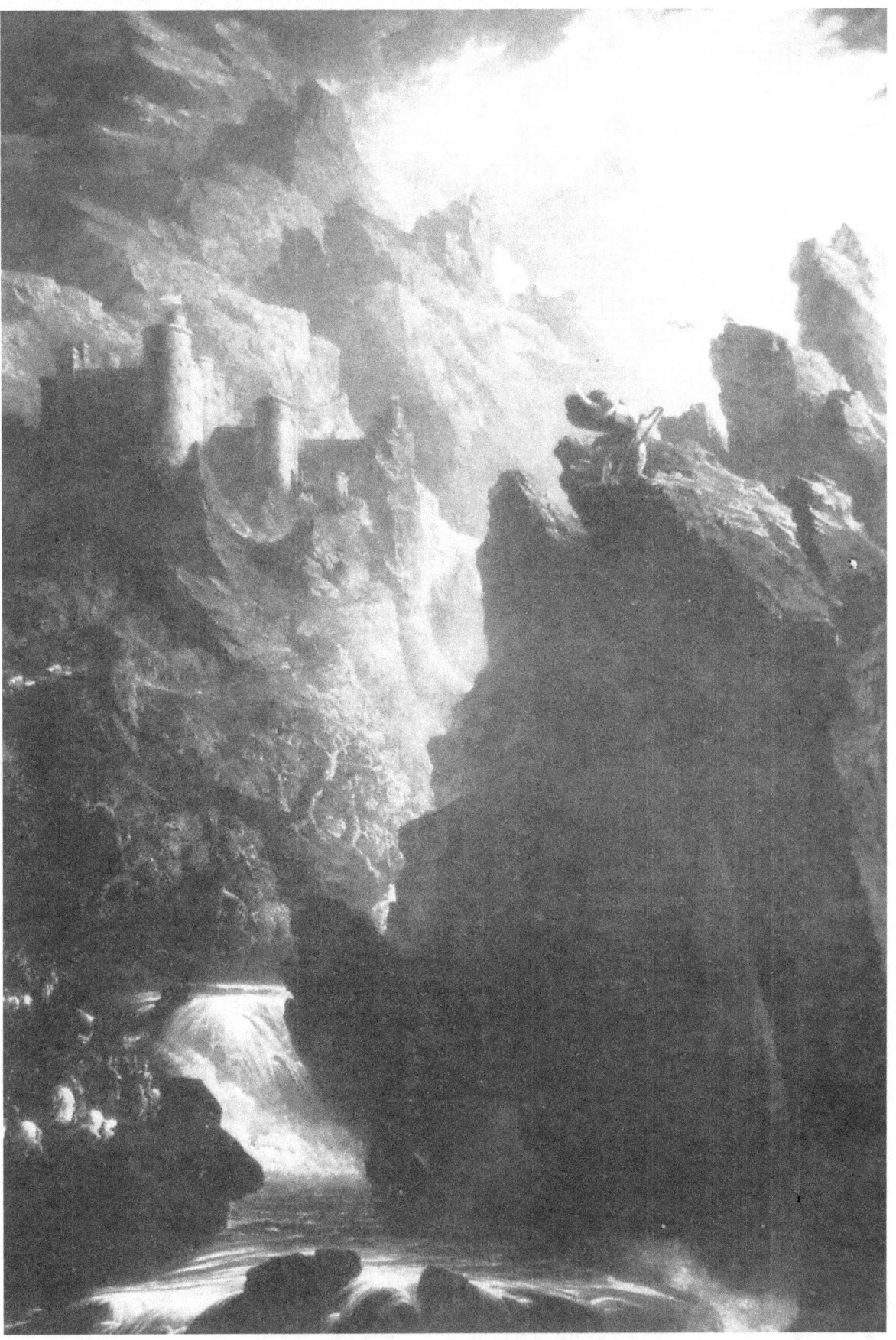

John Martin, The Bard, 1817

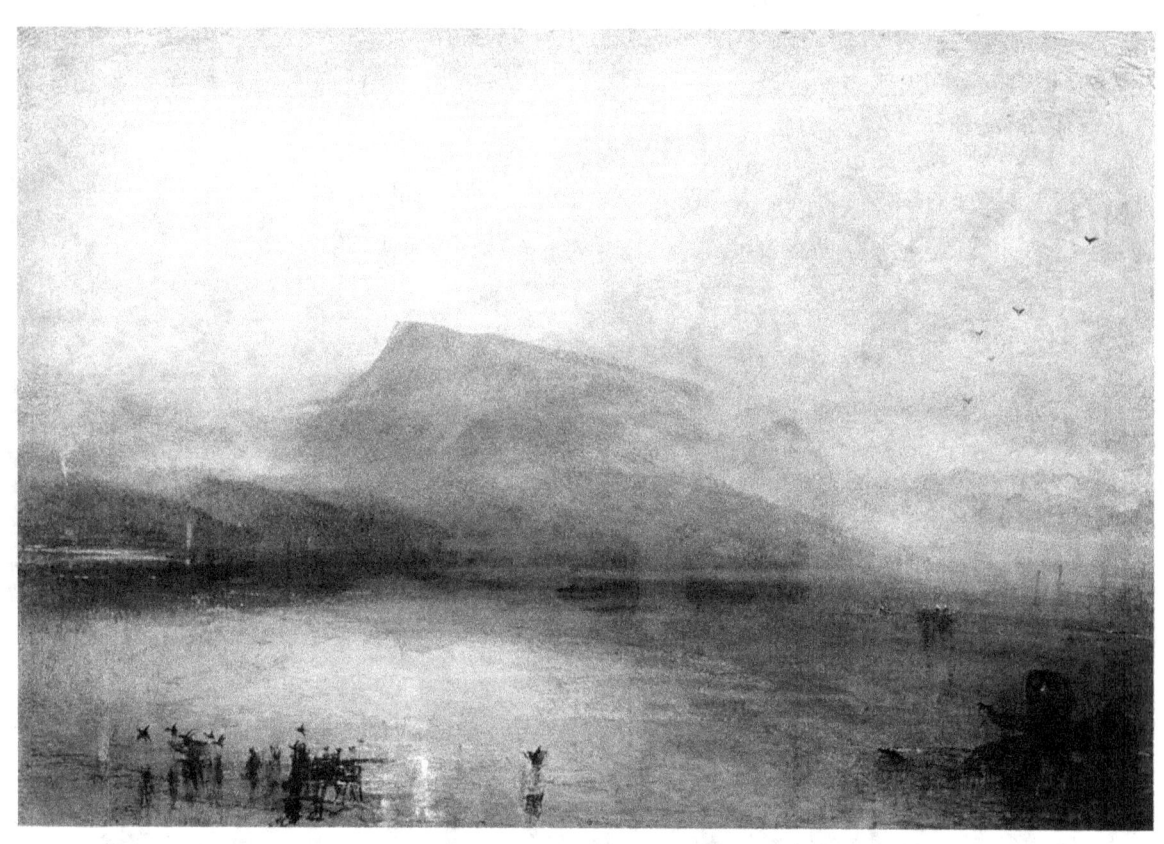

J.M.W. Turner, The Blue Rigi, Lake of Lucerne, Sunrise,
1842, Clore Gallery, London

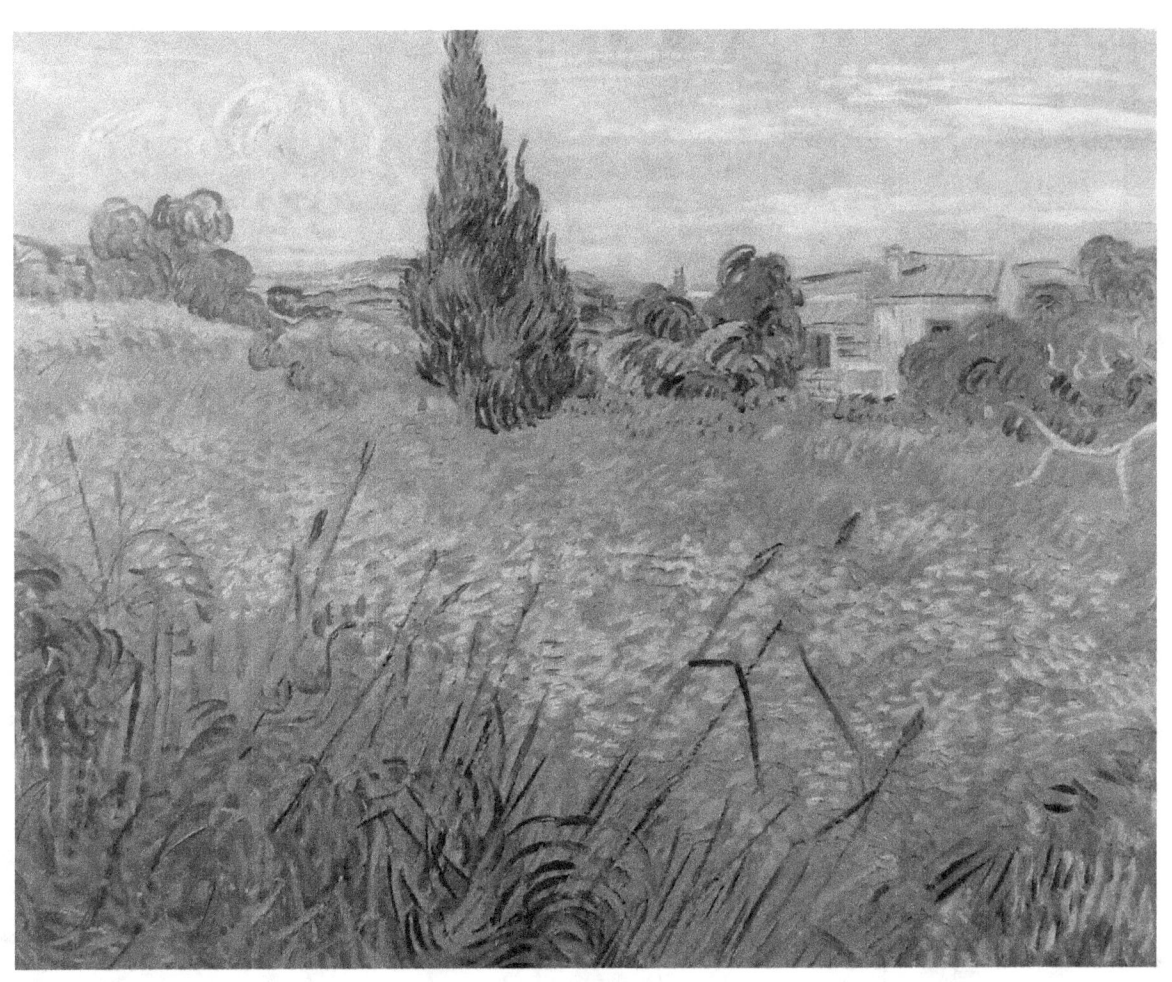

Vincent van Gogh, Wheatfield, Prague

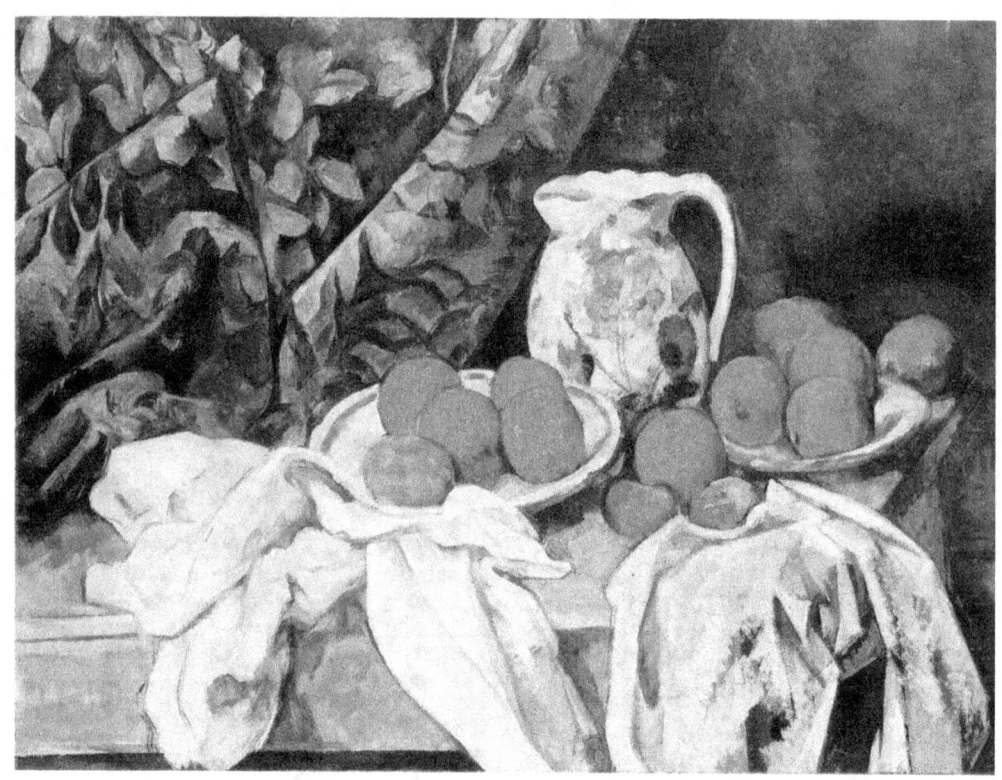

Paul Cézanne, Still Life with Curtain and Flowered Pitcher, c. 1899

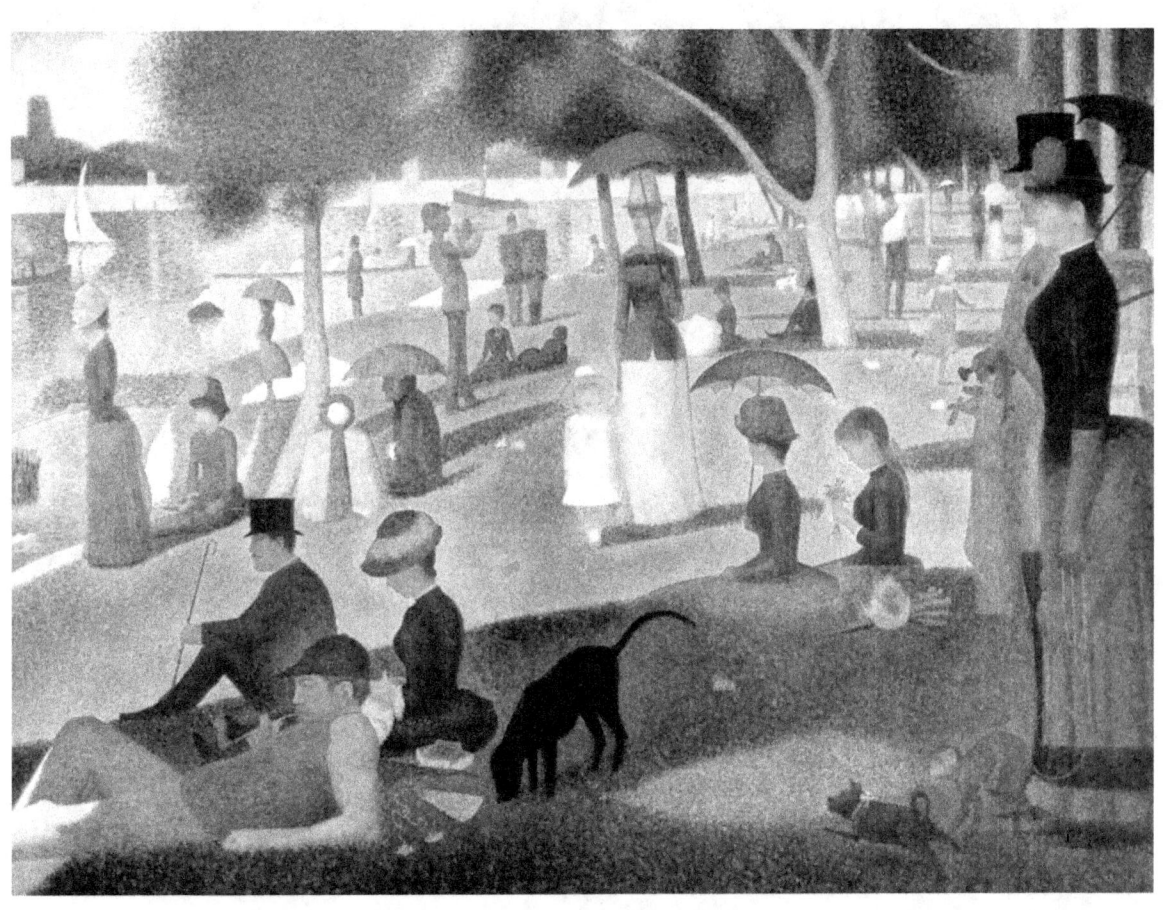

Georges Seurat, Sunday Afternoon On the Island of Grand Jatte, 1884-86
Art Institute, Chicago

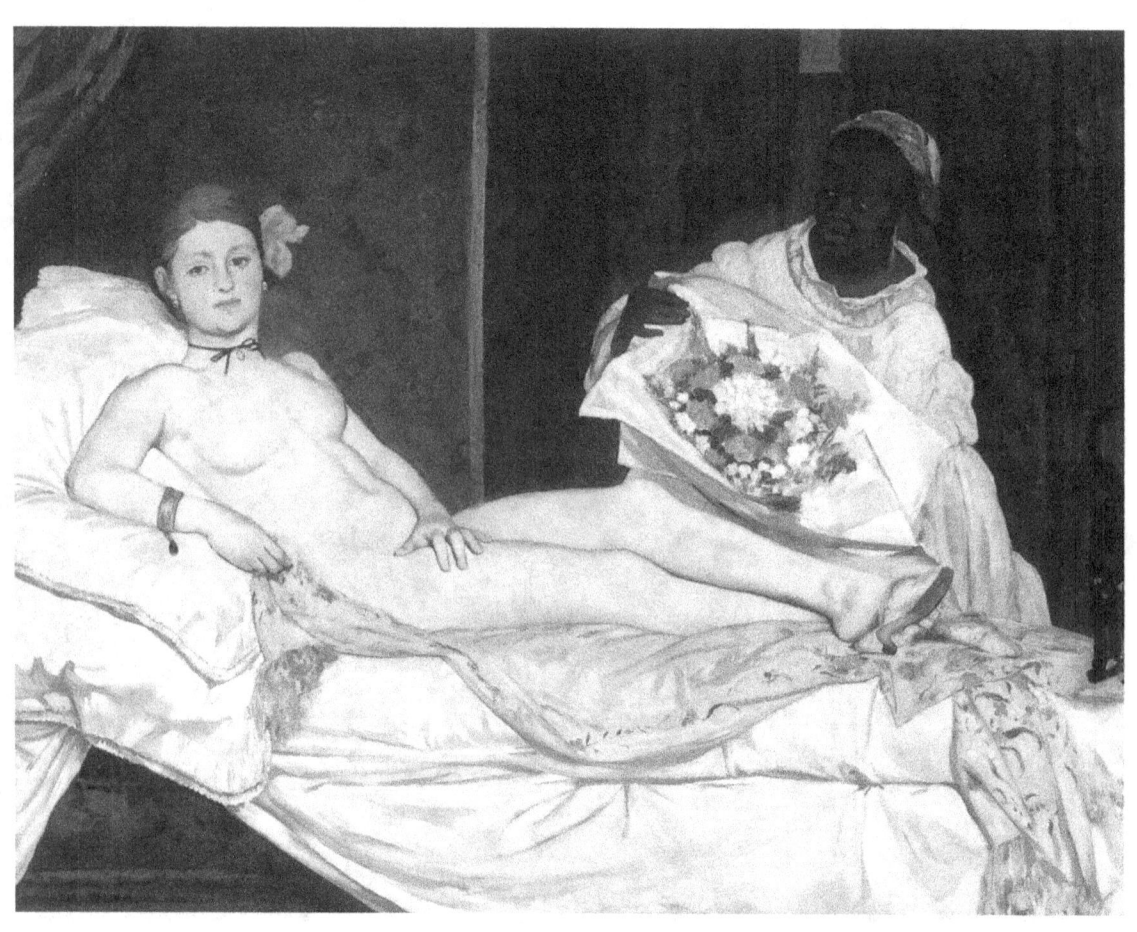

Edouard Manet, Olympia, Musée d'Orsay, Paris

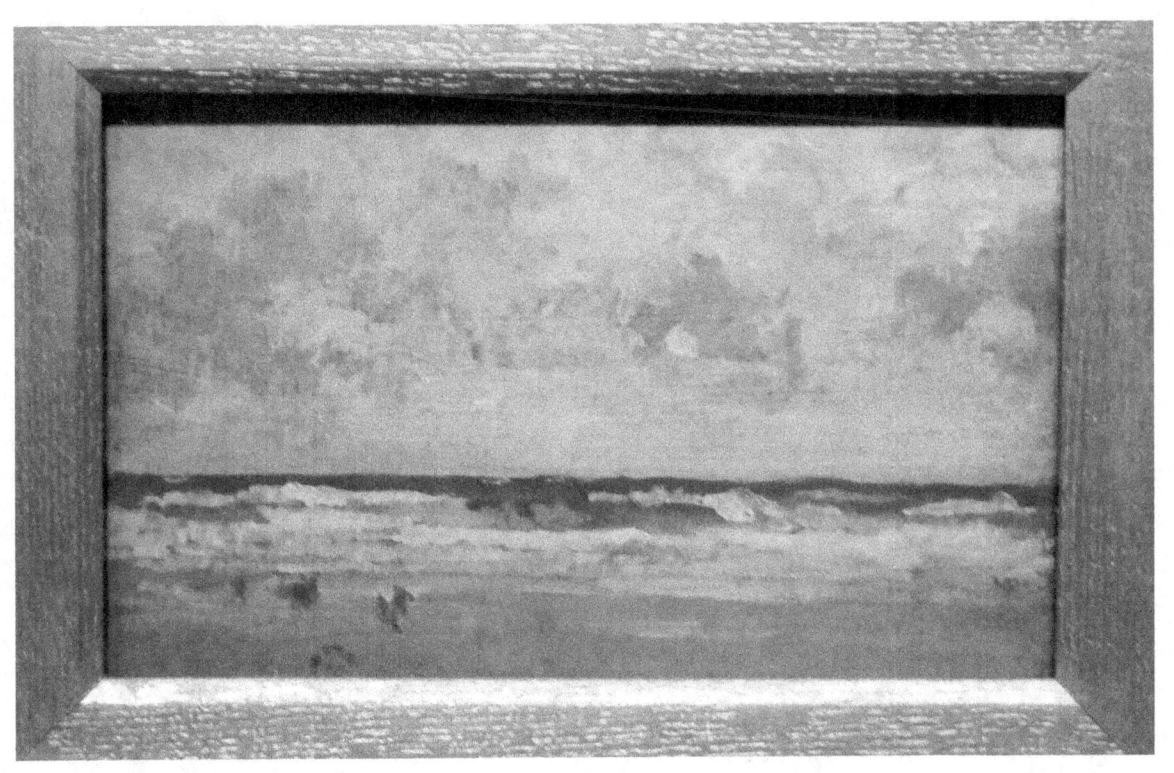

James Whistler, St Ives, Freer Gallery of Art, Washington, DC

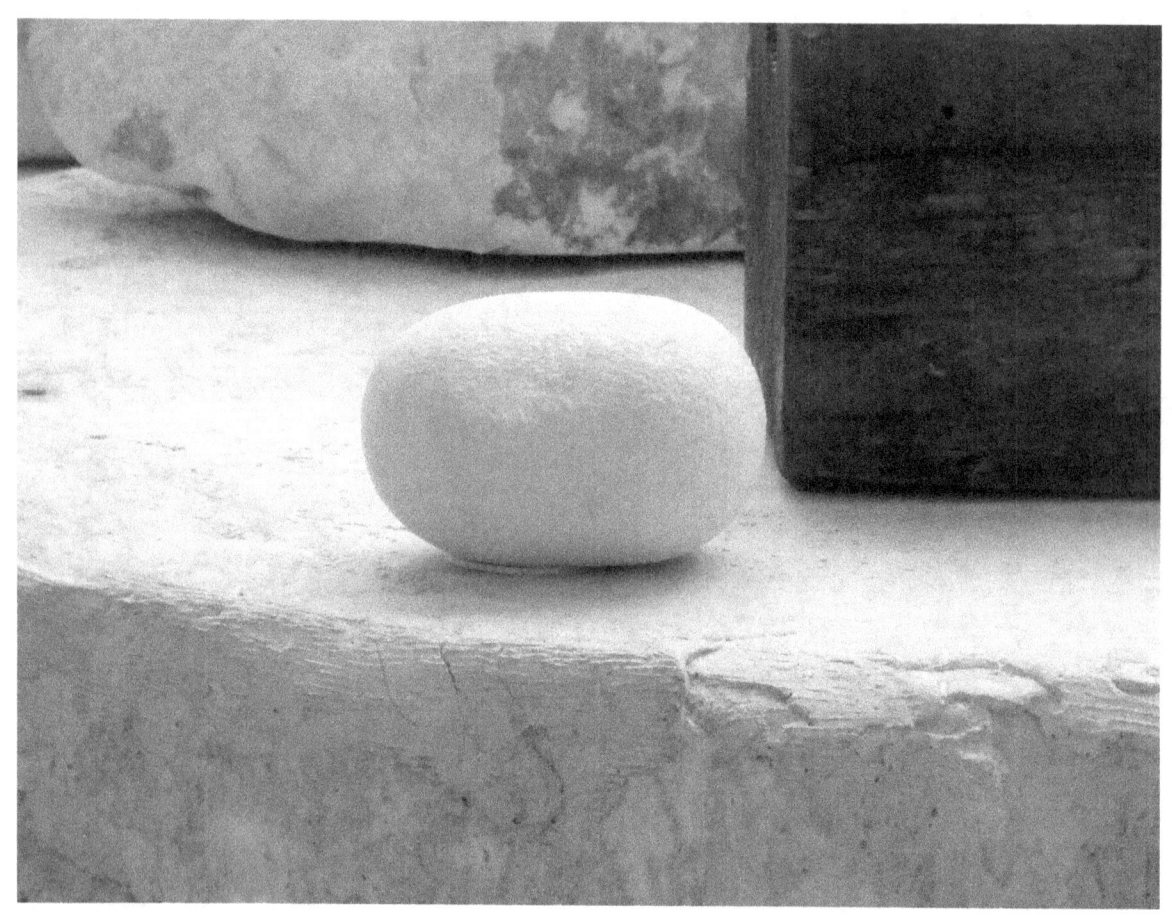

Constantin Brancusi, at the Brancusi Studio in Paris. This page and over.

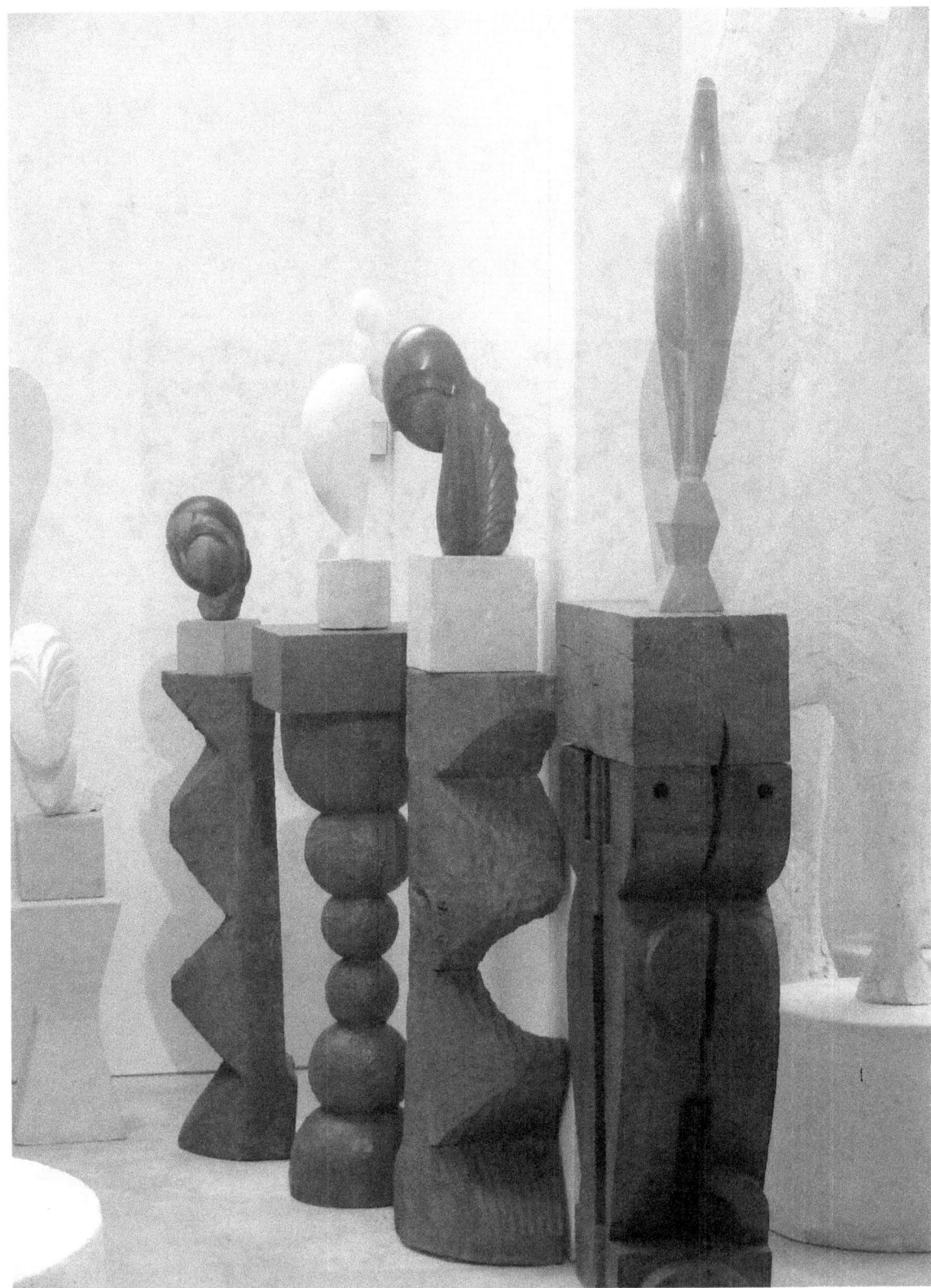

Kasimir Malevich, Black Painting, St Petersburg

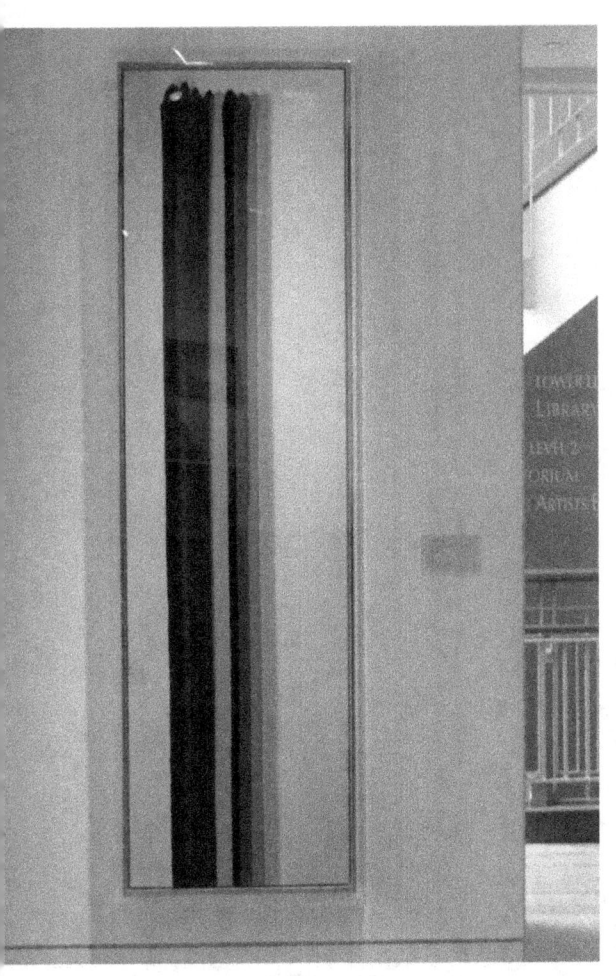

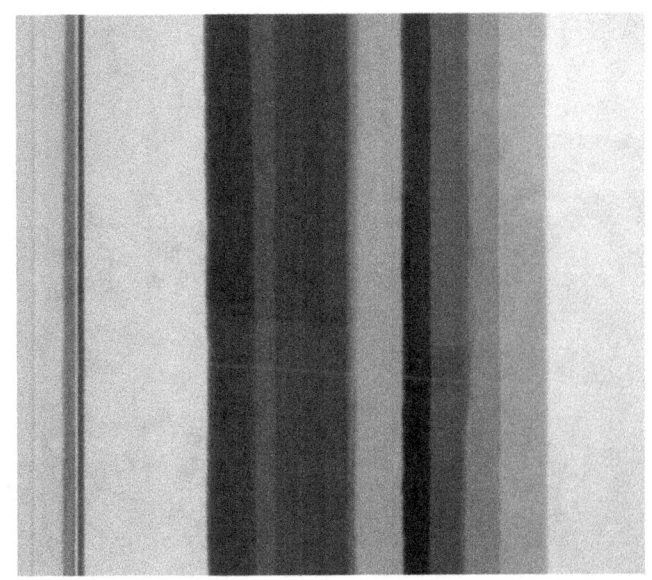

Morris Louis

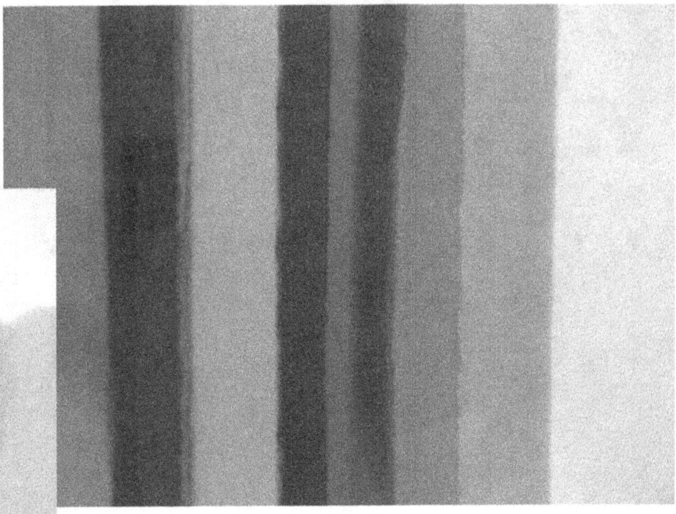

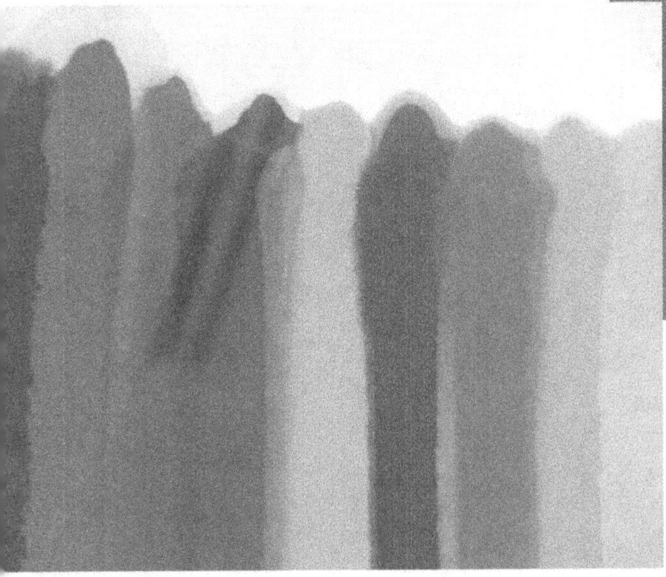

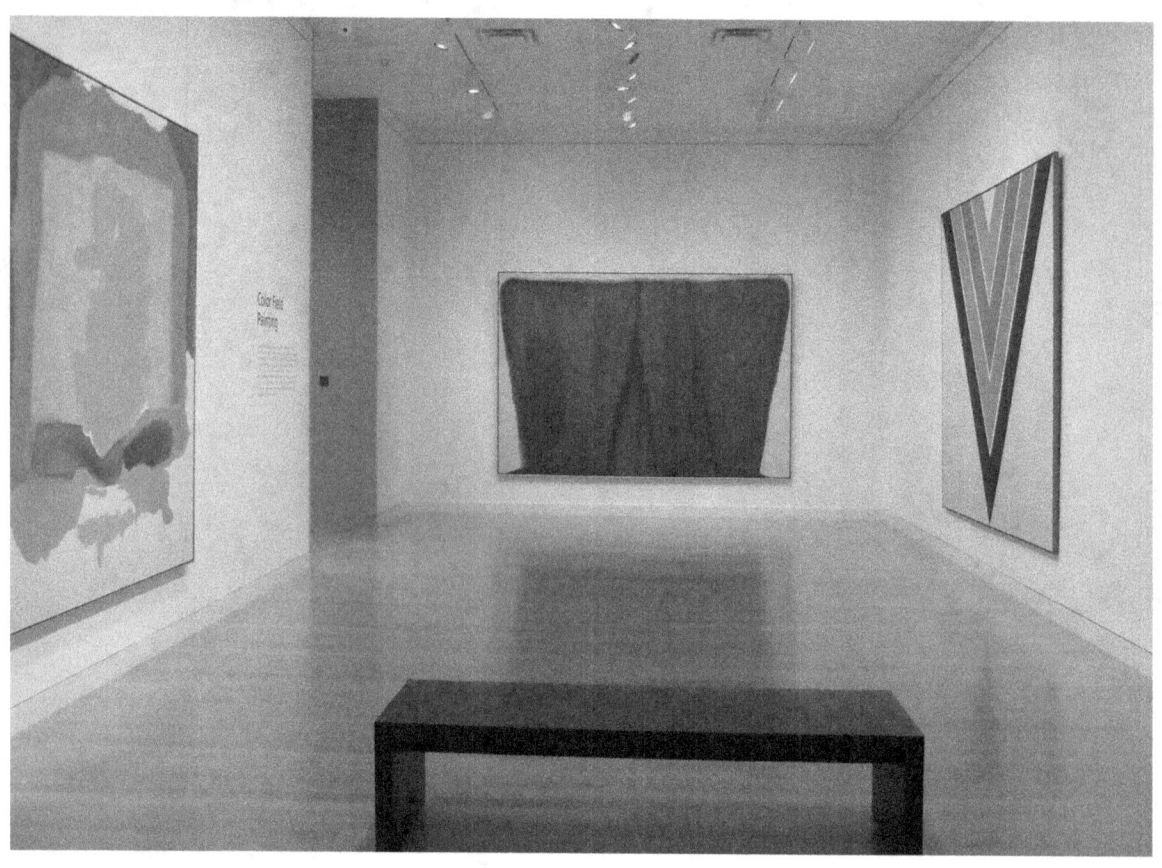

Helen Frankenthaler, Morris Louis and Kenneth Noland
at the wonderful Local Color show,
Smithsonian American Art Museum, Washington, DC, 2008

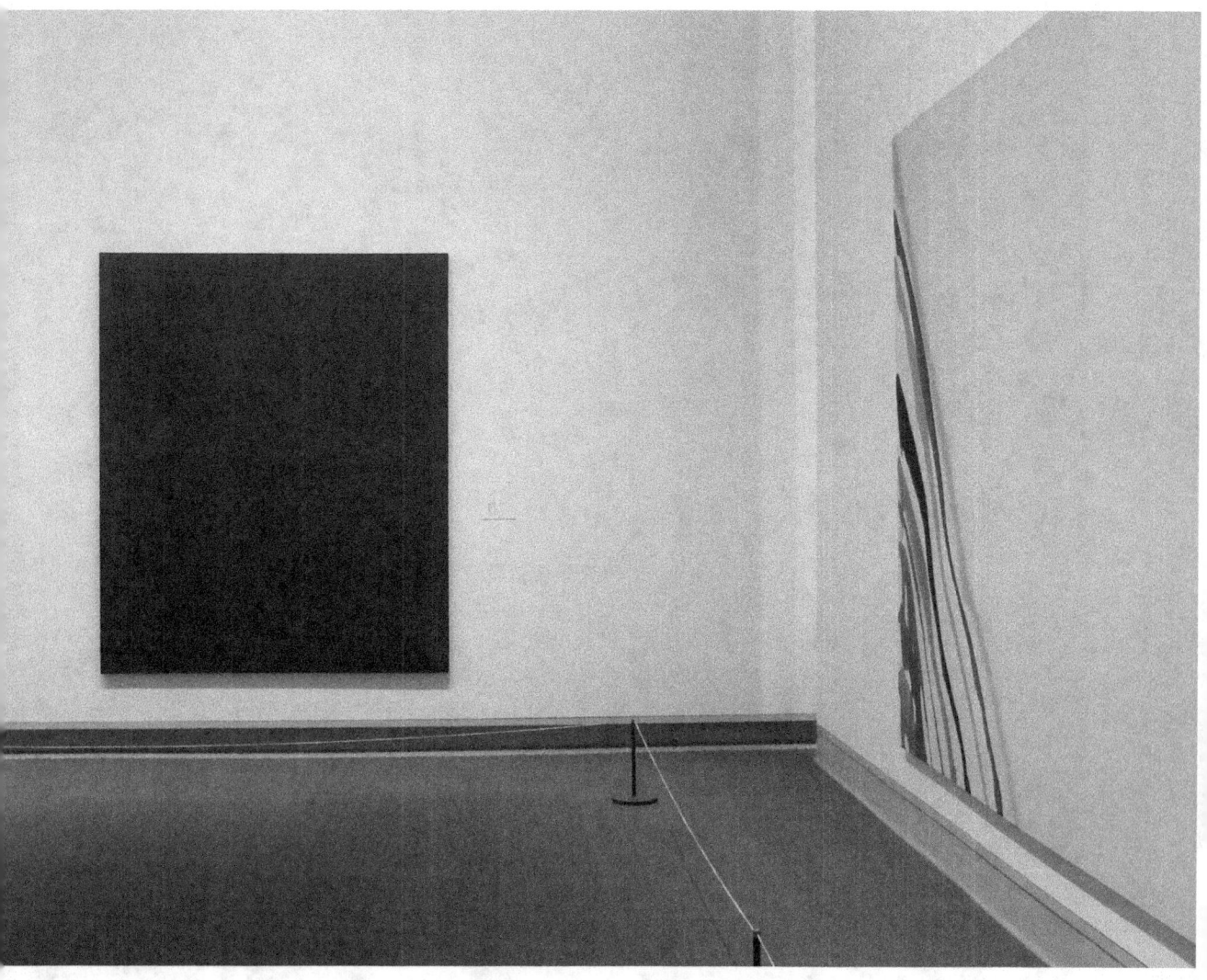

Ad Reinhardt in Gotham, at the Metropolitan Museum of Art, with Morris Louis on the right.

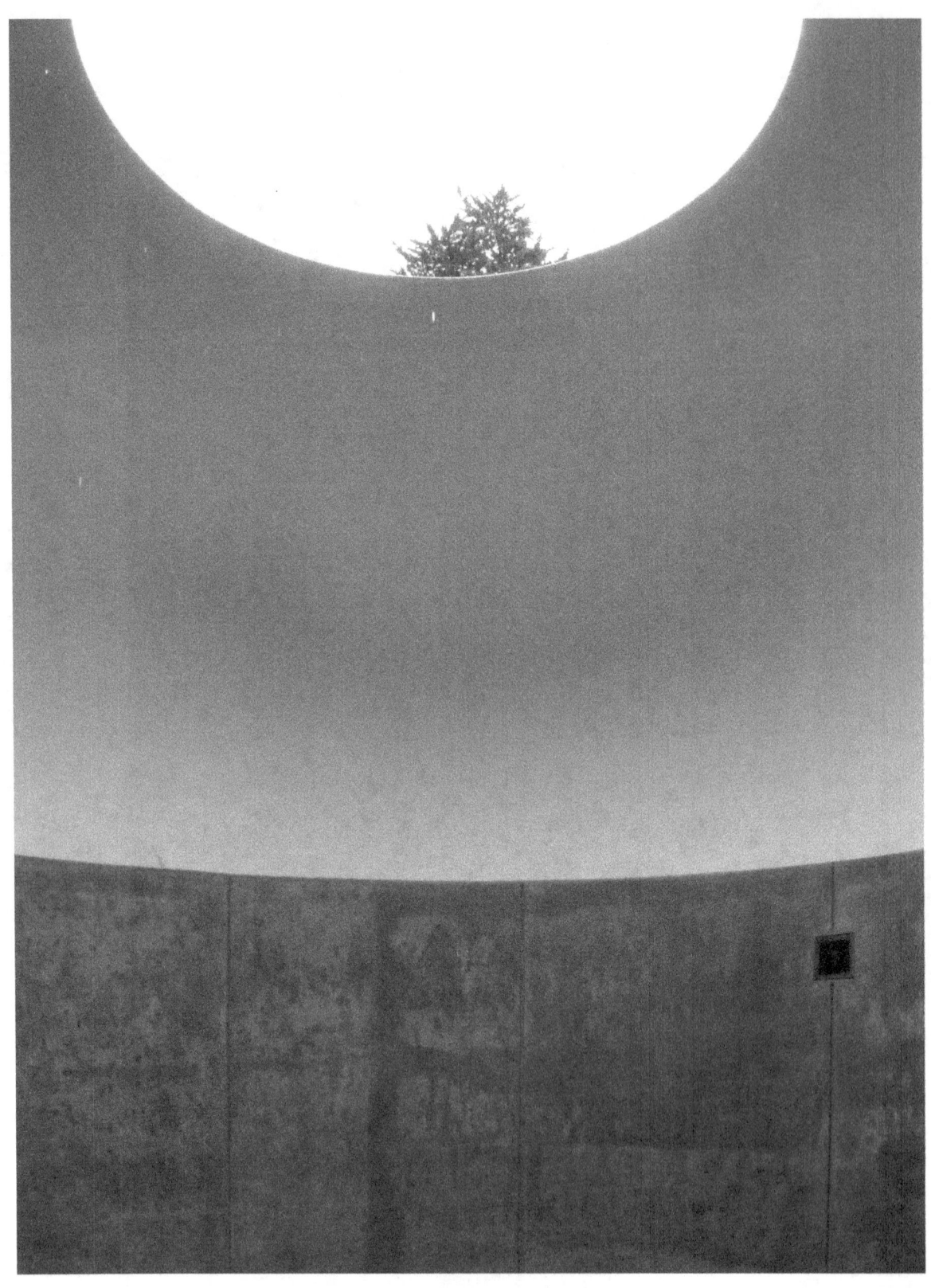

James Turrell, Skyspace, San Francisco.
This page and over.

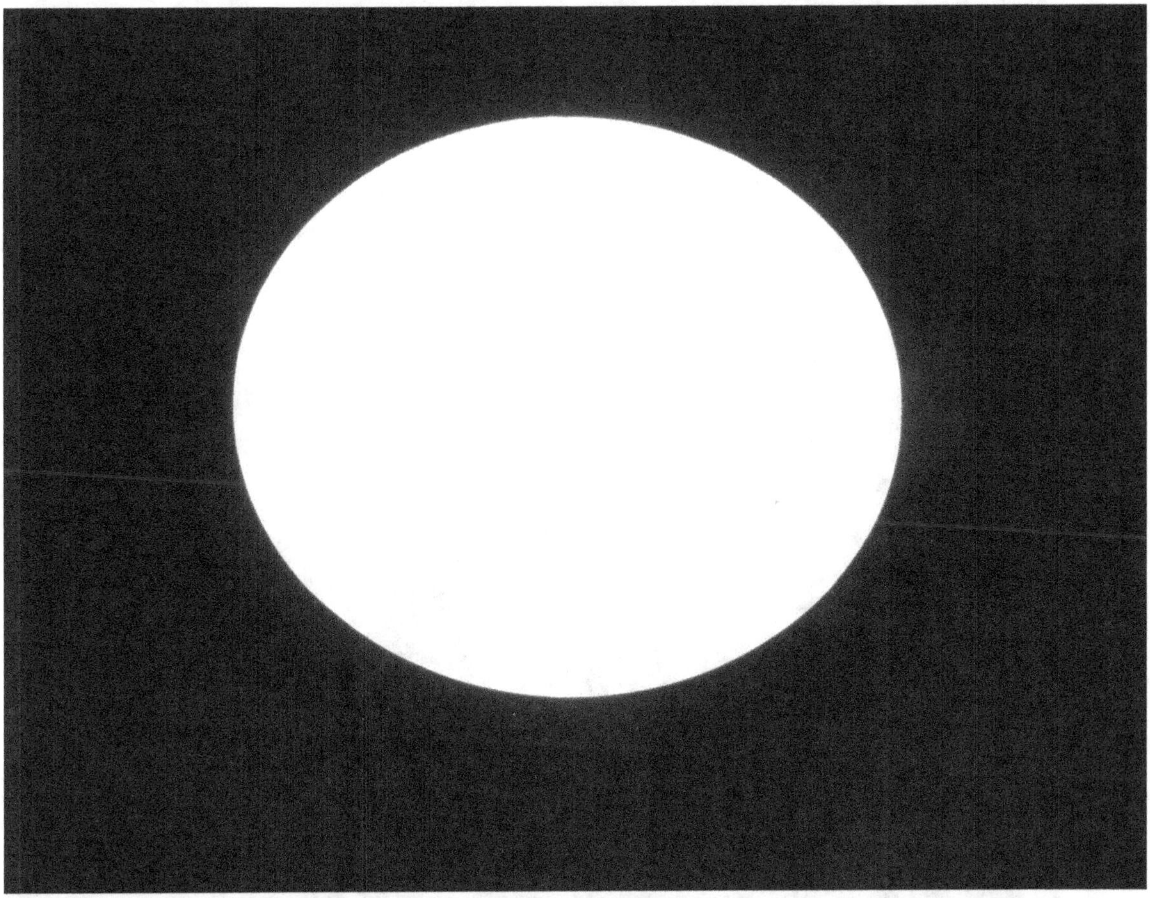

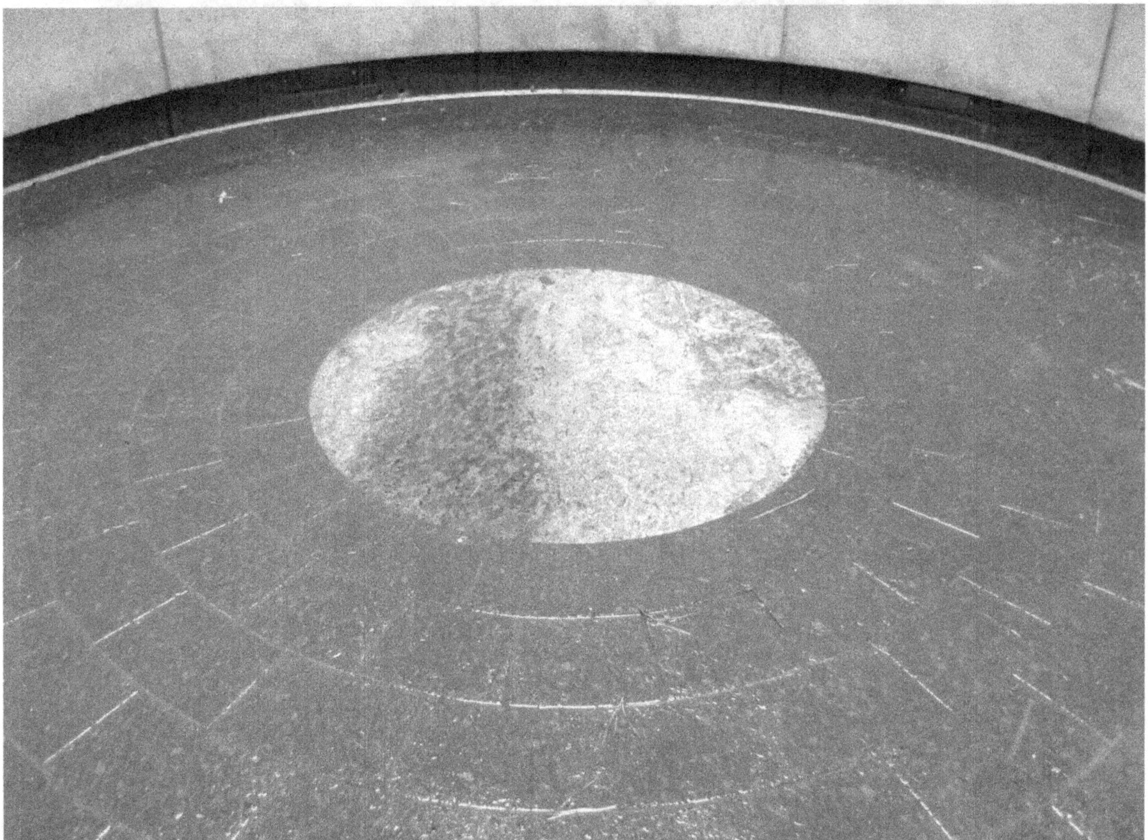

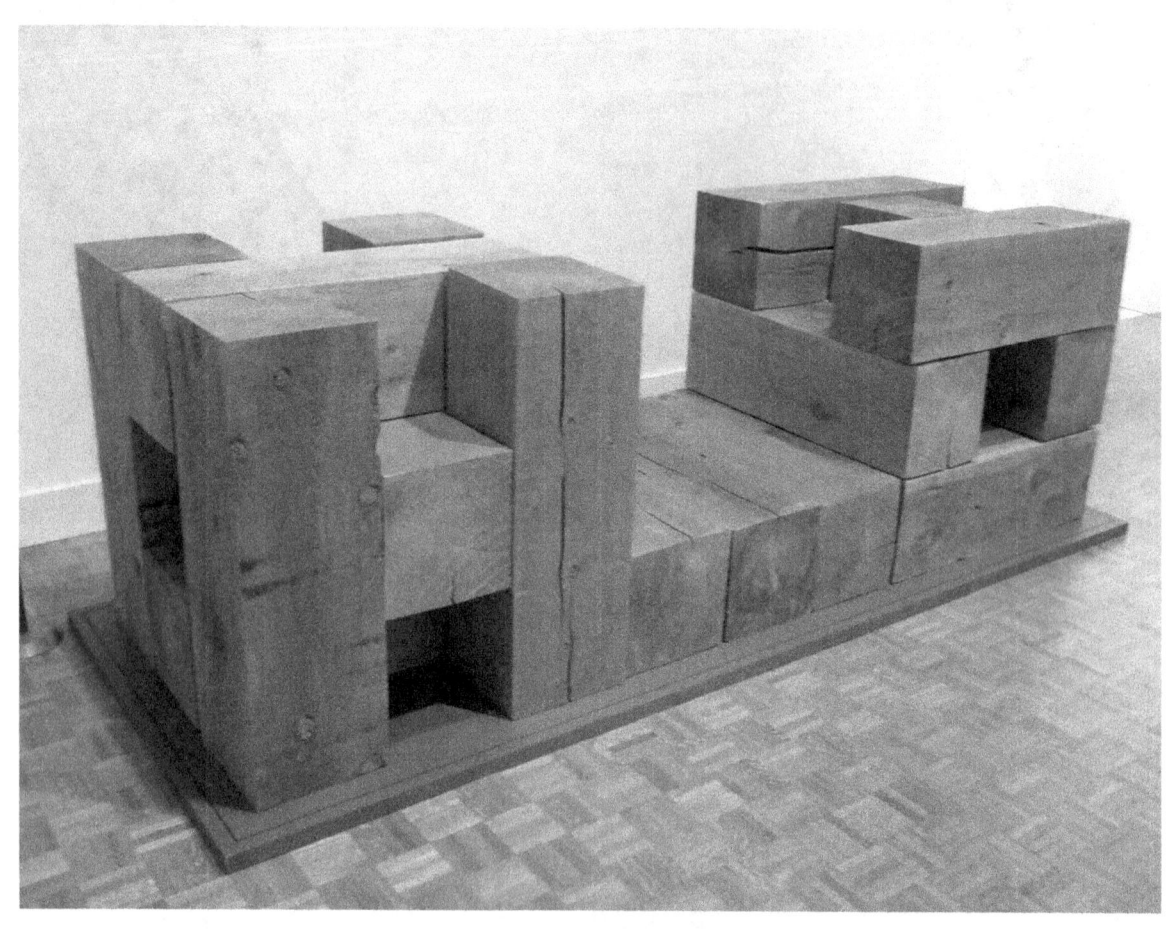

Carl Andre in the Art Institute, Chicago, IL

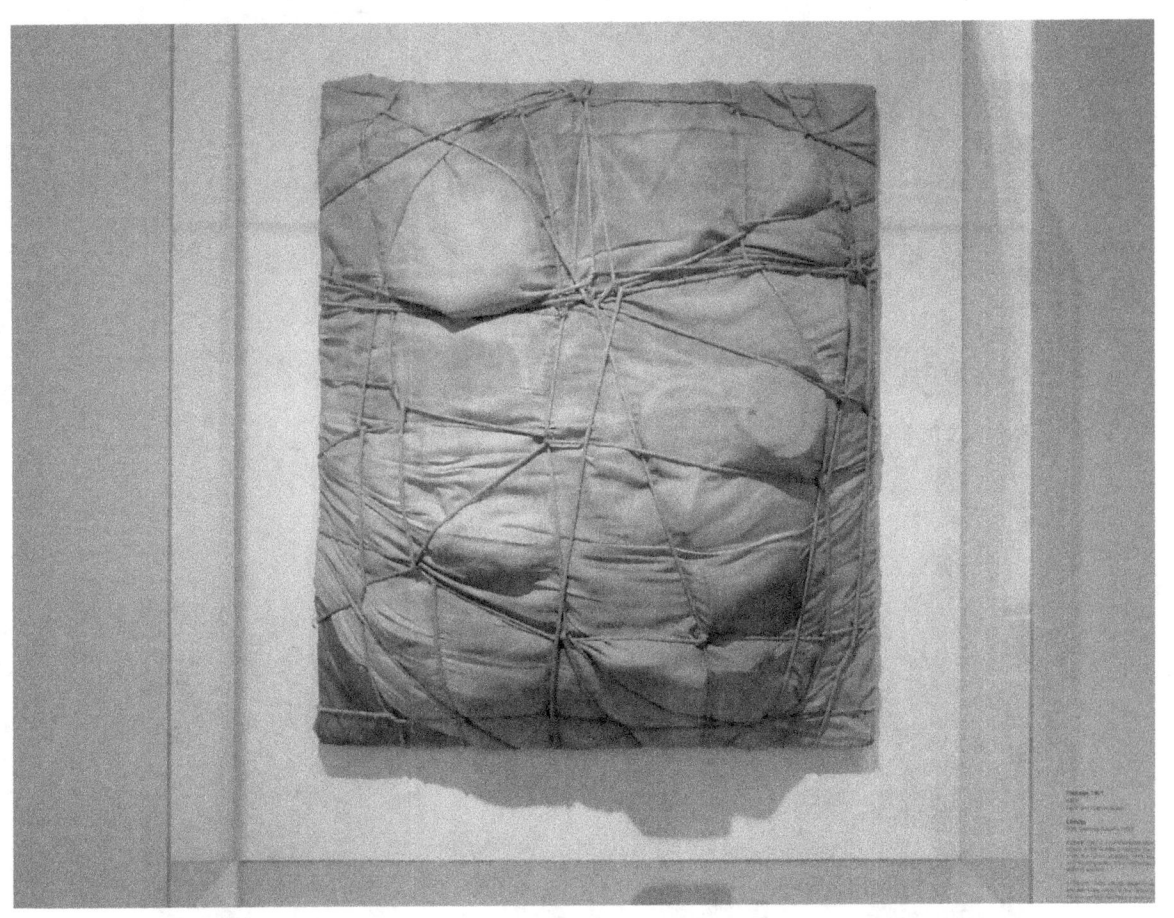

Christo, Package, 1961

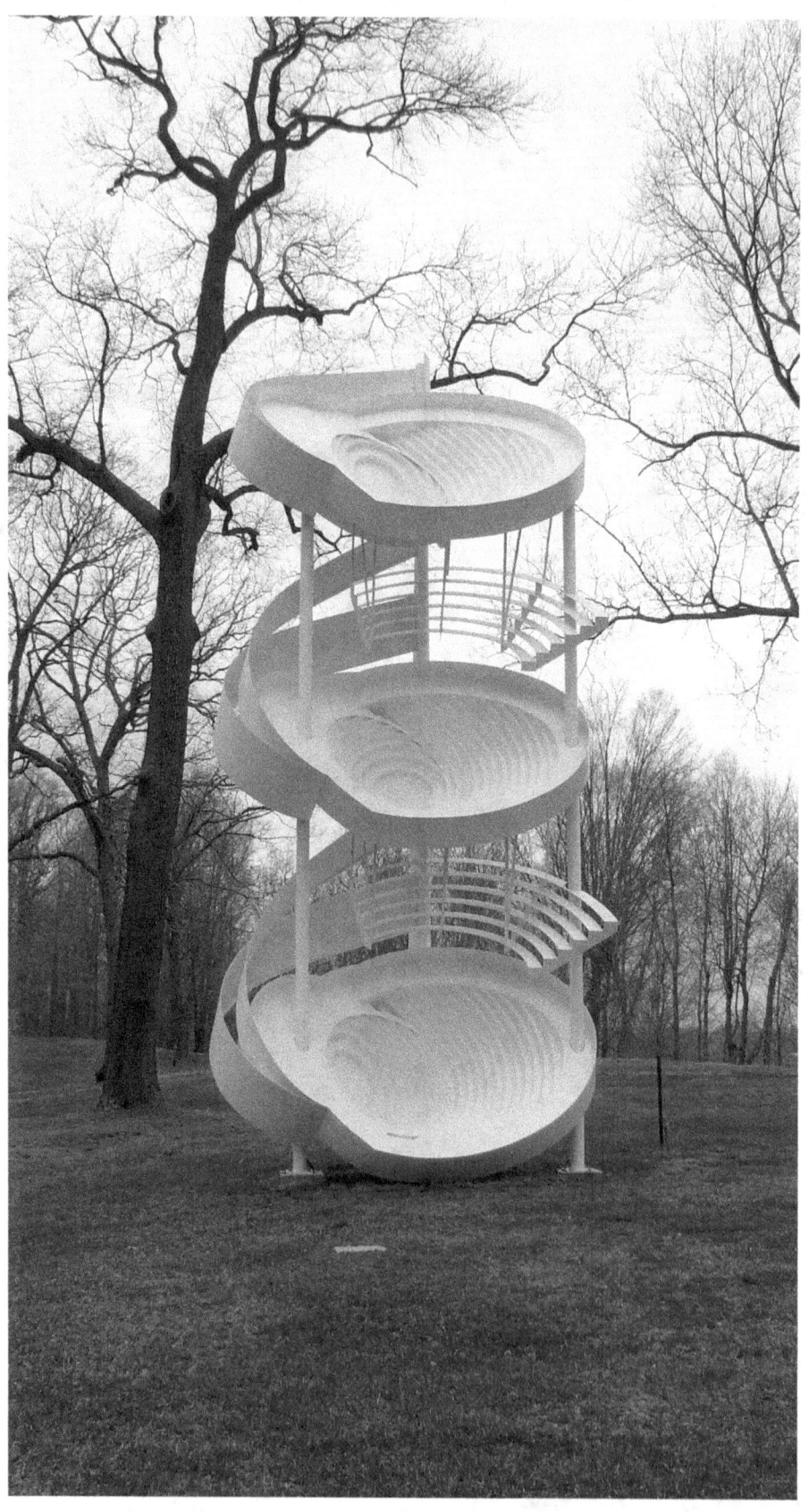

Alice Aycock at Storm King in New York state

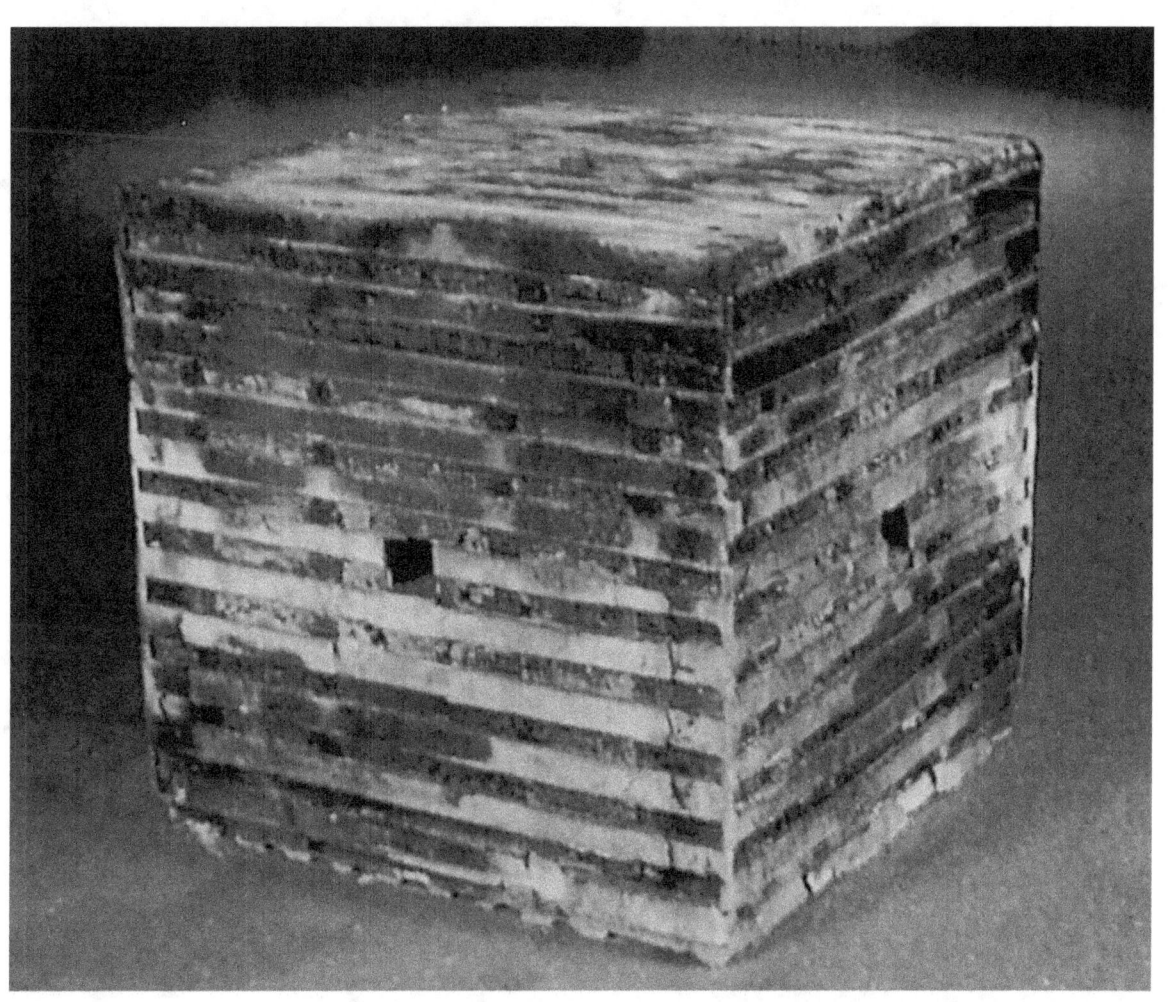

Jackie Winsor, Burnt Piece, 1977

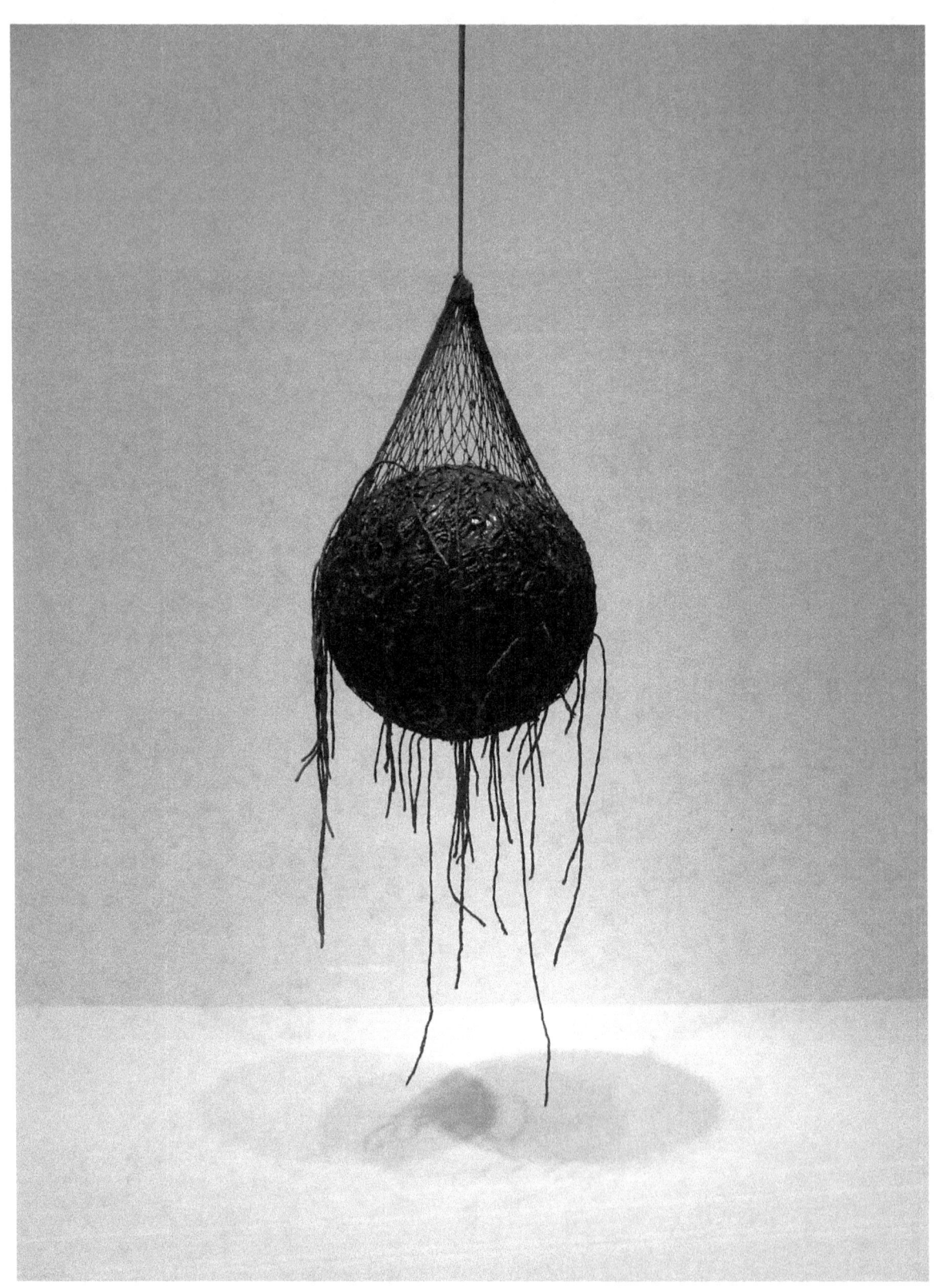

Eva Hesse, National Gallery of Washington, DC

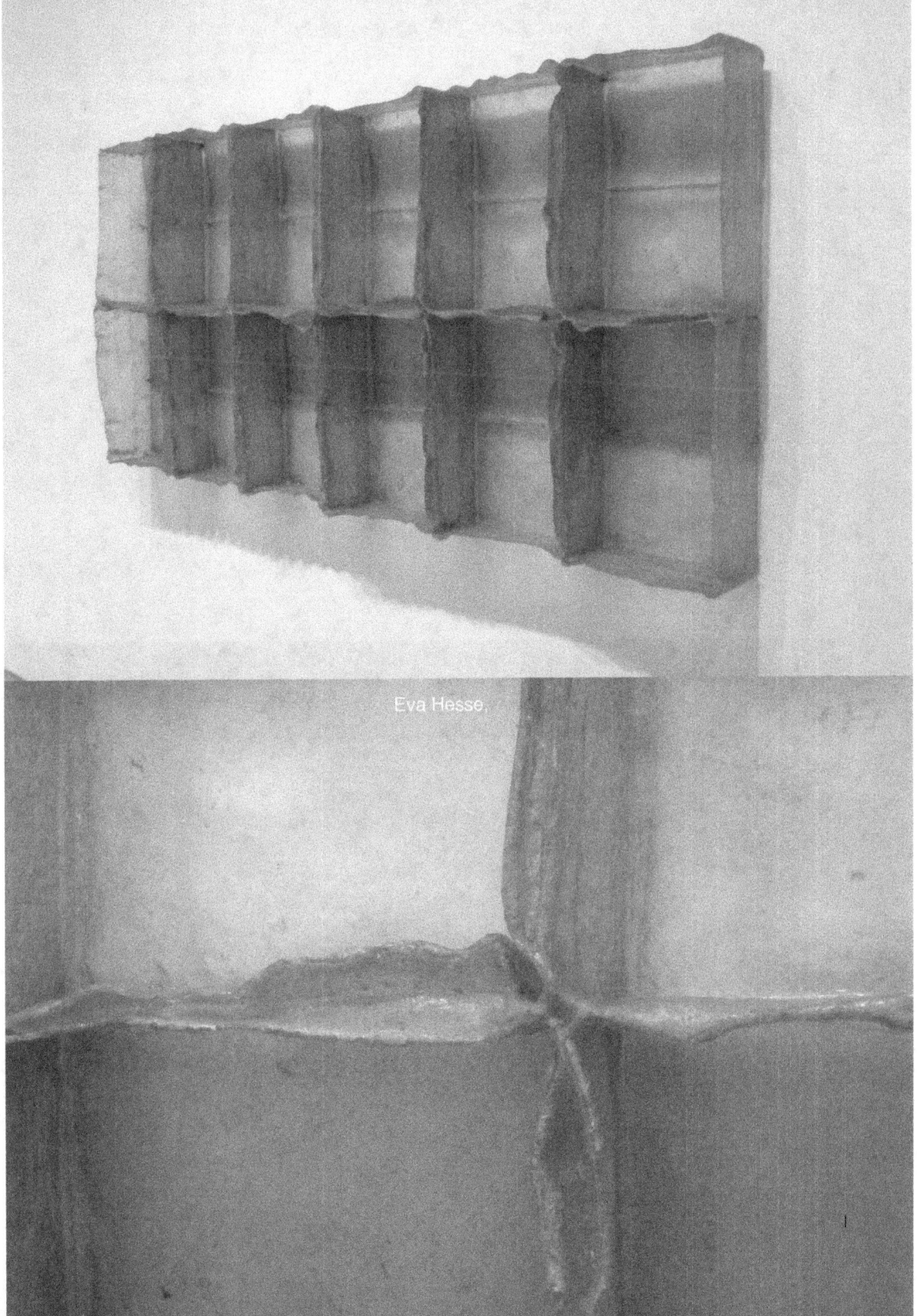

Eva Hesse.

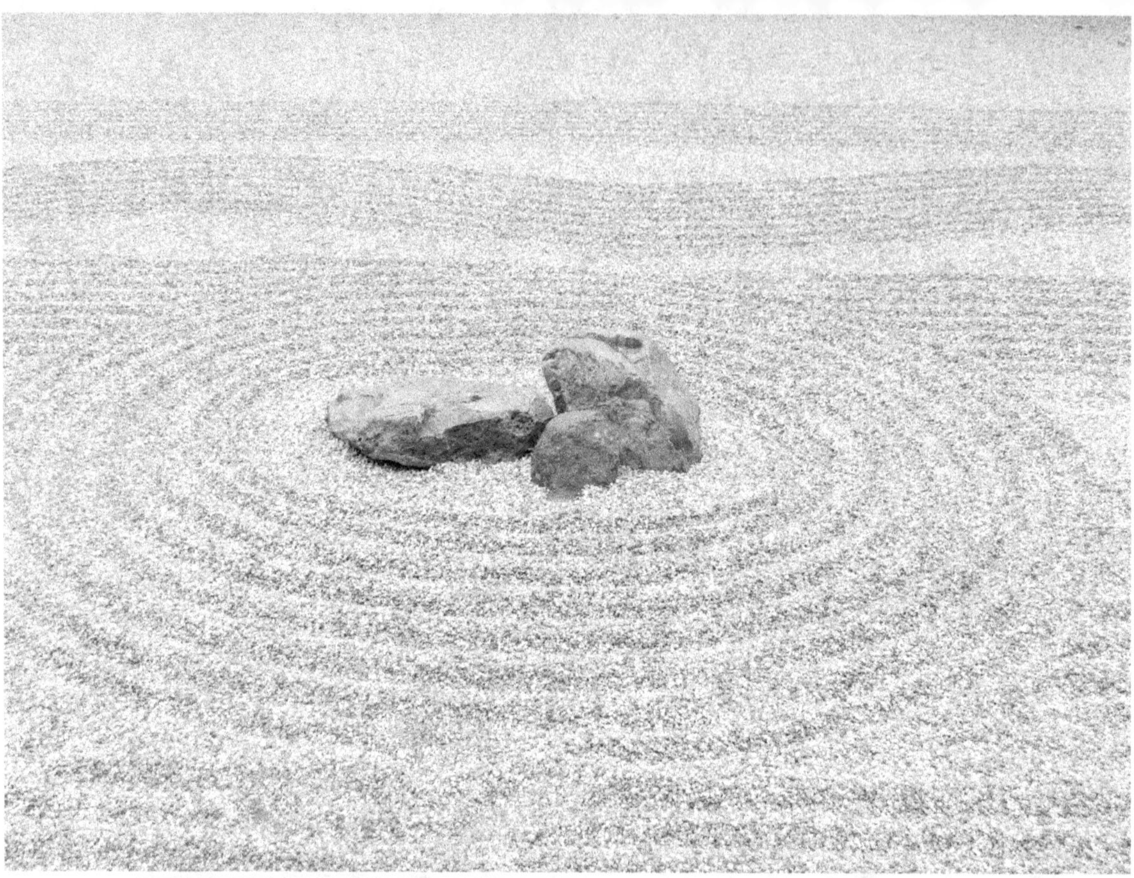

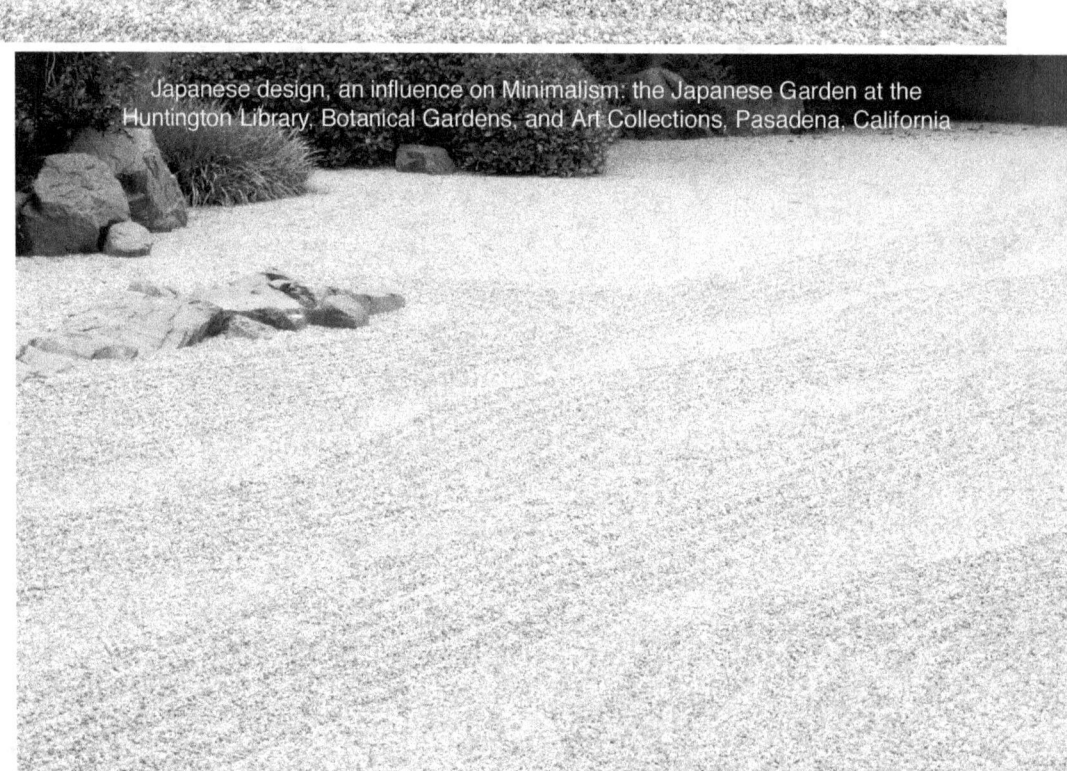

Japanese design, an influence on Minimalism: the Japanese Garden at the Huntington Library, Botanical Gardens, and Art Collections, Pasadena, California

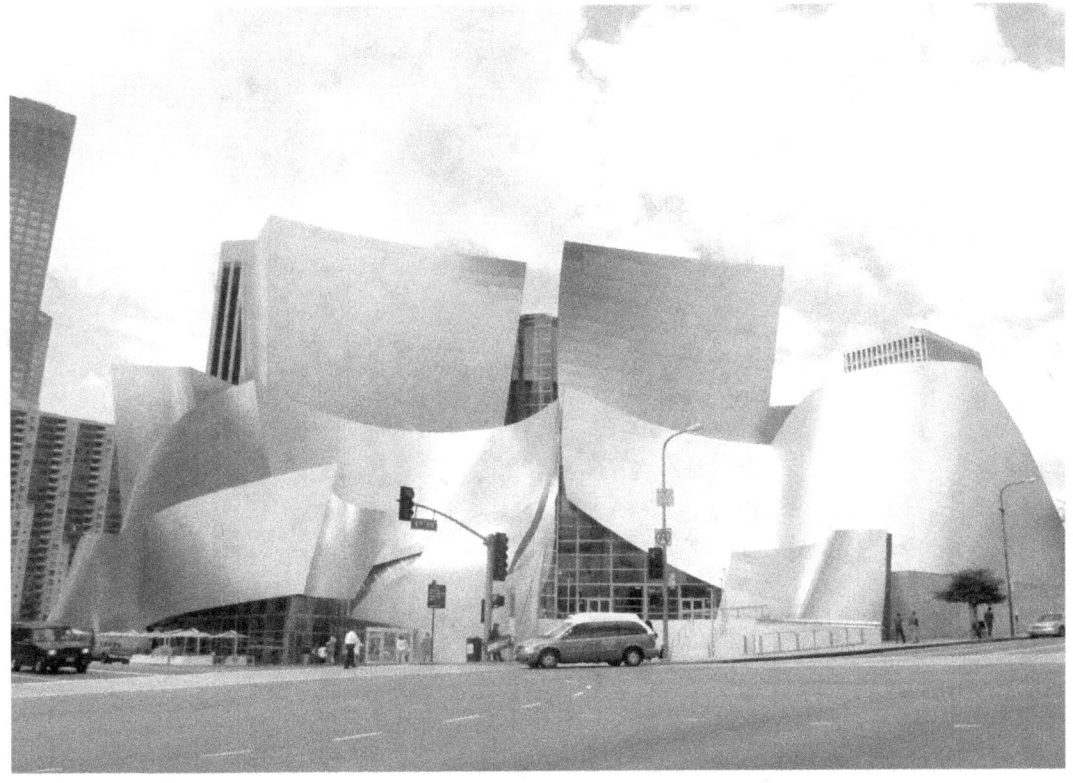

Examples of Minimalism in the contemporary era: the Walt Disney Concert Hall in L.A. (above).
Apple Computers (below left). IKEA furniture, so like a Donald Judd sculpture (below right).

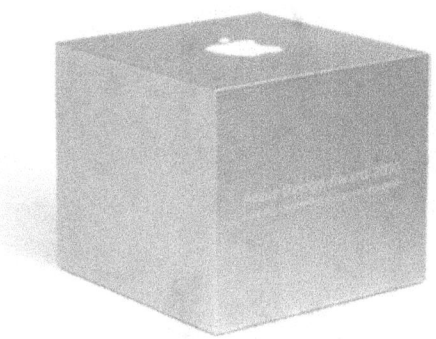

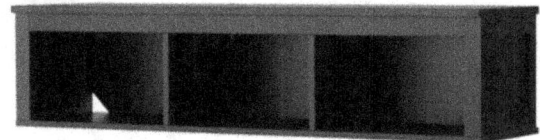

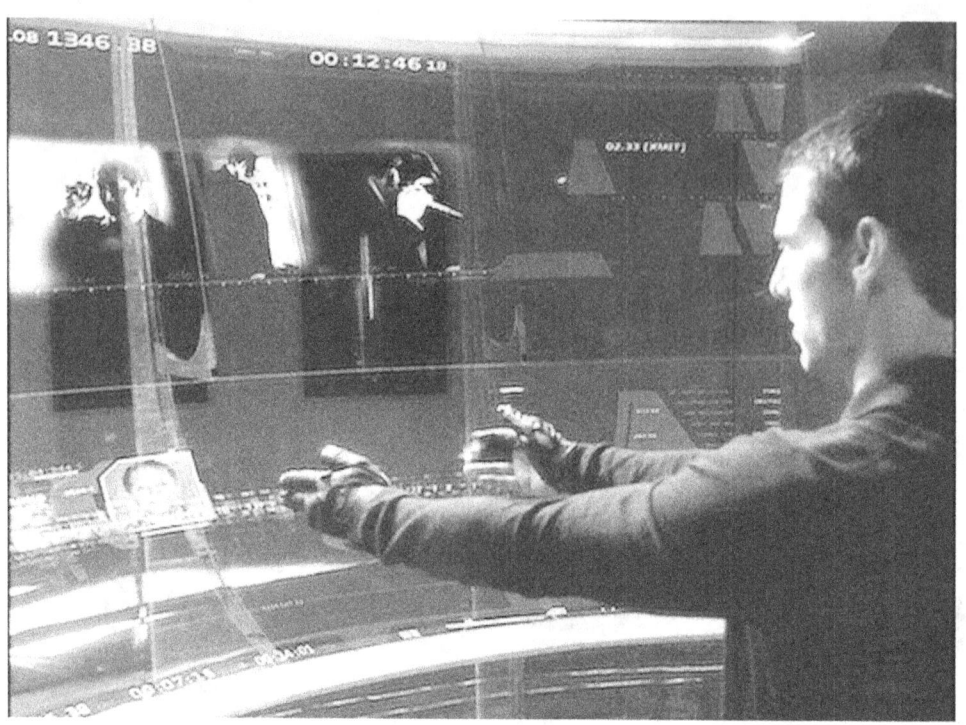

Minimal design in cinema: THX-1138 (1970), below.
Minority Report (2002), above.

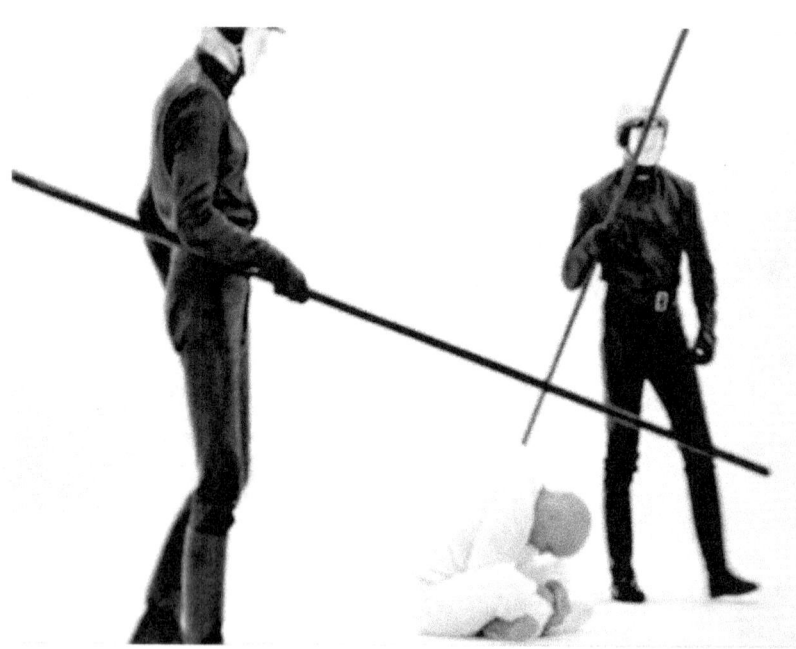

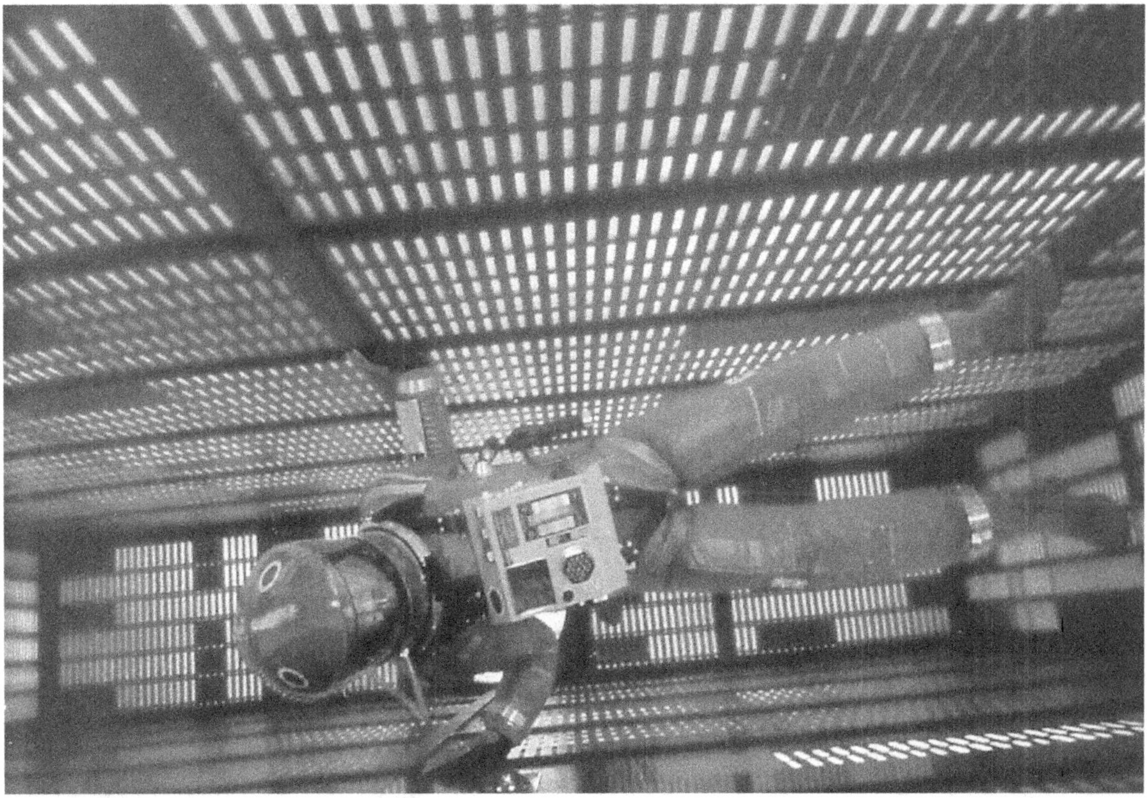

2001: A Space Odyssey (1968)

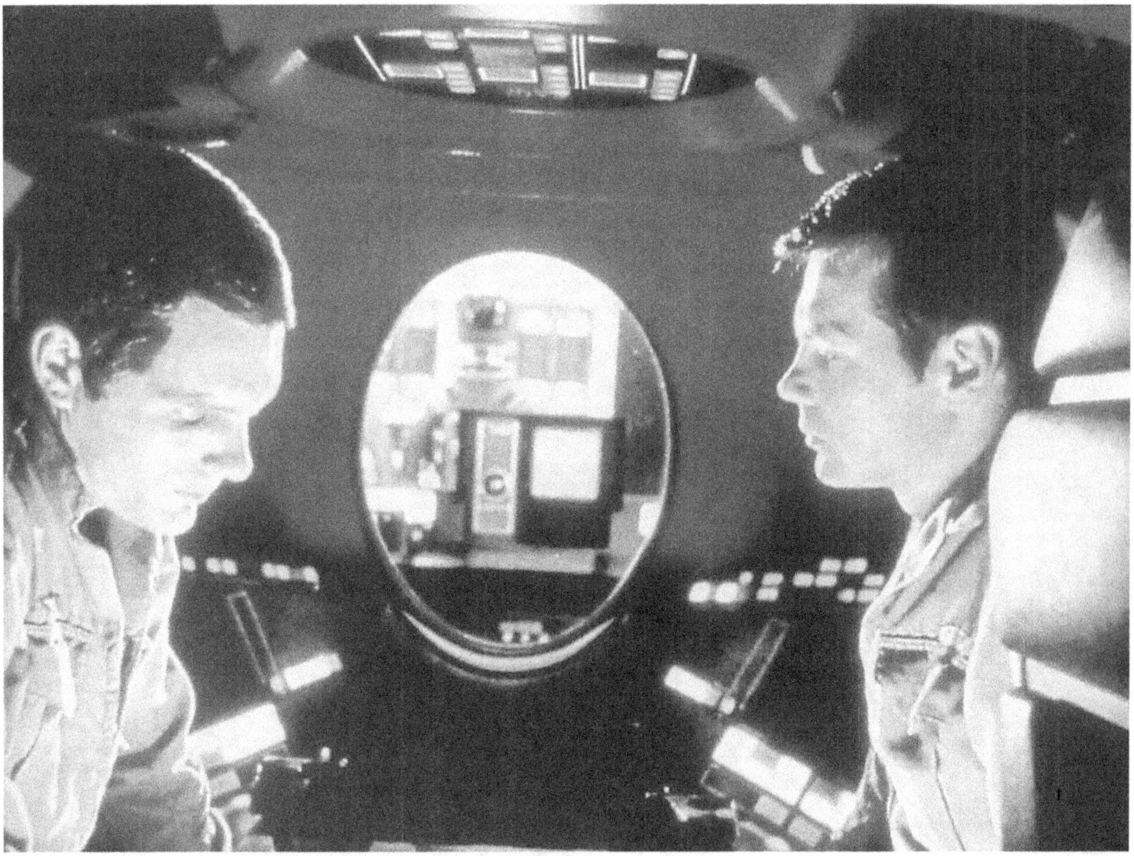

NOTES

1 MINIMAL ÆSTHETICS

MINIMAL ART AND ARTISTS

1. Is it me, or are there are a high proportion of Roberts and Richards among Minimal artists?: Smithson, Tuttle, Duran, Newirth, Grosvenor, Law, Murray, Morris, Irwin, Artschwager, Baringer, Mangold, Serra and Ryman.
2. Sculpture parks and gardens are other locations where Minimal art can be found. In the U.S.A., these include Grounds For Sculpture in New Jersey, Rockerfeller Estate, New York, the Storm King Art Center, New York, Empire State Plaza Art Collection, Albany, New York, Abington Art Center Sculpture Garden, Pennsylvania, Hirshhorn Museum and Sculpture Garden, Washington, DC, Des Moines Art Center, Iowa, Walker Art Center, Minneapolis, Laumeier Sculpture Park, St Louis, Sheldon Sculpture Garden, University of Nebraska, Lincoln, Florida International University, Miami, Chinati Foundation, Marfa, Texas, Oakland Museum, California, Franklin D. Murphy Sculpture Garden, UCLA, L.A., Los Angeles County Museum of Art and the Museum of Outdoor Arts, Colorado. In the UK, Goodwood in Sussex and the Yorkshire Sculpture Park are important sites.
3. H. Rosenberg, "Defining Art", 1967, in B, 306.
4. See. F. Colpitt, 1990, 4.
5. B. Kurtz, "Last Call At Max's", *Artforum*, 19, 8, Apl, 1981.

MINIMAL ART AND LITERATURE (AND SAMUEL BECKETT)

1. S. Beckett, *Dialogues*, in *Disjecta*, Calder, London, 1983, 139.
2. S. Beckett, *Company,* in *Nohow On*, Calder, London, 1992, 20.

MINIMAL ART AND PHILOSOPHY

1. Ludwig Wittgenstein took his work very seriously. Philosophy was a way of life for him, not just something you do in the academy, from nine to five, then forget about for the rest of your life. Wittgenstein disliked people who dabbled, who played with philosophy, who pursued bourgeois academic philosophy. Philosophy, for Wittgenstein, was something that you do. This strict, workaholic view of pursuing philosophy has something in common with the Minimal and Conceptual artists who merged their life and their art, and held similar views on combining life and work.
2. L. Wittgenstein, *Tractatus Logico-Philosophicus*, Routledge, London, 1961.

MINIMAL SCALE

1. "Donald Judd", *The New York Times*, Apl 1, 1977, C20.
2. J. Agee, 1975; P. Carlson, "Donald Judd's Equivocal Objects", *Art in America*, Jan, 1984, 114-8; B. Haskell, 1988; D. Kuspitt, 1985; B. Smith, 1975.
3. L. Lippard, 1972; G. Baro, "Toward Speculation in Pure Form", *Art International*, Summer, 1967, 27-31; E. Greene, "Morphology of Tony Smith's Work", *Artforum*, April, 1974, 54-59.
4. See I. Licht, "Dan Flavin", *Artscanada*, Dec, 1968, 50-57; W. Wilson, 48-51; J. Burnham, 1969, 48-55.
5. J.N. Chandler, "Tony Smith and Sol LeWitt", *Art International*, 12, 7, 1968; D. Kuspitt, 1975; A. Legg, 1978; L. Lippard, 1967; R. Pincus-Witten, "Sol LeWitt", *Artforum*, 11, 6, Feb, 1973.
6. R. Krauss, "Richard Serra: Sculpture Redrawn", *Artforum*, May, 1972, 38-43; D. Crimp, "Richard Serra: Sculpture Exceeded", *October*, Fall, 1981, 67-78.
7. K. Baker, 1980a, 88-94; D. Waldman, 1970, 60-62, 75-79; M. Tuchman, "Background of a Minimalist: Carl Andre", *Artforum*, Mch, 1978, 29-33; E. Develing, 1969.
8. See R. Williams, 2000, 86.
9. G. Battock, 1995, 150, 154.

THE PRESENCE OF THE OBJECT IN MINIMAL ART

1. W. Tucker, 1969, 12-13.
2. R. Morris, 1966, in B, 224.
3. R. Morris, 1966, 20-23.
4. T. Smith, quoted in B, 228-230.
5. R. Williams, 2000, 10.

MINIMAL ART AND CONSTANTIN BRANCUSI

1. D. Dudley, "Brancusi", *Dial*, 82, Feb, 1927, 124.
2. C. Brancusi, in P. Pandrea: "The Laws of Craiova", *Portraits and Controversies*, Bucharest, Romania, 194 vol. 1, 120.

3. B. Flanagan, quoted in the catalogue of *Entre el Objeto y la Imagen: Escultura britanica contemporanea*, Palacio de Velasquez, Madrid, 1986, 233.
4. S. Burton, "My Brancusi", *Art in America*, Mch, 1990.

MONOCHROME AND MONOTONOUS

1. See I. Sandler, *The Triumph of American Painting*, Harper & Row, New York, NY, 1970, 245f; L. Lippard, 1966, 62; R. Morris, "Notes on Sculpture"; K. McShine, 1966; R. Lund, "Why Isn't Minimal Art Boring?", *Journal of Aesthetics and Art Criticism*, 45, 2, Winter, 1986, 195-7.
2. A. Warhol, in K. Stiles, 1996, 340.
3. I. Sandler, *Concrete Expressionism*, Loeb Student Center, New York University, NY, 1965, 97.
4. J. Perreault, 1995, 260.
5. In K. McShine, 1966.
6. B. Boice, "The Quality Problem", *Artforum*, 11, 2, Oct, 1972.
7. M. Fried, in B, 142.
8. Quoted in C, 121.
9. M. Kozloff, 1964, 64; B. O'Doherty, 21.
10. A.S. Wooster, 1980, 143-7.
11. S. LeWitt, 1969, 1970; L. Lippard, 1967; R. Smith, 1975; A.S. Wooster, 1980.
12. L. Alloway, 1966.
13. L. Alloway, "Serial Forms", in M. Tuchman, 1967, 14.

CONCEPTUAL ART

1. C. Greenberg, 1961.
2. As anyone who has taken a photo will know, all manner of details can affect how one reads a photograph: how it is printed, light, dark, soft, hard, cropped, full frame, more red, more blue, burnt in, dodged, touched up, glossy or matt paper, and so on. The size of the photo affects it very much, as does the frame.
3. Quoted in D. Sylvester, op. cit, 15-16.
4. In C. Robins, 78.
5. David Nash discussed this indoor/ outdoor problem in a 1978 interview:

An object made indoors diminishes in scale and stature when placed outside. The reverse happens when an object made outside is brought inside, it seems to grow in stature and presence. It brings the outside in with it. The object outside has to contend with unlimited space, uneven ground and the weather. The sculpture I show inside is meant to be seen inside, it relates to the limited space, the peculiar scale, and the still air. (In A. McPherson, "David Nash: interviewed by Allan McPherson", *Artscribe*, 12, June, 1978, 30)

6. L. Weiner, in *Avalanche*, Spring, 1972, 67.

THE RELIGIOUS ELEMENTS IN MINIMAL ART

1. M. Basho, *The Narrow Road to the Deep North and Other Travel Sketches*, tr. N. Yuasa, Penguin, London, 1966, 33.
2. M. Ueda, *Matsuo Basho*, Twayne, New York, NY, 1970, 167.
3. John White, discussing Oriental art, makes points which can apply to Minimal art:

In Chinese art the surface emphasis is negative rather than positive. It is in close accordance with the calm acceptance, the contemplative natural mysticism, which reached its highest flowering in Taoism. The surface is left undisturbed. Colours are few, and soft. Ink, and delicate monotone washes are the characteristic media. Spiritual and decorative qualities are valued high above imitative naturalism, the evocative above the representational... The unmarked silk, or paper, is at once the atmosphere, the space, and the inviolate decorative surface. (J. White, *The Birth and Rebirth of Pictorial Space*, Faber, London, 1981, 67-69)

4. F. Stella, radio broadcast, 1964, in B, 158.
5. F. Stella, in B. Glaser, 58f.
6. C. Andre, 1984.
7. For Peter Fuller, Brice Marden and the Minimalists did not produce a positive æsthetic emptiness, but one which was spiritually bankrupt. Referring to Rudolf Otto's influential book *The Idea of the Holy,* Fuller wrote:

It seems to me that there is every difference in the world between this spiritually replete emptiness and the numbing vacuity of works by artists such as Carl Andre, Agnes Martin, Ellsworth Kelly or Brice Marden. (1993, xxxv)

LIGHT AND SPACE

1. S. Beckett, *Collected Shorter Prose,* Calder, London, 1984, 145.

MINIMAL CIRCLES

1. See M. Berger.
2. In L. Lippard, 1967, 26.
3. *Rosarium Philosophorum,* quoted in A. Mann, *Sacred Architecture,* Element Books, Shaftesbury, Dorset, 1993, 87.

2   MINIMAL PAINTERS

THE ÆSTHETICS OF MINIMAL PAINTING

1. In T. Hess, 1971, 24.
2. See M. Fried, 1965, 14-15.
3. T. Smith, in L. Lippard, 1972, 9, 23.
4. C. Robins, 1976, 19.

FRANK STELLA

1. D. Judd, 1962, 51.
2. S. Nodelman, 1967, 77.
3. W. Domingo, 44-45.
4. W. Rubin, quoted in E. de Antonio, 138.
5. J. Johns, in D. Sylvester, 1974, 14.
6. P. Fuller, "American Painting Since Last Year", *Art Monthly,* June, 1979, in D. Shapiro, 178.
7. William Rubin wrote:

    there's a vast difference in sensibilities and in aims, so I don't want to make this relationship too close, but I think [Jasper] Johns also had one other importance. That is, his flag pictures and some of the other images he made were the first paintings in which the field of the pictures is absolutely identical with the motif of the picture: the boundaries of the pictures are identical with the boundaries of the flag. The flag is laid out as a flat pattern on the surface, and although Johns is a representational painter in that sense and Frank became an abstract painter, I think the notion of making the motif identical with the shape of the field, even though that shape remains rectangular in Johns' flag, lurks somewhere behind what would become the principle of Frank's [Stella] shaped canvas. And that principle is, if I can define it in its simplest way, essentially that the boundary of the picture is going to be determined by the governing pattern of the surface, and that there will be an absolute reciprocity between the outer shape of the picture, which might be considered simply the outside line of a pattern that operates over the entire surface. (In E. de Antonio, 138-9)

8. K. Schwitters, quoted in F. Roh, 1968, 133.
9. J. Coplans, "Serial Imagery", 37.
10. B. Rose, "ABC Art", 59.
11. F. Stella: "The Pratt Lecture", 1960, in B. Richardson, 78
12. M. Kozloff, 1962, 34-36.
13. B. O'Doherty, 21.
14. F. Stella, in E. de Antonio, 144.
15. D. Judd, in G. Battock, 1995, 161.
16. F. Stella, in quoted in B. Glaser, 59.
17. M. Kozloff, 1964, 64; B. O'Doherty, 21.
18. F. Colpitt, 54.
19. F. Stella, quoted in G. Battock, 1995, 160.
20. F. Stella, quoted in D. Wheeler, 1991. 204.

MORRIS LOUIS

1. R. Hughes, 1990, 200.
2. In R. Hughes, 1990, 201.
3. C. Greenberg, in D. Wheeler, 192.
4. J. Elderfield, 1986, 27.
5   J. Elderfield, ibid.
6. A. Kagan, 138.
7. In D. Wheeler, 193.
8. M. Louis, in J. Gage, 267.
9. R. Hughes, 1990, 201.
10 F. Stella, in E. de Antonio, 139.
11. In N. Stangos, ed. *Concepts of Modern Art,* Thames & Hudson, London, 1981, 262.
12. A.J. Carmean, 1974, 9-15.
13. P. Fuller, "St Ives", *Artscribe,* no. 55, June, 1985.
14. P. Fuller, 1993, 217.

AD REINHARDT

1. A. Reinhardt, "Art-as-Art", *Art International,* 6, 10, Dec 20, 1960, in 1991, 56
2. A. Reinhardt, *Art as Art,* 1991, 205-6. Further extracts from *Art as Art* are cited in the text as 1991.
3. R. Hughes, 1997, 558.
4. R. Stankiewicz, *Sixteen Americans,* Museum of Modern Art, New York, NY, 1959
5. B. Newman, in H. Rosenberg, 1994, 59.

6. M. Benedikt, "New York Letter", in G. Battock, 1995, 91.
7. C. Greenberg, in G. Battock, 1995, 184.
8. M. Rothko, in D. Ashton, 1983, 179. Ad Reinhardt was less generous about Mark Rothko. In some undated notes, Reinhardt wrote:

   What's wrong with the art world is not Andy Andy Warhol or Andy Wyeth but Mark Rothko. The corruption of the best is the worst. Motherwell said someone said, "Rothko is the best Jewish artist in the world." ... How about Christians making synagogue murals? (Motherwell). How about Jews decorating Catholic churches? (Rothko). (1991, 190)

9. T. Merton, *Seeds of Contemplation*, Burns & Oates, London, 1962, 196.
10. P. Tillich, "Art", *Newsweek*, Feb, 1959, 54.
11. H. Frankenthaler, in E. de Antonio, 161.
12. A. Reinhardt, "Art-as-Art", *Environment*, 1962, 53.
13. A. Reinhardt, in *Art News*, May, 1957, and in G. Battock, 1995, 285.
14. A. Reinhardt, 1991, 108.
15. F. Stella, in G. Battock, 1995, 159.
16. M. Eliade, "The Sacred and the Modern Artist", in D. Apostolos-Cappadona, ed. *Art, Creativity and the Sacred*, New York, NY, 1984, 180f.
17. A. Reinhardt, 1991, 86-97, 108.
18. A. Reinhardt, interview, *Art International*, Dec, 1966, 18f
19. Robert Fludd, *Utriusque cosmi maiores et minors historia*, 1617, Frankfurt, Philosophical Research Library, Manley P. Hall Collection, Los Angeles, CA.
20. *Heart Sutra*, in E. Conze, *Buddhist Scriptures*, Penguin, London, 1959, 163.
21. S. Tillim, "Ad Reinhardt", *Arts*, Feb, 1959, 54.
22. P. Colt. "Notes on Ad Reinhardt", *Art International*, Lugano, 8, 8, Oct, 1964, 32f.
23. N. & E. Calas, 212f.
24. W. Kandinsky, *Concerning the Spiritual in Art*, Dover, New York, NY, 1977.
25. L. Alloway, 1960, 50.
26. A. Reinhardt in a lecture, Nov 5, 1965, in L. Lippard, 1966, 168.
27. L. Lippard, 1966, 154.

BRICE MARDEN

1. S. Burton, "Reviews and Previews" *Art News*, Feb, 1968.

2. J. Taylor *et al. Robert Rauschenberg*, Smithsonian Institute, Washington, DC, 1976, 66.
3. C. Greenberg, 1961, 134.
4. L. Fontana, quoted in J. Van der Marck, *Lucas Fontana*, catalogue, Walker Art Center, Minneapolis, MN, 1966.
5. C. Robins, 1984, 182.
6. L. Shearer, 1975, 19-20.
7. B. Marden, 1991a, 26-27.
8. C. Ratcliff, 1975, 85; C. Robins, 1984, 183.

ROBERT RYMAN

1. R. Ryman, in R. Storr, 16.
2. See B. Richardson, 1976, 3; F. Colpitt, 29.
3. See C. Huber. *Robert Ryman*, Kunsthalle, Basel, 1975; N. Grimes. "Robert Ryman's White Magic", *Art News*, Summer, 1968, 86-92; C. Ratcliff, 1986, 92-97.
4. L. Nead, "Getting down to basics: art, obscenity and the female nude", in I. Armstrong, ed. *New Feminist Discourses: Critical Essays on Theories and Texts*, Routledge, London, 1992, 206.
5. R. Ryman, in R. Storr, 48.
6. R. Ryman, in D. Wheeler, 207.
7. A. Danto, 1997, 154; R. Storr, 1993.

AGNES MARTIN

1. B. Rose, 1986, 138.
2. A. Martin, 1973, 23.

ELLSWORTH KELLY

1. D. Ashton, 1982, 89.
2. E. Kelly, 1980, 31.

GERHARD RICHTER

1. G. Richter, in *Gerhard Richter*, Tate Gallery, London, 1991.
2. G. Richter, *Gerhard Richter, Paintings*, Thames & Hudson, London, 1988.

OTHER MINIMAL PAINTERS

1. See P. Gardner, 1984, 47-55; R. Smith, 1987.
2. E. Murray, in R. Marshall, *50 New York Artists*, Chronicle Books, New York, 1986, 82
3. J. Baer, in *Paintings 1960-1998*, Stedelijk Museum, Amsterdam, 1999, 16.

3 MINIMAL SCULPTORS

TONY SMITH

1. H. Rosenberg, "Defining Art", 1967, in B, 307.

CARL ANDRE

1. C. Tomkins, 1989, 155.
2. C. Andre, statement, in Whitechapel Art Gallery exhibition catalogue, 2000.
3. M. Bochner, "Serial Art Systems".
4. L. Lippard, 1973, 157.
5. In L. Lippard, 1970, 7.
6. C. Andre, quoted in D. Bourdon, "The Razed Sites of Carl Andre", in B, 103.
7. L. Lippard, 1965, 58.
8. C. Andre, 1970, 61.
9. In E. Develing, 1969, 39.
10. M. Bochner, 1967, in B, 94.
11. M. Bochner, in B, 94.
12. D. Bourdon, 1978, 56. See M. Bochner, 1967, 39-43.
13. D. Bourdon, in B, 107.
14. R. Krauss, 1978, 271f.
15. E. Hesse, in C. Nemser, 1970, 59.
16. Quoted in B, 108.
17. In B, 386.
18. In B, 384.
19. David Lee said that 'Andre repeats one thing in each piece; Smithson repeats one thing but increases its size.' (1967, 44).

ROBERT MORRIS

1. R. Morris, quoted in M. Fried, 1967, in B, 126.
2. I. Sandler, "Gesture and Non-Gesture", in B, 311.
3. R. Morris, "Anti-Form", 24.
4. M. Friedman, 1966, 23.
5. D. Factor. "Los Angeles", *Artforum*, 4, 9, May, 1966, 13.
6. In M. Compton, 1971, 16.
7. In D. Wheeler, 1991, 221.
8. B. Rose, 1965.
9. D. Sylvester, 1996, 243.
10. British artist Rose Finn-Kelcey has also produced a steam work: her *Untitled* (1992, Chisenhalle Gallery, London) comprised water placed on a sheet metal base, with an extractor hood hung above it. In between the two was a cloud of steam, made dramatic by the lighting.

11. In M. Compton, 1971, 19.
12. J. Haldane, 1997, 56.

DAN FLAVIN

1. M. Bochner, 1967, in B, 99.
2. P. Hutchinson, 1966, in B, 193.

LAWRENCE WEINER

1. In E. Lucie-Smith, 1987, 117.
2. R. Long, 1985, 2, 24.

SOL LEWITT

1. "Notes on Sol LeWitt", 1978, 15-16.
2. Quoted in C, 121.
3. D. Wheeler, 1991, 227.

HANS HAACKE

1. H. Haacke, in J. Burnham, 1967.

EVA HESSE

1. See B. Barrette, *Eva Hesse's Sculpture: Catalogue Raisonné*, New York, NY, 1989; R. Krauss & E. Hesse, *Eva Hesse: Sculpture*, Whitechapel Art Gallery, London, 1979; C. Nemser, 1973, 12-13.
2. In C. Nemser, 1970, 62.
3. A. Chave, in H. Cooper, 1992, 100f.
4. In L. Lippard, *Eva Hesse*, 1976.
5. Quoted in ib., 6.
6. In C. Nemser, 1970, 59.

ANNE TRUITT

1. A. Truitt, *Daybook: The Journal of an Artist*, Penguin, London, 1982.

LOUISE NEVELSON, BARBARA HEPWORTH, REBECCA HORN, JACKIE WINSOR

1. Other artists who have worked in postmodern, feminist modes include Cindy Sherman, Mary Kelly, Marie Yates, Yves Lomax, Martha Rosler, Sutapa Biswas, Mitra Tabrizian, Zarina Bhimji, Mona Hatoum, Lubaina Himid, Barbara Kruger, Jenny Holzer, Rose Garrard, Susan Hiller, Nancy Spero, Rosa Lee and Rachel Whiteread.
2. See M. Roustayi, "Getting Under the Skin:

Rebecca Horn's Sensibility Machines", *Arts*, May, 1989, 58-68; M. Kimmelman, "A Sculptural Circus of Whips and Suspense", *New York Times*, Sept 23, 1988, C29.
3. H. Moore, in *The Listener*, 1937, quoted in H. Chipp, 595.
4. In A. Hammacher, 98.
5. In D. Wheeler, 1991, 323.

OTHER MINIMAL SCULPTORS

1. I. Sandler, 1996, 32.
2. Quoted in D. Waldman, 1966, 56.

4 MINIMALISM AND LAND ART

THE ECONOMICS OF MINIMAL ART AND LAND ART

1. A. Henri, 1974b, 81-82.
2. In American earthworks the key patrons were the Dia Art Foundation, Robert C. Scull and Virginia Dwan, director of the Dwan Gallery between 1966 and 1971.
3. In A. Haden-Guest, 40.
4. Surely that money would be better spent on a hospital? Or on feeding Third World countries? Isn't famine relief a better alternative? Perhaps one could make famine relief/ earthquake relief/ medical supply/ housing, and other 'charity' and 'aid' projects, an art event? Perhaps if Christo spent $26 million on providing food for the needy instead of wrapping a building in Berlin in a bit of plastic, people would not be so angry?

MINIMAL ART AND NATURE

1. C. Greenberg, "Abstract, Representational, and so forth", in 1961, 133.
2. C. Hussey, *The Picturesque*, Putnam's, New York, 1927.
3. Quoted in D. Wheeler, 1991, 324.
4. Quoted in N. Lynton, introduction to *Tony Cragg*, Fifth Triennale India, British Council, 1982, 2. On Tony Cragg, see also T. Neff, 1967; B. Jones, 1977; L. Ponti, "Tony Cragg", *Domus*, 611, Nov, 1980; I. Lamaitre, "Interview with Tony Cragg", *Artefactum*, 2, Dec, 1985; G. Celant,"Tony Cragg and Industrial Platonism", *Artforum*, 20, 3, Nov, 1981.
5. M. Eliade wrote: 'Nothing could convince Brancusi that a rock was only a fragment of inert matter; like his Carpathian ancestors, like all neolithic men, he sensed a presence in the rock, a power, an "intention" that one can only call "sacred"' (in "The Sacred and the Modern Artist", *Criterion*, 4, 1965, and in M. Eliade, 1988).
6. Another of Wolfgang Laib's installations is *The Passageway* (1988-93), made up of huge panels of beeswax.
7. W. Laib, in A. Benjamin, 91.

BRITISH MINIMAL ART AND THE BRITISH LANDSCAPE TRADITION

1. In A. Causey 1977, 126.

MINIMAL ART AND SCULPTURE IN THE U.K.

1. P. Fuller, "Likely Prospects: A British Art Questionnaire", *Artscribe*, 50, Jan, 1985, 27-28; "Onward Christian Soldiers", *Artscribe*, 52, July, 1985, 56.
2. J. Roberts, 1990, 111f.
3. Tony Cragg wrote:

   We consume, populating our environment with more and more objects, with no chance of understanding the making processes because we specialize in the production, but not in the consumption. (In E. Lucie-Smith, 1987, 130)

CHANGE, CYCLES, SEASONS

1. See J. Burnham 1971.

5 MINIMALISTS AND LAND ARTISTS

ROBERT SMITHSON

1. Robert Smithson, "A Sedimentation of the Mind: Earth Projects", in RS, 85
2. R. Smithson, "Discussion with Heizer, Oppenheim, Smithson", *Avalanche*, 1970, and in E. Johnson, 1982, 182.
3. C. Robins, 1984, 82.
4. In L. Lippard, 1973, 88.
5. See M. Gimbutas; *The Language of the Goddess*, Thames & Hudson, London, 1989.
6. R. Smithson, "The Spiral Jetty", unpublished MS, quoted in R. Krauss, 282. See R. Hobbs, 1981.
7. I. Sandler, 1990, 60.

8. In R. Hobbs, 212.
9. J. Coplans, "Robert Smithson: The Amarillo Ramp", in R. Hobbs, 53.

MICHAEL HEIZER

1. Sol LeWitt was sceptical of enormity: '[i]f it's so big that you can't really comprehend it except by its emotive force then I don't want it' (in F. Colpitt, 77). And Robert Morris wrote that 'beyond a certain size the object can overwhelm and the gigantic scale becomes the loaded term' (1966, 21).
2. See A. Sonfist, 1983; J. Beardsley, 1984.
3. See J. Brown, 1984; G. Muller, "Michael Heizer", *Arts Magazine*, Dec, 1969.
4. Quoted in H. Smagula, 1983, 286.
5. J. Bell, 1974, 55.
6. R. Hughes, 1997, 571.
7. R. Hughes, 1991, 386.

DENNIS OPPENHEIM

1. It's significant, for instance, that Dennis Oppenheim was the first US land artist to work with snow on a grand scale. Oppenheim began making snow works in the late Sixties. The only other important environmental artist who regularly used snow and ice, really, was Hans Haacke. But, more than any of the other first generation land artists, Oppenheim made snow one of his primary media.
2. In D. Oppenheim, 1992.
3. L. Lippard, 1983, 52.
4. Many of Dennis Oppenheim's land art pieces also existed as these framed photo-text-sketch-map works.
5. In M. Heizer, 1970.
6. Like many land artists, Dennis Oppenheim produced a maze (in 1970). But Oppenheim's *Maze* was just a little different: it was the design of a maze used in a scientific laboratory for rats transposed onto a large field, with cows as the rats, lured around the maze by the promise of food.
7. D. Oppenheim, in M. Heizer, 1970.
8. In D. Oppenheim, 1978.

JAMES TURRELL

1. Dia Foundation, the McArthur Foundation, the National Endowment for the Arts, the Lannan Foundation, the Canon Company, the Bohen Foundation, the Martin Bucksbaum Family Foundation, Count Guiseppe Panza di Buimo, Dr Pentti Kouri, Jean Stein, plus other donors.
2. J. Turrell, 1987.
3. M. Eliade, *Ordeal By Labyrinth*, University of Chicago Press, Chicago, IL, 1984, 162.

NANCY HOLT

1. "Sun Tunnels", 1977, 34
2. In T. Castle, 1982, 88.
3. See N. Holt, 1975, 1977; T. Castle, 1982.
4. The astronomical observatory has been an enduring theme in land art. Robert Morris, Michael Dan Archer and Julia Barton have also made viewing sites.
5. Again, Holt based the position of the concrete pits on a constellation (Hydra).
6. C. Robins, 1984, 104.

ALICE AYCOCK

1. A. Aycock, quoted in E. Johnson, 1982, 223.
2. *Maze* was partially based on a circular Egyptian labyrinth (designed as a prison), the Zulu *kraal* and the American Indian stockade. Aycock also cited a circular Greek temple at Epidarus, a 'Place of Sacrifice'.
3. A. Aycock in N. Rosen, 1975.
4. E. Johnson, 1982, 221.

MARY MISS

1. R. Onoratio, 1978, 32; see also K. Linker, "Mary Miss", *Mary Miss*, ICA, London, 1983.
2. See L. Anderson, 1973; M. Miss, 1981.

WALTER DE MARIA

1. Commentators have spoken of this cut as a 'wound' or 'scar' on the Earth.
2. Shown at Kassel Documenta 6 in 1977, de Maria's *Vertical Earth Kilometer* annoyed British artist Stuart Brisley so much he made *Survival in Alien Circumstances*. This was a hole in the earth dug with his bare hands, which Brisley lived in for 2 weeks, intending to mock de Maria's overblown American earthwork.
3. Quoted in H. Smagula, 289.
4. See D. Bourdon, 1968, 39-43, 72; M. Winton, "Sculptures That Blow Away", *Ark*, Spring, 1970; R. Smith, 1978.

5. W. de Maria, 1980.
6. *Lightning Field* is ambiguously related to the Dia Art Foundation, which financed its construction. The financing, by the Dia Art Foundation, came indirectly from military deals. 'Their elegant, potentially lethal forms stir associations of high-tech weaponry and its ancestry of spear, dart, and arrow', wrote Kenneth Baker of the poles (1988, 127), as well as the phallic connotations of Brancusi's *Endless Column* and *Birds in Space.*
7. Kenneth Baker related de Maria's *Lightning Field* to issues of philosophy and politics:

   The piece also serves as an instrument for intensifying one's grasp of the beauty of the earth... The *Lightning Field* acquaints the visitor with the possibility that beauty may be the only conscionable and feasible refuge from history. That is, the apprehension of reality as everywhere *radiant with its being* may be the only bearable consciousness of life that does not entail repressing awareness of the horrors of our time. Beauty in this sense is just what the *Lightning Field* makes available... (127)

8. See P. Redgrove, *The Black Goddess and the Sixth Sense*, Bloomsbury, London, 1987; *The Cyclopean Mistress*, Bloodaxe, Newcastle, 1993. De Maria himself thinks that a lightning strike is a 'false climax' to the work, which really needs to be seen over a period of time to appreciate its qualities.

CHRISTO

1. J. van der Marck, 1969.
2. 'When I was doing *Valley Curtain* everybody knew that this is a huge curtain crossing a valley. Now everybody knew what it is that is behind the valley. The thing that is behind is not so important...only that motion, the passing through' (Quoted in E. Johnson, 1982, 198).
3. A committee designed to 'stop Running Fence' brought the subject to the Superior Court of the State of California 3 times. The subsequent report on the environmental impact of the *Running Fence* project found that there were no endangered species in the region, except for the Brown Pelican, and virtually no wildlife would be affected by it. *Running Fence* went ahead, and stayed up for two weeks in Sept-

ember, 1976 (W. Spies, 1977).
4. In A. Haden-Guest, 40.

BIBLIOGRAPHY

W.C. Agee. *Don Judd*, Whitney Museum of American Art, New York, NY, 1968

—. "Unit, Series, Site: A Judd Lexicon", *Art in America*, May, 1975

—. *The Sculpture of Donald Judd*, Art Museum of South Texas, Corpus Christi, TX, 1977

—. *Donald Judd*, Hatje Cantz, 1999

L. Aldrich. *Cool Art: 1967*, Museum of Contemporary Art, 1968

P. Allison *et al. Beyond the Minimal*, Architectural Association Publications, London, 1998

L. Alloway. "Signs and Surface: Notes on Black and White Paintings in New York", *Quadrum*, 9, New York, NY, 1960,

—. "The American Sublime", *Living Arts*, 1, 2, June, 1963

—. *Morris Louis*, Guggenheim, New York, NY, 1963

—. *Systematic Painting*, New York, NY, 1966

—. "Residual Sign Systems in Abstract Expressionism", *Artforum*, Nov, 1973

L. Anderson. "Mary Miss", *Artforum*, Nov, 1973

W. Andersen. *American Sculpture in Process, 1930/1970*, New York Graphics Society, Boston, MA, 1975

C. Andre. "Frank Stella: Preface to Stripe Painting", in D. Miller, 1959

—. "Brice Marden Paintings", *57th Street Review*, Nov 15, 1966

—. "An Interview with Carl Andre", P. Tuchman, *Artforum*, 8, 10, June, 1970

—. *Carl Andre, Sculpture, 1958-1974*, Kunsthalle, Bern, 1975

—. "Object vs Phenomenon", *Sculpture Today*, The International Sculpture Center, Toronto, 1978

—. *Carl Andre: Sculpture*, State University of New York Press, Albany, NY, 1984

—. *Stichomythia, 12 Dialogues 1962-63*, Whitechapel Art Gallery, London, 2000

—. *Carl-Andre: works on land*, Exhibitions International, 2001

D. Anfam. *Abstract Expressionism*, Thames & Hudson, London, 1990

D. Antin. "Differences – Sames: NY, 1966-1967", *Metro*, 13, Feb, 1968

E. de Antonio & M. Tuchman. *Painters Painting*, Abbeville Press, New York, NY, 1984

J. Ashbery. "Gray Eminence", *Art News*, 71, 1, Mch, 1972

D. Ashton. *Modern American Sculpture*, Abrams, New York, NY, 1968

—. "Young Abstract Painters: Right On!", *Arts Magazine*, Feb, 1970

—. & A. Martin. *Agnes Martin*, Hayward Gallery, London, 1977

—. *American Art Since 1945*, Thames & Hudson, London, 1982

—. *About Rothko*, Oxford University Press, New York, NY, 1983

M. Auping. *Abstraction, Geometry, Painting: Selected Geometric Abstract Painting in America Since 1945*, Abrams, New York, NY, 1989

A. Aycock. "Work", "Maze", 1975, in A. Sondheim, 1977

J. Baer. "Letters", *Artforum*, 6, 1, Sept, 1967

E. Baker. "Judd the Obscure", *Art News*, 67, 2, 1968

K. Baker. "Andre in Retrospect", *Art in America*, Apl, 1980a

—. "Reckoning with Notation: The Drawings of Pollock, Newman, and Louis", *Artforum*, 18, 10, Summer, 1980b

—. *Minimalism: Art of Circumstance*, Abbeville, New York, NY, 1988

S. Bann. *Brice Marden: Paintings, Drawings, Etchings, 1975-80*, Stedelijk Museum, Amsterdam, 1981

—. & W. Allen, eds. *Interpreting Contemporary Art*, Reaktion Books, London, 1991

G. Baro. "American Sculpture", *Studio International*, 172, 896, 1968

D. Batchelor *et al. Sol LeWitt*, Museum of Modern Art, Oxford, 1993

—. *Minimalism*, Tate Publishing, London, 1997

C. Battaglia. "Tre Artisti: Ryman, Marden, Bell", *QUI Arte Contemporanea*, June, 1973

G. Battock, ed. *The New Art*, Dutton, New York, NY, 1966

—. "The Moral Integrity of Smudges", *New York Times*, Jan 25, 1968

—. *Idea Art*, Dutton, New York, NY, 1973

—. "Art in America: Confusions", *Domus*, Mch, 1975

—. ed. *New Artists Video*, Dutton, New York, NY, 1978

—. ed. *The Art of Performance*, Dutton, New York, NY, 1984

—. ed. *Minimal Art: A Critical Anthology*, University of California Press, Berkeley, CA, 1995

J. Beardsley. *Probing the Earth: Contemporary Land Projects*, Smithsonian Press, Washington, DC, 1977

—. *Art in Public Spaces*, Partners For Liveable Places, Washington, DC, 1981

—. *Earthworks and Beyond: Contemporary Art in the Landscape*, Abbeville Press, New York, NY, 1984/1998

D. Belgrad. *The Culture of Spontaneity:*

Improvisation and the Arts in Postwar America, University of Chicago Press, Chicago, IL, 1998

J. Bell. "Positive and Negative", *Arts Magazine*, Nov, 1974

A. Benjamin, ed. *Installation Art, Art & Design*, 30, 1993

M. Berger. *Labyrinths: Robert Morris, Minimalism, and the 1960s*, Harper & Row, New York, NY, 1989

—. *Minimal Politics*, University of Maryland, Fine Arts Gallery

R. Bersson. *Worlds of Art*, McGraw-Hill Education, 2003

M. Bochner. "Art in Process – Structures", *Arts Magazine*, 40, 9, 1966

—. "Primary Structures", *Arts*, June, 1966

—. "Systematic", *Arts Magazine*, 41, 1, Nov, 1966

—. "Serial Art Systems: Solipsism", *Arts Magazine*, 41, 8, Summer, 1967

—. "Mel Bochner on Malevich", interview with J. Coplans, *Artforum*, June, 1974

D. Bourdon. "The Razed Sites of Carl Andre", *Artforum*, 5, 2, Oct, 1966

—. "Walter de Maria: The Singular Experience", *Art International*, Dec 20, 1968

—"The Mini-Conceptual Age", *Village Voice*, Oct 17, 1974

—. "You Can't Tell a Painter By His Colors", *Village Voice*, Mch 24, 1975

—. *Carl Andre: Sculpture, 1959-1977*, Jaap Rietman, New York, NY, 1978

M. Bourel & S. Coudere. *Art Minimal II, De la Surface au Plan*, CAPC Musée d'Art contemporain de Bordeaux, 1986

J. Brown *et al. Michael Heizer: Sculpture in Reverse*, see M. Heizer

J. Burnham. *Beyond Modern Sculpture*, Braziller, New York, NY, 1968

—. "A Dan Flavin Retrospective in Ottawa", *Artforum*, 8, 4, Dec, 1969

—. "Robert Morris", *Artforum*, 8, 7, 1970

—. "Haacke's Cancelled Show at the Guggenheim", *Artforum*, June, 1971

J. Butterfield. *The Art of Light and Space*, Abbeville Press, New York, NY, 1993

N. & E. Calas. *Icons and Image of the Sixties*, Dutton, New York, NY, 1971

D. Campany, ed. *Art and Photography*, Phaidon, London, 2003

J. Campbell. *The Power of Myth*, with B. Moyers, ed. B. Flowers, Doubleday, New York, NY, 1988

A.J. Carmean. "Modernist Art: 1960-1970", *Studio International*, July, 1974

E. Castillo. *Minimalism Designsource*, Harper

Collins, London, 2004

T. Castle. "Nancy Holt, Siteseer", *Art in America*, Mch, 1982

A. Causey. "Space and Time in British Land Art", *Studio International*, 193, 98, Feb, 1977

—. *Sculpture Since 1945*, Oxford University Press, Oxford, 1998

G. Celant. "Introduction", *Arte Povera*, Praeger, New York, NY, 1969

—. *Dennis Oppenheim*, Edizioni Charta Srl, 1997

J.N. Chandler. "The Colours of Monochrome", *Artscanada*, 28, 160/1, Nov, 1971

A. Chave. "Minimalism and the Rhetoric of Power", *Arts*, Jan, 1990

H.B. Chipp, ed. *Theories of Modern Art,* University Press of California, Los Angeles, CA, 1968

R. Cohen. "Frank Stella", *ART News*, May, 1985

F. Colpitt. *Minimal Art: The Critical Perspective,* University of Washington Press, Seattle, WA, 1990

M. Compton & D. Sylvester. *Robert Morris*, Tate Gallery, London, 1971

H. Cooper, ed. *Eva Hesse*, Yale University Press, New Haven, CT, 1992

L. Cooke. "Between Image and Object: The "New British Sculpture"", in T. Neff, 1987

J. Coplans. "Serial Imagery", *Artforum*, 7, 2, Oct, 1968

—. *Donald Judd*, Pasadena Art Museum, CA, 1971

—. "Robert Smithson", *Artforum*, Apl, 1974

J. Cornell. *Theatre of the Mind: Selected Diaries, Letters and Files*, Thames & Hudson, London, 1994

M. Craig-Martin. *Minimalism*, Tate Gallery, Liverpool, 1989

M. Crichton. *Jasper Johns*, Thames & Hudson, London, 1977

T. Crow. *Modern Art in the Common Culture*, Yale University Press, New Haven, CT, 1996

P. Crowther. "Barnett Newman and the Sublime", *Oxford Art Journal*, 7, 2, 1984

—. ed. *The Contemporary Sublime, Art & Design*, 40, 1995

A. Danto. *After the End of Art*, Princeton University Press, Princeton, NJ, 1997

H. Davies *et al. Blurring the Boundaries: Installation Art 1969-1996*, Museum of Contemporary Art, San Diego, CA, 1997

R. Davies & T. Knipe, eds. *A Sense of Place: Sculpture in Landscape*, London, 1984

E. de Kooning. "Kline and Rothko: Two Americans in Action", *Art News Annual*, 27, 1958

W. de Maria. "The Lightning Field", *Artforum*, 18, 8,

Apl, 1980

A. Dempsey. *Styles, Schools Movements*, Thames & Hudson, London, 2002

N. de Oliveira *et al. Installation Art*, Thames & Hudson, London, 1994

—. *et al, Installation Art in the New Millennium*, Thames & Hudson, London, 2003

E. Develing. *Carl Andre*, Gemeentenmeuseum, The Hague, 1969

—. & L. Lippard. *Minimal Art*, Stadtische Kunsthalle, Düsseldorf, 1969

W. Domingo. "Brice Marden", *Arts Magazine*, Jan, 1971

—. "Color Abstraction", *Arts Magazine*, Jan, 1971

I. Dunlop. "Edvard Munch, Barnett Newman and Mark Rothko. The Search For the Sublime", *Arts Magazine*, 53, 6, Feb, 1979

J. Elderfield. *Contrasts of Form: Geometric Abstract Art, 1910-1980*, New York, NY, 1985

—. *Morris Louis*, New York, NY, 1986

—. *Helen Frankenthaler*, New York, NY, 1989

M. Eliade. *Ordeal by Labyrinth*, University of Chicago Press, Chicago, IL, 1984

—. *Symbolism, the Sacred and the Arts*, Crossroad, New York, NY, 1985

G. Evans. "Sculpture and Reality", *Studio International*, 177, 908, Feb, 1969

J. Fineberg. "Robert Morris Looking Back", *Arts Magazine*, 55, 1, 1980

—. *Art Since 1940: Strategies of Being*, Laurence King, London, 2000

J. Flam. "Old Artists, New Styles", *Wall Street Journal*, Mch 25, 1987

S. Foley. *Unitary Forms: Minimal Structures by Carl Andre, Donald Judd, John McCracken, Tony Smith*, Museum of Modern Art, San Francisco, CA, 1970

R. Francis. *Jasper Johns*, New York, NY, 1984

H. Frankenthaler. "Interview with Helen Frankenthaler", *Artforum*, 4, 2, Oct 1965

M. Fried. "New York Letter", *Art International*, 8, 3, Apl, 1964

—. *Three American Painters: Kenneth Noland, Jules Olitski, Frank Stella*, Fogg Art Museum, Harvard University, Cambridge, MA, 1965

—. "Shape as Form: Frank Stella's New Paintings", *Artforum*, 5, 3, Nov, 1966

—. "Art and Objecthood", *Artforum*, 5, Summer, 1967

—. *Morris Louis*, Abrams, New York, NY, 1970

M. Friedman. "Robert Morris: Polemics and Cubes", *Art International*, 10, 10, Dec, 1966

—. *14 Sculptors*, Walker Art Center, Minneapolis,

MN, 1969

E. Fry. *Alice Aycock*, University of South Florida Art Galleries, Tampa, FL, 1981

—. "The Poetic Machines of Alice Aycock", *Portfolio*, Nov, 1981

—. *et al. Robert Morris*, Museum of Contemporary Art, Chicago, IL, 1986

P. Fuller. *Peter Fuller's Modern Painters: Reflections on British Art*, ed. J. McDonald, Methuen, London, 1993

J. Gage. *Colour and Culture*, Thames & Hudson, London, 1993

P. Gardner. "Elizabeth Murray Shapes Up", *Art News*, Sept, 1984

C. Geelhaar. *Frank Stella, Workings, Drawings, 1956-1970*, tr. C. Hamlin, Kunstmuseum, Basel, 1980

A. Gibson. "Regression and Color in Abstract Expressionism: Barnett Newman, Mark Rothko and Clyfford Still", *Arts Magazine*, Mch, 1981

J. Gilbert-Rolfe. "Brice Marden, David Novros, Bykert Gallery", *Artforum*, May, 1974

—. "Appreciating Ryman", *Arts Magazine*, 50, 4, Dec, 1975

E. Gillen, ed. *German Art From Beckmann To Richter*, Dumont Buchverlag, Cologne, 1997

J. Giovannini. *Mary Miss*, Architectural Association, London, 1987

B. Glaser. "Questions to Stella and Judd", ed. L. Lippard, *Art News*, 65, 5, Sept, 1966

T. Godfrey. *Conceptual Art*, Phaidon, London, 1998

R. Goldberg. *Performance: Live Art Since the 60s*, Thames & Hudson, London, 1998

J. Goldman. *Frank Stella*, Princeton University Museum of Art, NJ, 1983

A. Goldstein & L. Mark, eds. *A Minimal Future?*, MIT Press, Cambridge, MA, 2004

A. Goldsworthy. *Hand to Earth: Andy Goldsworthy, Sculpture, 1976-1990*, Henry Moore Centre for Sculpture, Leeds, Yorkshire, 1990

M. Gooding & W. Furlong. *Song of the Earth*, Thames & Hudson, London, 2002

E.C. Goossen. *The Art of the Real: USA 1948-1968*, MOMA, New York, NY, 1968

C. Greenberg. "American-Type Painting", *Partisan Review*, Spring, 1955

—. "Modernist Painting", *Arts Yearbook*, 4, Art Digest, New York, NY, 1961

—. *Art and Culture*, Beacon Press, Boston, MA, 1961

—. *Post-Painterly Abstraction*, Los Angeles County Museum, Los Angeles, CA, 1964

—. *Three American Painters: Louis, Noland, Olitski,*

Norman Mackenzie Art Gallery, Saskatchewan, 1965

S. Guberman. *Frank Stella: An Illustrated Biography* Rizzoli, New York, NY, 1995

A. Haden-Guest. "The King of Wrap", *The Sunday Times Magazine*, Jan, 1994

K. Halbreich. *Affinities: Myron Stout, Bill Jensen, Brice Marden, Terry Winters*, Hayden Gallery, MIT, Cambridge, MA, 1983

J. Haldane. "Robert Morris", *Burlington Magazine*, Aug, 1997

A.M. Hammacher. *The Evolution of Modern Sculpture: Tradition and Innovation*, Abrams, New York, NY, 1969

B. Haskell. *Jo Baer*, Whitney Museum of American Art, New York, NY, 1975

—. *Donald Judd*, Whitney Museum of American Art, New York, NY, 1988

L. Hegyi. *Arte Povera, Minimal Art, Concept Art*, Art Data, 1995

M. Heizer, *et al.* "Discussion", *Avalanche*, 1, Autumn, 1970

—. *Sculpture in Reverse*, Museum of Contemporary Art, Los Angeles, CA, 1984

A. Henri. *Environments and Happenings*, Thames & Hudson, London, 1974a

—. *Total Art*, Praeger, New York, NY, 1974b

T. Hess. *Barnett Newman*, Walker, New York, NY, 1969

—. & L. Nochlin. *Woman as Sex Object: Studies in Erotic Art*, Newsweek, New York, NY, 1972

—. & E. Baker. *Art and Sexual Politics*, Art New Series, Macmillan, New York, NY, 1973

—. "Rules of the Game: Part II: Marden and Rockburne", *New York Magazine*, Nov 11, 1974

Galerie Max Hetzler. *Carl Andre, Gunther Forg, Hubert Kiecol, Richard Long, Meuser, Reinhard Mucha, Bruce Nauman and Ulrich Ruckreim*, Cologne, 1985

R.C. Hobbs. *Robert Smithson: Sculpture*, Cornell University Press, Ithaca, NY, 1981

N. Holt. "Amarillo Ramp", *Avalanche*, Fall, 1973

—. "Hydra's Head", *Arts Magazine*, Jan, 1975

—. "Sun Tunnels", *Artforum*, April, 1977

K. Honnef. *Concept Art*, Phaidon, Oxford, 1971

S. Hubbard, intr. *Sculpture At Goodwood: A Vision For 21st Century British Sculpture*, Sculpture At Goodwood, Sussex, 2002

R. Hughes. *Nothing If Not Critical: Selected Essays on Art and Artists*, Collins Harvill, London, 1990

—. *American Visions: The Epic History of Art In America*, Knopf, New York, NY, 1997

S. Hunter, ed. *American Art of the 20th Century*, Thames & Hudson, London, 1973

—. *Tony Smith*, Pace Gallery, New York, NY, 1979

—. *An American Renaissance: Painting and Sculpture Since 1940*, Abbeville Press, New York, NY, 1986

R. Irwin. *Being and Circumstance*, Lapis Press, California, CA, 1985

G. Johns. *In the Dim Void: Samuel Beckett's Late Trilogy*, Crescent Moon Publishing, 1993/ 2011

E.H. Johnson. *Modern Art and the Object*, Harper & Row, New York, NY, 1976

—. ed. *American Artist on Art*, Harper & Row, New York, NY, 1982

B. Jones. "A New Wave in Sculpture", *Artscribe*, 8, Sept, 1977

D. Joselit. *American Art Since 1945*, Thames & Hudson, London, 2003

D. Judd. "Frank Stella", *Arts Magazine*, 36, Sept, 1962

—. "In the Galleries", *Arts Magazine*, 37, 10, Sept, 1963

—. "Local History", *Arts Yearbook 7*, 1964

—. "Black, White and Gray", *Arts Magazine*, 38, 6, Mch, 1964

—. "Specific Objects", *Arts Yearbook*, 8, Art Digest, New York, NY, 1965

—. "Barnett Newman", *Studio International*, 179, 919, Feb, 1970

—. *Complete Writings, 1959-1975*, Nova Scotia College of Art and Design, Halifax, Canada, 1975

—. *Complete Writings, 1975-1986*, Van Abbemuseum, Netherlands, 1987

A. Kagan. *Absolute Art*, W.H. Green, St Louis, 1995

J. Kastner, ed. *Land and Environmental Art*, Phaidon, London, 1998

E. Kelly. *Ellsworth Kelly*, Stedelijk Museum, Amsterdam, 1980

M. Kozloff. "Pop Culture, Metaphysical Designs and the New Vulgarians", *Art International*, Mch, 1962

—. "New York Letter", *Art International*, 8, 3, Apl, 1964

—. *Jasper Johns,* New York, NY, 1969

Z. Kraus, ed. *From Nature to Art, From Art to Nature*, Venice Biennale, Milan, 1978

R.E. Krauss. *Passages in Modern Sculpture*, Thames & Hudson, London, 1977

—. "Sculpture in the Expanded Field", *October*, 8, Spring, 1978

—. *et al. Robert Morris*, Abrams, New York, NY, 1994

D. Kuspitt. "Sol LeWitt", *Art in America*, 63, 5, 1975

—. "Authoritarian Abstraction", *Journal of Aesthetics and Art Criticism*, 36, 1, Autumn, 1977

—. "Robert Smithson's Drunken Boat", *Arts Magazine*, Oct, 1981

—. "Aycock's Dream Houses", *Art in America*, Sept, 1985

—. "Donald Judd", *Artforum*, 23, 5, Feb, 1985

J. Kutner. "Brice Marden, David Novros, Mark Rothko: The Urge to Communicate through Non-Imagistic Painting", *Arts Magazine*, 50, 1, Sept, 1975

D. Lee. "Serial Rights", *Art News*, 66, 8, Dec, 1967

A. Legg, ed. *Sol LeWitt*, Museum of Modern Art, New York, NY, 1978

P. Leider. "Literalism and Abstraction: Frank Stella's Retrospective at the Modern", *Artforum*, 8, Apl, 1970

—. "For Robert Smithson", *Art in America*, Nov, 1973

—. *Stella Since 1970*, Fort Worth Art Museum, TX, 1978

K. Levin. "Robert Smithson", *Art News*, Sept, 1982

—. "Reflections on Robert Smithson's *Spiral Jetty*", *Arts Magazine*, May, 1978

S. LeWitt. "Paragraphs on Conceptual Art", *Art Language*, May, 1969

—. *Sol LeWitt*, Gemeentemuseum, The Hague, 1970

L. Lippard. "New York Letter: April-June, 1965", *Art International*, 9, 6, 1965

—. "New York Letter: Recent Sculpture as Escape", *Art International*, Feb, 1966

—. *Ad Reinhardt*, Jewish Museum, New York, NY, 1966

—. "An Impure Situation", *Art International*, May 20, 1966

—. "The Silent Art", *Art in America*, 55, 1, Jan-Feb, 1967

—. "Sol LeWitt: Non-Visual Structures", *Artforum*, Apl, 1967

—. "Tony Smith", *Art International*, Summer, 1967

—. "Rebelliously Romantic?", *New York Times*, June 4, 1967

—. "Escalation in Washington", *Art International*, 12, 1, Jan, 1968

—. ed. *Surrealists on Art*, Prentice-Hall, Englewood Cliffs, NJ, 1970

—. *Tony Smith*, Thames & Hudson, London, 1972

—. *Grids*, Philadelphia Institute of Contemporary Art, PA, 1972

—. *Six Years: The Dematerialization of the Art Object from 1966 to 1972*, Praeger, New York, NY, 1973

—. *From the Center: feminist essays on women's art*, Dutton, New York, NY, 1976

—. *Eva Hesse*, New York University Press, New York, NY, 1976

—. "Complexities: Architectural Sculpture in Nature", *Art in America*, Feb, 1979

—. *Ad Reinhardt*, Abrams, New York, NY, 1981

C. Loeffler, ed. *Performance Anthology*, Contemporary Art Press, San Francisco, 1979

R. Long. *Richard Long: In Conversation*, Parts 1 & 2, MW Press, Noordwijk, Holland, 1985-86

—. *Richard Long*, text by R.H. Fuchs, Thames & Hudson, London, 1986

—. *Old World New World*, Anthony d'Offay, London, 1988

—. *Richard Long: Walking in Circles*, Hayward Gallery/ Thames & Hudson, London, 1992

—. *Richard Long - Walking the Line,* Thames & Hudson, London, 2002

E. Lucie-Smith. *Sculpture Since 1945*, Phaidon, London, 1987

—. *Art Today,* Phaidon, London, 1989

—. *Movements In Art Since 1945*, Thames & Hudson, London, 1995

S.H. Madoff. "The Return of Abstraction", *Arts News*, Jan, 1986

J. van der Marck. *Wrapped Museum*, Museum of Contemporary Art, Chicago, IL, 1969

B. Marden. *Paintings, Drawings and Prints, 1975-1980*, ed. N. Serota, Whitechapel Art Gallery, London, 1981

—. *Brice Marden: The Grove Group*, text: Robert Witten, Gagosian Gallery, New York, NY, 1991a

—. *Brice Marden: Recent Drawings and Etchings*, Matthew Marks Gallery, New York, NY, 1991b

—. *Paintings and Drawings*, ed. D. Whitney, Harry N. Abrams, New York, NY, 1992a

—. *Brice Marden: Prints, 1961-1991: A Catalogue Raisonné*, text: J. Lewison, Tate Gallery, London, 1992b

—. *Cold Mountain*, Houston Fine Arts, TX, 1992

—. *Brice Marden: Paintings, Drawings, Etchings*, Matthew Marks Gallery, New York, NY, 1993

—. *Work Books*, Richter, 1997

A. Martin. *Agnes Martin*, Institute of Contemporary Art, Philadelphia, PA, 1973

D. Marzona & E. Carlini. *Minimal Art*, Taschen, Cologne, 2004

L. Masterson *et al*, eds. *Investigating Modern Art*, Yale University Press, New Haven, CT, 1996

D. Mayall. *The Minimal Tradition*, Aldrich Museum of Contemporary Art, Ridgefield, CT, 1979

D. McKinney. *Yves Klein, Brice Marden, Sigmar Polke*, Hirschl & Alder Modern, New York, NY, 1989

K. McShine. *Primary Structures*, Jewish Museum,

New York, NY, 1966

J. Mellow. "New York Letter", *Art International*, Apl 20, 1966

F. Meyer. *Frank Stella*, Kunsthalle, Basel, 1976

J. Meyer, ed. *Minimalism*, Phaidon, London, 2000

U. Meyer. *Conceptual Art*, Dutton, New York, NY, 1972

D.C. Miller, ed. *Sixteen Americans*, Museum of Modern Art, New York, NY, 1959

C. Millett. "De Kooning, Newman, Rothko: des bâtards", *Art Press International*, 26, Mch, 1979

M. Miss. *Mary Miss: Interior Works*, Bell Gallery, University of Rhode Island, Autumn, 1981

K. Moffet. *Kenneth Noland*, New York, NY, 1977

—. *Jules Olitski*, New York, NY, 1981

R. Morris. "Notes on Sculpture", *Artforum*, Feb, 1966, Oct, 1966, June, 1967, Apl, 1969

—. "Anti-Form", *Artforum*, Apl, 1968

—. "Aligned with Nazca", *Artforum*, Oct, 1975

—. *Robert Morris: Mirror Works, 1961-1978*, Leo Castelli Gallery, New York, NY, 1979

—. *Continuous Project Altered Daily*, MIT Press, Cambridge, MA, 1993

R. Murdoch. *Modular Painting*, Albright-Knox Art Gallery, Buffalo, CO, 1970

L. Nead. *Female Nude: Art, Obscenity and Sexuality*, Routledge, London, 1992

T.A. Neff, ed. *A Quiet Revolution: British Sculpture Since 1965*, Thames & Hudson, London, 1987

C. Nemser. "An Interview with Eva Hesse", *Artforum*, May, 1970

—. "My Memories of Eva Hesse", *Feminist Art Journal*, Winter, 1973

B. Newman. *The Stations of the Cross*, Guggenheim, New York, NY, 1966

—. *Selected Writings and Interviews*, ed. J.P. O'Neill, Knopf, New York, NY, 1990

M. Newman. "New Sculpture in Britain", *Art in America*, Sept, 1982

M. Nixon. *Eva Hesse*, The MIT Press, Cambridge, MA, 2002

S. Nodelman. "Sixties Art: Some Philosophical Perspectives", *Perspecta, The Yale Architectural Journal*, 11, 1967

—. *Marden, Novros, Rothko: Painting in the Age of Actuality*, Institute for the Arts, Rice University, Houston, TX, 1978

P. Noever, ed. *Donald Judd: Architecture*, Hatje Cantz, 2003

I. Noguchi. *A Sculptor's World,* Harper & Row, New York, NY, 1968

G. Nordland. *Fourteen Abstract Painters*, Frederick S. Wright Art Gallery, University of California, Los Angeles, CA, 1979

—. *Richard Diebenkorn*, New York, NY, 1987

B. Oakes, ed. *Sculpting the Environment*, Van Nostrand Reinhold, New York, NY, 1995

B. O'Doherty. "Frank Stella and a Crisis of Nothingness", *New York Times*, Jan 19, 1964

R. Onoratio. "Illusive Spaces: The Art of Mary Miss", *Artforum*, Dec, 1978

—. *Mary Miss – Perimeters/ Pavilions/ Decoys*, Nassau County Museum, 1979

F. Orton. *Jasper Johns: The Sculptures*, Henry Moore Institute, Leeds, Yorkshire, 1996

P. Osborne, ed. *Conceptual Art*, Phaidon, London, 2002

A.C. Papadakis, ed. *British and American Art: The Uneasy Dialectic*, Art & Design, 3, 9/1, Academy Group, London, 1987

—. ed. *Abstract Art and the Rediscovery of the Spiritual*, Art & Design, 3, 5/6, Academy Group, London, 1987

—. ed. *The New Romantics*, Art & Design, 4, 11/12, Academy Group, London, 1988

—. et al, eds. *New Art*, Academy Group, London, 1991

R. Parker & G. Pollock. *Old Mistresses: Women, Art an Ideology*, Routledge & Kegan Paul, London, 1981

—. *Framing Feminism: Art and the Women's Movement, 1970-1985*, Pandora Press, London, 1987

P. Patton. "Robert Morris and the Fire Next Time", *Art News*, 82, 10, Dec, 1983

J. Pawson. *Minimum*, Phaidon, London, 1996

J. Perreault. "A Minimal Future? Union-Made: Report on a Phenomenon", *Arts Magazine,* 41, Mch, 1967

—. "Minimal Abstracts", in G. Battock, 1995

J. Perrone. "Seeing Through Boxes", *Artforum*, 15, Nov, 1976

—. "Review", *Artforum*, Dec, 1976

K. Petersen & J.J. Wilson: *Women Artists: Recognition and Reappraisal from the Early Middle Ages to the Twentieth Century*, Women's Press, London, 1978

R. Pincus-Witten. "Systematic Painting", *Artforum*, 5, 3, Nov, 1966

—. "Ryman, Marden, Manzoni: Theory, Sensibility, Mediation", *Artforum*, 10, 10, June, 1972

—. *Postminimalism*, Out of London Press, New York, NY, 1977

—. *Entries: Maximalism*, Out of London Press, London, 1983

—. *Post-Minimalism into Maximalism*, UMI Research Press, Ann Arbor, MI, 1987

M. Poirier. "Color-coded Mysteries", *Art News*, Jan, 1985

—. "The Ghost in the Machine", *Art News*, Oct, 1986

—. & J. Necol. "The '60s in Abstract Painting: 13 Statements... Brice Marden", *Art in America*, Oct, 1983

G. Pollock. *Vision and Difference: femininity, feminism and histories of art*, Routledge, London, 1988

C. Ratcliff. "Robert Ryman's Double Positive", *Art News*, Mch, 1971

—. "Once More With Feeling", *Art News*, 71, 4, Summer, 1972

—. "Abstract Painting, Specific Spaces: Novros and Marden in Houston", *Art in America*, 63, 5, Nov, 1975

—. *In the Realm of the Monochrome*, Renaissance Society, University of Chicago, Chicago, IL, 1979

—. "The Compleat Smithson", *Art in America*, Jan, 1980

—. "Mostly Monochrome", *Art in America*, 69, 4, Apl, 1981

—. "Robert Ryman Making Distinctions", *Art in America*, June, 1986

—. *Out of the Box*, Allworth Press, 2001

A. Reinhardt. *Art as Art: The Selected Writings of Ad Reinhardt,* University of California Press, Berkeley, CA, 1991

G. Reinhardt *et al. Eva Hesse*, Ulmer Museum, Ulm, 1994

B. Reise. "Untitled, 1969: A Footnote on Art and Minimal Stylehood", *Studio International*, 177, 910, Apl, 1969

—. "The Stance of Barnett Newman", *Studio International* 179, 920, Mch, 1970

B. Richardson. *Frank Stella: The Black Paintings*, Baltimore Museum of Art, Baltimore, MD, 1976

N. Rifkin & E. Hirsch. *Agnes Martin: the Nineties and Beyond,* The Menil Collection, Houston, Hatje Cantz, 2002

C. Riley II. *Color Codes,* University Press of New England, Hanover, NH, 1995

H. Risiatti. "The Sculpture of Alice Aycock", *Woman's Art Journal*, Summer, 1985

A.C. Ritche. *Salute to Mark Rothko*, Yale University Art Gallery, New Haven, CT, 1971

J. Roberts. *Postmodernism, Politics and Art*, Manchester University Press, Manchester, 1990

C. Robins. "Object, Structure or Sculpture: Where Are We?", *Arts Magazine*, 40, 9, 1966

—. "Empty Paintings", *SoHo Weekly News*, Apl 22, 1976

—. *The Pluralist Era: American Art, 1968-1981,* Harper & Row, New York, NY, 1984

F. Roh. *German Art in the Twentieth Century: Painting, Sculpture, Architecture*, Thames & Hudson, London, 1968

A. Rorimer. *New Art in the 60s and 70s*, Thames & Hudson, London, 2001

B. Rose. "ABC Art", *Art in America*, 53, 5, Nov, 1965

—. *A New Aesthetic*, Washington Gallery of Modern Art, Washington, DC, 1967

—. *American Art Since 1900*, Thames & Hudson, London, 1967

—. *American Painting*, Skira/ Rizzoli International, New York, NY, 1986

—. *Robert Morris*, Corcoran Gallery, Washington, DC, 1990

N. Rosen. "A Sense of Place: Five American Artists", *International Sculpture*, Merriewold West, 1975

H. Rosenberg. *The De-Definition of Art*, Horizon Press, New York, NY, 1972

—. *Barnett Newman*, Abrams, New York, NY, 1978/ 1994

—. *The Tradition of the New*, Da Capo Press, New York, NY, 1994

R. Rosenblum. "Frank Stella: Five Years of Variations on an Irreducible Theme", *Artforum*, 3, 6, Mch, 1965

—. *Frank Stella*, Penguin, London, 1971

—. "Notes on Sol LeWitt", in A. Legg, 1978

—. *Modern Painting and the Northern Romantic Tradition*, Thames & Hudson, London, 1978

—. *Jasper Johns' Paintings and Sculptures, 1954-1974*, Ann Arbor, Michigan, MI, 1985

—. "Romanticism and Retrospective: An Interview with Robert Rosenblum", in A. Papadakis, 1988

M. Roth. "Robert Smithson on Duchamp", *Artforum*, Oct, 1969

M. Rothko. *Mark Rothko, 1903-1970: A Retrospective*, Guggenheim, New York, NY, 1979

—. *Mark Rothko, 1903-1970*, Tate Gallery, London, 1987

L. Rubin. *Frank Stella Paintings: 1958-1965*, New York, NY, 1986

W.S. Rubin. *Frank Stella*, New York Graphic Society, Greenwich, CT., 1970

—. *Frank Stella: 1970-1987*, Museum of Modern Art, New York, NY, 1987

A. Ruby *et al. Minimal Architecture*, Prestel Publishing, 2003

M. Ryan, ed. *Gravity and Grace: The Changing Condition of Sculpture, 1965-1975*, Hayward Gallery, London, 1993

R. Ryman. "An Interview with Robert Ryman", P. Tuchman, *Artforum*, 9, 9, May, 1971

—. "The 60's in Abstract", *Art in America*, 71, 9, Oct, 1983

A. Saalfield. *Mary Miss*, Fogg Art Museum, Cambridge, MA, 1980

I. Sandler. "The New Cool-Art", *Art in America*, 53, 1, Feb, 1967

—. *American Art of the 1960s*, Harper & Row, New York, NY, 1988

—. *Art of the Postmodern Era: From the 1960s to the Early 1990s*, HarperCollins, London, 1997

P. Schjeldahl. *Art in Our Time: The Saatchi Collection*, Lund Humphries, London, 1984

H. Senie & S. Webster, eds. *Critical Issues in Public Art*, Smithsonian Institution Press, Washington, DC, 1998

N. Serota, ed. *Donald Judd*, Tate Publishing, London, 2003

P. Selz. *Art in Our Times: A Pictorial History 1890-1980*, Thames & Hudson, London, 1982

E. Shanes. *Constantin Brancusi*, Abbeville, New York, NY, 1989

D. Shapiro & C. Shapiro, eds. *Abstract Expressionism: A Critical Record*, Cambridge University Press, Cambridge, 1990

G. Shapiro. *Earthworks: Robert Smithson and After After Babel*, University of California Press, Berkeley, CA, 1995

L. Shearer & R. Pincus-Witten. *Eva Hesse*, Guggenheim Museum, New York, NY, 1972

—. *Brice Marden*, Guggenheim Museum, New York, NY, 1975

P. Sims. *From Minimalism to Expressionism*, New York, NY, 1963

H.J. Smagula. *Currents: Contemporary Directions in the Visual Arts*, Prentice-Hall, Englewood Cliffs, NJ, 1983

B. Smith. *Fluorescent Light, etc, from Dan Flavin*, National Gallery of Canada, Ottawa, 1969

—. *Donald Judd*, National Gallery of Canada, Ottawa, 1975

D. Smith. *Sculpture and Drawings*, ed. J. Merkert, Prestel-Verlag, Munich, 1986

R. Smith. "Sol LeWitt", *Artforum*, Jan, 1975

—. "Review", *Artforum*, Dec, 1975

—. "De Maria: Elements", *Art in America*, May, 1978

R. Smithson. "Entropy and the New Monuments", *Artforum*, 4, 10, June, 1966

—. "Incidents of Mirror-Travel in the Yucatan", *Artforum*, Sept, 1967

—. "The Monuments of Passaic", *Artforum*, Dec, 1967

—. "Toward the Development of an Air Terminal Site", *Artforum*, Summer, 1967

—. "A Museum of Language in the Vicinity of Art", *Art International*, 12, 3, Mch, 1968

—. *The Writings of Robert Smithson*, ed. N. Holt, New York University Press, New York, NY, 1979

—. *Robert Smithson*, ed. J. Flam, University of California Press, Berkeley, CA, 1996

T. Sokolowski *et al. Robert Morris*, New York University Press, New York, NY, 1989

A. Solomon & C. Greenberg. *Morris Louis*, Whitechapel Art Gallery, London, 1965

E.M. Solomon. *Recent Drawings: William Allan, James Bishop, Vija Celmins, Brice Marden, Jim Nutt, Alan Saret, Pat Steir, Richard Tuttle*, American Foundation of Art, New York, NY, 1975

A, Sondheim, ed. *Post-Movement Art in America*, Dutton, New York, NY, 1977

A. Sonfist, ed. *Art in the Land: A Critical Anthology of Environmental Art*, Dutton, New York, NY, 1983

N. Spector. *Robert Ryman,* Whitechapel Art Gallery, London, 1977

W. Spies. *The Running Fence Project, Christo,* Abrams, New York, NY, 1977

F. Stella. *Working Space*, Harvard University Press, Cambridge, MA, 1986

—. *Frank Stella*, Madrid, 1995

K. Stiles & P. Selz, eds. *Theories & Documents of Contemporary Art: A Sourcebook of Artists' Writings*, University of California Press, Berkeley, CA, 1996

—. *Out of Actions: Between Performance and the Object, 1949-1979*, Thames & Hudson, London, 1998

R. Storr. *Robert Ryman*, Abrams, New York, NY, 1993

E. Suderburg, ed. *Space, Site, Intervention*, University of Minnesota Press, Minneapolis, MN, 2000

D. Sylvester. "Interview", *Jasper Johns Drawings*, Museum of Modern Art, Oxford, 1974

—. *About Modern Art*, Chatto & Windus, London, 1996

G. Tiberghien. *Land Art*, Art Data, London, 1995

The Tibetan Book of the Dead, tr. W.Y. Evans-Wentz, Oxford, 1957

C. Tomkins. "Profiles", *New Yorker*, Sept, 1984

—. *Post- to Neo-: The Art World of the 1980s*, Penguin, London, 1989

M. Toy. *Aspects of Minimal Architecture*, Wiley-Academy, 1999

E. Tsai. *Robert Smithson Unearthed*, Columbia University Press, New York, NY, 1991

M. Tuchman. *American Sculpture of the Sixties*, Los

Angeles County Museum of Art, Los Angeles, CA, 1967

—. *The New York School*, Thames & Hudson, London, 1971

—. *The Spiritual in Art: Abstract Painting 1880-1985*, Los Angeles County Museum of Art/ Abbeville Press, New York, NY, 1986

P. Tuchman. "Minimalism and Critical Response", *Artforum*, 15, 9, May, 1977

M. Tucker. *Robert Morris*, New York, NY, 1970

W. Tucker. *The Language of Sculpture*, Thames & Hudson, London, 1974

G. de Vries, ed. *On Art: Artists' Writings on the Changed Notion of Art After 1965*, Cologne, 1974

A.M. Wagner. *Three Artists (Three Women): Modernism and the Art of Hesse, Krasner and O'Keeffe*, University of California Press, Berkeley, CA, 1996

S. Wagstaff. "Paintings to Think About", *Art News*, 62, 9, Jan, 1964

D. Waldman. *Carl Andre*, Guggenheim, New York, NY, 1970

—. "Holding the Floor", *Art News*, Oct, 1970

—. *Robert Mangold*, New York, NY, 1971

—. *Robert Ryman*, New York, NY, 1972

—. "Color, Format and Abstract Art: An Interview with Kenneth Noland", *Art in America*, 65, 3, May 1977

—. *Mark Rothko*, Thames & Hudson, London, 1978

J. Walker. *Art & Outrage: Provocation, Controversy and the Visual Arts*, Pluto Press, London, 1999

—. *Art and Celebrity*, Pluto Press, London, 2003

L. Weiner. *Lawrence Weiner, Works,* Anatol AV und Filmproduktion Hamburg, 1977

L. Weintraub. *The Maximal Implications of the Minimalist Line*, Edith C. Blum Art Institute, New York, NY, 1985

D. Wheeler. *Art Since Mid-Century: 1945 to the Present*, Thames & Hudson, London, 1991

R. Williams. *After Modern Sculpture: Art in the United States and Europe 1965-70,* Manchester University Press, Manchester, 2000

W. Wilson. "Dan Flavin: Fiat Lux", *Art News*, Jan, 1970

G. Woods *et al*, eds. *Art Without Boundaries*, Thames & Hudson, London, 1972

A.S. Wooster. "Sol LeWitt's Expanding Grid", *Art in America*, 68, 5, May, 1980

WEBSITES

Donald Judd <chinati.org>
Donald Judd <juddfoundation.org>
Robert Smithson <robertsmithson.com>
Alice Aycock <aaycock.com>
Walter de Maria <lightningfield.org>
Christo <christojeanneclaude.net>
James Turrell <rodencrater.org>
Mary Miss <marymiss.com>
Carl Andre <carlandre.net>
Gerhard Richter <gerhard-richter.com>
Michael Heizer <doublenegative.tarasen.net>
Dennis Oppenheim <dennis-oppenheim.com>
Richard Long <richardlong.org>
Earthworks <earthworks.org>
The Artists <the-artists.org>
Crescent Moon Publishing <crmoon>
Richard Diebenkorn <diebenkorn.org>
Kenneth Noland <kennethnoland.com>
DIA <diacenter.org> and <diaart.org>
Female Artists <female-artists.net>

THE ART OF
ANDY GOLDSWORTHY

COMPLETE WORKS: SPECIAL EDITION
(PAPERBACK and HARDBACK)

by William Malpas

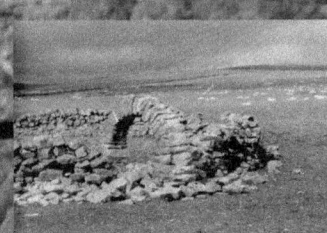
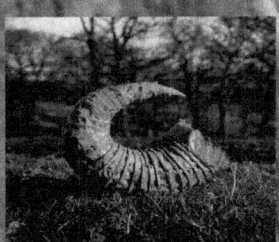

A new, special edition of the study of the contemporary British sculptor,
Andy Goldsworthy, including a new introduction, new bibliography and many
new illustrations.

This is the most comprehensive, up-to-date, well-researched and in-depth
account of Goldsworthy's art available anywhere.

Andy Goldsworthy makes land art. His sculpture is a sensitive, intuitive
response to nature, light, time, growth, the seasons and the earth. Goldsworthy's environmental art is becoming ever more popular: 1993's art book
Stone was a bestseller; the press raved about Goldsworthy taking over a
number of London West End art galleries in 1994; during 1995 Goldsworthy
designed a set of Royal Mail stamps and had a show at the British Museum.
Malpas surveys all of Goldsworthy's art, and analyzes his relation with other
land artists such as Robert Smithson, Walter de Maria, Richard Long and
David Nash, and his place in the contemporary British art scene.

The Art of Andy Goldsworthy discusses all of Goldsworthy's important and
recent exhibitions and books, including the *Sheepfolds* project; the TV docu-
mentaries; *Wood* (1996); the New York Holocaust memorial (2003); and
Goldsworthy's collaboration on a dance performance.

Illustrations: 70 b/w, 1 colour. 330 pages. New, special, 2nd edition.
Publisher: Crescent Moon Publishing. Distributor: Gardners Books.

ISBN 1-86171-059-3 (9781861710598) (Paperback) £25.00 / $44.00

ISBN 1-86171-080-1 (9781861710802) (Hardback) £60.00 / $105.00

ANDY GOLDSWORTHY IN CLOSE-UP

SPECIAL EDITION (HARDBACK and PAPERBACK)

by William Malpas

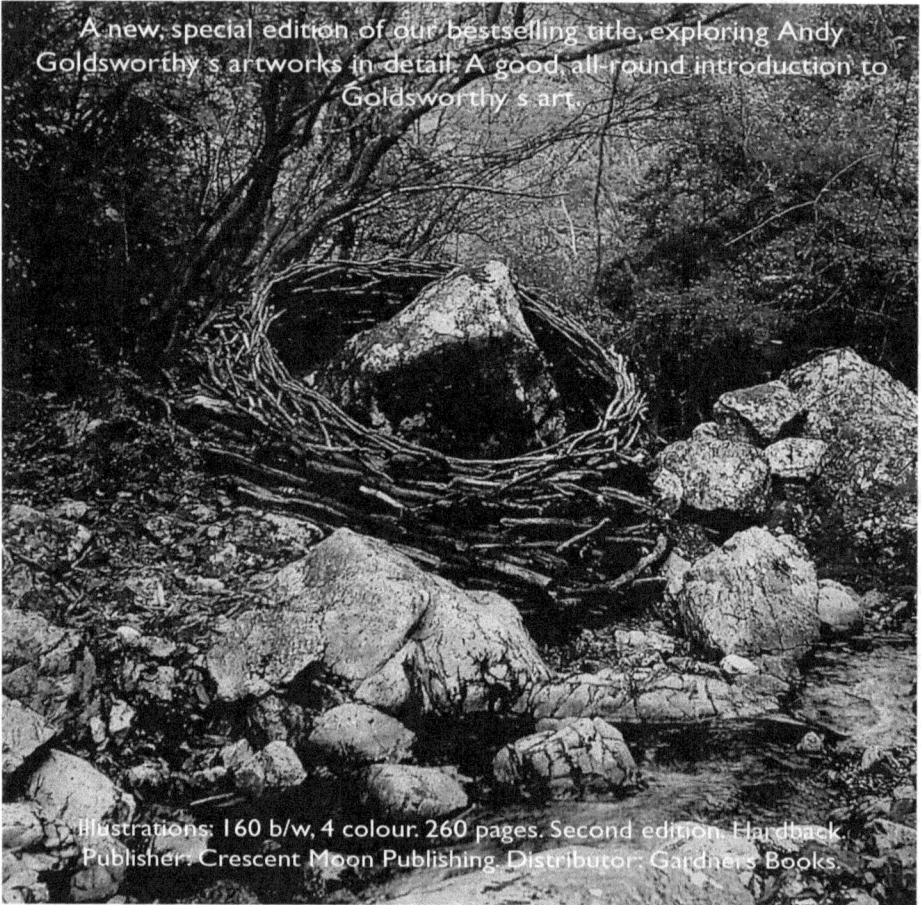

A new, special edition of our bestselling title, exploring Andy Goldsworthy's artworks in detail. A good, all-round introduction to Goldsworthy's art.

Illustrations: 160 b/w, 4 colour. 260 pages. Second edition. Hardback. Publisher: Crescent Moon Publishing. Distributor: Gardner's Books.

ISBN 1-86171-094-1 (9781861710949) (Hbk) £60.00 / $105.00

ISBN 1-86171-091-7 (9781861710919) (Pbk) £25.00 / $44.00

Available from bookstores. amazon.com, play.com, tesco.com, and other websites.
In the United States from Baker & Taylor, (800) 7753760 or (800) 7751100 or (908) 5417062. electser@btol.com or btinfo@btol.com.

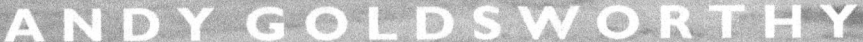

ANDY GOLDSWORTHY

TOUCHING NATURE:
SPECIAL EDITION

(PAPERBACK and HARDBACK)

by William Malpas

A new, special and updated edition of our bestselling title, providing
an excellent general introduction to the art of Andy Goldsworthy.

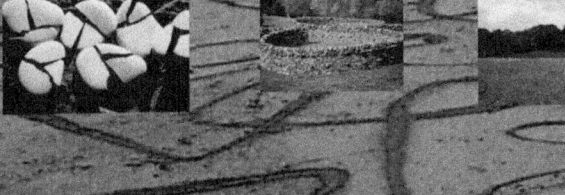

Illustrations: 75 b/w, 2 colour. 354 pages. Third edition. Paperback.

Publisher: Crescent Moon Publishing. Distributor: Gardners Books.

ISBN 1-86171-056-9 (9781861717) (Paperback) £25.00 / $44.00

ISBN 1-86171-087-9 (9781861710871) (Hardback) £60.00 / $105.00

LAND ART

A COMPLETE GUIDE TO LANDSCAPE, ENVIRONMENTAL, EARTHWORKS, NATURE, SCULPTURE AND INSTALLATION ART

by William Malpas

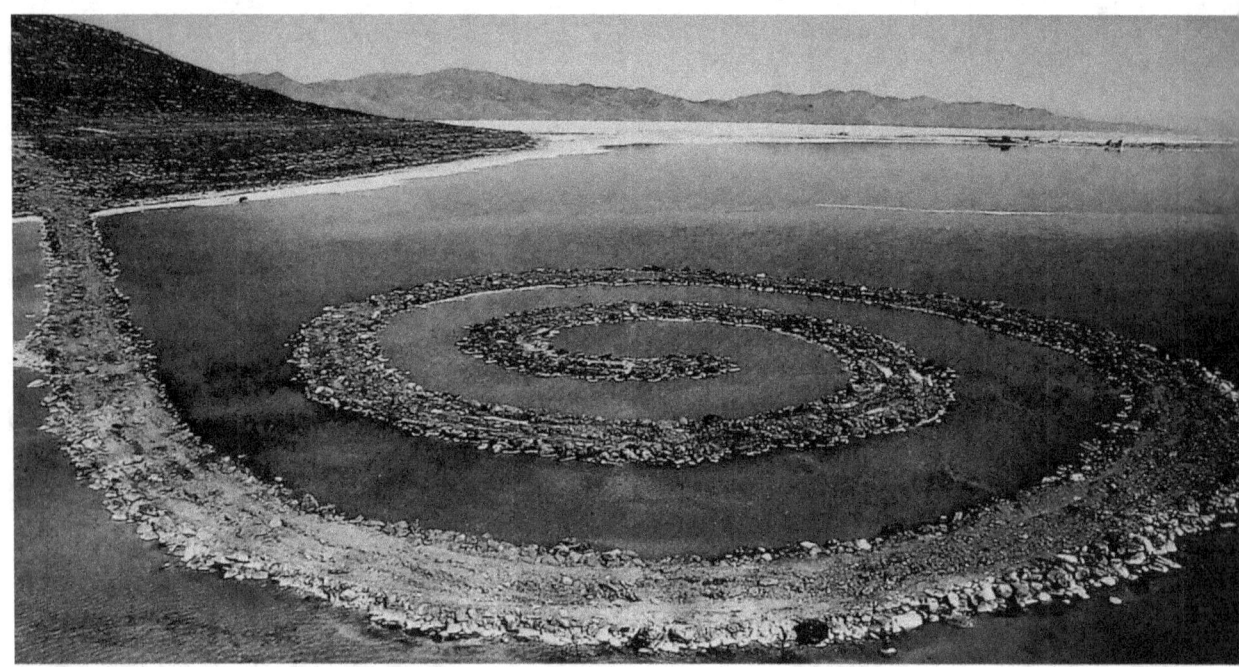

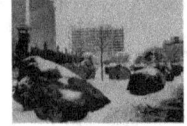 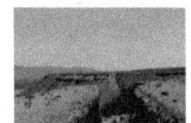 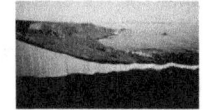 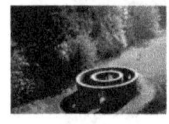 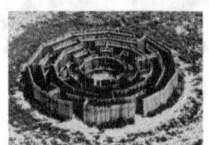

A new, special edition of our popular book on land art.
Chapters on land artists such as Robert Smithson, Walter de Maria, Christo,
Michael Heizer, Richard Long and Andy Goldsworthy.

Illustrations: 35 b/w, 2 colour. 314 pages. First edition. Paperback.

Publisher: Crescent Moon Publishing. Distributor: Gardners Books.

ISBN 1-86171-062-3 (9781861710628) £25.00 / $44.00

LAND ART IN CLOSE-UP

SPECIAL EDITION (PAPERBACK)

by William Malpas

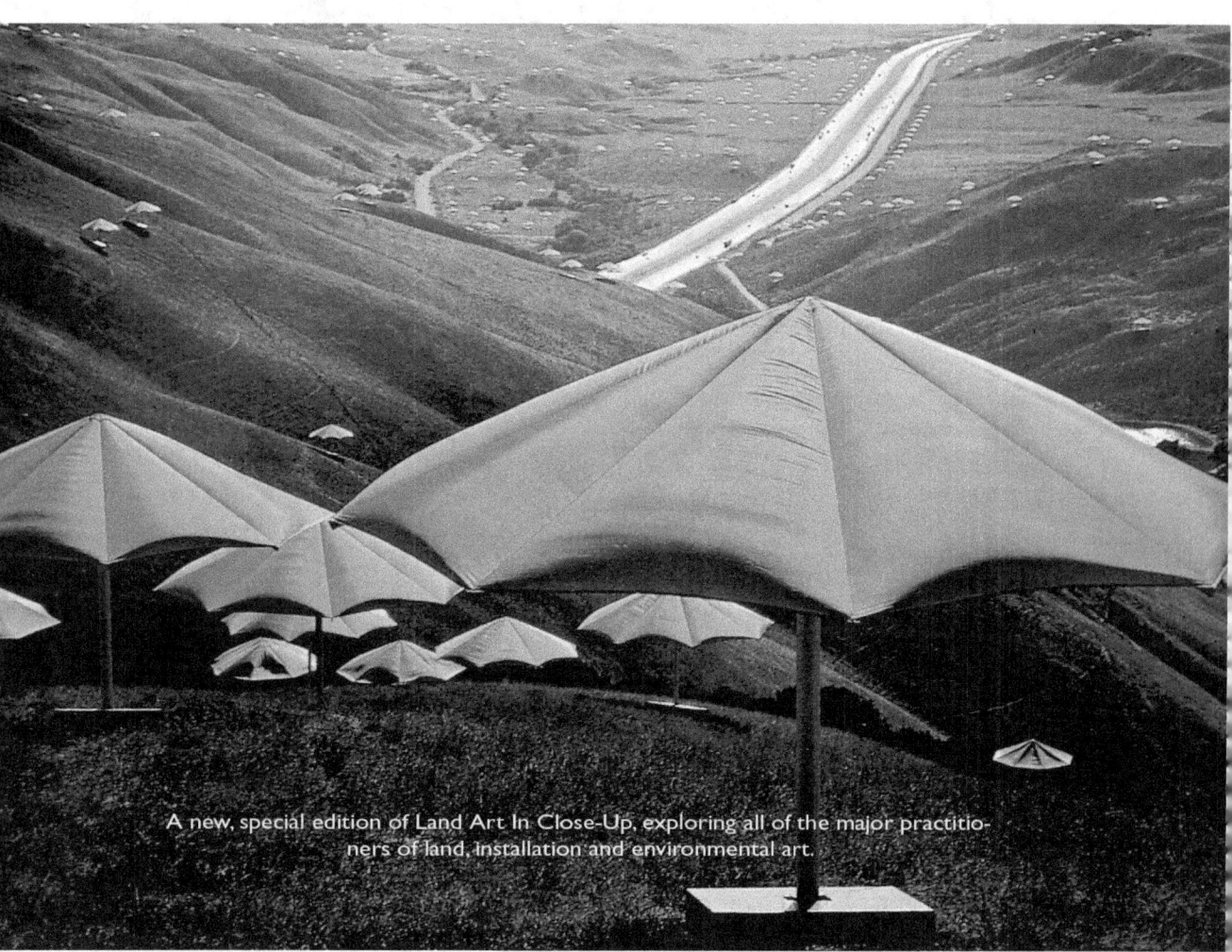

A new, special edition of Land Art In Close-Up, exploring all of the major practitioners of land, installation and environmental art.

Illustrations: 161 b/w, 2 colour. 248 pages. Second edition. Paperback.

Publisher: Crescent Moon Publishing. Distributor: Gardners Books.

ISBN 1-86171-092-5 (9781861710925) £25.00 / $44.00

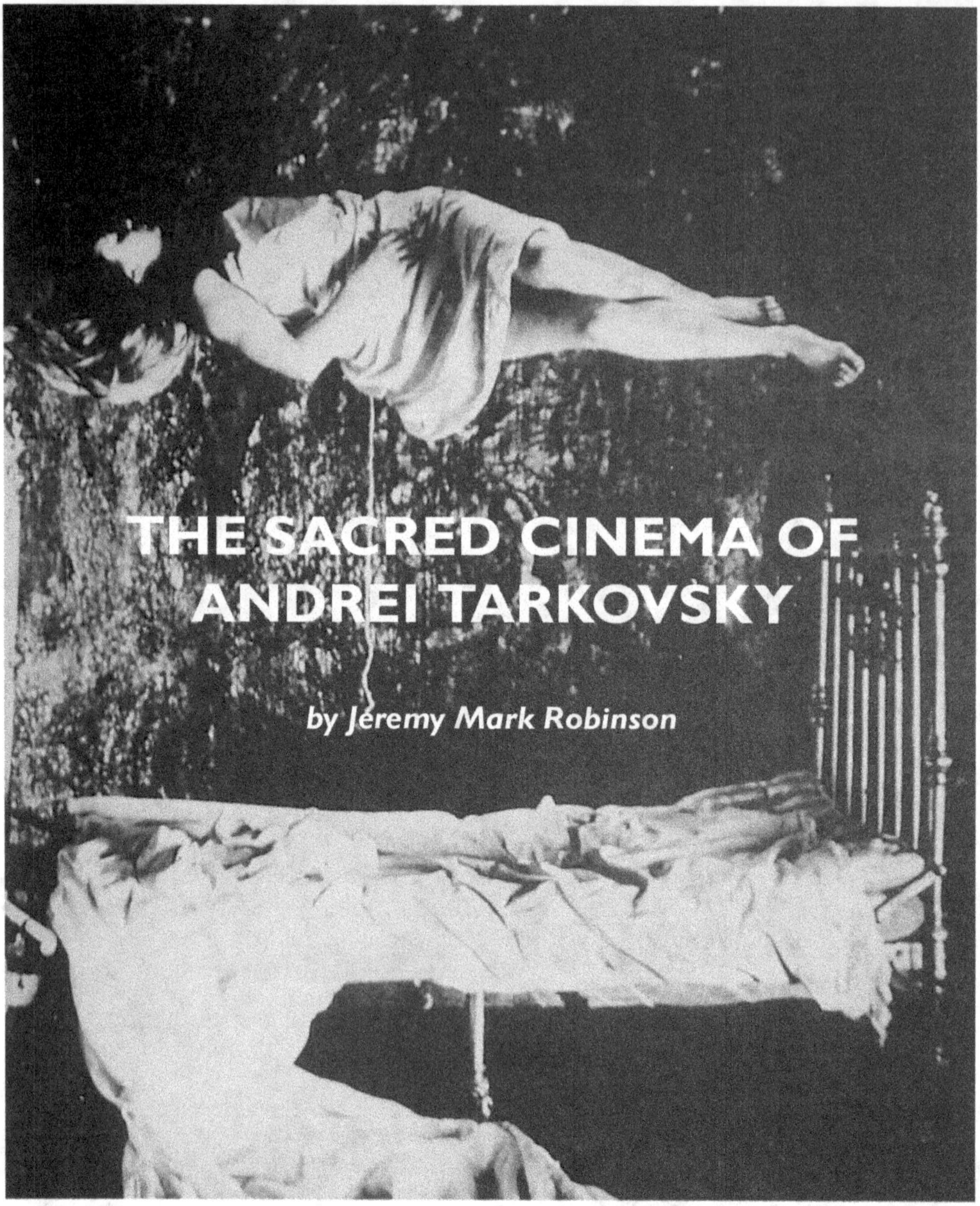

THE SACRED CINEMA OF ANDREI TARKOVSKY

by Jeremy Mark Robinson

A new study of the Russian filmmaker Andrei Tarkovsky (1932-1986), director of seven feature films, including *Andrei Roublyov, Mirror, Solaris, Stalker* and *The Sacrifice*.

This is one of the most comprehensive and detailed studies of Tarkovsky's cinema available. Every film is explored in depth, with scene-by-scene analyses. All aspects of Tarkovsky's output are critiqued, including editing, camera, staging, script, budget, collaborations, production, sound, music, performance and spirituality. Tarkovsky is placed with a European New Wave tradition of filmmaking, alongside directors like Ingmar Bergman, Carl Theodor Dreyer, Pier Paolo Pasolini and Robert Bresson.

An essential addition to film studies.

Illustrations: 150 b/w, 4 colour. 682 pages. First edition. Hardback.

Publisher: Crescent Moon Publishing. Distributor: Gardners Books.

ISBN 1-86171-096-8 (9781861710963) £60.00 / $105.00

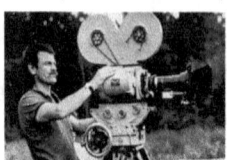